LATINO LANGUAGE
AND COMMUNICATIVE
BEHAVIOR

LATINO LANGUAGE AND COMMUNICATIVE BEHAVIOR

Edited by Richard P. Durán
Educational Testing Service

ABLEX Publishing Corporation
355 Chestnut Street
Norwood, New Jersey 07648

Latino Language and Communicative Behavior

editor: Richard P. Durán

Volume 6 in ADVANCES IN DISCOURSE PROCESSES
Series editor: Roy O. Freedle, *Educational Testing Service*

ISBN: 0-89391-038-4(C)

ISBN: 0-89391-093-7(P)

ABLEX Publishing Corporation
355 Chestnut Street
Norwood, New Jersey 07648

Contents

To Jane, Mother and Father

Preface

The present volume is an outgrowth of proceedings from the National Conference on Chicano and Latino Discourse Behavior sponsored by Educational Testing Service in 1978. The purpose of the original meeting was to provide an intimate opportunity for a moderate size group of thirty or so researchers to share their research ideas and findings on Latinos and their language behavior in an interdisciplinary setting. The organizational theme of the meeting centered on the use of Spanish or English in functional contexts of relevance to the education and everyday welfare of Latinos.

The contributions of the present volume provide us clear, objective evidence that Latinos use of English and Spanish is strongly linked to numerous factors such as Latino subgroup identity, generations in the U.S., geographical region of residence, familial structure, individual social and educational history and proficiency in two languages. The findings that emerge are indeed complex, but uniformly suggest an immense diversity of adaptibility of Latinos to life in the U.S.

While the volume in its language and style of presentation is intended for readers primarily interested in social science and applied linguistics research on Latinos, its contents should nonetheless be of value to persons concerned with general policy issues surrounding access of Latinos to educational and social services and the applications of research to practice.

Gratitude is extended to Educational Testing Service for sponsorship of the conference leading to this work and as well for support of the editor during production of the volume. Acknowledgements are also extended to the Public Health Service for postdoctoral fellowship support of the editor at ETS during the early stages of this project. Finally, and most importantly, thanks are extended to Roy Freedle for his original suggestion to create this volume and for his colleagual support in its production.

Richard P. Durán

INTRODUCTION

The contributions to the volume investigate language and language functioning among Latinos. Disciplines represented by the authors include sociolinguistics, cognitive psychology, anthropology, and education. A recurrent theme occurring in the volume's works is the need for sensitivity to sociocultural and language background factors which mediate the Latino's proficiency in Spanish and English and general communicative behavior. While the emphasis of papers is largely on language behavior, in a very strong sense, cultural issues surrounding rules for appropriate communication are equally implicated in virtually every analysis presented.

Part I of the volume addresses some general sociolinguistic issues of relevance to the study of Spanish and English of Latinos and goes on to focus on the study of codeswitching as a particular example of a linguistic phenomenon affected by social factors. The first two papers of Part I, by Peñalosa and Ornstein-Galicia, stress the extreme heterogeneity which exists in the Spanish and English of the Southwest among Latino inhabitants— largely Mexican-Americans. Both of these authors take strong issue with previous research which has not recognized that appropriateness of language form (phonology, syntax, and vocabulary) in Spanish and English among U.S. Latinos is subject to historical, geographical, and social influences. Both authors, as well, go on accordingly to stress the need for more intensive sociolinguistic research on Latinos and on the development of more adequate theoretical basis for such research.

Reyes and Lavandera, in their separate chapters, bring forth evidence that the spoken Spanish of their bilingual informants reveals an essential mastery of Spanish rules for word formation and grammar, while at the same time demonstrating influences of English. The implications of these phenomena for studying the spoken Spanish of Latinos is elaborated in both papers. The remaining six chapters of Part I exclusively concern codeswitching, or alternative use and intermixture of Spanish and English among Latinos.

McClure presents a review of previous research on codeswitching and goes on to present codeswitching data from her own research which demonstrates that codeswitching systematically occurs according to conversational participants, setting, discourse type and topic. In addition, attention is given to citation of example codeswitches which mark specific functions in discourse related to enhancement of meaning and management of conversation. Valdés, in her chapter, discusses how codeswitching among Latino interlocutors can be used as a specific strategy to either mitigate or aggravate the making of requests, and how information marked by codeswitching references the rights and obligations shared by interlocutors in their social and conversational expectations.

Zentella and Genishi separately present findings of research on codeswitching in bilingual classrooms. Zentella, in one of the few existing studies of Puerto Rican children's codeswitching, finds that children's perception of appropriateness of a given language and preference for language mixture is strongly related not only to children's relative proficiency in either language, but as well to a bilingual teacher's own relative proficiency in two languages and to the social prestige assigned to use of one language versus another. Genishi, in her work, carefully documents how four six year old Mexican-American children choose the language best understood by other children addressees in conversation and how codeswitching thereby occurs in conversation.

Huerta-Macias discusses codeswitching data obtained in a Chicano family context. Her work reveals that codeswitches may serve a number of discourse functions in conversation. The function of signalling change from casual to formal mode of speech is found to be the most frequently occurring purpose of codeswitching among her informants. In the second section of the paper Huerta-Macias cites examples of codeswitching by a two and one half year old child which suggest early evidence of discrimination between the Spanish and English language systems.

Poplack in the concluding chapter of Part I examines codeswitching among members of the oldest Puerto Rican community in the U.S. Mainland located in East Harlem. Her work leads to the specification of a number of syntactic constraints which govern the relative frequency and acceptability of intrasentential and intersentential forms of codeswitching among her informants. Her paper, as well, discusses how social identity of interlocuters affects codeswitching.

Part II of the volume examines Latino's communicative skills and cognitive performance in home, community and school settings. Marcos and Trujillo are both practicing psychiatrists serving bilingual Latino patients. In their paper they review their own and other's previous research which show that quality of communication in diagnostic and therapeutic mental health settings is seriously affected by inability of patients to use their preferred language and by practitioner's cultural familiarity with the background of patients.

Maryellen Garcia investigates conversational patterns surrounding leave-taking at a Christmas gathering of an extended Mexican-American family. Her work reveals that stage of leave taking and social roles played by family members affect the direction and interpretation of conversation. The conclusion of the paper offers suggestions on further work needed to understand how Mexican ethnic background might affect the discourse observed.

Ramírez overviews his and other's previous research on attitudes towards Spanish and English spoken by Latino bilingual classroom students. His review cites accumulating findings showing that both teachers and students often attribute lower esteem and unfavorable personality or intellectual characteristics to children who speak accented English or varieties of Spanish other than formal Spanish. Ramírez concludes with comments on the need for teacher sensitization training to overcome the negative classroom implications of typecasting children's learning ability by speech style.

Carrasco, Vera and Cazden report an analysis of the communicative competence of a first grade bilingual child in teaching another child spelling in a language arts task. Following an ethnographic methodology, the authors study the structure of the peer tutoring sequence involved and then go on to describe the intent shown by children in their utterances. Their results show that the child in question displays communicative skills and knowledge of lesson content which the bilingual classroom teacher is unaware of based on her isolated interaction with the child.

Garcia and Carrasco study control of turn taking and choice of language in discourse between four Mexican-American mothers and their preschool children in a preschool setting. They find that mother's speech and children's replies in an instructional setting generally match discourse patterns found in previous research on teacher's control of recitation by students. This finding is most noticeable in situations where mothers overtly undertook to teach children vocabulary in their weaker language, Spanish.

Lindholm and Padilla investigate mother-child discourse in a home setting among twelve Mexican-American families. They report that approximately one-third of all discourse between mother-child dyads is of relevance to the socialization of children. Such discourse termed mastery skill communication is found to involve an elaborate coordination between mastery skill topic, grammatical form of utterances, and social function of discourse. The authors argue that the kind and complexity of coordination in speech they observe is contrary to expectations generated by some previous research which hypothesizes that working class family status restricts the range of communication between the mothers and children.

Laosa analyses data on connections between mother's teaching strategy to five year old children and cognitive styles of both mothers and children. The results reveal that there are significant associations between mother's degree of field independence-dependence and preferred teaching strategy. Evidence is discussed which suggests that children's degree of field independence-dependence may be influenced by mother teaching strategies.

Durán presents results of a study of mainland Puerto Rican bilingual college student's ability to solve verbal deductive reasoning problems in either Spanish or English. The results show that level of reading ability in a language significantly affects how well students perform on verbal reasoning tests in the same language, and that the pattern of these effects is similar across both Spanish and English languages.

In the final chapter, DeAvila and Duncan discuss research findings, including their own, which support the conclusion that high proficiency in two languages is coupled with stimulation of cognitive abilities related to breaking or creation of mental set. The authors suggest that a proper understanding of how to design effective bilingual education programs need consider ways of stimulating the positive effects of bilingualism that have begun to emerge consistently in the research literature.

Richard P. Durán

Preface to the Series

Roy Freedle
Series Editor

This series of volumes provides a forum for the cross-fertilization of ideas from a diverse number of diciplines, all of which share a common interest in discourse—be it prose comprehension and recall, dialogue analysis, text grammar construction, computer simulation of natural language, cross-cultural comparisons of communicative competence, or other related topics. The problems posed by multisentence contexts and the methods required to investigate them, while not always unique to discourse, are still sufficiently distinct as to benefit from the organized mode of scientific interaction made possible by this series.

Scholars working in the discourse area from the perspective of sociolinguistics, psycholinguistics, ethnomethodology and the sociology of language, educational psychology (e.g., teacher-student interaction), the philosophy of language, computational linguistics, and related subareas are invited to submit manuscripts of monograph or book length to the series editor. Edited collections of original papers resulting from conferences will also be considered.

Volumes in the Series

Vol. I. Discourse production and comprehension. Roy O.Freedle (Ed.), 1977.
Vol. II. New directions in discourse processing. Roy O. Freedle (Ed.), 1979.

I LATINO SOCIOLINGUISTICS AND CODESWITCHING

1 Some Issues in Chicano Sociolinguistics

Fernando Peñalosa
California State University, Long Beach

There are two principal competing viewpoints in the social sciences. One, that they should model themselves after the physical and biological sciences and be as objective and unbiased as possible. The other, that it is neither possible nor desirable to do so, that human affairs are inherently controversial, and that to take no position is in fact to take a position. Thus not to condemn oppression is to condone it. And because scientific research of any sort affects people, all of us, natural and social scientists alike, must consider the possible effects of our research on the welfare of human beings. Since I subscribe to this viewpoint, I cannot claim complete objectivity, only honesty as I state my biases: a firm commitment to cultural pluralism and a belief in the inherent worth of every human being, ethnic group, and variety of language; further, that sociolinguistic research pertaining to the Chicano must be judged in terms of its potential to benefit or harm the Chicano people. Social research is thus considered inseparable from social action.

Material bearing on Chicano sociolinguistic questions appears not only in scholarly journals but also in the popular press. For example, some time ago while reading the Los Angeles *Times,* a headline on the last page of the movie and theater review section caught my eye: "Uprooted Melodrama in Spanglish." It was an unfavorable, insensitive review of J. Humberto Robles Arenas' play *Uprooted* by an Anglo reviewer (Christon, 1977), who characterized the play as "1950's family melodrama," and said, "It may as well have concerned a Jewish, Italian, Irish, or Black family, or any minority whose problem is assimilation into the mainstream, except that its dialect is 'Spanglish,' a contemporary barrio mix of English and Spanish."

One may raise a number of questions concerning this review. In the first place, why did the *Times* send an Anglo reporter to the play? The paper has several very competent Chicano reporters. Then, *is* the problem of the Chicano family *really* the same as that of the Black family, or of the Jewish, Italian, or Irish family in earlier times, and is its problem assimilation? Are not the problems of Chicanos rather economic prosperity, political power, dignity, cultural autonomy and efflorescence? Chicano speech is denigrated by the use of the pejorative term *dialect*, even more so by the term *Spanglish*. The latter is reminiscent of terms like *Franglais*, used in France to refer to French with a heavy admixture of English vocabulary. Regarded as abnormal by prescriptivists, it is the converse of what might be called "Franglosaxon," the Anglo-Saxon language after the Norman Conquest, saturated with French words, an earlier version of the very same language in which this paper is written. This "contemporary barrio mix" then is looked down on because the Chicano himself and his culture are looked down on. Of course, those of us who are sociologists, linguists, etc., are more enlightened and perhaps ought not to be too concerned about statements made in the popular media. But this is precisely the point: the Los Angeles *Times* has the largest circulation of any newspaper in the West. Not only that, its distribution area coincides with the largest concentration of Chicanos in the United States.

Another case in point: commenting on the catastrophic effects of Proposition 13 on California public libraries (hundreds of library workers laid off and many libraries completely closed or open for limited hours with skeleton staffs) the head of the Los Angeles County Public Library recently emphasized the great variety of readers served, ranging from "sophisticated patrons in Claremont to bilinguals in East Los Angeles" (Spiegel, 1978). The implication was clearly that "bilingual" was symptomatic of the lowest possible cultural status. Ms. Moss could have contrasted the high socioeconomic status of Claremont residents and the low socioeconomic status of East Los Angeles residents. Instead, she chose to look at bilingualism as a "problem" and communicated this attitude to hundreds of thousands of readers of the Los Angeles *Times*. Thus, the Anglo (non-Hispanic white) who learns a second language in school may be praised, whereas the Chicano child who comes to school or library with two languages may be considered "deprived."

So a strategic dilemma suggests itself. Should those of us who consider ourselves Chicano sociolinguists concentrate on enlightening the general public, work on specific problems of concern to the Chicano community, or sit in our ivory towers constructing theoretical models? What are the relationships among theory, research, and public responsibility? These questions must ultimately be answered in the spirit of Chicano self-definition and self-determination. We can no longer allow others to define us and determine our fate. Someone has quoted Thomas Szasz to the effect that in the animal kingdom it is eat or be eaten; in human society it is define or be defined.

For almost a decade now I have been engaged in research on the published literature on Chicano bilingualism and related topics, being by nature a library scholar and synthesizer rather than an empirical researcher and analyst. It is now possible to identify some of the major ideological, theoretical, and practical sociolinguistic issues related to the Chicano. (For a fuller account see my recent text, Peñalosa, 1980.)

As a sociologist, I am not particularly interested in linguistic minutiae as such, but where important ideological, social, and other practical implications are to be drawn from linguistic studies, I feel it my duty and right to comment. It is these implications and the welfare of the Chicano which are my express concern, rather than potential contributions to linguistic theory, valuable as these may be in their own right.

SOME THEORETICAL ISSUES

Any new area of study necessarily abounds in typologies. We have typologies of Chicano language varieties and typologies of Chicano speakers. But nomenclature and taxonomy is only the first step. We need explanations, that is, theories. Theories enable us to predict and thus extend some measure of control over our own destiny. We await the development of a self-conscious Chicano sociolinguistic theory. Even the lengthy proceedings of the First National Exploratory Conference on Chicano Sociolinguistics (1974) disappointingly reveal no concern with developing theory, although several first-rate Chicano theoreticians were at the conference.

No sociolinguistic theoretical framework appropriate to the Chicano situation is presently available. Existing models are generally assimilationist and functional. Even such a champion of the oppressed as Labov (1972) accepts the functionalist interpretation. Marxist models of society abound in Chicano intellectual circles, but none has encompassed sociolinguistics as yet, with the exception of Rosaura Sánchez (1978). To refer to Chicanos as a *speech community,* for example, is to assume a consensus among Chicanos as to norms for the choice and use of speech varieties. Such a consensus cannot be simply postulated, it must be empirically established. But whatever norms vary or are shared among Chicanos, or which may overlap with nonChicano norms, it is still likely that there is no overall United States norm system into which Chicanos might fit. Thus the prevailing consensus model must be rejected in favor of a more realistic conflict model. For example, the Anglo backlash over bilingual education is best understood in these terms. Anglos and Chicanos are in effect competing for limited resources, that is, school funds and the benefits they bring. One sometimes hears, "Why don't they do something for the majority for a change?" as well as "This is America, why don't they speak English?"

Transformational grammar has scarcely made an impact on Chicano sociolinguistics. Judging from available published sources at least, contrastive analysis, Hispanist and taxonomic models still predominate. More than two decades after the publication of *Syntactic Structures* (Chromsky, 1957) we have yet to see a proposed model for phrase structure rules and transformations that would generate sentences in a Chicano mixed code, let alone studies done in a generative semantic framework. Rather, what we have for the most part is a series of studies contrasting Chicano forms with their counterparts in so-called Standard Spanish and Standard English. Although such studies are of much potential practical value, they do not address themselves to the question of the possibility of a single linguistic system (for many Chicanos) with an underlying deep structure subject to a variety of transformations and lexicalizations (including relexification) derived from Spanish, English, and more unique Chicano sources. The ideological question here is whether the Chicano is unique and autonomous, or merely marginal, an outsider to two cultures, the Mexican and the American.

These remarks should not be interpreted to impute uniformity to Chicano linguistic behavior. The tremendous heterogeneity of the Chicano population is too well known to require comment, yet many studies lack socioeconomic information regarding subjects and fail to report variations in style, for like all speakers, no Chicano is a single-style speaker.

Cultural and linguistic relativists contend that there are no universal standards with which to judge the worth or adequacy of cultures or language varieties. All peoples have developed societies and cultures which they find satisfying and which they are ordinarily reluctant to change. As part of their culture, they have fashioned language and speech norms fully adequate for instrumental and expressive communication. In this sense no language variety is more adequate than another. Hymes (1973) has denied this axiom. He has pointed out that communities may lack specialized styles of language for scientific work, public affairs, etc. The purposes for which it is proper to use certain language varieties is of course a matter of social definition (Hymes, 1976). But if language varieties in use by the Chicano are not adequate for his needs, he is being shortchanged, and means need to be developed to overcome whatever inadequacies of code may exist. And what are we to make of the findings of Grebler, Moore, and Guzmán (1968) who claim that 1–4 percent of their adult samples in San Antonio and Los Angeles could carry on a conversation in neither English nor Spanish? We must reject the vile canard of certain school officials and others that some Chicano children are actually "alingual," without language at all, but Chicano performance as well as competence must be studied.

SOME METHODOLOGICAL ISSUES

The basis of most studies of Chicano speech is a comparison of Chicano Spanish and English with the corresponding standard language. Yet in any idiolect or sociolect the standard and nonstandard forms together form a system, and it is a moot point whether a given speaker is conscious of which are which, and whether this makes any difference, except in very self-conscious speech. Chicano speech, particularly Chicano Spanish, needs to be looked at—by somebody—as a self-contained system. Attention to deviant forms only will not give us a balanced picture. We need to relate both standard and nonstandard linguistic variables to their social and social-psychological correlates, where such can be established.

Here I would like to enter a plea for Labovian-type studies of Chicano speech in a natural setting. Experimental and interview settings although necessary, do bias findings. For example, the practice of having Chicano university students write essays in Spanish beyond the limits of their ordinary vocabulary (Craddock, 1976) can lead to exaggerated estimates of the amount of English influence on their normal Spanish lexicon. I say *normal,* because for such students Spanish is predominantly a spoken language, which many speak well, but they are used to expressing themselves on paper in English. The resulting high degree of relexification which takes place as they try to write Spanish is clearly artificial, as artificial as the exercise itself. Extensive training in formal Spanish would, of course, be a prerequisite for utilizing a written exercise as an estimate of the student's competence.

Scattered throughout the literature are correlation studies involving very small samples—for example, McMenamin's (1973) paper on code-switching—which are neither randomly chosen nor have employed any tests of statistical significance. Linguists are ordinarily not as picayune about such matters of sociologists; hence the latter are likely to accept the reported associations with considerable skepticism. Such findings cannot be regarded as conclusive, only suggestive or impressionistic, unless of course a number of such studies are consistent in the same direction. Where studies contradict each other, we have little basis for choice. We don't know whether the contradictory findings are due to different methodology or other bias, or whether the situations studied are inherently different, say as between Texas and California, between rural and urban, or between middle- and working-class subjects. This is not to belittle available studies, but rather to plead for larger-scale studies based on probability sampling and standard statistical procedures.

It is next to impossible to generalize concerning the linguistic behavior of the Chicano. This is an exceedingly heterogeneous population, and the linguistic variables complex and multifarious. Especially we cannot generalize on the basis of studies of poverty-level families, or of children considered "problems" by school authorities. Oppression of such people is a reality, but the behavior of our more affluent Chicanos is also worthy of study.

CHICANO ENGLISH

The most obvious discrepancy in the field of Chicano sociolinguistics is that between the extensive use of English in the community and the paucity of serious studies concerning the varieties of English used by Chicanos, just a handful compared to those dealing with Chicano Spanish. The main theoretical dispute here appears to be whether Chicano English, the fluent kind spoken by many as their first language, is simply English with Spanish interference, or whether it is a social variety which represents not imperfect learning of Standard English, but rather competent learning of a variety of English current and standard in the community. In its origins this variety was of course influenced by Spanish. This latter conceptualization would depend to a considerable extent on empirically establishing that this variety, if it exists, is passed on by, and to, Chicanos dominant or monolingual in English. How is English learned in the majority of Chicano homes where English is now the only or primary language? We obviously need to know a great deal more about this before we can make definitive statements about the nature of Chicano English.

These are not just theoretical questions; some Chicano students taking the speech test required for teacher certification in California have been failed because of their supposed foreign accent. Had their accent been that of Boston or Charleston, they would undoubtedly have passed. A case can certainly be made for ethnic language varieties as well as for social and regional varieties. It would seem that the *nature* of linguistic differences, rather than their *origins* should be the critical factor, especially in the realm of practical affairs.

If we are looking for variables to study, the phonology of Spanish loanwords in English, as used by Chicanos may be a possible social indicator. Whether a particular word is given a pronunciation closer to Spanish or English may be a Labovian type of indicator of language attitudes, linguistic insecurity, or position in the social structure. I have in mind for example whether in speaking English a Chicano friend says [enčilada] or [enčəladə], or [bai̯yo] [vario] or [baRiyo]. We must look to the social system rather than the linguistic system for an explanation of the patterning of these variables.

It is difficult for speakers of one language to perceive phonemic contrasts in another language which do not exist in their own. Thus a Spanish speaker may have trouble hearing the differences among the words ship/sheep/chip/

cheap or between the sentences "Did you watch that card?" and "Did you wash that car?" Matluck and Mace (1973) deduce from this that the Chicano child's linguistic and hence academic problems stem from perception difficulties. This is possible, yet contrastive analysis is not empirical proof. Homonyms are ordinarily distinguished from context. For example, monolingual speakers of English seem to have no difficulty in perceiving the differences among the various homophonous lexemes which we write "fair" (as in state fair, fair price, fair maiden, fair complexion) or "fare" (as in pay your fare, fare thee well, bill of fare). Certainly this is of the same level of difficulty as distinguishing ship/sheep/chip/cheap by the context. It seems to me this is another attempt to blame the failures of the school on the Chicano child himself.

It is difficult to understand on linguistic grounds alone why so many Chicano children fail to acquire adequate command of English, given the natural propensity of children to learn a second language with ease and alacrity. Likewise, given the English-dominance profile sketched for a majority of young Chicanos, it may be that the apparent language deficit is one in the academic language area. This is a deficit working-class Chicanos share with many working-class people of all backgrounds, and which derives as much from class as ethnic discrimination. Thus López (1976) has pointed out that, in Los Angeles, middle-class–raised Chicanos brought up in Spanish average a year more of schooling than Chicanos who were lower-class English monolinguals. It has often been observed also that middle-class students with prior schooling in Mexico have relatively little problem acquiring English and adjusting successfully to American schools. Thus we need to study the effects of class discrimination as well as of ethnic and racial discrimination. And yet the question remains: What is primarily responsible for the teacher's belief that Juanito is likely to be a low achiever? Is it his poverty, his physical appearance, his culture, or the way he speaks? We need further to investigate such attitudes, not merely condemn them. Yet as Hymes (1976) points out, "If linguistic discrimination is a culturally deep-seated way of maintaining social distinctions, then discrimination is likely to continue."

Although most announcers are imported, Chicano vernacular Spanish is used to a considerable extent on Spanish-language radio and television. Nevertheless, Chicano announcers (as well as other minority announcers) on English language media invariably speak accent-free Standard English. Chicano and other minority children are in effect being told, "You don't have to be white to be a TV announcer as long as you shed all traces of ethnic accent." Some of these announcers Anglicize their own names and Spanish place names, others use Spanish phonology for these. Some use English phonology for proper names when speaking English and Spanish phonology when speaking Spanish. These are sociolinguistic variables worthy of study.

CHICANO SPANISH

So much research emphasizes the Chicano as deviant, as marginal. For example, the number of English words borrowed into Spanish by Chicanos seems to be considerably exaggerated in existing studies which list words culturally adopted throughout the Hispanic world, or even words that are not from English at all, but which happen to be Spanish cognates of English words. For example, even such a careful scholar as Beltramo (1972) lists *doctor* (in the sense of "physician") and *educación* (in the sense of "schooling") as loanshift extensions, but both of these are listed in Standard Spanish dictionaries of four decades ago (Cuyás, 1940). And Ornstein (1951) claimed *borlote* was derived from "brawl" by jocular metonymy, although the expression is current in the informal standard Spanish of Mexico. Tzusaki (1971) likewise cites [xol] "hall," [sweter] "sweater," and [mofle] "muffler" as local borrowings in Detroit, thereby exaggerating the extent of cultural assimilation. The extreme relexification which Chicano Spanish *is* undergoing, however, suggests that we may be developing a creole without having to go through a previous process of pidginization, if that is not a contradiction in terms.

One problem making needed reforms difficult is that, in general, Chicanos do poorly in high school and college Spanish classes because of the devaluation of their vernacular. As a result, at the graduate school level Chicanos are vastly outnumbered by Anglos in Spanish M.A. and Ph.D. programs. Spanish departments thus are typically dominated by non-Chicanos: Anglos, Spaniards, or Latin-Americans interested primarily in literature and generally holding narrowly prescriptive attitudes toward language. Chicano self-determination in the linguistic area might well start in Spanish departments as well as in departments of English and Speech.

It is not the case, however, that barrio Spanish must be taught in the classroom. In most instances Standard Spanish will be taught. What is often lacking is teachers' respect for the local vernacular and enough knowledge of it to lead students toward bidialectalism. In some bilingual programs, Spanish is used for teaching Mexican history and literature, for example, but English for mathematics and the sciences, thus fostering the misleading impression that English is the language of a modern scientific, technological society, but Spanish suitable only for literary, folkloristic, and traditional, "impractical" purposes. Certainly this is not the type of diglossia that we wish to promote.

Solé (1975) claims that Texas Spanish does not have Standard Mexican Spanish as an underlying dialect, rather that it must be analyzed in terms of the underlying rules of both English and Spanish. In this Chicano Spanish variety the interlingual identification of Spanish and English lexical items is thus said to be almost complete; as children have unlearned Spanish under the impact of English, they are able to maintain their Spanish only by means of constant cross reference to English. If this analysis is correct, we may be justified in postulating another L3 in addition to *pocho* (mixed speech) as part of the linguistic repertoire used and created by Chicanos.

Matluck and Mace (1973) believe that a large number of Chicano Spanish constructions not found elsewhere in the Hispanic world, but which coincide exactly with English structure, constitute evidence for large-scale English influence on syntax. They cite such constructions as:

fueron puestos libres	(they were set free)
mi chiquito hermano	(my little brother)
estoy esperando por Juan	(I am waiting for John)
he perdido mi tiempo	(I have lost my time)

Contrariwise, Hernández-Chávez (1972) and Ornstein (1974) interpret these as lexical borrowings in the sense that they are complex lexico-semantic units imported *in toto* with no necessary knowledge of English grammar. They do not involve performance errors and involve interference only in a historical sense. Interpreting such cases as syntactic interference again only serves to characterize Chicano Spanish as more deviant or exotic than it really is. Studies of codeswitching rather have demonstrated the Chicano's competence in keeping the two syntactic systems separate (Gingras, 1974; Reyes, 1976; and this book, especially Chapters 3–10).

PUBLIC USE OF SPANISH

An area which needs more research concerns the laws requiring the use of Spanish for the proceedings of legislative and judicial bodies, public notices, public services, ballots, etc., the extent of conformity with such laws, and the extent to which such use of written Spanish actually meets people's needs. In the written notices and literature of a number of private and public organizations, one finds strange versions of Spanish, often obviously translated literally from English with the aid of a dictionary, and probably incomprehensible to anyone lacking a firm command of both languages. The Health Department of San Bernardino County for example has bilingual signs posted in public restrooms throughout the county: "Wash Your Hands. Lava Sus Manos." It must take a special kind of competence to make three syntactic errors in a three-word sentence. Such constructions, and sadly, they are not rare, reflect neither lively barrio Spanish nor anybody's Standard Spanish.

But the assault on the Spanish language in the Southwest is not confined to public notices. Real estate developers in California, and presumably elsewhere, have the awesome authority, subject to the review of no person competent in the Spanish language, to name apartment buildings, condominiums, housing tracts, streets, and towns. The eye of the sensitive Spanish-speaking person is constantly assailed by such linguistic atrocities as La Habra, Don Diablo, San Domingo, Los Flores, La Posadas, and Lado de Loma. It is inconceivable that French would be treated in such a manner in Canada. If we Chicanos do strange things to the Spanish language, that is our own concern. Spanish is not, however, the property of Anglo businessmen to do with as they please, evoking the so-called "Spanish" past of the "days of the Dons" for monetary gain.

MIXED CODES

Sophisticated linguistic analyses of Chicano code-switching are becoming increasingly available. But we need to understand more about the social correlates of both switching situations and the code switchers themselves. Obviously the code-switcher possesses not only competence in the two languages, he possesses switching competence as well. Does this type of competence help to maintain coordinate bilingualism and/or vice versa?

In a now classic paper, Chacón (1969) said in reference to *pocho,* "It is my mother tongue." Should this statement be taken literally or metaphorically? There is a tendency in some segments at least of the Chicano community to disregard the technicalities of interference, borrowing, and codeswitching and to regard mixed speech as a code with an identity of its own. There are ideological forces working both for and against this idea. Creation of a unique code might be considered a cultural achievement emphasizing the specialness of the Chicano community, leading to a deemphasis of concepts referring to Chicano marginality. The poetry of people like Alurista is merely the tip of this creative iceberg. We now have an extensive literature, both prose and poetry, in mixed Spanish/English, as well as Chicano literature in both Spanish and English. A literary renaissance has truly taken place, and mixed codes are playing a significant role in this movement.

Two Chicano creations typical of barrio youth await definitive study, youth jargon or *caló*, and the famous Chicano wall graffiti. Whereas *caló* is regarded as a "snarl language" by writers like Álvarez (1967), the graffiti are commonly referred to in the Anglo press as "juvenile vandalism." We need to cast aside both insensitive criticism and unmitigated admiration and examine these creative responses to ethnic discrimination and economic exploitation in terms of their social functions, for their sociological dimensions are as significant as their linguistic ones.

Phillips (1972) asserts that the phoneme [v] occurs less in the speech of female than of male Spanish speakers in Los Angeles; the word *frasquito* is more frequently used by males and *vasija* by females to refer to a small jar in San Antoñito, New Mexico, according to Bowen (1952); according to McMenamin (1973), women code switch more than men. And *caló* is primarily a male speech variety. Otherwise, we know very little about sex differences in the language use of Chicanos. To what extent do Chicano men and women speak differently? We should expect to find differences in language both by, and about, the two sexes, but Chicano sociolinguistics has yet to produce a study of Chicano male/female language as such.

DIGLOSSIA AND BILINGUALISM

Is diglossia an appropriate model for characterizing the Chicano situation? To what extent is there functional allocation of varieties? With English now the primary language of most Chicano homes, but Spanish and English both being used in the home, along with extensive switching and mixing, and with bilingual education expanding in the public schools, diglossic allocation seems increasingly to be a phenomenon of the past. The major allocation appears to be an intergenerational one. These remarks pertain to out-diglossia (cf. Kloss, 1967). The concept of in-diglossia is perhaps irrelevant to the Chicano situation, and what we have is something on the order of a social dialect continuum or variable usage as conceptualized by Labov (1972) and exemplified for the Chicano by such scholars as Ornstein (1973) and Hensey (1973).

Fishman (1967) has noted that bilingualism without diglossia typically occurs in immigrant communities undergoing rapid social change. Despite my earlier statement on this subject (Peñalosa, 1973), this latter characterization may well apply to the Chicano situation.

López (1976), Hernández-Chavez (1979), and others have clearly shown the attrition of Spanish use from one generation to the next. The primary cause of the extraordinary Spanish language loyalty in the United States, they contend, is the continuing immigration from Mexico. If these analyses are correct, what does this portend for our linguistic future? Will bilingual education keep Spanish alive and in use? And how can we justify the future maintenance of two languages without functional allocation? Clearly we need to develop a cadre of Chicano futurologists.

One area for potential research might be the relationships among language attitudes, the compound/coordinate distinction, and the phenomenon of covert and passive bilingualism (Sawyer, 1978). Yet it seems to me that the question of the validity of the compound/coordinate distinction in the study of bilingualism has not been completely resolved, despite recent studies such as that of Jacobson (1975). This distinction, undoubtedly better conceptualized as a continuum, needs to be related to social variables. Perhaps on the other hand it ought to be allowed to die a natural death, as should perhaps also the Sapir-Whorf hypothesis. Influence of the latter has led to such logical absurdities as claiming (Jaramillo, 1972), that because the Spanish-speaking person for example says, *El camión me dejó*, where the English-speaking person would say "I missed the bus," the former disclaims any responsibility for having missed the bus, since the bus left *him* behind. This merely perpetuates the stereotype of the irresponsible, nonfuture-oriented, fatalistic Chicano.

LANGUAGE MAINTENANCE, BILINGUAL EDUCATION, AND SOCIAL ADVANCE

We need to examine the changing proportions of Spanish and English-dominant Chicano bilinguals. Is English dominance a step on the road to English monolingualism? Or put more appropriately, under what conditions is it so?

By federal law Chicanos are now a language minority and their political, educational, and economic disparities officially ascribed primarily to language problems (López, 1976). At one time, the Chicano's difficulties were ascribed to biological inferiority (i.e., our part-Indian ancestry), later to cultural deprivation, then to cultural differences—all racist "explanations" in disguise. Now they say we have a language problem. So we're being funded for bilingual education. As an enthusiastic supporter of bilingual education, I hope I am not labeled a heretic or as pessimistic or disloyal for suspecting that bilingual education will not do the job. The problem is not the Chicano's language. The problem lies in the discrimination against the poor and the ethnically different which is so endemic in our socioeconomic system as well as prejudice against Chicanos by Anglo teachers and students alike. Some problems are perhaps better attacked directly than indirectly and this may be one of them. Bilingual education is valuable in and of itself but may not solve fundamental problems. Especially now there may be a conflict in some large cities between the goals of bilingual education on the one hand and school integration involving extensive long-distance busing on the other. Because linguistic goals and educational, occupational, and economic goals may be in conflict, the Chicano community must order its own priorities.

Surveys of parent attitudes concerning bilingual education (e.g., Adorno, 1973) have shown parents believing English important for their children to get ahead, whereas the main reason for wanting their children to learn Spanish is for them to be able to speak to family members. Parents want the schools to take this responsibility (Carrillo, 1973). If this is generally true, then the community vernacular rather than academic Spanish ought to be taught. If the latter is taught, where will it be used? For diglossia to be effective, the two languages must be allocated to different functions.

At the university level, perhaps a student might have a choice of which variety of Spanish on which to concentrate. If he is interested in becoming a bilingual secretary or in working in the Foreign Service, then he might concentrate on the standard variety. If on the other hand, he wants to be a social worker in the barrio, he might want to concentrate on the local vernacular. A case may also be made for trilingual/tricultural education at both the secondary and university levels: exposing the student to the languages and cultures of Mexico, of the barrio, and of Anglo society. But in the last analysis the decision must be based on what the community wants, after it has been made aware of the possible alternatives.

As Ulibarri (1968) has pointed out, students prohibited from, and punished for, speaking Spanish at school become painfully aware that Spanish is the language of deviancy. Such prohibitions are becoming a thing of the past and even being replaced by bilingual education programs, but the Chicano child may still be made to feel deviant because of the variety of Spanish which he speaks.

The United States Commission of Civil Rights (1972) found that a no-Spanish rule was more likely to be enforced the higher the proportion of Chicanos in the school and the lower the socioeconomic status of the population being served. This pattern again suggests class as well as ethnic bias, the solution to which is perhaps school integration and economic advance. In a materialistic society, economic achievement rather than linguistic versatility is prized.

The desire to get ahead is linked in many Chicanos' minds with the learning and use of English. In the popular mind, poverty is linked with Spanish. Militant and other socially conscious Chicanos, however, are trying to make people aware of the necessity and desirability of maintaining Spanish, and people in a good economic position appear to have more positive attitudes toward vernacular Spanish (Elías-Olivares, 1976). The research evidence however consistently reveals a definite negative attitude on the part of both Anglos and Chicanos toward Chicano English, despite the positive attitudes usually found toward Standard Spanish and other varieties of Chicano Spanish. Lower-income people are generally less tolerant of nonstandard varieties than are higher-income people.

Published reports showing negative associations between social status and measures of Spanish language use and retention have assumed, without any empirical evidence, that language loyalty is negatively correlated with status and mobility. But as López (1976) indicates, "these reports include larger proportions of Mexican immigrants who rank low on indicators of social status and, since they were raised in Mexico, were hardly subject to home/school bilingualism." He has further shown that Spanish language upbringing and loyalty in Los Angeles are positively correlated with upward mobility among working-class men, even though both are negatively correlated with years of schooling. Intergenerational occupational mobility was not positively associated with language shift. Thus it would seem that retention of Spanish does *not* impede social mobility, and that social mobility in turn promotes linguistic security and favorable attitudes toward popular speech varieties.

In conclusion, even if inequalities due to language are wiped out, will the Chicano suffer any less from discriminatory attitudes and practices in education, government, employment, and social life? Can we afford to be as pessimistic as Christian (1972) who has written: "The ideal of linguistic democracy, in which the speech of every citizen is regarded with equal respect by all others, is perhaps the most unrealistic of all social ideals. Speech is one of the most effective instruments in existence for maintaining a given social order involving social relationships, including economic as well as prestige hierarchies." Thus a dilemma manifests itself, whether to attack language policy, which is a secondary symptom of ethnic and linguistic prejudice and discrimination or whether to attack directly the political and economic institutions which are themselves the root causes of this oppression. From the viewpoint of socially concerned Chicano researchers, political action, research, and soul searching are all needed. In their role as researchers they must document the processes and agents of linguistic oppression as well as its effects on the Chicano population.

REFERENCES

Adorno, W. *The attitudes of selected Mexican and Mexican American parents in regards to bilingual/bicultural education.* Unpublished doctoral dissertation, United States International University, San Diego, Calif., 1973.

Álvarez, G. R. Caló: The "other" Spanish. *ETC: A review of General Semantics,* 1967, *24,* 7–13.

Beltramo, A. F. *Lexical and morphological aspects of linguistic acculturation by Mexican Americans in San Jose, California.* Unpublished doctoral dissertation, Stanford University, 1972.

Bowen, J. D. *The Spanish of San Antoñito, New Mexico.* Unpublished doctoral dissertation, University of New Mexico, 1952.

Carillo, R. A. *An in-depth survey of attitudes and desires of parents in a school community to determine the nature of a bilingual-bicultural program.* Unpublished doctoral dissertation, University of New Mexico, 1973.

Chacón, E. Pochismos. *El Grito,* 1969, *3*(1), 34–35.

Chomsky, Noam. *Syntactic structures.* The Hague: Mouton, 1957.

Christian, C. Language functions in the maintenance of socio-economic hierarchies. In R. W. Ewton, Jr., & J. Ornstein (Eds.), *Studies in language and linguistics, 1972-1973.* El Paso, Texas: Texas Western Press, 1972.

Christon, L. "Uprooted": Melodrama in Spanglish. *Los Angeles Times,* March 26, 1977, pt. II, p. 9.

Craddock, J. Lexical analysis of Southwest Spanish. In J. D. Bowen & J. Ornstein (Eds.), *Studies in Southwest Spanish.* Rowley, Mass.: Newbury House.

Elías-Olivares, L. *Language use in a Chicano community: A sociolinguistic approach.* (Working papers in sociolinguistics, No. 30) Austin Texas: Southwest, Educational Development Laboratory, 1976.

Fishman, J. A. Bilingualism with and without diglossia: Diglossia with and without bilingualism. *Journal of Social Issues,* 1967, *2,* 29–38.

Gingras, R. C. Problems in the description of Spanish-English intra-sentential code-switching. In G. D. Bills (Ed.), *Southwest areal linguistics.* San Diego Calif.:, Institute for Cultural Pluralism, 1974.

González, G. Analysis of Chicano Spanish and the "problem" of usage; a critique of "Chicano Spanish dialects and education." *Aztlán,* 1972, *3*(2), 223–231.

Grebler, L., Moore, J., & Guzmán, R. C. *The Mexican American people; the nation's second largest minority.* New York: Free Press, 1970.

Hensey, F. Grammatical variation in Southwestern American Spanish. *Linguistics,* 1973, *108,* 5–26.

Hernández-Chávez, Eduardo. *Early code separation.* (Unpublished manuscript, 1972.)

Hernández-Chávez, E. Language maintenance, bilingual education, and philosophies of bilingualism in the United States. In J. E. Alatis (Ed.), *International dimensions of bilingual education.* Washington, D.C.: Georgetown University Press, 1979.

Hymes, D. Speech and language: On the origin and foundations of inequality in speaking. *Daedalus,* 1973 (Summer), 59–85.

Hymes, D. *Ethnographic monitoring.* Paper presented for the Symposium on Language Development in a Bilingual Setting, California State Polytechnic University, Pomona, California, March 19–21, 1976.

Jacobson, R. *Semantic compounding in the speech of Mexican American bilinguals: A reexamination of the compound-coordinate distinction.* Paper read at the Annual Meeting of the Rocky Mountain Modern Language Association, Denver, 1975 (ERIC: ED 115 112).

Jaramillo, M. L. *Cultural differences revealed through language.* New York: National Center for Research and Information on Equal Education Opportunity, 1972.

Kloss, H. Bilingualism and nationalism. *Journal of Social Issues,* 1967, *23*(2), 39–47.

Labov, W. *Sociolinguistic patterns.* Philadelphia: University of Pennsylvania Press, 1972.

López, D. E. *Language loyalty and the social mobility of Chicanos.* Paper read at the Annual Meeting of the American Sociological Association, New York, 1976.

Matluck, J., & Mace, B. J. Language characteristics of Mexican American children: Implications for assessment. *Journal of School Psychology,* 1973, *11,* 365–386.

McMenamin, J. Rapid code-switching among Chicano bilinguals. *Orbis,* 1973, *22,* 474–487.

McMenamin, J. Spanish English bilingualism in California's Imperial Valley. In H. H. Key, G. G. McCullough, & J. B. Sawyer (Eds.), *SWALLOW VI; Proceedings of the sixth southwest areal language and linguistics workshop: the bilingual in a pluralistic society.* Long Beach, Calif.: California State University, 1978.

Ornstein, J. The archaic and the modern in the Spanish of New Mexico. *Hispania,* 1951, *34,* 137–142.

Ornstein, J. Toward a classification of Southwest Spanish non-standard variants. *Linguistics,* 1973, *93,* 70–87.

Ornstein, J. Mexican American sociolinguistics: A well kept scholarly and public secret. In B. L. Hoffer & J. Ornstein (Eds.), *Sociolinguistics in the Southwest.* San Antonio, Texas: Trinity University, 1974.

Peñalosa, F. Chicano multilingualism and multiglossia. *Aztlán,* 1973, *3,* 215–222.

Peñalosa, F. *Chicano sociolinguistics; A brief introduction.* Rowley, Mass.: Newbury House, 1980.

Phillips, R. The influence of English on the /v/ in Los Angeles Spanish. In R. W. Ewton, Jr., & J. Ornstein (Eds.), *Studies in language and linguistics, 1972-1973.* El Paso, Texas: Texas Western Press, 1972.

Reyes, R. Language mixing in Chicano bilingual speech. In J. D. Bowen & J. Ornstein (Eds.), *Studies in Southwest Spanish.* Rowley, Mass.: Newbury House, 1976.

Sánchez, R. Bilingualism in the Southwest. In H. H. Key, G. G. McCullough, & J. B. Sawyer (Eds.), *SWALLOW VI; Proceedings of the sixth Southwest areal language and linguistics workshop: The bilingual in a pluralistic society.* Long Beach, Calif.: California State University, 1978.

Sawyer, J. Passive and covert bilinguals; A hidden asset for a pluralistic society. In H. H. Key, G. G. McCullough, & J. B. Sawyer (Eds.), *SWALLOW VI; Proceedings of the sixth Southwest areal language and linguistics workshop: The bilingual in a pluralistic society.* Long Beach, Calif.: California State University, 1978.

Solé, Y. R. Sociolinguistic perspectives on Texan Spanish and the teaching of the standard language. In G. C. Harvey & M. F. Heiser (Eds.), *Southwest languages and linguistics in educational perspective.* San Diego, Calif.: Institute for Cultural Pluralism, 1975.

Solé, Y. R. Language attitudes towards Spanish among Mexican American college students. *Journal of the Linguistic Association of the Southwest,* 1977, *2* (2), 37–46.

Solé, Y. R. Hispano organizational interest in language maintenance. In H. H. Key, G. G. McCullough, & J. B. Sawyer (Eds.), *SWALLOW VI; Proceedings of the sixth Southwest areal language and linguistics workshop: The bilingual in a pluralistic society.* Long Beach, Calif.: California State University, 1978.

Spiegel, C. County library faces prop. 13 budget peril, *Los Angeles Times,* August 7, 1978, pt. 2, pp. 1, 8.

Tsuzaki, S. M. *English influence on Mexican Spanish in Detroit.* The Hague: Mouton, 1971.

Ulibarrí, H. Bilingualism. In E. M. Birkmaier (Ed.), *The Britannica review of foreign languages.* Chicago: Encyclopaedia Britannica, 1968.

U.S. Commission on Civil Rights. *The excluded student: Educational practices affecting Mexican Americans in the Southwest. Report III.* Washington, D.C.: Government Printing Office, 1972.

2 Varieties of Southwest Spanish: Some Neglected Basic Considerations[1]

Jacob Ornstein-Galicia,
University of Texas, El Paso

INTRODUCTION

It is fitting to begin by noting that the amount of sociolinguistic research on United States varieties of Spanish, spoken by perhaps more than 15 million persons who constitute our largest foreign-language ethnic group, has been slow in developing and pales in comparison with that in Black English. A major reason for this is that, due to intimate contact with English and resultant interference, the varieties appear "mixed." Except for some dialectologists, linguists have until recently avoided all but "standard languages," both in the Bloomfieldian structural tradition and in the transformational model of Chomsky, who emphasizes that the science focuses on "... an ideal speaker-listener in a completely homogeneous community who knows his language perfectly" (Chomsky, 1965: 3). Sociolinguistics has made us keenly aware of both social and regional dialects, sometimes merging into one, sometimes remaining separate. Political and social developments, such as the Bilingual Education Act of 1968 and the Supreme Court decision in *Lau* vs. *Nichols* (and related legislation), have also in a short time propelled the neglected Latino varieties

[1]Acknowledgment is here made of the material support provided for research reflected in this paper by University of Texas, El Paso; Hogg Foundation for Mental Health, University of Texas, Austin; Spencer Foundation, Chicago, and the Cross-Cultural Southwest Ethnic Study Center, founded with the aid of the Spencer Foundation and our university's administration. Colleagues and speakers of different varieties of both Spanish and English in the Southwest are also gratefully recognized, but they are too numerous to permit individual mentions. The writer takes full responsibility for the content, however.

into the forefront. The majority of the 800-odd bilingual education programs in the country are concerned with Spanish-English speakers, and with the millions allocated to these projects, it was inevitable that an alarming ignorance should be discovered regarding the children's home language or dialect, notably differing from the standard book or formal Spanish taught in our curricula.

Fortunately, work on Spanish varieties can build on an excellent foundation provided by such scholars, mostly sociolinguists, as Haugen, Mackey, Fishman, Gumperz, Labov, Shuy, Fasold, Wolfram, Gilbert, Cedergren, the Sankoffs, Bright, and others. Uriel Weinreich's ground-breaking *Languages in Contact* (1953) was both a guide and a clarion call for more work in this area. At any rate, sociolinguistics, or the *sociology of language,* as Fishman prefers to call it, is self-defining, and it is doubtful that linguistic science can ever return to a day when language was regarded and analyzed in a detached vacuum. There is no time here to discuss differences within the field, but adequate anthologies exist, as well as several articles reviewing some of the leading sociolinguistic models of field research (Ornstein & Murphy, 1973; Murphy & Ornstein, 1975). Studies, pronouncements, conferences, and publications on bilingualism per se are also proliferating, with approaches ranging from naive to rigorous, with sociolinguistics well represented.

Returning to Spanish, sociolinguistic work offers numerous lacunae, given the vastness of the areas in which it is spoken. As a matter of fact, Spanish is the official and generally dominant language of some nineteen nations, and reflects as many varieties and numerous regional and social dialects. In the United States it appears to be the only language save English with solid prospects of maintenance and growth. Craddock (1973) in a recent review of research, divides United States varieties into Mexican-American, Puerto Rican, and Cuban, with the number of speakers in that order, followed by *Isleño,*spoken by Canary Island immigrants and their offspring in Louisiana and elsewhere, and Ladino, or Judeo-Spanish, well on its way toward extinction as a spoken language. A monograph by Cárdenas (1970) is useful for its description of linguistic features. A few years ago, an Academy of North American Spanish was established, based in New York, which will attempt some degree of standardizing, maintain a working relationship with the Real Academia Española, and whose dictionary will also reflect United States usage.[2]

---

[2]Against such a seemingly chaotic background to "US Spanish" a welcome development is seen in the recent formation of the Academia Norte-americana de la Lengua Española made up of scholars and teachers concerned with the Spanish of the United States and the literary and folkloric traditions of "hispanohablantes" here. Its Director Provisional is Carlos F. McHale; Bibliotecario Provisional, Theodore S. Beardsley, and Secretario Provisional, Gumersindo Yépez. The editor of the *Boletín de la Academia Norte-americana de la Lengua Española* is

To a large extent, as a result of years of contact with English, and concomitant interference and codeswitching, the aforementioned varieties are realized by most speakers as what Haugen has termed "bilingual dialects" (1969) or "contactual dialects" (1971). Looking at them from the Saussurean viewpoint of language, they have developed norms of their own, as Gumperz (1967: 48–57) has so ably pointed out; from the standpoint of *parole* however, the performance of any given speaker can be posited along a linguistic continuum, or spectrum, where standard and nonstandard features are clustered toward either extreme, and varying amounts of codeswitching occur.

Fortunately, an annotated bibliography of research and writing on United States varieties is now available in Teschner, Bills, and Craddock, *Spanish and English of U.S. Hispanics* (1975), as well as an updated article (Teschner, 1977). Consequently, no review of research as such, is needed here. The remainder of the paper can be devoted to a discussion of Chicano varieties and to a research project carried out at this university.

A TAXONOMY OF SOUTHWEST SPANISH VARIETIES

In a paper presented at the Second International Congress of Applied Linguistics Cambridge, 1969, the writer presented a schema of the language varieties of the Southwest (1971). (It is also presented in Appendix Figure 1 in modified form, although it has not been radically altered.) At this point, the schema is still presented in levels, owing to the difficulties encountered in arriving at a satisfactory horizontal continuum. These levels are not meant to reflect value judgments in the sense that one variety is superior or inferior to another. Suffice it to say, that this is still not the definitive form of the schema. Moreover, our discussion here will be confined to Spanish.

Standard (Mexican) Spanish. This is the idealized variety of the schoolroom and of formal written materials, from which even educated individuals diverge in varying degrees, especially in spoken interaction. At the same time, in the United States Southwest, where Spanish is used mostly as a spoken vernacular, relatively few of the 5 to 7 million Chicanos are able to

Eugenio Chang-Rodrigues, Queens College, City University of New York, Flushing, N.Y. 11367 (subscriptions are handled by Sr. D. Odon Betanzos, 125 Queens St. Staten Island, N.Y. 10314; Distributor: Interbook, Inc., 545 Eighth Avenue, New York, 10018). Interested readers are particularly urged to consult the first issue for further elaboration of its aims and a sample of its contents (Cf. *Boletín,* No 1, 1976). A link with the rest of the Spanish-speaking world is provided by the contact maintained with the Real Academia Española, so that North American lexical innovations may also appear in the authoritative dictionary produced periodically by the former.

control this variety, except for priests, teachers, some professional people, or immigrants with higher education from south of the Border.

At any rate, this variety corresponds largely to the northern dialect of Mexican Spanish. Like other New World varieties, this developed basically from rustic Spanish speech of the sixteenth century, although Mexico city's serving as the court and center of the *virreinato* (viceroyalty) of Nueva España somewhat modified that rusticity. Linguistically it, like the other dialects of Mexico, is distinguished by strong *conçonantismo,* meaning that consonants, especially stops, are retained to a striking degree in intervocalic positions and elsewhere. In addition, one notes a distinctive intonational or melodic pattern, immediately recognized by speakers of other national varieties, with supposed Nahuatl influence reflected. Matluck says that it is "..una especie de canto con su curiosa cadencia final, muy parecido al nuhuatl mismo" (1951: 120–121). In addition, considerable lexical borrowing occurs from Nahuatl and other Amerindian languages. Finally, the distinguished dialectologist Juan Lope Blanch (1973) disputes the commonly held view that of all the New World varieties it is the most "archaic."

Dialects and Subdialects.   Even more than "language," the very concept of "dialect" is vigorously disputed by many linguists, since the lines of demarcation between these two often become so nebulous. Humorously, but not without basis, it has been suggested that a *language* be defined as a dialect "with an army and a navy." For reasons similar to this, "variety" is increasingly employed for all of these. Charles-James Bailey (1971) suggests that "isolect" or merely "lect" replace "dialect" which is so unacceptable to many.

At any rate, two main dialects are indisputably to be identified in the Southwest. One of these is a vestige of the sixteenth-century Spanish of the conquistadors and their foot soldiers and is spoken north of Socorro, New Mexico, and in the San Luis valley of Southern Colorado. *New Mexican Spanish,* as it is labeled, has attracted considerable scholarly attention, being well described in philological terms by scholars like Hills (1938) and Espinosa and Rosenblat (1930:1946).

The other I called *General Southwest Spanish Koine* in the Cambridge paper, but it seems preferable to delete the last word as excessively technical; we can conveniently abbreviate GSWS as merely SWS. Synonyms from English to Spanish, in my view, are part of Chicano Spanish, Mexican-American Spanish, or as Elías-Olivares would have it, *Español Mixtureado* (1976). In the same paper she maintains that the influence of English and English loans differentiates *Español Mixtureado* from Popular Spanish, used by persons of limited eduation throughout the Spanish-speaking world. In an exhaustive study conducted in the Chicano community of East Austin, Texas, she was unable to find any feature of the structure not duplicated elsewhere in Spanish-speaking countries, except for English loans.

In my opinion, SWS qualifies fully as a *bilingual* or *contactual* dialect, to use Haugen's term, and to apply it disposes of the problem of how to deal with codeswitching, which is then taken for granted as an aspect of the variety. Nevertheless, Peñalosa (1972) and Elías-Olivares (1976) prefer to treat codeswitching as another variety or mode. Studies on what triggers switching have come relatively late to United States Spanish, with significant work done by Gumperz and Hernández-Chávez (1969) and Valdés-Fallis (1977). It can be stated categorically that there can be virtually no situation where two or more languages are in intimate contact and codeswitching does not occur.

From the linguistic point of view, SWS is based on the northern dialect, Mexican-Spanish, with heavy borrowings from English lexicon. Loans are of two types: integrated and nonintegrated. For Example, *suera* for "sweater" is the normal term, relexified and rephonemicized from English, whereas *Voy al movie* is nonintegrated. As usually occurs in linguistic borrowing, syntax is most resistant, although English influence on syntax is often considerable, but not to the same degree as lexicon.

Although assertions are often heard regarding the great differences between Chicano Spanish in different localities, it is, compared to subdialects existing in many languages of the world, extremely homogeneous. I would venture to say that over 95 percent of the vocabulary in Galván and Teschner's *Diccionario del Español Chicano* (1977) would be recognizable to any Spanish-speaking Southwesterner from Corpus Christi or Galveston to Palo Alto. Nevertheless, there is need for research on this problem because variation does exist. The writer has missed no opportunity to urge faculty wherever he lectures to investigate the language varieties in their own backyards. In addition, it would be possible to mount a meaningful research project which would gather theses and dissertations on local varieties of Spanish and create concordances of lexical and syntactic usage throughout the Southwest and in Spanish-speaking pockets of the Middle West and elsewhere.

It should also be noted that the term *Spanglish* is being increasingly employed to signify a variety with heavy English interference and borrowing from English, hence applicable to SWS and the Puerto Rican (Boricua) and Cuban varieties of Spanish. Rose Nash (1974), University of Puerto Rico, Hato Rey, in her studies of Puerto Rican Spanish, for example, utilizes Spanglish in this sense. Another term which is acquiring increasing respectability for SWS is pocho Spanish and courses so listed have been offered by at least one Calfornia university. The origin of *pocho* appears with little doubt to be Mexican usage south of the border, with at least mild disapproval of things Mexican-American.

Contact Vernaculars or Pidgins. These varieties are employed by monolinguals, so that one is Spanish-based whereas the other is English-based (English-Spanish-Amerindian also occurs in the Southwest), with approximations of one another's language, within limited structure and lexicon. They are, of course, utilized on both sides of the border in work situations, buying and selling, and tourist-type situations of limited range. Unfortunately, not a single description of these exists, to my knowledge, thus adding another item to our list of significant desiderata.

An extremely important sociolinguistic fact about pidgins is that they have been grossly confused with SWS, and both varieties have been termed indiscriminately *Tex-Mex, Border Lingo,* as well as *pocho,* and the more recent Spanglish. Other pejorative terms also exist.

Special Codes. These are varieties developed by particular socio-economic classes or occupations and to a large extent are distinguished by their special lexicon rather than syntactic differences. Another characteristic is that, like teenage slang among most ethnic groups, including Mexican-Americans, the vocabulary is extremely changeable, with some lexical terms inexplicably maintaining themselves in usage. Numerous occupational codes exist, such as those of cattlemen and migrant workers. Various "street" and underworld codes are found on both sides of the border: Mexican-Spanish border criminal code is sometimes referred to as *caliche.* Best known, however, and perhaps most misunderstood, has been *Pachuco* (also termed *Tirilí, Tirilongo, bato, Cholo,* and so on). *Pachuco* has been a term for some reason identified with El Paso, where the Spanish-speaking "zoot-suiters" of World War II first came to national attention when the Pachucos of that Texas city, in difficulties with the police, moved on to Los Angeles, where they warred and were apparently absorbed by the local *Califas,* or Mexican-Americans of the area. It seems fairly clear that the Pachucos received very severe treatment, particularly in California, not only from the police but from self-appointed law enforcers. It is ironic that their then "garish" attire and hairdress would seem conservative at present!

At any rate, much has been written, some of it naive and some of it sound, on the *caló* or argot of the Pachucos, although egregious errors have been made, even by some scholars who have classified colloquial informal SWS terms as Pachuco. There is no question that this *caló* originated as a secret code of a marginal or outgroup, in some cases delinquent, and that the etymology of the colorful lexicon derives from multiple sources since Spanish is spoken in more sovereign nations than any other language. With lexical innovation and imagery (not syntactic changes) as its distinguishing feature, it is not strange that it should have borrowed from informal varieties of Spanish and English, underworld *caliche* or *germanía* (the Penisular term) as well as the Romany (Gypsy) language. A welcome and rigorous study of the etyma or origins of Pachuco has been completed by John Terrance Webb (1974) at Berkeley.

By now, as ordinarily occurs with colorful varieties of speech which maintain themselves, a large percentage of Pachuco terms have lost their original secrecy, being understood and, in varying degrees, used by males in their fifties and under; some terms have undergone "upward mobility," becoming integrated into informal Spanish discourse, with new creations replacing old ones. Even female Spanish speakers, or at least some of them, understand *chante* and *cantón* as "house," *ranfla* as "car," and so on. Again we need to examine the geographical distribution of elements integrated into informal SWS, for example, in my experience, few college students in the El Paso area appear to know *huisa* or *guisa* as "girl" ("gal"), but New Mexico speakers have assured me that it is alive and well in their state. Works on Pachuco worthy of consultation, in addition to Webb, are Barker (1958); Coltharp (1965); Trejo (1968); and Sharp (1970), among others,

Some colleagues will note that so far there has been no mention of any creole. My contention is that there is not, in the true sense of a mother tongue transmitted from generation to generation, a Spanish creole in the Southwest, nor perhaps anywhere else in the United States with the possible exception of Louisiana. In the case of SWS, creolization is impeded by what I have called a "sociocultural linguistic matrix" (1972) across the border, namely, Mexico. Puerto Rico serves a similar function.

Following a descriptive taxonomy paradigm, these in briefest outline, are, the principal varieties of Southwest Spanish. Although I basically agree with Peñalosa (1972; 1976) that it is time to move on from taxonomy, as a linguist I can only make a plea that societal discussions be based on more and better descriptions than we now have of most of these varieties, with the possible exception of New Mexican Spanish, where updating is also needed. For example (to make my point), to date only two books—anthologies in this case—have appeared on Southwest Spanish: *El lenguaje de los Chicanos,* edited by Hernández, Beltramo, and Cohen (1975) and *Studies in Southwest Spanish* edited by Bowen and Ornstein (1976). Much more work is needed along the lines followed by Rosaura Sánchez in her dissertation "A generative study of the Spanish dialects" (1974), Lucía Elías-Olivares, in her "Ways of Speaking in a Chicano Speech Community" (1975), and others. Elías-Olivares, in particular, although following in a broad framework Dell Hymes's "Ethnography of Speaking" model, also addresses herself to John Gumperz's felicitous concept of the "linguistic repertoire," as that sum total of varieties of language(s) controlled by an individual.

Finally, it goes without saying that, given the recency of bilingual education and the often old-fashioned methods of teaching Spanish in Southwest classrooms, the repertoire of a Southwestern Chicano may vary radically, in some cases even excluding any functional command of Spanish. As a rule of thumb, however, it can be maintained that in most cases, the repertoire includes only informal varieties of Spanish, and formal and informal varieties of English. This is a reality and needs to be either accepted or modified. An eloquent proof of this is that at the University of Texas at El Paso, as elsewhere, attempts at conducting a Chicano conference entirely in Spanish have become mired as vocabulary and conceptual demands forced some reliance on English. Be that as it may, it is also true that Chicanos in the Southwest as Elías-Olivares (1976: 5) affirms for speakers in East Austin, have "access to a language repertoire that includes English and four varieties of the Spanish language." These are, in her formulation: Northern Mexican Spanish, Popular Spanish, *Español Mixturado* (a term used in that locality when English influence is marked), and (Pachuco) *caló*). No two scholars would be likely to agree on any classification, but it is to the credit of Elías-Olivares that she stresses rather than minimizes the basic unity of these varieties with the Popular Spanish spoken throughout the Hispanic world. As a native Chilean familiar with a number of varieties, she insists that she has not yet encountered a feature which is not duplicated elsewhere in a region where Spanish is employed.

In Table 1 (Appendix) some of the leading features common to most of the varieties except formal Spanish are listed, in somewhat technical linguistic terms. Further discussions of these are available in various writings by the author, Valdés-Fallis, and Solé (1975), among others.

Another way of looking at the problem of varieties is suggested by Jacobson (1975), who remarks that Mexican-American bilinguals are in essence employing a Spanish-English and English-Spanish continuum, embracing different varieties or registers, and switching from one to another, in accordance with their competence and situational needs. In his continuum, Standard formal English is at one polarity, Standard formal Spanish at the other.

Research on the Varieties and their Status

Attention is called to some of Rosaura Sánchez's investigations of Southwest varieties, in addition to her dissertation analyzing two specific varieties in as many communities. In "Spanish Codes in the Southwest" (1976), she formulates an extremely simple and basically sound division. For prestigious social roles and functions, according to her, English is the appropriate language, except for a few special situations, such as mass media, the church, and school instruction, inclusion bilingual education in large part. Chicanos as a group, in her view, use a varied range of codes, which are not necessarily shared by each individual. For the most part, Southwest Spanish speakers employ a Spanish-English codeswitching variety, with the same base as Spanish throughout the rest of the world, except for the English component, in integrated, nonintegrated, or codeswitching mode. The other variety is the highly creative *caló*, in which, as she puts it "Clichés and worn-out expressions are defamiliarized through the addition of suffixes and prefixes and argot terminology is substituted for common items." One may note her example of the substitution of *Ahí nos vemos* (we'll see each other there) by *Ahí nos vidrios*. In another essay on "Bilingualism in the Southwest" (1978) she addresses herself mainly to maintenance of Spanish in this area, choosing to term the bilingualism of the region *dynamic* rather than *stable,* as does this worker, since for upward mobility and status, Chicanos may, given the opportunity, shift to the English language entirely. Her facts are hard to dispute, yet one would have to quality this by studying and comparing the geographical distribution of the bilingualism. For example, bilingualism in El Paso is mostly stable, since the city is situated on the border, but in Los Angeles, except in some pockets dominated by recent migrants, bilingualism is dynamic.

As for Jacobson's proposal, it is basically sound and even helpful, but I have had great difficulties in attempting to construct an adequate continuum for Chicano bilinguals. That offered by Jacobson is satisfactory if one is willing to consider the matter in *grosso modo* and in a very generalized and even idealized sense. It seems to me that Gumperz's notion of "linguistic repertoire" (1969) is still the most effective when dealing with an individual's control of varieties of styles. It can be assumed that some of them are not controlled by certain individuals. In our Southwest, for example, older Mexican-American females of lower-middle-class orientation may be expected not to have any effective control of the Pachuco *caló*. Bilingual persons' profiles contrasted with their linguistic repertoire thus might illustrate such phenomena most clearly.

Enrique López, an international lawyer and free-lance writer, reflects upon the growing use of *pocho*, originally employed in Mexico to denote Mexican-Americans, in a somewhat pejorative sense. Pleading that we need more research on the home language of Chicano children (López, 1975), he suggests that their varieties are

1. Conventional English of a particular locale, Texas dialect, for example;
2. Conventional Spanish as it is widely spoken in New Mexico;
3. Southwest Spanish as it is spoken in New Mexico or northern Colorado;
4. *pocho* Spanish, an amalgam of Spanish and English, which may be total *pocho,* with continuous codeswitching; moderate *pocho,* with only occasional phrases, or, minimal *pocho,* in which Spanish phrases are used for emphasis from time to time or for affective purposes.

In this connection, it is my understanding that some California colleges have offered courses listed formally as *Pocho Spanish,* for example, California

State Polytechnic University at San Luis Obispo. Like the term *Chicano, pocho* then is apparently reflected in an upward mobility in the bilingual community itself, although perhaps to a lesser degree.

Thus it can be seen that even among the limited number of individuals who have written on the taxonomy of varieties of Southwest Spanish, there is anything but overwhelming agreement.[3] It is my opinion that it is, however, less important to spend time wrangling over terminology than to arrive eventually at some consensus on what refers to what. As it is, widespread confusion exists both among Anglos and Mexican-Americans as to the sorts of Spanish utilized here. Most of the attitudinal research on Chicano language use has addressed itself to reactions of both Anglos and Mexican-Americans to Mexican-American English, a variety covering a wide range, going from mild divergence of intonation or pronunciation to heavy interference. On the other hand, it is the view of many linguists, including the author, that Mexican-American English is a legitimate variety on its own merits, and remedial and "correctional" measures should not be forced, but if undertaken should represent an individual choice.

Research on attitudes is conveniently summarized in Amastae and Elias-Olivares (1978). Investigators who have performed attitudinal research on SWS include Ryan and Carranza (1976); MacIntosh and Ornstein (1974); Amastae and Elias-Olivares (1970); Williams (1970), and Ramirez (Chapter 13). Further references may be found in the appropriate sections of Teschner, Bills, and Craddock (1975).

Very little has been done on reactions to varieties per se, and that, again, is mostly summarized by the scholars just cited. Nevertheless, in a sociolinguistic survey carried out at this university and described briefly in the following section, some interesting reactions to Southwest varieties came to light.

Research and New Perspectives

Repeatedly, orally and in writing, I have pleaded that scholars in the behavioral sciences join linguists in attacking language problems on the widest possible front. I have recommended a network of sociolinguistic teams, consisting minimally of a language scientist and a social scientist, collaborating in gathering, storing, and analyzing language varieties in their areas. Targets should not be monolithically uniform, but they should include the most significant sociological, psychological, and political interrelations along with hard linguistic data. In this regard, Peñalosa argues (Chapter 1) for applications of a conflict model, rather than a consensus or functionalist one, such as Labov and Fishman follow, or a purely descriptivist framework.

---

[3]Constructive suggestions and corrections are sincerely solicited.

My notions on regional sociolinguistic consortia are most explicitly presented, in narrative and diagrammatic form, in Ornstein (1975: 40–42; 44–45). In essence, the idea is that the teams, each with a coordinating committee and computer facilities, would address themselves to the following targets:

1. Linguistic variation and change,
2. Bilingual bidialectal communciation patterns,
3. Attitudinal factors,
4. Interrelations between ethnolinguistic communities, in a sociological sense,
5. Power relationships at various levels of sociopolitical organizations,
6. Investigations of sociopolitical and linguistic universals wherever languages and dialects converge, coexist harmoniously, and conflict. (Cf. Appendix Figure 2).

The last-named target is undoubtedly the most difficult, yet it should somehow be addressed, much as Joseph Greenberg (1963) has done.

In speaking of collecting data, it needs to be emphasized that it is not necessary to invent the wheel all over again. Much up-to-date data on local types of Spanish and English (also Ameridian languages) is available in periodical literature, published reports, and particularly in theses and dissertations. A fascinating and extremely useful project needs to be funded to gather these sources and, above all, make reliable information in them available, perhaps somewhat in the manner of the ERIC system, but going beyond that. Funding for such research undertakings must, of course, be sought from the Education Department, National Institute of Education, National Endowment for the Humanities, National Science Foundation, private foundations, and state and local resources, including one's own institution.

Returning now to the concept of mounting interdisciplinary teams to investigate local varieties, it is relevant to describe briefly the sociolinguistic survey carried out in El Paso—not as one to be imitated slavishly, but as one supporting the feasibility of our notion, and which at the same time reports on the confusions and misconceptions of Anglo and Chicano students, the *flor y nata* of regional youth, reflected throughout the study.

A small interdisciplinary team was organized at this university, to undertake a broad-gauge investigation of the characteristics of Anglos and Chicanos attending it, with special emphasis on language varieties, attitudes toward them and their respective cultures, as well as of demographic characteristics, including age, sex, socioeconomic status, college major, and year of enrollment. A *Sociolinguistic Background Questionnaire,* mostly of multiple-choice type, and including 106 items, was devised by Brooks,

Brooks, Goodman, and Ornstein (1972), an educational administration specialist, an educational psychologist, a sociologist specializing in the culture of poverty, and a language scientist.

With the assistance of the registrar's office, our social scientists sought to secure a 5 percent sample of the fulltime undergraduate enrollment, resulting in a total of 301 subjects, almost evenly distributed between Chicanos and Anglos (in our area, anyone but Chicanos). All these completed the questionnaire, which, it should be added, also contained numerous questions of distributive use of Spanish vs. English in specific situations of various domains of activity and living. In addition, a subsample—similarly stratified—was taken, mounting to 30 subjects, representing about 10 percent of the overall sample, or 20 percent of the total bilinguals. The latter group agreed to participate in our battery of linguistic elicitation, consisting of an open-ended interview (20 minutes to an hour) in the two languages, respectively, conducted by male and female peer interviewers. This was followed by an exercise in writing in the two languages, a component usually slighted by American sociolinguists in favor of oral samples only. In part B (Optional) of our questionnaire involving essay writing, two identical sets of three groups of themes in English and Spanish were presented, from which subjects could choose, and which were arranged in ascending order of complexity, both ideologically and grammatically. Three independent judges then rated the written language skills shown in essays individually and globally, largely following the United States Foreign Service Institutes' five-point scale, in which 1 is slight, and 5 represents native fluency. Peñalosa (1977) is right in criticizing expectations of good performance in writing skill in Spanish, since often few have training in it. At any rate, from all I know, this has resulted in apparently the most extensive (although limited to the population studied) set of written and spoken samples of adult Chicano speech yet. It has been exploited in part by a grammatical analysis by Hensey, a phonological one by Foster, and an exhaustive analysis and classification of Southwest Spanish lexicon by Craddock, all these appearing in Bowen and Ornstein (1976). The project as a whole is discussed in a monograph and an article by Ornstein (1974, 1976), a doctoral dissertation by Murray (1972), two essays, one by Goodman and Brooks (1974) and another by Goodman and Renner (1979), as well as by Ornstein and Goodman (1979).

Having presented the foregoing, we can now limit ourselves to the results of the attitudinal items of the questionnaire. We assumed no linguistic technical background on the part of our informants and asked them to choose one of four terms which best describes the Spanish spoken in this area. The results, given in Table 1, follow:

As may be noted, the students believed that all four varieties were available in the Southwest. A mere seven, considered that "formal, educated" Spanish is used, but this did not include a single Anglo. The most frequent response, unhappily, was "Border slang" (41 percent), comprising 51 percent of Anglo

TABLE 1
Student's Evaluations of Types of Spanish Used in the Area

	Anglo		Mexican-American		Total	
	N	%	N	%	N	%
Formal, educated	0	0	7	5	7	2
Informal, everyday	46	32	62	40	108	37
Southwest dialect	24	17	36	24	60	20
Border slang	72	51	48	31	120	41
Total	142	100	153	100	295	100

(Kolmogorov-Smirnov one-tailed test) $X^2 = 11.01$ $p < .001$

and 31 percent of Chicano respondents. Second in frequency was far more realistic, being "informal, everyday," chosen by 37 percent of the entire sample, representing 32 percent of Anglos and 40 percent of Chicanos. The remaining subjects chose "Southwest dialect," again favored by more Chicano than Anglo respondents, 24 percent vs. 17 percent. It is regrettable that "informal, everyday" and "Southwest dialect" criss-cross each other somewhat semantically, but no set of labels would have been without its perils. A statistically significant difference between the two overall groups existed at the $p < .001$ level.

Actually, the preceding data tend to agree with the results of most studies of attitudes toward Chicano Spanish and English (however, most of the investigations have concerned the latter). In general, there was a tendency to rate Southwest Spanish somewhat, although not altogether, low in the El Paso study. Reasons for this are well known, but one should not fail to take into account the general and abysmal ignorance of even the educated layman about the most elementary facts regarding modern linguistics and the field of languages. This was reflected, not only by Anglos but also by Chicanos, and stems in part from the failure of our school system to incorporate such knowledge in the curricula.

In the following chart, Table 2, we have the best opportunity of perceiving the contradictions in the views of many Southwesterners about regional varieties, especially SWS:

With respect to the foregoing, the choice of either "Informal, everyday" or "Southwest dialect" is quite realistic. Nevertheless, the remaining choices clash with informants' perceptions of the types of varieties employed in the region. The most glaring contradiction was afforded by the 49 or 31 percent claiming control of "formal, educated" Spanish, although only 7 (Chicanos), or 5 percent of the overall sample had thus characterized the regional variety. Furthermore, although 48 Mexican-Americans, or 31 percent had termed it *border slang,* a mere step from the more pejorative *Tex-mex,* only 3, or 2

TABLE 2
Bilingual Students' Self-report on Variety Best
Controlled by Them

	Number	Percent
Formal, educated	49	31
Informal, everyday	87	57
Southwest dialect	14	9
Border slang	3	2
Cannot	1	1
	153	100

percent, cared to claim an obviously stigmatized variety. Here again, even the term *dialect* is distasteful to many, and Bailey (1971) has proposed that we substitute "isolect" or "lect" (these terms are not original with him). The semantics of any labeling system are extremely delicate and from experience thus far, it occurs to me that in data collection like the foregoing, one should, provide a bit of orientation orally without venturing into technical linguistics.

It will only be noted, in addition, that contrary to the findings of Grebler, Moore, and Guzman (1970) with Los Angeles bilinguals, a high degree of professed, loyalty to Spanish language and its regional culture had no significant correlation with performance in this language. A possible tendency to overrate language as the overwhelming symbol of solidarity is dangerous; for example, Irish solidary in Eire and Ulster does not depend upon Gaelic (Erse) anymore than that of American Jews relies on Yiddish or Hebrew. In any event, the author had prepared two essays going into more detail on attitudes toward Spanish varieties in the United States (Ornstein, 1978a, 1978b).

The parameters of this paper have already been dangerously extended, and it is appropriate to bring it to its conclusion. This consists merely of reiterating the need to proceed to more systematic approaches in order to replace the chaos now existing in research on Southwest language varieties and their cultures. Perhaps the best all-around plan for achieving this has been prepared by an interdisciplinary team funded by the National Institute of Education. This valuable source—*Spanish-English Bilingual Education in the United States: Current Issues, Resources and Recommended Priorities for Research* (Ramirez, Macaulay, et al., 1974)—is based on visits to sites of principal activity, clearly suggesting priorities and urging a greater degree of planning, centralization of efforts, and dissemination of results. (A briefer summary is available in Macaulay and Ramirez, 1977.) Since the initial preparation of this paper, the National Institute for Education has invited proposals for establishing a National Research Center for Bilingualism.

Finally, one should not fail to take into consideration the report of the First National Exploratory Conference on Chicano sociolinguistics, organized by Sergio Elizondo, at New Mexico State University, Las Cruces, in 1974 (Peña, 1975). Interdisciplinary in nature, this conference probably resulted in the most extensive discussion of the relative roles of Southwest varieties and other United States varieties of Spanish and English in existence. Moderate in its recommendations, it urged (among other things) intensified teaching and/or awareness of both informal and formal varieties of Spanish, and proper cognizance of, and attention to, English in our schools. The sociological and political issues ancillary to this were also addressed by both Chicano and Anglo scholars and spokespersons. There is, in sum, good reason for looking at the many unfinished tasks in Chicano and Latino linguistics with anticipation and a sense of excitement.

REFERENCES

Amastae, J., & Elías-Olivares. L. Attitudes toward varieties of Spanish. In M. Paradis (Ed.), *Fourth LACUS Forum 1977*. Charleston, S.C.: Hornbeam Press, 1978.

Bailey, C. J. *Variation and language theory*. (Monograph presented at LSA Summer Institute, 1971, SUNY-Buffalo, (Typescript).

Barker, G. C. *Pachuco: An American Spanish argot and its social functions in Tucson, Arizona*. Tucson: University of Arizona Press, 1958.

Bowen, J. D., & Ornstein, J. (Eds.), *Studies in Southwest Spanish*. Rowley, Mass. Newbury, 1976.

Brooks, B. S., Brooks, G. Goodman, P. W. & Ornstein, J. *Sociolinguistic background questionnaire: A measurement instrument for studying bilingualism* (Rev. ed.). El Paso, Texas: University of Texas, Southwest Ethnic Study Center, 1972.

Cárdenas, D. *Dominant Spanish dialects spoken in the United States*. Arlington, Va.: Center for Applied Linguistics, 1970. ERIC Ed 042-137).

Chomsky, N. *Aspects of the theory of syntax*. Cambridge, Mass. : MIT Press, 1965.

Coltharp, L. *The tongue of the Tirilones*. University, Ala.: University of Alabama Press, 1965.

Craddock, J. Spanish in North America. *In Current Trends in Linguistics*, 1973, *10*, 305–339.

Craddock, J. Lexical analysis of Southwest Spanish. In J. D. Bowen & J. Ornstein, *Studies in Southwest Spanish*. Rowley, Mass.: Newbury, 1976.

Elías-Olivares, L. Chicano language varieties and uses in East Austin Texas. Presented at SWALLOW IV, Center for Cultural Pluralism, San Diego State University, 1977, (Typescript.)

Elías-Olivares, L. *Ways of speaking in a Chicano speech community*. Unpublished doctoral dissertation, University of Texas, Austin, 1975.

Espinosa, A., & Rosenblat, A. *Estudios sobre et al Español de Nuevo Méjico*. (2 vols.). Buenos Aires: Instituto de Filología, Española, 1930–1946.

Foster, D. The phonology of Southwest Spanish. In J. D. Bowen &. J. Ornstein, *Studies in Southwest Spanish*. Rowley, Mass.: Newbury, 1976.

Galván, R., & Teschner, R. *Dictionary of Chicano Spanish*. Silver Spring. Md.: Institute of Modern Languages, 1977.

Goodman, P., & Brooks, B. S. A comparison of Anglo and Mexican-American students attending the same university. *Kansas Journal of Sociology*, 1974, *10*, 181–203.

Goodman, P. W., & Renner, K. S. Social factors and languages in the Southwest. In G. Gilbert & J. Ornstein (Eds.), *Problems in applied educational sociolinguistics.* The Hague and Berlin: Mouton and de Gruyter, 1979.

Grebler, L., Moore, J. & Guzmán, R. *The Mexican-American people: The nation's second largest minority.* New York: Free Press, 1970.

Greenberg, J. H. (Ed.). *Universals of language.* Cambridge, Mass.: MIT Press, 1963.

Gumperz, J. J. On the linguistic markers of bilingual communication. *Journal of Social Issues,* 1967, *23,* 48–57.

Gumperz, J. J., & Hernández-Chávez, E. *Cognitive aspects of bilingual communication. Working paper* 28. Language Behavior Research Laboratory, 1969. University of California, Berkeley.

Hernández-Chávez, E., Cohen, A. D., Beltramo, A. (Eds.). *El lenguaje de los Chicanos.* Arlington, Va.: Center for Applied Linguistics, 1975.

Hannum, T. Attitudes of bilingual students toward Spanish. *Hispania,* 1978, *61,* 90–94.

Haugen, E. *The Norwegian language in America: A study in bilingual behavior.* (2nd ed.). Bloomington Ind.: Indiana University Press, 1969.

Haugen, E. The ecology of language. *Linguistic Reporter,* 1971, Supplement 25, 19–26.

Hensey, F. Toward a grammatical analysis of Southwest Spanish. In J. D. Bowen & J. Ornstein, *Studies in Southwest Spanish.* Rowley, Mass.: Newbery, 1976.

Hills, E. C. *El Española de Nuevo Méjico.* Buenos Aires: Instituto de Filología Española, 1938.

Jacobson, R. Research in Southwestern English and the sociolinguistic perspective. In B. L. Dubois & B. Hoffer (Eds.), *Papers in Southwest English I: Research techniques and prospects.* San Antonio, Tex.: Trinity University, Department of English, 1975.

Lope Blanch, J. El supuesto arcaísmo del español American. In J. Lope Blanch (Ed.), *Estudios sobre el español mejicano.* Mexico, D. F.: Centro de Filología Hispanica, 1972.

López, E. & Ortego, F. Pocho Spanish: The case for a 'third' language in the classroom. *Interracial Books for Children Bulletin* (Special Issue), 1975, 5, 7, 18, 15–16.

MacIntosh, R. J., & Ornstein, J. A brief sampling of West Texas teacher attitudes toward Southwest Spanish and English language varieties. *Hispania,* 1974, *57,* 902–926.

Macaulay, R. K. S., & Ramirez, M. S. III. Research priorities in bilingual education in the United States: Patterns and prospects. In *The bilingual education movement: Essays on its progress.* El Paso, Texas: Texas Western Press, 1977.

Matluck, J. *La pronunciación en el español del valle de Mexico.* Mexico, D.F.: Imprenta de Adrián Morales Sánchez, 1951.

Murphy, R. P., & Ornstein J. A survey of research in sociolinguistics: A partial Who's Who in sociolinguistics. In Peter A. Reich, (Ed.), *Second LACUS Forum 1975.* Columbia, S.C.: Hornbeam Press, 1976.

Murray, W. *Ethnic and sex differences as related to perceptions of a university environment.* Unpublished doctoral dissertation, New Mexico State University, Las Cruces, 1972.

Nash, R. Spanglish: Language contact in Puerto Rico. *American Speech,* 1974, *46.*

Ornstein, J. La investigación de actitudes hacia el español Mexico-Americano (Chicano) del sudoeste de los Estados Unidos. Eighth International Congress ALFAL, Caracas, Venezuela, January 9–13, 1978.

Ornstein, J. A cross-disciplinary sociolinguistic investigation of Mexican-American bilinguals/biculturals at a U.S. border university. *La Linguistique* (Paris) 1976a, *12,* 131–145.

Ornstein, J. A sociolinguistic study of Mexican-American and Anglo students in a border university. In Will Kennedy (Ed.), *Occasional Paper,* 3 San Diego, Calif.: San Diego State University, Institute of Public and Urban Affairs Press, 1976b.

Ornstein, J. Sociolinguistics and the study of Spanish and English language varieties and their use in the U.S. Southwest. In J. Ornstein (Ed.). *Three essays on linguistic diversity in the Spanish-speaking world.* The Hague: Mouton, 1975.

Ornstein, J. Language varieties along the U.S. Mexican border. In J. L. M. Trim & G. M. Perren (Eds.), *Applications of linguistics. Selected papers of the second international congress of linguistics.* Cambridge: Cambridge University Press, 1971.

Ornstein, J. Murphy, R. P. Models and approaches in sociolinguistic research on language diversity. *Anthropological Linguistics,* 1974, *16,* 141–167.

Peña, Salvador (Ed.) *Proceedings of the First National Exploratory Conference on Chicano Sociolinguistics,* Las Cruces, N.M., 1975. (ERIC/CRESS).

Peñalosa, F. Sociolinguistics and the Chicano community. 6th Annual Southwest Area Linguistics Workshop. Long Beach, Calif., April 16, 1976 (Typescript.)

Peñalosa, F. Chicano multilingualism and multiglossia. *Aztlán,* 1972, *3,* 215–222.

Ramirez, M. S., Macaulay K. S., Gonzalez A., Cox, B., & Perez M. Spanish-English bilingual education in the United States: Current issues, resources and recommended funding priorities for Research (Contract No. NIE-C-74-0151), Washington D.C.: National Institute of Education, 1974. (Available from Systems and Evaluation in Education. P.O. Box 2148, Santa Cruz, Calif. 95063).

Ryan, E. B. & Carranza, M. Evaluative reactions of adolescents toward speakers of Standard English and Mexican-American accented English. *Journal of Personality and Social Psychology,* 1975, *31,* 855–863.

Sánchez, R. *A generative study of two Spanish dialects.* Unpublished doctoral dissertation, University of Texas, Austin, 1975.

Sánchez, R. (Typescript.) 1976. *Spanish codes in the Southwest.*

Sánchez, R. Bilingualism in the Southwest. In H. H. Key, G. McCullough, & J. B. Sawyer (Eds.), *Proceedings of 6th Annual Workshop,* 1978.

Sharp, J. M. The origin of some non-standard lexical items in the Spanish of El Paso. In R. L. Ewton, Jr., & J. Ornstein (Eds.), *Studies in language and linguistics 1967-70.* El Paso, Texas: Texas Western Press, 1970.

Solé, Y. Sociolinguistic perspectives on Texas Spanish and the teaching of the standard language. In G. C. Harvey & M. Heiser (Eds,), *Southwest language and linguistics in educational perspective.* San Diego, Calif,: San Diego State University, Institute for Cultural Pluralism, 1975.

Teschner, R. V. Current research on the languages of U.S. Hispanos. *Hispania,* 1977, *60,* 347–358.

Teschner, R. V., Bills, G. & Craddock, J. *Spanish and English of U.S. Hispanos: A critical, annotated, linguistic bibliography.* Arlington, Va.: Center for Applied Linguistics, 1975.

Trejo, A. D. *Diccionario etimológico latino-americano de la delincuencia.* Mexico, D.F.: UTEHA, 1968.

Valdés-Fallis, G. Social integration and code-switching patterns: A case study of Spanish-English alternation. In G. Keller, R. Teschner, & S. Viera (Eds.), *Bilingualism in the bicentennial,* 1977.

Webb, J. T. *The origin of nonstandard elements in Southwest Spanish.* Unpublished doctoral dissertation, University of California Berkeley, 1974.

Weinreich, U. *Languages in contact.* New York: Linguistic Circle of New York, 1953.

Williams, F. *Language and poverty.* Chicago: Markham, 1970.

APPENDIX

TABLE 1
Common Variants in Southwest Spanish

1. Deaffricatization of /č/ to [š]: *oš* < *ocho*.
2. Labiodental /v/ for /b/ and [b]: *lavo* < *laβo*, *vos* < *voz*.
3. [ǥ] as velar stop: /g/.
4. /∅/ as phonological correlate of /y/ intervocalically after a front vowel: *eia* < *ella*.
5. Frequent devoicing of vowels.
6. Aspiration of /s/ between vowels; *pahamos* < *pasamos*.
7. Analogical leveling of /e/ to /i/ in radical-changing verbs of the *ir* class: *sirvir* < *servir*, *sirvimos* < *servimos*.
8. Nonstandard semantic shifts (loanshifts); *grosería* < *grocery*.
9. Reduplication of plurals: *pieses* < *pies*.
10. Massive borrowing from English (direct loans and calques) *pučar* < (to push); *tener un buen tiempo* < (to have a good time.)
11. In syntax, tendency toward congruence with English, e.g., fusing of subjunctive and indicative (or vacillation in use of former); *Quiero que vaya* ~ *Quicro que va.*
12. Metatheses of certain high-frequency lexemes; *estógamo* < *estómago*.
13. Inventory of nonstandard lexemes: *aigre* (aire): *viento*.

FIGURE 1

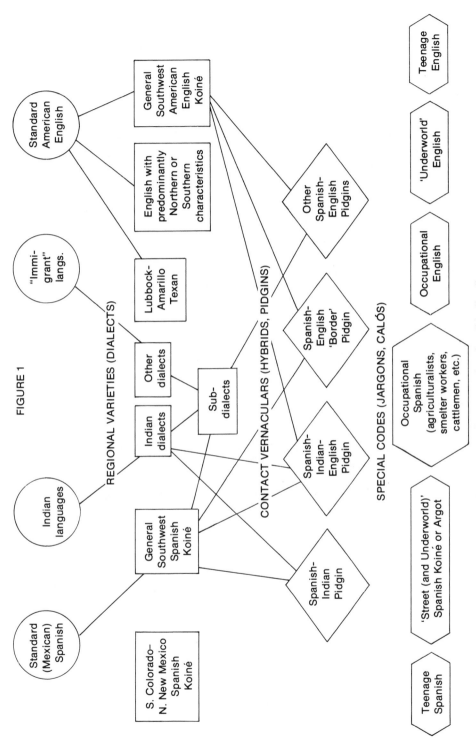

STANDARD (Mexican) Spanish

Indian languages

"Immigrant" langs.

Standard American English

S. Colorado–N. New Mexico Spanish Koiné

General Southwest Spanish Koiné

Indian dialects

Other dialects

Lubbock–Amarillo Texan

English with predominantly Northern or Southern characteristics

General Southwest American English Koiné

REGIONAL VARIETIES (DIALECTS)

Sub-dialects

Spanish-Indian Pidgin

Spanish-Indian-English Pidgin

Spanish-English 'Border' Pidgin

Other Spanish-English Pidgins

CONTACT VERNACULARS (HYBRIDS, PIDGINS)

SPECIAL CODES (JARGONS, CALÓS)

Teenage Spanish

'Street (and Underworld)' Spanish Koiné or Argot

Occupational Spanish (agriculturalists, smelter workers, cattlemen, etc.)

Occupational English

'Underworld' English

Teenage English

Southwestern language situation (idealized)

37

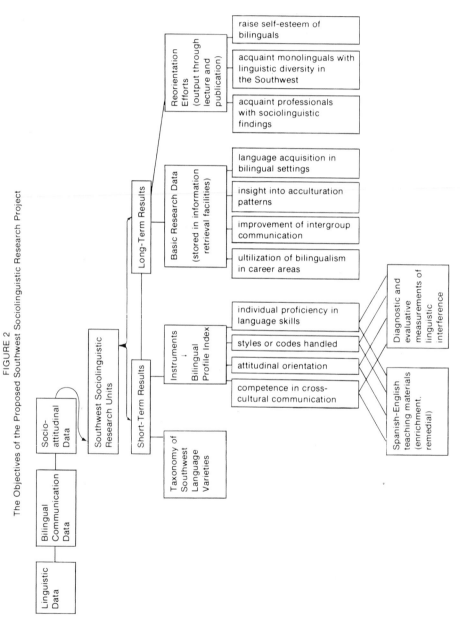

FIGURE 2
The Objectives of the Proposed Southwest Sociolinguistic Research Project

3 Independent Convergence in Chicano and New York City Puerto Rican Bilingualism[1]

Rogelio Reyes
University of San Francisco

SUMMARY

The present study is an attempt to demonstrate that in two separate bilingual speech communities in the United States—i.e., the Chicano or Mexican-American communities of the Southwest and the Puerto Rican community of New York City—there is a tendency toward the exclusive use of the formative /ea/ suffixed to an English bare infinitive in the formation of new verbs borrowed from English. This similarity of development in spite of the two communities' geographical separateness from each other seems to suggest the possible existence of a unifying influence in both communities that guides bilingual phenomena in the same direction.

Other authors, cited in this study, have observed similar phenomena (which I call *independent convergence* as a general term) in other speech communities of the world. They have not, however, isolated these phenomena explicitly as their object of study.

1. The Problem

In two separate dialects of Spanish in the United States—Chicano Spanish in the Southwest and Puerto Rican Spanish in New York City (NYCPR)—there

---

[1]The research for this paper was made possible through a fellowship from the Institute of Comparative Human Development, the Rockefeller University, New York. Essentially the same data presented in this paper, with less analysis, appear also in the appendix of my *Aspects of Chicano and New York City Puerto Rican Bilingualism,* presented at the VIII Annual Linguistics Conference, University of Wisconsin, Milwaukee, March 17, 1978.

is evidence of the formation of new verbs through the adaptation of English forms to Spanish phonology and morphology; a high number of these new verbs follow the same pattern in both dialects. This pattern may be represented as

X-*ear* (*se*)

e.g., NYCPR[2]/*biteár*/ (to beat [a rap],) /*likeár*/ (to leak), /*parkeár*/ and /*parkeárse*/ (to park), where X stands for an English suffixless root, morphologically adapted to fit the Spanish pattern, followed by the sequence /ea/ and an inflectional ending (additionally, some forms include a reflexive pronoun, exemplified above as *se*).

On first appearance, it might seem unexpected that two separate bilingual communities should independently develop the same pattern of borrowing from the dominant language. In some instances not only the pattern is identical but also the specific forms themselves (except for differences of phonetic detail—e.g., NYCPR [*palkyál*] compared to Chicano [*parkyár*]. These differences are irrelevant to the present discussion, thus making it unnecessary for me to indicate them in the phonological transcriptions.

The scanning of a Standard Spanish dictionary, however, reveals a relatively high number of verbs derived from a native base through the addition of this same sequence /ea/ and, in some instances, a reflexive pronoun (e.g., *balanza* (weighing scale) *balancear* (*se*) (to tilt, sway). In Chicano and NYCPR Spanish new verb formation, its productiveness is further developed and extended almost to its exclusive use.

2. The Formative /ea/ in New York City Puerto Rican Spanish

Consider the following examples of NYCPR speech:

(1) [*palkéalo*] *aquí* (Park it here.)
(2) *yo lo voy a* [*m̃apyál*] (I'm going to mop it).
(3) [*čekéelo*] (Shake it.)
(4) , *esta goma se* [*likea*] (This tire leaks.)

The segments [*palkéa*], [*mapyál*], [*čekée*], [*likea*] are obviously borrowings from English /park/, /mop/, /šeyk/, and /lik/, respectively (questions of phonetic detail will be addressed wherever relevant).

As examples of bilingual speech these segments represent a phenomenon distinct from that of forms like

---

[2]In this paper, the terms *New York City Puerto Rican Spanish, Chicano Spanish,* and *Standard Spanish,* will be abbreviated NYCPR, Ch., and SS, respectively. When referring to all three, the general term *Spanish* (abbreviated Sp.) will be used.

(5) NYCPR *cogimos un* [breyk] (We took a break.)

In (5), the borrowed term retains its English morphophonological form. The NYCPR speaker attempts to reproduce the English segment exactly as it sounds in English.

In the segments under discussion from examples 1–4 on the other hand, the borrowed forms are morphophonologically modified to fit the Spanish patterns—for discussion of this same distinction in Chicano Spanish see Reyes (1976), The forms focused on in examples (1) through (4) function in NYCPR speech as completely Spanish forms, there being no indication in their contextual behavior, as far as can be ascertained, of their non-Spanish origin. How much a speaker of NYCPR Spanish is aware of the non-Spanish origin of these forms is irrelevant to his competence as a speaker of this particular dialect.

As I shall demonstrate in the following discussion, the NYCPR forms studied in this paper may be properly analyzed from the point of reference of Standard Spanish (SS) derivational morphology as exemplified in pairs like SS

paso (step): *pasearse* (to stroll, to ride)
tanto (so much): *tantear* (to estimate)
buzo (diver): *bucear* (to dive)
lado (side): *ladear* (to tilt)
chistoso (funny): *chistear (to joke)*
chismoso (gossiper): *chismear* (to gossip)
sonda (sound): *sondear* (to fathom, to sound)
falso (false): *falsear* (to falsify)
balanza (scale): *balancear* (to balance)
chispa (spark): *chispear* (to let off sparks)

The verbs listed are formed through the addition of a suffix /ea/ (more accurately two suffixes /e/ and /a/ as will be demonstrated) constituting a stem, to which the inflections are added.

The reason for segmenting /ea/ into two morphemic units /e/ and /a/ is that in Spanish there already exist two independent suffixes /e/ and /a/. The existence of /e/ as a separate morpheme is seen in the SS pairs

pase (pass): *pasar* (to pass)
desagüe (drainage): *agua* (water)
parte (part): *partir* (to cut into parts)
chiste (joke): *chistoso* (funny)
corte (cut): *cortar* (to cut)

The existence of a separate morpheme /a/ is seen in the SS pairs

amar (to love): *amor* (love)
pasar (to pass): *paso* (step, pass)
desaguar (to drain): *desagüe* (drainage)
saltar (to jump): *salto* (jump)
brincar (to jump): *brinco* (jump)

In the preceding discussion I have pointed out the separate nature of the Spanish suffixes /e/ and /a/. This was done in order to explain the separate nature of /e/ and /a/ in NYCPR Spanish. Since these two morphemic units are attested in the morphology of Standard Spanish and are current in the speech of NYCPR Spanish speakers as well, there is no reason to posit a separate NYCPR Spanish morpheme /ea/ to account for the verbs borrowed and adapted from English. It is more logical to assume that these verb forms consist of a root (borrowed from English) plus two separate suffixes /e/ and /a/; e.g., /park+e+a/, map+e+a/, /ček+e+a/, /lik+e+a/, etc., followed by the appropriate inflectional ending.

If we accept this analysis, the existence of a related stem with only the suffix /e/ is not necessary to positing two separate morphemes in the NYCPR segment /ea/. In the case of NYCPR /parkéa/, for example, the separate existence of a stem */park+e/ may or may not be found in SS. /párke/ meaning park, recreation grounds, is a current form among NYC Spanish speakers. This is a question of semantics, with which—strictly speaking—we are not concerned here. Furthermore, the answer to this question is not crucial to positing a separate morpheme /e/ in the sequence /ea/ of the NYCPR Spanish verbs we are concerned with.

Historically we know that SS /párke/ and NYCPR /parkeár/, /parkeárse/ have separate origins.[3] /párke/ entered the Spanish language through earlier contact with French.[3] NYCPR /parkeár/, /parkeárse/, however, is a direct borrowing from English /park/.

Synchronically, on the other hand, we must ask ourselves whether SS. /párke/ and NYCPR /parkeár/, which coexist in NYCPR Spanish, are to be considered derivations of the same root /park/.

I have been unable to find any evidence of such a relationship.

It seems, therefore, that in NYCPR Spanish, the forms /párke/ and /parkeár/ coexist as two independent lexical items with two correspondingly separate roots /park/₁ (park recreation grounds), and /park/₂ (to park [a vehicle]).

One cannot always, however, analyze a Spanish verb ending in /eár/ as having the suffixes /e/ and /a/. Spanish /pelear/ (to fight), /desear/ (to desire), /afear/ (to make ugly), /apearse/ (to dismount), for example, more

---

[3]See Corominas (1954:671–672).

probably have a root ending in /e/ followed by the verb formative /a/; i.e., /pele+a/, /dese+a/, /a+fe+a/, respectively. From Sp. /feo/ (ugly) we know that the root is /fe+/ and not */afe+/. In /a+pe+a/ (the root /pe/ is probably related to Sp. [pyé] (foot), although in the verb forms derived from this root there is no (e) ~ (ye) alternation—e.g., apéo (I dismount), not *apyéo, apéas (you dismount), not *apyéas, etc.). I include the /e/ as part of the root in these forms because, as far as I am aware, there are no related forms without /e/. Such forms, if they could be found, would warrant positing the roots */pel/, */des/, */f/, and */p/, respectively.

For the NYCPR Spanish examples cited, I have been unable to find related forms without the suffix /e/, except for NYCPR [mápo] "mop" (noun), which is obviously related to NYCPR /mapear/ (to mop). Thus, in this example the root should be represented as /map/, whereas the other examples should be represented with the roots /parke/, /čeke/, and /like/, respectively. The speaker of NYCPR Spanish may be aware to a greater or lesser degree that these roots are somehow related to the English suffixless roots /park/, /šeyk/, and /lik/, respectively; but this awareness is inconsequential to the view that the borrowed forms in NYCPR Spanish have a root ending in /e/. The English forms /park/, /šeyk/, and /lik/, are not part of the same code as that in which NYCPR /parkeár/, /cekeár/, /likeár/, etc., occur, although both of these codes do cooccur in the same speech community.

In the foregoing discussion, the segment /e/ in NYCPR /ea/ was analyzed as a suffix or as part of the root, depending on this segment's presence or absence in other related forms. This criterion is, admittedly, negative. Serious consideration must be given to the alternative of considering all occurrences of the verb formative /ea/ as two separate suffixes, irrespective of the separate attestation of other forms without /e/ in other related forms, considering the confirmed existence of each in other undisputable forms.

Given the high productiveness of the Spanish formative /ea/ in the creation of new verbs, it is not surprising to find that virtually all the attested NYCPR verbs borrowed from English are formed in this way.[4]

3. The Formative /ea/ in Chicano Spanish

After the preceding discussion on NYCPR /ea/, it is interesting, but again hardly surprising, to find that this same suffixal complex is used in the

---

[4]Chicano Spanish, as will be explained in Section 3, also makes use of the formative /ea/ in the formation of new verbs from English bases, but in Ch. there are a few exceptions to this pattern (see p. 11).

formation of new verbs in another dialect of Spanish in the United States—Chicano Spanish of the Southwest (Ch.).[5]

In certain instances, the Chicano borrowed verbs correspond to identical forms (aside from phonetic detail) of identical meaning in NYCPR Spanish; e.g.,

Ch and NYCPR
/párkeár/, /parkeáse/, (to park)
/mapeár/ (to mop)
/cĕkeár/ (to check)
/likeárse/ (to leak)

In other instances, a specific form is found in only one or the other of the two dialects (as far as I am aware); e.g.,

Ch. only
/blofeár/ (to bluff)
/kwiteár/ (to quit)
/čayneár/ (to shine)
/dičeár/ (to ditch [school])
/pičeár/ (to pitch)
/swičeár/ (to switch)
/čiteár/ (to cheat)
/espateár/ (to spot [a billiard ball])
/weldeár/ (to weld)
/mokeár/ (to muck)
/plogeár/ (to plug up)
/r̄ayteárse/ (to ride)
/r̄ekeár/ (to wreck)
/sayneár/ (to sign)
/tapeár/ (to top, remove the top of [a plant])
/taypeár/ (to type)
/trineár/ (to train)

NYCPR only
/biteár/ (to beat [a conviction])
/cĕkeár/[6] (to shake)
/estokeárse/ (to get stuck; to butt in)
/frikeárse/ (to freak out)
/tripeár/ (to trip [on drugs, etc.])

---

[5]My data are mainly from recordings of the speech of Chicanos from the Globe-Miami area in Arizona.

[6]Although NYCPR /cĕkeár/ (to shake), if used in a Ch. context for English /šeyk/ would correspond to the regular Ch. pattern of adaptation, I have no knowledge of a Ch. */cĕkeár/ (to

In NYCPR virtually all of the attested borrowed verbs from English follow the /ea/ pattern; the only exception I am aware of is NYCPR /frisár/, /frisárse/ (to freeze).

As far as exceptions in Ch. Spanish are concerned, I have encountered the following borrowed verbs without the /ea/ formative:

/wačar/ (to watch), /wačo/ (I watch)
/wačarse/ (to watch out) /me wačo/ (I watch out)
/pončar/ (to punch [a hole, etc.]), /pončo/ (I punch)
/pučar/, /apučar/ (to push); /pučo/, /apučo/ (I push)
/mistir/ (to miss); /misto/ (I miss)—(Arizona variant of Ch. /misteár/, which follows the expected pattern.

Arizona Ch. /mistir/ is particularly interesting since it is the only form of which I am aware which has the suffix /i/ rather than /ea/, i.e., which follows the pattern of the Spanish third conjugation rather than the first. All other attested borrowed verbs, including Ch. /wačár/, /wačárse/, /pončár/, and /pučár/ are of the first conjugation, i.e., have the verb formative /a/. This itself attests to the high productiveness of the /a/ suffix in new verb formation in Chicano compared to the second (with the suffix /e/) and the third (with the suffix /i/) conjugation.

Bowen (1977:103) has noted the high frequency of verbs with what—in my analysis—is essentially the same /ea/ formant, in New Mexican Spanish (NMS)—14 percent of his total corpus. And he states that it is the most productive pattern of new verb formation in this dialect of Chicano Spanish.

It is important to note here that although Bowen's analysis of his New Mexican Spanish examples differs from mine, in some respects, we are speaking of essentially the same phenomenon. Bowen begins with the surface representations [y] and [e] of forms like [batyár]: [batéo] to justify his "vocalization" rule

---

shake). The only attestation of Ch. /čekeár/ I have is with the meaning (to check), which also follows the regular Ch. sound correspondences for English /ček/.

For the regular correspondence of Ch. /č/ for English /š/, compare also (Bowen, 1976:118):

Chicano	English
[pučár] (to push)	[pʊs]
[čaynyár] (to shine [shoes])	[šyn]
[čutyár] (to shoot [pool])	[šut]
[kročár] (to crush)	[krʌš]

Another possible example, although borrowed probably from Nahuatl rather than English, is NMS [čokokár] (to sour [as milk]) (Bowen, 1976:121), which I suspect to be from Nahuatl [šókok] (sour-thing), found also in Arizona Spanish [xokóke] (milk curds), with [x] rather than [č] for original [š].

(1) /y → e/.

Forms like NMS [*pičár*] (to pitch): [*pičéo*] (I pitch) are accounted for by Bowen by assuming a rule

(2) / čy → č/.

Thus, in Bowen's terms, forms like NMS [*pičár*]; [*pičéo*], [*swičár*] (to switch): [*swičéo*] (I switch), etc., are to be derived from underlying /*pičyar*/: /*pičyo*/, /*swičyar*/: /*swičyo*/, etc.

In my analysis of verbs of this pattern I prefer to posit /e/ as the underlying representation of the surface alternation [y] ~ [e] ~ [φ] (as in NMS [*pičár*], [*swičár*], etc.) because this same phonological alternation is seen in other instances of Chicano Spanish vowel sandhi in which unstressed surface (y) is clearly to be represented as underlying /e/ e.g.,

> Ch. *d*(yá)*lgo* for *d*/e#á/*lgo* (of something);
> *tóm*(yó)*tro* for *tóm*/e+ó/*tro* (take another one).

On the other hand, stressed /e/ does not become surface [y]; e.g.,

> Ch. *d*(éá)*lgo,* not **d*(yá)*lgo* for *d*/é#á/*lgo* (give something!);
> *tom*(éó)*tro* not **tom*(yó) *tro* for *tom*/é#ó/*tro* (I took another one).

As can be seen by these examples, the surface alternation [y] ~ [e] for underlying /e/ depends on whether or not it is stressed. This is precisely the condition that determines the alternation [y] ~ [e] in NMS *bat*[y]*ár* (to bat): *bat*[é]*o* (I bat), etc.

Bowen himself suggests the possibility of this analysis when he states, "... perhaps the NMSp verb ending /-yar/ compared to SSp /-ear/ is an effect of this (vowel) reduction..." (1977:114).

In my analysis, instead of Bowen's vocalization rule (1), I assume a Chicano "vowel reduction" rule

(3) e → y/ _____   V
       [– stress]   [– front]

which applies generally to all vowel sequences that meet the description, across as well as within word boundaries.

Once we establish the general validity of rule (3) in Ch. Spanish phonology, we can account for all [y] ~ [e] alternations of Ch. *bat*[y]*ár:bat*[é]*o,* *parqu*[y]*ár:parqu*[é]*o* etc. without the need of Bowen's rule (1). All Chicano forms with stressed suffix /e/ e.g., /*batéo*/, /*parkéo*/, etc., are exempt from rule (3) since the environment of this rule does not fit these forms.

Now, by means of Bowen's Chicano rule

(2) čy → č

we can account for the [e] ~ [φ] alternation of forms such as Ch. [pičár]:
[pičéo], [swičár]: [swičéo], etc. To be explicit, Bowen's rule (2) would be
ordered after my rule (3) so that it would apply to the intermediate forms
/pičyár/, /swičyár/, etc., but not to Ch. /pičéo/, /swičéo/, etc., with the
stress on /e/.

Besides Bowen's statistical attestation of the productiveness of this pattern
of new verb formation, it should also be pointed out that in New Mexican
Spanish as well as in Arizona Spanish, verbs which in Standard Spanish
follow other morphophonological patterns have been reformed to follow the
pattern with the /ea/ formative, e.g.,

SS	= Ch
cop[y]ár (to copy):cóp(y)o (I copy)	cop[y]ár: cop[é]o
camb[y]ár (to change): camb(y)o (I change)	camb[y]ár: camb[é]o
roc[y]ár (to spray): roc (í)o (I spray)	roc[y]ár: roc[é]o
cocinar (to cook): cocino (I cook)	cocin[y]ar: cocin[é]o
sangrar (to bleed): sangro (I bleed)	sangr[y]ar: sangr[é]o

Chicano verbs of these types seem to be in a state of transition, for not all
follow the same pattern, e.g., Ch. conf[y]ár (to trust): conf[í]o (I trust); f[y]ár
(I give credit); f(í)o (I give credit); enfr[y]ár (to make cold): enfr[í]o (I make
cold); etc., to my knowledge, have nowhere been adapted to the /ea/ pattern
and consequently there are no Chicano *conf[é]o (I trust): *f[é]o (I give
credit); *enfr[é]o (I make cold), etc.

With respect to the NYCPR Spanish data, until further research on this
question is available, I believe it is fairly safe to say that my analysis for the
Chicano data will be essentially the same for that of NYCPR data.

4. Conclusion

In the preceding discussion I have demonstrated how two separate dialects of
Spanish in the United States have independently developed and extended
almost to exclusive use the same pattern of borrowing English verbs. This fact
seems to point toward a unifying influence in the two dialects in spite of their
geographical isolation from each other. I shall refer to this influence as
independent convergence.

To conclude this study, I shall present data from other studies in other
dialects and languages that indicate the possible influence of independent
convergence.

Lapesa (1968:356) observes "la independencia de evolucion" of assibilated
/ř/ and /ř̯/ in the Spanish provinces of Rioja and Navarra and the Basque

provinces, on the one hand, and in American Spanish, on the other. He also points out the independent development of dialectal forms, such as *cáido, máiz, pior, tiatro, cuete,* in peninsular and in American Spanish presumably for Standard Spanish *caído, maíz, peor, teatro,* and *cohete,* respectively. (Lapesa does not cite the Standard Spanish equivalents). According to Lapesa, these same two separate dialectal areas of Spanish have also developed independently, forms such as *gáina, biete, amario, botea,* etc. for SS *gallina,* (hen), *billete* (bill, ticket), *amarillo* (yellow), and *botella,* (bottle), respectively.

In another part of the world, Gumperz (in press), observes that in India among bilingual Hindi-English speakers, the use of expressions such as *us-ne fix kiyā* "he fixed it." A similar pattern—i.e., the use of an unassimilated English bare infinitive accompanied by the appropriate forms of the verb *hacer* (to make) (corresponding to *karnā* in Hindi)—is found in Chicano bilingual speech e.g., *hizo improve mucho* (she improved a lot)—see Reyes (1978).

All of this seems to suggest that human linguistic behavior shows a tendency toward preference for certain linguistic structures (as opposed to other possible ones) when two languages are combined in speech.

REFERENCES

Bowen, J. D. Structural analysis of the verb system in New Mexican Spanish. In J. D. Bowen & J. Ornstein (Eds.), *Studies in Southwest Spanish.* Rowley, Mass.: Newbury, 1976.

Corominas, J. *Diccionario crítico etimológico de la lengua castellana* (Vol. III: 671–672), Madrid: Editorial Gredos, 1954.

Gumperz, J. *Conversational strategies.* New York: Academic Press, in press.

Hymes, D. *Foundations in sociolinguistics.* Philadelphia, University of Pennsylvania Press, 1974.

Key, H. *Vocabulario de la sierra de Zacapoaxtla, Puebla.* Mexico: Instituto Lingüístico de Verano, 1953.

Lapesa, R. *Historia de la lengua española* (7th ed.) Madrid: Escetier S.A., 1968.

Reyes, R. Language mixing in Chicano speech. In J. D. Bowen & J. Ornstein, (Eds.), *Studies in Southwest Spanish.* Rowley, Mass.: Newbury, 1976.

Reyes, R. *Studies in Chicano Spanish,* Bloomington Indiana: Indiana University Linguistics Club: 1978.

4 Lo Quebramos, but Only in Performance*

Beatriz R. Lavandera
Stanford University

"Being a bilingual" may mean many different things. Many who control and use two languages to varying degrees consider bilingualism a positive advantage economically, or as a mark of identity as non-Anglos in an American environment. Others consider the coexistence of two languages neutrally, as an undeniable fact. The Chicano speakers whose speech I shall be describing, share a series of less positive beliefs about their use of language. They are convinced that there is something wrong with the way they speak. They tend to consider themselves to be either primarily English or primarily Spanish speakers, and they acknowledge that they do "a lot of mixing," the implication being that this mixing is related to an incomplete proficiency in either language. The speakers I studied, like many Chicanos, are poor and socially limited. Furthermore, they believe there is a connection between the negative evaluation of their speech and the negative aspects of their socioeconomic situation.

As I have indicated elsewhere with examples from the Italian–Spanish-speaking community in Buenos Aires for some bilinguals it may be true that, because of the specialization of each code to a set of domains, neither code has fully developed stylistic variation within their performance (Lavandera, 1978). The stylistic and other nonreferential meanings are instead

---

*I thank the John Solomon Guggenheim Foundation for supporting this research with a Fellowship during 1977–1978. The final version of this article was edited by John J. Attinasi and other members of the Language Policy Task Force, Centro de Estudios Puertoriqueños, CUNY.

49

systematically expressed by means of switching. As speakers of at least three varieties (in the Chicano case, Spanish, English, and the mixed variety), their stylistically richest variety would probably be the mixed variety rather than either of the codes separately. These speakers who feel that "switching" languages is the most comfortable and natural way of expressing themselves may be only a subset of the Chicano community. I met many other Chicano bilinguals for whom switching plays only a reduced role, and they find all the necessary means of expression within monolingual English. To what extent these speakers who understand both languages but use only one of them in production are still to be considered bilinguals is an open issue which I will not discuss here. I would rather address once more the issue of what it takes to be a bilingual who feels more at ease when mixing languages and how much knowledge of each of the languages is exploited. In this paper I restrict the analysis to Spanish.

Labov has resisted the suggestion that the competence of those bilinguals who produce fragments of what he calls "strange mixtures" includes rules for alternating between the two languages. He considers the mixture itself "unsystematic," and he is right in saying that its systematicity has not been proved in a definite way. He reserves the notion of system for the codes which are involved in the mixture. We would thus have unsystematic mixture of two systematic codes. Labov finds it methodologically useful to show examples of "unsystematicity," since only the absence of "system" makes the notion of "systematic" justifiable. He writes: "It would be meaningless to say that linguistic relations are systematic if there were not also forms of communication which are unsystematic" (1971:451). Thus, he contrasts the unsystematicity of the mixture with the systematicity of the codes that are mixed.

The work of Gumperz and his coworkers focuses on the meanings of codeswitching, and therefore on its systematicity. I want to explore the other side of the issue, the extent to which the systematicity of the codes involved in the switching is preserved. I can show the use of Spanish past tenses by one of these bilingual speakers to be systematic and consistent with the distribution of tenses in monolingual dialects of Spanish. On the other hand, some extensions of the distribution of tenses are characteristic of this variety of Spanish and can be understood in terms of its "convergence" with English.

The choice of the Spanish tense system as a starting point to establish the systematic character of the Spanish used in situations of intense codeswitching is motivated by the observation that one of the most difficult areas of the Spanish language for a monolingual English speaker to learn is the distinction among past tenses of the indicative; take, for example, some of the past tense forms for *buscar* (to search, to look for [something]):

Tense	Spanish	English
imperfect indicative	*lo buscaba*	he looked for it / he was looking for it
preterite	*lo buscó*	he looked for it
past continuous (with imperfect)	*lo estaba buscando*	he was looking for it
past continuous (with preterite)	*lo estuvo buscando*	he was looking for it
present perfect	*lo ha buscado*	he has looked for it / he looked for it
pluperfect	*lo había* buscado	he had looked for it

The Spanish forms and their English translations show that there is not a one-to-one correspondence between the English and the Spanish meanings. The confusion in the use of these tenses, like the distinction between *ser* and *estar* (to be), is one of the typical grammatical "mistakes" of a native English speaker's Spanish. But whereas *ser* and *estar* sometimes appear used by bilingual speakers in ways divergent from the distribution found among monolingual speakers—see line 36 of the narrative, *yo ya era arriba* (I was already at the top), bilinguals who switch extensively use the tense system to make the same distinctions monolingual Spanish speakers make. Although the Spanish tense forms are sometimes combined with those of the English tense system, even in the same clause, the Spanish tense forms are not known fragmentarily but as members of the whole linguistic system of past tenses.

We are now approaching an issue which is far from having been investigated clearly. What does a bilingual speaker of Spanish and English know when s/he professes to know "some" Spanish? What are the characteristics of the at times incomplete native knowledge of a language by a native bilingual that nevertheless makes it different from the incomplete knowledge of that same language by a nonnative bilingual?

Some of the speakers who produced the corpus I am analyzing here can be said to know less Spanish than some monolingual English speakers who have studied Spanish systematically for several years. They are aware of this and comment on it. Yet, they do show total mastery of some of the core subsystems of the language in a native way. Which are these subsystems? How are they preserved? When are they acquired? Can the selection of some systems for preservation be explained on any functional basis? For instance, are the systems for which there is no equivalence in the other language better preserved? Or is their preservation related instead to the kinds of meanings these systems are apt to convey? Or are those systems employed more frequently in situations which favor the use of Spanish exercised more thoroughly and therefore better preserved?

An example of this last kind of correlation might be the following. The bilingual speakers analyzed here generally prefer to use Spanish to tell childhood stories, to talk about things which happened many years ago, or to describe living conditions in the old days. Since this type of narration in Spanish implies a thorough mastery of the opposition imperfect indicative/preterite, these speakers are very competent in the use of this Spanish tense opposition. It is impossible to talk about the past in Spanish without knowing this tense distinction, and switching to English in these reminiscent or evocative passages would probably fail to convey the desired effect. We would have here an instance of the relationship between the development of competence in a code or part of a code and the opportunities to exercise it. I have suggested elsewhere (Lavandera, 1978) that if a code is not applied in a wide enough range of very different situations, the competence involving the ability to vary so as to indicate different registers may remain underdeveloped even if potentially the speaker were to have the means to make such distinctions. Likewise, if one code is especially used to talk about the past and talking about plans and the future is relegated to another code, we can predict that in the first code the past system will be better preserved than the nonpast system.

The data I shall now discuss represent a family gathering which lasted four and a half hours and which I recorded semi-surreptitiously in February 1978. (The hosts agreed to the use of a recorder, which was not hidden, but the guests were told explicitly that we had taped everything only at the end of the gathering, at which time they gave their permission for me to keep the tapes.)

The speech analyzed was produced by four Chicano men, four Chicano women, and me. My contribution to the talk was minimal and consisted in answering questions about how long I had been in the country, about my job, etc. There were also some children in the house who occasionally made short entrances. They were encouraged to introduce themselves to me in Spanish, but they refused, and I hastened to introduce myself in English to them. These young people spoke English in my presence and were addressed in English by their parents. The adults, who ranged in age from forty to fifty, had all been migrant farm workers and now held better jobs, varied in their preference for one or another of the languages when speaking among themselves, but they all resorted to switching so often that this can be considered a situation conducted primarily in codeswitching. I chose to analyze one of the very few speech events which involved only Spanish.

It is interesting to note that, as a rule, recollections of the past were verbalized mainly in Spanish with switching into English, whereas descriptions of their present jobs or of people they meet at work were conducted in English, always with switching into Spanish. At one point, one of the women is describing a fellow worker in English, but she switches to Spanish to comment on what she knows about this person's childhood. This preference for using Spanish to talk about the past resulted in a high frequency of Spanish forms of the verbal past tense system.

Before turning to the examination of the text, it is important to point out that however subtle the distinction between imperfect indicative and preterite may appear to a foreigner, it is one area of the grammar where practically no variation has been reported among the different native dialects of Spanish. Use of the imperfect indicative for a preterite or vice versa is perceived as a foreign usage and there is no geographic or social variation. On the other hand, the imperfect indicative appears in socially and stylistically conditioned variation with nonpast, forms such as the conditional and the present indicative.

I shall present an analysis of past forms used to refer to the past in one of the narratives in this corpus. Past forms are also used to refer to the nonpast, and vice versa, but I shall not report on these areas of tense distribution here. It was told by Pepe, a Texan, who was characterized by others as preferring Spanish, and who in fact did use more Spanish than the others at the gathering. His narrative shows two main features: the use of tenses to organize discourse is consistent with the meanings and distribution of these forms for monolingual Spanish speakers, furthermore, a skillful use of tenses makes a narrative out of what otherwise has very few elements which would be assigned to a narrative in terms of content. It is told like a narrative and it sounds like a narrative, even though as we shall see, really very little is being told.

Pepe's story is directed mainly to Tom, another Chicano at the gathering. Dolores makes the final comment. I use *vua* as the contracted form of the paraphrastic future *voy a* (I will, I'm gonna,) and other renderings to capture the sound of the narrative such as *pa que* (*para que*) and *lotro* (*lo otro*). (A full translation of the text is found at the end of the article.)

At the Alamo

Fíjate, Tom, hablando de ese Alamo te vua platicar una historia (T... storias) Okay? Ese Alamo ahí hicieron el el ser ahí en en un lado del del río en un pueblito que se llama Bracketville *este y luego estaban estaban eh fueron ahí andaban los de esos ah carrotes y y y y este y luego las station wagons y cuanto, con la Columbia o Paramount Pictures en las puertas (T. Sí) y luego este andaban queriendo agarrar gente, especialmente muchos mejicanos porque los mejicanos los mejicanos iban a hacer los soldados mejicanos, ves? (T. Hm, hm) que iban a estar peleando contra los tejanos (T. Sí) en el Alamo (T. Sí) y luego después de casados a los cinco años que fuimos pa llá me encontré a este muchacho que era muy amigo mio y era grandote y prietote y luego tenía unas narizotas como indio... puro chicano... este y luego ya comenzamos a hablar de esto y lotro y luego ya me comenzó a platicar de la vista del Alamo y dice "No*

pos si ya, hasta trabajé en películas yo también" Digo "Ah, frega" (All. laughter)
*y luego me platicó de un incidente que iban los soldados mejicanos iban ya a
entrar al Alamo y luego ponían escaleras (T. Escaleras) Ahá! Y luego subían pa
arriba (T. Pa arriba) y luego les habían hecho pozos y luego habían puesto
colchones y luego arriba de los colchones sus cartones, y luego ee le tiraban (T.
Poca tierra) tierra pa que se miraran como que estaban quedando en el suelo (T.
Aha!) Dice "Pues yo y era arriba y luego me pusharon la escalera y ya no alcancé
a caer en el en el colchón." (B. En el colchón.* All. Laughter and comments) *En el
Alamo. (D. Quería ser estrella y se estrelló.)*

The analysis has three parts:

1. A broad examination of the structure of this narrative in Labov's terms
   (1972) which allows us to conclude that there does not seem to be
   anything specific to this particlar one which makes it different from the
   structure of narratives that have been analyzed for English and
   Spanish.
2. An attempt to establish how the use of tenses contributes to the
   structuring of the narrative.
3. From the use of Spanish past tenses to structure a narrative, some
   generalizations are made as to the distribution of past tense forms in
   this variety of United States Spanish.

A complete narrative begins when an orientation proceeds to the
complicating action, is suspended at the focus of evaluation before the
resolution, concludes with the resolution, and returns listener to the present
time with the coda (Labov, 1972:369)

The narrative structure of Pepe's discourse follows Labov's outline of
narrative elements with a few modifications. An abstract presents the capsule
summary of the narrative to follow; it may be considered part of the
orientation. The orientation section (here there are several orientations) sets
the stage of the narrative often with topic-comment or descriptive sentences.
In this narrative, the evaluation element, the point or rationale foretelling the
narrative, is rather weak, and is present in the pseudo action. Rather than
being an element of complicating action, the *pseudo action* serves to
introduce a narrative within the narrative, about an incident related to the
Alamo. This internal narrative has its own orientation, in several descriptive
clauses. The complicating action, which in developed narratives is the bulk of
the discourse, is here quite short. It is actually three short sentences conjoined
by *y* (and). Finally, the coda serves as a resumé or punch line to the entire
narrative. The punch line (line 40), which exhibits the preterite/imperfect
tense distinction, was actually uttered by neither Pepe nor Tom, but by
Dolores, another person seated at the table.

Narrative	At the Alamo
Abstract	(lines 1–3)
1st Orientation	(lines 4–13)
2nd Orientation	(lines 14–19)
Pseudo Action	(lines 22–25)
3rd Orientation	(lines 26–34)
Action	(lines 36–38)
Coda	(lines 39–40)

Abstract
1. *Fíjate, Tom*
   (Listen, Tom)
2. *hablando de ese Alamo*
   (speaking about the Alamo)
3. *te vua platicar una historia*
   (I'm gonna tell you a story)

First Orientation
4. *Ese Alamo, ahí hicieron el el ser*
   (That Alamo there they made the the be)
5. *ahí en un lado del río en un pueblito que se llama Bracketville*
   (there by the side of the river in a small town called Bracketville)
6. *y luego estaban estaban fueron ahí andaban los de esos carrotes*
   (and then they were were, went the ones who have those big wagons)
7. *y luego las station wagons y cuanto,*
   (and then the station wagons and all that,)
8. *con la Columbia o Paramount Pictures en las puertas*
   (with Columbia or Paramount pictures at the doors)
9. *y luego andaban queriendo agarrar gente*
   (and then they went around wanting to grab people)
10. *especialmente muchos mejicanos*
    (especially a lot of Mexicans)
11. *porque los mejicanos iban a hacer los soldados mejicanos*
    because they were going to make the Mexican soldiers,)
12. *ves?*
    (you see?)
13. *que iban a estar peleando contra los tejanos*
    (that were going to be fighting against the Texans)

    Second Orienation
14. *y luego después de casados a los cinco años que fuimos pa llá*
    (and then after getting married, five years after we went there)
15. *me encontré a este muchacho*
    (I met this guy)

16. *que era muy amigo mío*
(who was a very good friend of mine)
17. *era grandote y prietote*
(and was very large and very dark)
18. *y luego tenía unas narizotas como indio*
(and then he had a great big nose like an Indian)
19. *...puro chicano...*
(...pure Chicano....)

Pseudo Action
20. *y luego ya comenzamos a hablar de esto y lotro*
(and then we started to talk about this and that)
21. *y luego ya me comenzó a platicar de la vista del Alamo*
(and then he began to tell me about the movie of the Alamo)
22. *y dice*
(he says,)
23. *No pos si ya, sta trabajé en películas yo también*
("Yea, you know, I even worked in the movies already.")
24. *digo Ah, frega!*
(I say, "Oh, you're kidding!")
25. *y luego me platicó de un incidente*
(And then he told me about an incident)

Third Orientation
26. *que iban los soldados mejicanos iban ya a entrar al Alamo*
(where the Mexican soldiers were going just then to enter the Alamo)
27. *y luego ponían escaleras*
(And then they placed ladders)
28. *y luego subían pa arriba*
(and went up them)
29. *y luego les habían hecho pozos*
(and the trenches had been dug)
30. *y luego habían puesto colchones*
(and they had placed mattresses in them)
31. *y luego arriba de los colchones sus cartones*
(and then on top of the mattresses [they put] cardboards)
32. *y luego les tiraban tierra*
(and then they were throwing some earth)
33. *pa que se miraran*
(so that it would look)
34. *como que estaban quedando en el suelo*
(as if they were landing on the ground)
35. *Dice*
(He says.)

Action
36. *Pues yo ya era arriba*
    ("Well I was on top")
37. *y luego me pusharon la escalera*
    (and then they pushed my ladder
38. *y ya no alcancé a caer en el colchón.*
    (and I didn't manage to fall on the mattress.")

Coda
39. *En el Alamo.*
    (At the Alamo.)
40. (D. *Quería ser estrella y se estrelló.*)
    (D. He wanted to be a star and he splattered himself.)

The first three lines can be interpreted as the "abstract" insofar as they state in precise terms that the reason for telling the story is not to make any particular point but that mentioning El Alamo has reminded Pepe of a story about El Alamo. Pepe gets the floor by calling out to one of the participants, Tom, who, significantly, is across the room, which means that if Tom is to hear the story, everybody else must shut up and listen to it as well. The choice of the main interlocutor is furthermore justified by Tom's being the one who had been talking about El Alamo.

Lines 4–13 provide the first orientation of this narrative. Pepe gives a more precise location, *en un lado del río en un pueblito que se llama Bracketville* (by the side of the river in a small town called Bracketville) and introduces the time indirectly. No clause expresses the temporal information but the description of the activities leads to the inference that they took place at a time when they were trying to make a movie about the battle at El Alamo.

It is important to point out that the occurrence of the preterite *hicieron ser ahí* (made be there) in an utterance which is never completed nevertheless contributes to establishing when all the activities which make up the story actually took place. This constitutes an interesting example of the functionality in real communication of "ungrammatical" incomplete utterances.

This orientation section also provides information about the participants in this story. The fact that the Americans (represented by *la Columbia o Paramount Pictures*) and the *mejicanos* are going to make a movie which involves both *mejicanos* and *tejanos* is an "evaluation" of Pepe's narrative as being relevant to the ethnic concerns of his audience. In fact, the point of his story is totally unrelated to the issue of *mejicanos* and *tejanos* but Pepe's skill as a narrator becomes evident here since mentioning the different ethnic groups serves to suspend the action and to gain the attention of his listeners.

Lines 14–19 provide a second orientation which itself has the form of an embedded narrative. Thus, in the setting described by the first orientation an event takes place: the meeting of Pepe and his Chicano friend. As we see, however, this event is only a speech event in which the original narrative, that which contains the punch line, was told.

There are several things to be pointed out here. First, Pepe again uses his strategy of referring to ethnic characteristics to suggest that the story may be relevant to ethnic issues. He insists on describing his friend as *grandote y prietote* (big and dark) with *narizotas como indio* (a great big nose like an Indian) *puro Chicano* (pure Chicano) and he devotes three clauses to this description. As we see at the resolution of the story, the friend's Chicano identity or his Indian traits play no role in the comic incident. Another interesting strategy is the precision with which Pepe dates this encounter: *después de casados, a los cinco años que fuimos pa llá* (after getting married, five years after we went there). This date relates to a very important event in his life, his marriage, and creates the expectation that he will narrate a personal experience, rather than the vicarious experience which it turns out to be. The effect of personal involvement is emphasized by the clause *este muchacho que era muy amigo mío* (this guy who was a very good friend of mine)

Line 20 points, once more misleadingly, to the initiation of complicating action. No action really gets started except for a friend talking to Pepe about an incident. It is the incident itself which will constitute the complicating action, which contains the point of the story, and which is only three clauses long (36–38), all of them narrative clauses.

But lines 23 and 24 describe a "pseudo action" and thus serve another function which contributes more directly to the point made at the end: they provide the necessary contrast to make the friend's fall from the ladder more ridiculous and hilarious. An evaluation is contained in the direct quote in these lines which present Pepe's friend as showing off about this participation in the film as well as making Pepe come through as being quite impressed with the news that his friend had been an actor.

Line 26 is the beginning of the story as narrated by the friend who provides an orientation describing the time: the moment in the filming when *los soldados mejicanos iban ya a entrar al Alamo* (the Mexican soldiers were about to enter the Alamo) as well as a series of activities carried out before the main event. This orientation covers lines 26–34.

Lines 36–38 (three clauses) can be analyzed as the complicating action of the larger story, or as a story in itself, reported here within a larger speech structure by means of a direct quote. The direct quote introduced by *dice* (he says), line 35, makes the story into the narration of a personal experience, although as I have already pointed out, when we see the whole turn as a narrative, this direct quote is just a component of the narration of a vicarious experience.

Finally, by way of a coda, Pepe repeats his justification for telling the story: *En el Alamo* (in the Alamo)—line 39. They were talking about El Alamo, well, here is something that happened at El Alamo.

The basic mechanism of the narrative, which as I have already suggested, is based on unfulfilled expectations and contrast, is well captured by one of the women in a very good coda: *Queria ser estrella y se estrelló,* literally (he wanted to be a star and he crashed), but there is a pun involved which might translate as "he wanted to be a smash and he got smashed." This in itself expresses a contrast and refers to the unfulfilled expectations of fame and glory of the protagonist which matches the unfulfilled expectations of the listeners for some serious ethnic relevance in the story.

The factors which lead to isolating this fragment of speech as a single speech event identifiable as a narrative are at least the following:

1. It is explicitly introduced as a narrative: *te vua platicar una historia* (I'm gonna tell you a story.)
2. The name of the place at the very beginning, *ese Alamo* (that Alamo,) which has been mentioned in the conversation, indicates that he is going to report something that took place in *ese Alamo.* As long as Pepe keeps locating the action in the Alamo, he is interpreted as still being involved in the same story.
3. It is told without interruptions by a single person. That is, Pepe holds the floor throughout this period although he allows his listeners to intersperse brief comments and feedback.
4. The use of *luego* (then) conveys the idea of a connected succession of events, although *luego* can be shown not to have a referentially temporal meaning here. As a matter of fact, if *luego* were to be read with a referentially temporal meaning, the story would sound incoherent. The temporality of *luego* is text-oriented, it is there to indicate the connection among the different sentences.
5. Finally, I shall show that the cohesion of the narrative derives to a large extent from the appropriate use made of the tenses, specifically of the opposition imperfect indicative/preterite.

Table 1 shows that we have 18 instances of the imperfect indicative, only one of which occurs within the action, in what can, however, also be analyzed as a final orientation. Sixteen of the other 17 examples occur in sections which must in Labov's terms be labeled "orientation sections." On the other hand, of the 10 preterites, 6 occur in the telling of actions, and 4 in orientation sections. The imperfect indicative seems to be specialized for the contexts that provide the orientation, the preterites seem to have a more unmarked use, occurring in both the orientation and narration parts. This distribution is predictable from

TABLE 1
Distribution of Tenses within Narrative Elements

Structure (line numbers)	Future	Present	Imperfect	Preterite	Pluperfect
Abstract (1–3) 1st Orientation (4–13)	voy a platicar (3)	llama (5)	estaban (6) estaban (6) andaban (6) andaban queriendo (9) iban a hacer (11) iban a estar peleando (13)	hicieron (4) fueron (6)	
2nd Orientation (14–19)			que era (16)* era (17) tenía (18)	que fuimos (14)* encontré (15)	
Pseudo Action (20–25)		dice (22) digo (24)		comenzamos (20) comenzó (21) trabajé (23) platicó (25)	
3rd Orientation (26–34)			iban (26) iban ya a entrar (26) ponían (27) subían (28) tiraban (29) pa que se miraran (33)† estaban quedando (34)		habían hecho (29) habían puesto (30)
Action (35–38)		dice (35)	era (36)	pusharon (37) alancé (38)	
Coda (39–40)			quería (40)^c		
Totals	1	4	18	11	2

*The que is not subordinating the following clause (Lavandera, 1971).
†Imperfect subjunctive.

the characterization of these forms provided by the general grammars of Spanish. Thus, Bello (1847) says about the preterite only that it is "anterior" to the speech act:

> 624. *Canté, pretérito, significa la anterioridad del atributo al acto de la palabra.*
> *(Canté* (I sang), preterite, means the anteriority of the attribute to the time of speaking (Bello, 1847:210).

He does however engage in more subtle qualifications consistent with the data above when he describes the imperfect (which for Bello is called the *co-pretérito*):

> 632: *En las narraciones el co-pretérito pone a la vista los adjuntos y circunstancias y presenta, por decirlo así, la decoración del drama.*
> (In narratives, the co-preterite reveals the adjuncts and circumstances and presents, so to speak, the decoration of the drama [Bello, 1847:211]).
> 633. *Análogo es a este uso del co-pretérito el de aplicarse a acciones repetidas o habituales, que se refieren a una época pretérita que se supone conocida.*
> (Analogous to this use of the co-preterite is that of applying it to repeated or habitual actions which refer to a preterite time which is assumed to be known. [Bello, 1847:211; see also Kany, 1945, chap. V–VIII and Ramsey, 1956]).

In a very general way it can be said that in Spanish the imperfect indicative occurs mainly in contexts where background actions are described, in descriptions where several simultaneous or partially overlapping actions are enumerated, etc. It helps the inference that the limits of the action are not relevant either because the action is presented as seen from the past or because what matters is only its partial or total overlap with other actions which can be expressed with either the imperfect indicative or the preterite. Thus, the imperfect indicative is favored by contexts of habitual actions, ongoing actions which provide the background for other events to take place. In these different contexts, the imperfect indicative receives different English translations:

1. With a *would* fom for the habitual actions
   *Venía a visitarnos a menudo. Se **sentaba** en la cocina y nos **contaba** historias.*
   (He would visit us often. He would sit in the kitchen and tell us stories.)
2. With a *was....-ing* form in contexts of actions which serve as background for other actions.
   Dormía *cuando él* **entró.**
   Imperfect   Preterite
   (I was sleeping when he came in.)

Notice that in these contexts the Spanish imperfect indicative can occur either in the auxiliary *estar* with the main verb expressed by a gerund in *-ndo* (directly translatable by an -*ing* participle in English) or in the main verb itself.

Dormía ~ **estaba** *durmiendo*
Imperfect   Imperfect

Spanish grammars distinguish these two contexts of the imperfect indicative as different forms: only the main verb contexts are considered imperfect indicatives; the auxiliary + gerund forms are analyzed as "past continuous." Since, however, there are two possible forms for this "past continuous" in Spanish, one with the auxiliary inflected as an imperfect indicative, *estaban peleando* (they were fighting) and another with the preterite, *estuvieron peleando* (they were fighting), the choice of auxiliary for these two forms must be accounted for along the same lines as for the other contexts where imperfect indicative and preterite contrast.

3. With a past tense for a series of actions which are represented as simultaneous or as partially overlapping; in the narrative under analysis *ponían escaleras, subían pa arriba, le tiraban tierra* (they were placing ladders, going up them, throwing earth on them)

The effect achieved by the use of the imperfect indicative is to list the actions as unordered, as a description of the general activities that were going on. Although the meaning of the lexical items of the verb may lead to infer some temporal order in the actions in the referent, this order is skillfully deemphasized in this narrative by the choice of the imperfect indicative. The reading of these clauses is that while some of them were placing ladders against the walls, others were throwing earth down, and still others were climbing up the ladders which were already up.

If we compare Labov's comments on the English forms in his anlaysis of English narratives with the distribution of imperfect in our narrative, we can observe that the forms he predicts for the nonnarrative clauses are precisely those that translate the Spanish imperfect indicative and we find a match in the structure of narratives between the distribution of the Spanish imperfect indicative and the distribution of its equivalent forms in English.

As opposed to these uses of the imperfect indicative, the preterite tense places a situation in the past only with respect to the moment of the utterance. It is used to refer to past actions or events as told from the vantage point of the present. This perspective leads to interpreting a series of actions in the preterite as sequentially ordered. Thus, two main clauses with preterites become ordered and cannot be reversed without disturbing the temporal order. For example, *leyeron, escribieron tareas y sacaron sus libros* (they read, wrote their lessons, and took out their books) exhibits this fact of sequencing. The books in the third verb phrase are necessarily not the material read in the first phrase. In other words, two clauses in the preterite are separated by a temporal juncture and would be considered narrative clauses in this analysis. It is easy to see why half of the preterites occur in actions belonging to the section Labov calls the "complicating action." A series of preterites advances the action while the accompanying clauses that provide the evaluation, or the orientation, are placed in perspective by means of the imperfect indicative. As I shall point out, the narrative in this case exploits the marginal ordering effect of the preterites to convey the impression that action is taking place when no events are actually being reported.

Pepe starts his turn with a description containing imperfect tense forms which provide the background for some action which can be expected to be reported (first orientation). We thus have a first sequence of imperfect indicatives. This sequence by itself could have been interpreted as a description of the habitual activities at El Alamo. But, in the second orientation, the preterite *fuimos* (we went,) dated by *a los cinco años* (five years after,) indicates that the imperfect indicatives provide only the background events against which some set of actions will be developed. The first preterite leads the listener to expect others.

What is especially interesting about this narrative is that a sequence of preterites is used *only to give the impression* that a series of events is developing, since when we pay attention to the semantics of the lexical items we see that they are not really descriptions of actions:

1. *fuimos pa llá* (we went there)—line 14—does not refer to the movement involved in going there, but to the state of being there;
2. *me encontré a este muchacho* (I met this guy)—line 15—does not refer to the event of the two men meeting and could instead be replaced by (a friend of mine was there);
3. the following actions are all performatives which continue to advance the narrative only insofar as they contain more preterites which keep the discourse *sounding* like a narrative:
   comenzamos a hablar . . . y luego me comenzó a platicar . . . y luego me platico de un incidente (line 20, 21, 25).
   (we started to talk . . . and then he started to tell me . . . and then he told me of an incident.)

Finally, a present tense (which is often used as an alternate of the preterite to advance the action of the narrative) is used to express the last performative, *dice* (he says), line 35, and we get a narrative embedded as direct discourse with one orientation clause in the imperfect indicative, line 36 and two narrative clauses in the preterite, lines 37–38.

The preceding description of the different structural inferences favored by the use of one of the simple past tenses as opposed to the other does not allow us to write rules that predict the occurrence of one tense vs. another. As in the case of codeswitching (see Poplack, Chapter 10), we cannot predict when the imperfect indicative will be chosen instead of the preterite but we can predict where it is more likely to occur.

The preceding analysis shows that the meanings of the contexts in which the imperfect indicative is chosen does not contradict the general statement of Spanish grammars as to its distribution and distinction from the preterite. In this last sense we can conclude that the use Pepe makes of the preterite and the imperfect indicative in his narrative is perfectly consistent along general lines with the distribution on which all Spanish grammars agree. I can, however, point out some ways in which this distribution does not exactly match that of Spanish spoken in monolingual areas, away from contact with English. If we compare the dialect of Spanish represented by Pepe's narrative to the other dialects of Spanish, we find a skewing toward a higher frequency of occurrence of the imperfect indicative in an auxiliary than in the main verb itself. True, the forms *estar... -ndo, ir... -ndo, andar... -ndo,* etc., can be found in most monolingual dialects of Spanish, it is also quite true that their frequency in this text is noticeably higher. Although these forms are frequent in monolingual Mexican Spanish usage, it can be reasonably hypothesized that this higher frequency is related to the fact of contact with English. In fact, English has more structures which split tense and lexical meaning into an auxiliary and a main verb. I want to distinguish this case of influence of English on the distribution of a native Spanish form, however, from cases of interference which lead to forms or distributions which are alien to monolingual Spanish, i.e., gross incorporations of structures of English into the rules of Spanish. The increase in verbs with auxiliaries does not violate any of the Spanish constraints on the use of the imperfect. The interpretation of these constructions with the auxiliary in the imperfect vs. those with the auxiliary in the preterite can be carried out along the same lines as the choice between these two forms in other linguistic environments of Spanish. In the case under analysis, we may claim that United States Spanish is undergoing processes of change, as any other dialect of Spanish is, and that one of the factors influencing changes is contact with English structures. Indeed, contact with English must be seen as merely an accelerating factor, since the very same processes are found to be taking place in other dialects of Spanish.

A more general hypothesis to be discussed elsewhere is that bilingual Spanish-English speakers make more frequent use of those structures of Spanish which are equivalent to English structures than those which diverge more radically so that they minimize the grammatical structural and lexical differences between Spanish and English. If we keep in mind that these same speakers may opt to switch codes in the appropriate social circumstances, and if it proves to be correct that codeswitching is constrained to those points where there is structural equivalence between the two languages (Chapter 10), it is likely that their use of each code in monolingual situations may be affected by some need for consistency with the use of these same codes in codeswitching situations. If the occurrence of the very frequent English verb form auxiliary + main verb is increased in a speaker's Spanish production, s/he would have more potential loci for codeswitching. (This phenomenon of linguistic convergence was first reported in Gumperz (1967, 1971), describing the Kannada-Marathi situation in India).

To sum up this preliminary analysis of Pepe's narrative, I can say that it reveals an effective exploitation of the possible distinctions which can be made by choosing between the imperfect indicative and the preterite in Spanish, that insofar as it can be demonstrated, these distinctions fit into the general meanings pointed out for these tenses in the different dialects of Spanish, and they reveal the command which the speaker has of the language.

On the other hand, the analysis of the distribution of these tenses also suggests that United States Spanish is an independent variety in which some changes, such as the replacement of simple forms by periphrastic forms, are more advanced than in other dialects of Spanish. The faster rate of change in this area of the grammar must be accounted for by including contact with English as one of the favoring factors. Therefore I conclude both that this story was told making an effective use of the Spanish tense system, and that this use in this narrative has some special characteristics which would justify a separate analysis of the dialect of Spanish spoken by United States bilinguals as an independent dialect of Spanish.

The practical educational relevance of this conclusion is that it may not be adivsable to abstract the norm for United States Spanish speakers from the Spanish used in Spain, Colombia, or other monolingual Spanish-speaking communities, nor from the Spanish described in the general grammars. Neither can it be looked for among the Mexican dialects spoken by the parents of these bilinguals, or by their relatives who are still in Mexico. The Mexican norm is as independent from the Unites States norm as any other monolingual norm may be (even though the Mexican dialect may be more similar to the United States dialect of Spanish than to any other) because all monolingual norms have been and are undergoing their own processes of change; among other differences which could be pointed out, those processes lack the influence of contact with English as an accelerating factor. Finally, Spanish spoken in a monolingual situation, such as that encountered in Mexico, does not, like United States Spanish, need to fufill the functions of providing areas of equivalency of structure where codeswitching can take place.

REFERENCES

Bello, A. *Gramática de la lengua Castellana.* (With notes by Rufino J. Cuervo, rev. Niceto Alcaláamora y Torres.) Buenos Aires: Editorial Sopena. 1958. (Originally published, 1847.)

Gumperz, J. J. On the linguistic markers of bilingual communication. In J. Macnamara (Ed.), Problems of bilingualism, *The Journal of Social Issues,* 1967, *23*(2), 48–57.

Gumperz, J. J. Communication in multilingual societies. In J. J. Gumperz, *Language in Social Groups* (Selected and introduced by Anwar S. Dil). Stanford, Calif.: Stanford University Press, 1971. Also in S. Tyler (Ed.), *Cognitive anthropology.* New York: Holt, Rinehart & Winston, 1969.

Kany, C. E. *American-Spanish syntax.* Chicago: University of Chicago Press, 1945.

Labov, W. The transformation of experience in narrative syntax. In W. Labov, *Language in the Inner City.* Philadelphia: University of Pennsylvania Press, 1972.

Lavandera, B. La forma *que* del español y su contribución al mensaje. *Revista de Filología Española* 1977, *34,* 13–36. Also in J. M. Lope Blanch (Ed.), *Estudios sobre el español hablado en las principales ciudades de América.* México: Universidad Nacional Autonoma de México, 1977.

Lavandera, B. The variable component in bilingual performance. In J. Alatis (Ed.), *Proceedings of the Georgetown University Round Table on Languages and Linguistics, 1978,* Washington, D.C.: Georgetown University Press, 1978.

Ramsey, M. M. *A textbook of modern Spanish.* (Rev. R. K. Spaulding) New York: Holt, Rinehart & Winston, 1956.

APPENDIX

Look here, Tom, speaking of that Alamo, I'm gonna tell you a story. (T . . . stories) Okay? That Alamo there they made the the the be there by by one side of the river in a small town called Bracketville and then they were were, uh, went to the ones who have those big wagons were around and and and and, uhm, and then the station wagons and all that, with Columbia and Paramount Pictures at the doors. (T. Yes) And then they went around wanting to grab people, especially a lot of Mexicans because they were going to make the Mexicans Mexican soldiers, you see, that were going to be fighting against the Texans at the Alamo. (T. Yes) And then after getting married, five years after we went there. I met this guy who was a very good friend of mine and was large and very dark and then he a had a great big nose like an Indian . . . pure Chicano . . . uhm and then we started to talk about this and that and then he began to tell me about the movie of the Alamo and he says "Yeah, you know, I even worked in the movies already" I say, "Oh, you're kidding!" (All. Laughter) and then he told me about an incident where the Mexican soldiers were going they were going to enter the Alamo. And then they were placing the ladders (T. ladders) Yeah! And then they were going up them (T. Up them) and then trenches had been dug for them and then they had placed mattresses and then on top of the mattresses some cardboard and then they were throwing (T. some earth) earth so it would look as though they were staying on the ground. (T. Yeah!) He says "Well, I was standing on top and then they pushed my ladder and I no longer managed to fall on the mattress" (B. On the mattress. All. laughter and comments) In the Alamo. (D. He wanted to be a smash (lit. *star)* and he smashed himself.)

5 Formal and Functional Aspects of the Codeswitched Discourse of Bilingual Children

Erica McClure
University of Illinois, Urbana-Champaign

Scholarly interest in codeswitching has been on the increase since the fifties. That decade witnessed the publication of three seminal books in the study of multilingualism, Einar Haugen's *The Norwegian Language in America* (1953) and *Bilingualism in the Americas* (1956) and Uriel Weinreich's *Language in Contact (1953)*. In the sixties, a series of works concerned with the alternation between codes in multilingual verbal repertoires appeared (e.g., Rubin, 1962; Diebold, 1963; Ervin-Tripp, 1964; Gumperz, 1964, 1967; Clyne, 1967, 1969). By the seventies the spate of publications focusing on this issue (e.g., Gumperz, 1970, 1976; Blom & Gumperz, 1972; Gumperz & Hernandez-Chavez, 1972; Hasselmo, 1970; Rayfield, 1970; Annamalai, 1971; Gingrás, 1974; Kachru, 1975; Timm, 1975; Lance, 1975; Pfaff, 1976; Valdés-Fallis, 1976; Lipski, 1978; Poplack, 1977; Shaffer, 1978) showed that codeswitching had become an important topic in sociolinguistics. A substantial data base with respect to both the formal and functional aspects of codeswitching has now been developed.[1]

Nevertheless, a gap remains. Most researchers have collected their data from adults. Fewer authors have discussed codeswitching among children (e.g., Swain, 1972; Swain & Wesche, 1975; Cornejo; 1975; Fantini, 1974, 1978; McClure & McClure, 1975; McClure & Wentz, 1975, 1976; Wentz & McClure, 1976a, 1976b, 1977; McClure, 1977; Wentz, 1977; Genishi, 1976;

---

[1]This data base is affected by one problem. It is heavily skewed toward studies involving alternate use of Spanish and English in the United States. Studies involving other languages, particularly non-Indo-European ones are necessary in order to test the cross-linguistic validity of the constraints which have been formulated.

Huerta, 1977; Lindholm & Padilla, 1978; Zentella, 1978). A theory of the acquisition of codeswitching by bilingual children has yet to be developed. This paper will briefly summarize the author's research on this topic and compare it with the findings of other researchers. First, however, a discussion of some of the difficulties in conducting research on children's codeswitching is in order.

Two basic problems exist. First, there is no consensus among researchers as to what constitutes a codeswitch. Some (e.g., Rubin, 1962; Ervin-Tripp, 1964; Blom & Gumperz, 1972) have been concerned with the alternate choice of codes occasioned by shifts in factors, such as topic, setting, and participants. Such alternation, termed "situational switching" by Gumperz is highly unlikely to occur within a sentence but instead occurs between structurally identifiable stages or episodes of a speech event. It is therefore excluded from consideration by those whose primary interest is the formulation of the linguistic constraints on codeswitching (e.g., Gumperz, 1976; Poplack, 1977; Lipski, 1978). The latter tend to focus on "conversational codeswitching" in which "the items in question form part of the same minimal speech act, and message elements are tied by syntactic and semantic relations apparently identical to those which join passages in a single language (Gumperz, 1976). Dissension is also rife among those focusing on conversational code-switching. Two points are at issue here: (a) what constitutes a minimal codeswitch; and (b) at what linguistic level is a codeswitch defined. The first concerns the status of single lexical items from one language inserted in discourse in another. At one extreme, we have the position of Shaffer:

> . . . it has been argued that the language of elements surrounding a head word, including proper concord and agreement as marked by structure words and affixes within the phrase is a more accurate indicator of switching as opposed to borrowing. Switching would therefore seem to involve entire phrases rather than single words. It is not without good reason that Clyne (1967, p. 19) referred to switching as "multiple transference" (Schaffer, 1978:268).

At the other extreme, Pfaff (1975:17) concludes that rather than segregating language contact phenomena it may be advantageous to study their interplay. Thus in her tripartite classification of styles of codeswitching, she notes that in the third type, "Spanish street talk," "switching to English is mainly for *single* nouns, verbs, adjectives and set phrases." Somewhere in the middle is a position which does not exclude the possibility of single word switches but which seeks to distinguish them from borrowings. Generally the distinction rests on two grounds: borrowings are phonologically and morphologically integrated into the borrowing language and within the speech community they are accepted as bona fide elements of and are in general use in the borrowing language. Both these criteria are slippery. With respect to phonology, Shaffer points out

As noted by Diebold (1963) and Hasselmo among others, the phonology of switches may spill over across lexemes, especially where the switches are in close proximity rather than having been separated by a pause. Thus, some instances which researchers still wanted to classify as switches exhibited some measure of overlap. Phonology was not a totally consistent guide to identifying switches (1978: 268).

The attempt to ascertain the status of a word as borrowing or codeswitch by investigating norms of usage is also hazardous. Depending on their linguistic sophistication and attitudes, in questioning members of the same speech community about a lexeme, one may receive responses ranging from an indication of no awareness that it was ever not part of the language, through claims that it is a well-integrated borrowing, to statements that it is not part of the language at all (McClure, 1972; McClure & McClure, 1977).

Morphology does however appear to be a good indicator of the status of a lexeme. Wentz and McClure (1977) postulated a constraint on bicodal words. Poplack (1977) has formulated a similar free morpheme constant which states

CS [codeswitching] may occur at any point of the discourse at which it is possible to make a surface constituent cut and still retain a free morpheme (1977:11).

The authors cited follow Haugen (1956) in accepting morphology as a good indicator of the status of a lexeme, but Shaffer (1975, 1978) has suggested that syntactic considerations afford a better index. Indeed Shaffer's emphasis on syntax brings up the second issue. At what linguistic level is a codeswitch defined? Most researchers define it to be at the level of the lexicon. Shaffer (1978:270) suggests that higher-order, prelexical switching occurs. He gives the following three arguments in support of this position:

First...why should syntactic borrowing be assumed to have come about through *lexical* switching? It is simpler to assume that integration at a given level has been effected through switching at the same level.

Second why should it be assumed that higher order transfers require lower order transfers in the process? Lexical switching indeed suggests prior formation at higher levels in sentence generation....

Third, loan translations—including the semantic transfer of idioms—likewise indicate prelexical switching (1978:271)

Although the problem of definition plagues all researchers alike, whether their subjects be adults or children, the problem of data collection weighs more heavily on the language researcher who deals with children. A number of techniques which can be employed with adults meet with little success with child subjects. Recording naturalistic conversations or manipulated conversations (conversations in which the investigator varies characteristics of the speech event, such as topic, participants, and setting, or language to be used) appears to be successful with children as well as with adults. With children, however, it is much more difficult to obtain judgments about the meaning of recorded switches. Likewise, ratings of grammaticality or judgments about the language or languages of an utterance are very difficult to obtain from children, whether these utterances are presented in isolation or embedded in a conversational context. Indeed, such ratings can be hard to obtain from adults, for multilinguals from many speech communities tend to stigmitize all codeswitching as incorrect. Without native speakers' judgments about the grammaticality of an utterance, it is often difficult to determine whether the utterance clearly reflects the speaker's competence and so should be included in the corpus for which rules must account or whether it has been affected by performance factors, such as lapses of attention, and hence should be excluded from consideration. It appears likely that some of the lack of agreement among researchers with respect to the formulation of linguistic constraints on codswitching may be the result of the attempt by some to account for things that others have relegated to the sphere of performance. The problem of distinguishing competence from performance is greater in the child than the adult not only because of the difficulty of eliciting metalinguistic judgments from children but also because their systems may be in flux, thus making it more difficult to infer competence from performance. One technique which shows some promise in working with children is a sentence-repetition task, such as that used by researchers studying first-language acquisition. With this technique the investigator can manipulate his sentences to test hypotheses about allowable codeswitches. He need not await the fortuitous occurrence of a pattern in naturalistic conversation. Furthermore, if sentences are long enough, or sufficient time elapses between when the child hears the sentence and when he repeats it—so that he can not store it in short-term memory—it is likely that what he produces reflects his competence.

Research Design.   The data to be discussed here consist of a transcribed corpus of 90 hours of tape. This corpus was collected through a variety of techniques, including recording naturalistic and manipulated conversations, elicited sentence repetitions, and elicited sentence completions. Transcripts of conversations were situationally annotated and divided into turns of speaking. Attempts were made to elicit judgments about grammaticality and meaning of codeswitches and language(s) of utterances. These attempts met, however, with limited success. Research was conducted in two communities. The first community is a small city of about 45,000 inhabitants whose

Spanish-speaking population of over 2000 comes from Mexico and the Southwestern United States and is employed primarily in the local canneries. The second community is a small town of about 1400 inhabitants. Its Spanish-speaking population also comes both from Mexico and the southwestern United States. This population fluctuates between 100 and 200 persons and is composed of two groups: families, who are more or less permanently resident, and migrant men. The local nurseries are the main sources of employment for both groups. In the first community, research was conducted with eight three- and four-year-old children in their Head Start classrooms over a period of six months. In the second community, the researchers worked with the 39 Mexican American children enrolled in kindergarten through fourth grade during the two-year period of research and also with three preschool children who were in the care of older children in the sample. These children ranged in age from three to fifteen. Research was conducted in the school, the children's homes, the local park, and the project mobile home.

Data were collected on both the functions of and the linguistic constraints on the children's codeswitching. With respect to function, attention was paid both to the alteration of codes as they relate to changes between speech events or structurally identifiable stages of speech events, and as they occur within minimal speech acts. That is, both "situational" and "stylistic"[2] codeswitching were investigated. When we investigated the formal properties of codeswitching, a middle position was taken on what to consider a true codeswitch. An attempt was made to exclude *borrowings*, forms phonologically and morphologically integrated into the language by the speaker.[3] Single words, however, were not arbitrarily excluded from consideration. Two formal types of codeswitching, codemixing and codechanging, were also differentiated and will be discussed. Both involve lexical switching. Let us, however, turn first to a consideration of the functional properties of children's codeswitching.

Situational Codeswitching.   Language selection by adult bilinguals has been shown to be partially determined by situational factors: the social characteristics of the *participants* in the speech event (kinsmen, friends, strangers; social inferiors, equals, or superiors; juniors, age mates, or elders; etc.), *setting* (job, school, church, public place, home, etc.), *discourse type* (conversation, interview, public address, ceremony, etc.), and *topic.* Participants and topic have also been found to be important in the register variation of monolingual Anglophone children (Fischer, 1958; Weeks, 1971).

---

[2]"Stylistic" codeswitching is similar to what Gumperz (1976) terms "conversational" or "metaphorical" codeswitching.

[3]Community consensus was not criterial in deciding that a form had the status of a borrowing.

Code Selection and Participants. Among the children we studied, it appears that the earliest systematic codeswitching is a function of the category *participants*. Such switching occurs not only at junctures between conversations but also between and within turns of speaking. Examples of the latter two types are:

1. CS (girl, 7):   I want to play checkers.
   E (Anglo researcher): Ask Roli if you can.
   CS: *¿Puedo jugar* checkars? (to boy, 4)
                          (Can I play checkers?)
2. P (girl, 9):   You have to king me.
   D (girl, 6):   Do what?
   P: You gotta put one on top.
                          Mira, cómete éste. (to boy, 4)
                          (Look, eat this)

Three characteristics of participants are important: language proficiency, language preference, and social identity.

Code Selection and Langauge Proficiency. Inappropriate choice of languge when addressing a monolingual is rare. For example, although upon first entering school, children with little prior experience with the Anglo community occasionally used Spanish with Anglophone school teachers and pupils, such behavior was no longer observed after the first month of classes. Children lacking even minimal facility in English quickly resorted to one of two strategies: silence and passivity, or the use of nonverbal communication devices such as gesture to supplement one- or two-word telegraphic utterances. Fantini (1978:284–285) has noted similar findings.

In determining whether it is possible to use a particular language with an individual, young children appear to rely on binary judgments of linguistic competence—either a person knows a language or he does not. Assessments of relative ability do not enter into their decisions about language choice as they tend to do among adults and older children. Thus, those children five or younger who were Spanish dominant spoke to the author in Spanish, the language in which they were most comfortable, although in most cases their English was more fluent than her Spanish. Older children make finer discriminations in selecting a code for use with a given person. They seem to consider both the absolute degree of the hearer's proficiency in both languages and the relative language proficiencies of speaker and hearer. The older children in the second group studied used English almost exclusively in interacting with the author and Spanish almost exclusively in interacting with the four children of the group whose English was rudimentary. Zentella (1978:17) has also observed sensitivity to linguistic ability among older children. Fantini (1974:288–289) has noted increasing sophistication in assessment of linguistic ability with increasing age, but he states that his children were competent to assess language fluency by about four years of age.

Assessments of language facility also appear to account at least partially for older children using Spanish predominantly with preschoolers. Since this pattern obtains even in the case of the one preschooler in the second group who is equally proficient in Spanish and English, it would appear that the social identity,[4] preschooler, is also a factor. A random selection of 15 one-hour recordings contained 188 utterances directed to preschoolers, 67 percent of which were in Spanish. The English addressed to preschoolers is generally restricted to short, routinized expressions; Spanish is used for most utterances with high information content. Siblings of preschoolers tend to address more English to them than do other children. In our corpus, 43 percent of the 118 utterances addressed by siblings to preschoolers were in English. Only 22 percent of the 70 utterances addressed by nonsiblings to preschoolers were in English. Perhaps in interaction among siblings the social identity preschooler is not always salient. Other identities, such as sibling, may take precedence, or identity itself may not be salient and code selection may be more strongly influenced by other factors. Zentella (1978:5–6), however, notes that among the children she studied, the typical pattern was for children to use English with older siblings and Spanish with younger ones.

Code Selection and Language Preference. A good illustration of language preference and not merely ability as an important consideration is that in the second community one child who is quite fluent in English but prefers Spanish is addressed far more frequently in Spanish than are her peers who prefer to use English. Furthermore, even the very young Spanish-dominant children use English in addressing a young girl who, although she knows Spanish, refuses to use it with anyone but a monolingual.[5] Interestingly, there is a difference in the language preference trends reported by Zentella (1978:7) among Puerto Rican children and those we observed among the children we studied. Zentella found that younger children (third graders) preferred English, but the majority of the older children (sixth graders) preferred Spanish. We found instead an increasing preference for English with increasing age.

---

[4]*Social identity* is used here as in Goodenough (1969).

[5]This child's teenaged siblings are, together with the teenaged children of the Mexican-American teacher's aide, the most integrated into the Anglo community. They use English almost exclusively even in the home despite their parents' strong preference for the use of Spanish as the home language.

Code Selection and Social Identity.   Social identity is the third property of participants which influences language choice. There appears to be a characteristic pattern of language use associated with every identity relationship.[6] In most families, child-parent interactions take place in Spanish. Interactions between children and adults from the Mexican-American community also take place in Spanish.

For teacher-pupil interactions, English has been established as the appropriate language. The advent of a bilingual-bicultural program in 1972 complicated the situation. The instructors in this program were a female Anglo teacher and a Mexican-American teacher's aide, both fluent bilinguals. The former has had great difficulty in sustaining conversations in Spanish with children who know English, especially those who began school before the bilingual program started. The latter has not, although children occasionally address her in English (see Table 1). The difference may be that there is an alternate identity relationship, child–Mexican-American adult, associated with the use of Spanish which can obtain between the children and the teacher's aide. The corresponding relationship between the children and the teacher, child–Anglo adult, is associated with the use of English.

With the researchers, Anglos and Hispanos alike[7], who attempted to define for themselves an identity outside the children's previously established categories, the children generally used a mixed register in which discourse alternated between Spanish and English with frequent codemixing and codechanging. However, when interactions with them were defined in terms of the identity adult member of the community, codeswitching was minimal.

Identity also affects language choice in interactions among children. Shifting identity relationships among children are often marked by code alternation just as Blom and Gumperz (1972) have demonstrated among adults. Both peer and sibling interactions are carried on in a mixed register. Children at play have been observed to switch from Spanish to English when switching from a peer relationship to a teacher-pupil relationship. Interactions between children which involve caretaker-child relationships are almost always in Spanish. We observed that if a younger child were hurt, he was comforted by an older child in Spanish even though an immediately preceding interaction between the children might have taken place in English. The following sequence is tyical:

3. P (girl, 9):　　　　Stop it Roli, You're stupid!
　　R (brother, 3):　　You stupid Pat.
　　P:　　　　　　　　Don't hit me! (laughing and holding R off)

---

[6]The use of the term *identity relationship* also follows Goodenough (1969).

[7]The research staff included a female Mexican-American, a male Mexican-American, a female Puerto Rican, a female Peruvian, two male Anglos, and one female Anglo.

TABLE 1
Percentages of Spanish and English Used in Various Contexts*

	English	Spanish	English with Spanish elements	Spanish with English elements	Changes at sentence boundary	Changes within sentences
Interview-Family A (only the children control any English)	9	90	0	0	1	0
Interview-Family B (adults and children control English)	40	41	0	2	17	0
Bilingual classroom (Anglo teacher only)	61	10	0	10	16	3
Bilingual classroom (Mexican American teacher's aide)	4	95	0	1	0	0
Regular kindergarten	90	7	1	0	1	1
Boys† at project mobile home (interview situation)	17	72	4	3	3	0
Girls at project mobile home (interview situation)	2	91	0	7	0	0
Boys at project mobile home (free conversation)	78	22	0	0	4	0
Girls at project mobile home (free conversation)	60	31	2	1	5	1

*Figures may not add to 100 owing to rounding.
†Since girls and boys came to the project mobile home at different times, our data lack interactions between the sexes.

R: (trips and begins to cry)
P: ¡Ay, Roli! Mi hijito ¿qué pasó?
      (Oh Roli! Honey what happened?)

Corroboration of this pattern may be found in the literature (Zentella, 1978:18; Fantini, 1978:286, 289). Fantini notes that his children "displayed a propensity to speak Spanish even with American girls who baby-sat, despite awareness that the babysitters spoke only English."

Children also used Spanish for commands when assuming a position of authority. Thus, when one of our research assistants went alone to collect data from a group of children in the project mobile home, rather than as usual in the company of several other researchers, one of the older boys spontaneously assumed the role of the one responsible for keeping order among the re... His orders in this role were issued in Spanish.

It would appear that behavior in the caretaker-child relationship is modeled after that between parent and child. This pattern appears to contradict one found by both Fantini (1978:288) and Zentella (1978:18). Fantini found that his children used Spanish to convey intimacy. He states that although they used English appropriately with intimate English-speaking interlocutors, they yet displayed "an inclination—almost a desire—to switch intermittently to Spanish." Zentella notes that at least in one interactional dyad she studied, Spanish serves the *tu* (solidarity) function and English the *ud* (power) function for one of the interlocutors.

Language alteration to mark a shift in identify relationship is, of course, more common among older children than among younger children since the former have access to more identities. We found that as children become older their knowledge of English increases and so does the number of English-associated identity relationships accessible to them. Thus their use of English increases. Since in the children's culture English is less commonly used in those relationships in which females may participate (those being generally associated with the home) than in which men participate, the sex difference between the amounts of English and Spanish used by the children in free conversation (see Table 1) is not surprising.

The children studied also recognize an ethnicity component in social identity. There is an expectation that those whose physical characteristics indicate that they are of Mexican descent will speak Spanish, and those whose physical characteristics indicate that they are Anglo will speak English. In addressing a stranger, children will use physical characteristics as a guide in the selection of the appropriate language. When the bilingual teacher—a green-eyed redhead—went to visit the family of one of her pupils, a four-year-old boy asked her, *¿Cómo es que hablas como nosotros?* (How come you talk like we do?) Furthermore, it appears on the basis of interactions with the research staff and visitors that it is harder for Anglos, even those proficient in Spanish, to establish Spanish as the language of conversation than it is for Hispanos. Fantini's data (1978:287) also indicate the importance of ethnicity. He found that for his children the physical characteristics of interlocutors were more important than setting in determining language choice and mentions that his boy spontaneously greeted a Black maid in Caracas in English. Zentella (1978:15) and Poplack (1977:9) note that codeswitching among adults occurs less often with interlocutors of differing ethnicity.

Code Selection and Setting. Setting alone does not determine language choice. Thus although Spanish is used with greater frequency in the home than in any other place, English is also heard there—more in the case of some families, less in the case of others. Similarly, although English is the only language of instruction and response in the school outside the bilingual classrooms, interactions among Mexican-Americans in the classroom and on the playground are often in Spanish. The community park and project mobile home, the other settings in which observations were made, appeared to be neutral with respect to language choice. Fantini (1978:287) also found that setting had an effect, but did not by itself determine language choice. Relevant setting variables included "whether an event took place in a predominantly Spanish-speaking locale (e.g., Bolivia or Mexico)... if an English-speaking setting, whether an event occurred in the home or in a public location," and "whether at a gathering of obvious Spanish-speakers."

Code Selection and Discourse Type.   Discourse type also affects language use. During interviews[8] and narratives[9] codeswitching was strongly inhibited, but in conversations it occurred freely. The inhibition of codeswitching during formal adult-directed interviews was also observed by Zentella (1978:14) as was its relative frequency during child-centered play activities (1978:16). Fantini (1978:286) has observed related phenomena. He described a variable, "message form," which affects language choice. This category covers messages "couched in a special form distinct from that used in normal conversation," such forms as narration, role play, quotation, story telling, play, song, and jokes.[10]

Code Selection and Topic.   The topic of a discourse does not have as large an influence upon language selection in the children studied as does who is present. The children are able to and in fact do converse about anything in their experience in both languages. The discussion of a few topics is, however, more likely to occur in one language than in the other. Topics related to the family, child care, kinship, and food preparation are most often discussed in Spanish; whereas sports, school, and holidays such as Halloween and Thanksgiving are more often discussed in English. When a topic which is habitually discussed in one language happens to come up in a conversation in the other language, there is a higher incidence of codemixing and codechanging. Fantini's (1978:291) observations are similar. He found no evidence that his children related a specific language to a specific topic. He did note that an increase in interference (codeswitching?) was associated with specific topic areas, particularly those whose discussion required "culturally bound" words. As topic has been found to be an important factor in adult

---

[8]Interrogation in English of the preschool children in the small city was an exception. The children often answered English questions with Spanish responses even when they were able to respond in English.

[9]Codeswitching could, however, be artifically induced in narration by request. See McClure and Wentz (1976) for details.

[10]Some of these we have classified as aspects of stylistic switching, and they will be discussed under that heading.

bilingual usage, these findings are somewhat surprising. Fantini hypothesizes that "as the children's experiences increase (and education fosters specialized areas of knowledge), topic will probably become increasingly important as a determinant." It is, however, possible that the two sets of children studied learned their languages in a way different from that of adults whose speech patterns are reported in the literature. If so, this difference might mean that topic will never constrain these children to a particular language although it may occasion switching.

Stylistic Codeswitching. In discussing the conversational functions that codeswitching has among adults, Gumperz (1976:19–24) introduces a preliminary typology which includes the following six main headings: quotation, addressee specification, interjections, repetition, message qualification, and personalization vs. objectivization. Valdés-Fallis (1976) in discussing patterns of adult codeswitching combines in her list both situational and stylistic factors affecting codeswitching, but the stylistic patterns she mentions overlap to a great extent those just cited. Included are such categories as quotation, discourse marker (similar to Gumperz's interjections), repetition, paraphrase (related to Gumperz's message qualification and repetition), and parenthetical or personal use (related to Gumperz's personalization vs. objectivization). Unlike Gumperz, Valdés-Fallis does not mention addressee specification but does mention emphasis, contrast, narration, and preformulation (linguistic routines) as factors which affect codeswitching. Fantini (1978:286–287) has noted some of the same functions in the codeswitching of his two chldren. In his list of variables affecting their codeswitching, he includes whether an utterance was a quotation or narration; intended to exclude or include the participants (related to Gumperz's addressee specification), to underscore (Valdés-Fallis's emphasis) an utterance or replicate a previous statement (repetition), or to be self-expressive or private speech (related to Gumperz's personalization vs. objectivization and Valdés-Fallis's parenthetical or personal use). Additionally, Fantini found that role play, storytelling, song, and jokes had an effect on language choice as did whether an act "was one of 'normal' communication (i.e., unmarked verbal behavior) or intended to shock, amuse, or surprise the participants."

In our data, children's conversational codeswitching also overlapped functionally with that reported by Gumperz and Valdés-Fallis. Codeswitching appeared to take place for quotation, address specification, emphasis, clarification,[11] elaboration (Gumperz's message qualification), focus, attention attraction or retention, parenthesis of personalization vs.

---

[11]Both emphasis and clarification can be accomplished by a codeswitched repetition as indicated by Gumperz.

objectivization, and topic shift. A major difference does, however, exist between Gumperz's findings and those reported here. Gumperz has found that as a result of the "we" status of one code and the "they" status of the other, the direction of shift carries clear semantic meaning. We have not found this to be the case in our data, perhaps because our subjects are children whose systems are not fully developed. There is some evidence in Valdés-Fallis (1976) that direction is not always important; perhaps differing social parameters of communities affect the existence of this rule. (Examples of code-switching for each purpose follow.)

Quotation. Almost everyone working with codeswitching has noted that a code change often occurs marking a direct quotation. An example from our data:

4. R (girl, 9):   Then Michael told Don Pablo,¿ *Sabes quién es la novia de Hector?* (Do you know who Hector's girlfriend is?)

Addressee Specification. We have already mentioned that the characteristics of the addressee influence a child's language selection. If s/he switches addressees and the relevant characteristics of the new addressee are different from those of the previous addressee, a language switch is common. Sometimes, however, the relevant characteristics of two sequential addressees are the same, yet a language switch takes place. It seems likely that such a language switch is sometimes used to help clarify that a new person is being addressed, thereby avoiding the necessity of a later message, such as "I'm not talking to you; I'm talking to Maria." The following instance of codeswitching appears to have occurred for that reason:

5. H (girl, 13):   *Pregúntale a* Patty. *Pregúntale.* (To Rosa)
(Ask Patty. Ask her)
Wasn't I at the house? (to Patty)

We also find codeswitching associated with a change in addressee when there is an alternation between messages in the second person and messages in the third person:

6. Cr (girl, 6):   *Mira, Rosa está sacando la lengua.* (to Anglo researcher)
(Look, Rosa is sticking out her tongue)
You like Jim; you like Jim (to Rosa)

7. R (girl, 7):   Why you cry baby? (to Anglo researcher)
Está llorando. (to audience of researchers and Mexican-American girls)
(He is crying)

Emphasis.   The majority of emphatic codeswitches involve commands. Sixteen of our corpus of 74 codeswitched commands involve repetitions of commands in translation. Sentence 8 is an example:

  8. P (girl, 9):   Stay here Roli. *¡Te quedas aquí!*

There are 17 switches for commands which begin new turns of speaking:

  9. R (boy, 4):   I go get it.
      P (girl, 9):   *¡Hazte, hazte pa'allá!*
                            (Get over, get over there)

The remainder are switches for commands within a turn of speaking:

  10. C (girl, 7):   Who is that? *¡Pégalo!*
                            (Hit him)

The following examples show emphatic codeswitches which are not commands. There are only six which seem clear-cut in our entire corpus. All involve repetitions in translation, as in:

  11. T (boy, 8):   *Yo soy segundo.* (I'm second.)

Clarification.   The repetition of an utterance in translation also functions to resolve ambiguity or clarify a potential or apparent lack of understanding.

  12. C (girl, 7):   You(r) dog.
       J (Anglo researcher):   You dog? My woof?
       C: You(r) dog! *¡Tu perro!* (Your dog!)
       J: OK. What about him?
  13. I (Anglo researcher):   *¿Dónde fuiste?* (Where did you go?)
       R (boy, 3):   *A* school. (To school.)
       I: Huh?
       R: *A (la) escuela.* (To school.)

Elaboration.   Occasionally codeswitching is used when a child wishes to

  14. R (girl, 7):   *Yo lo puedo quebrar. Yo lo también...*
                            lo pu(edo) quebrar.
                            (I can break it. I can break it too...)
                            I can break this easy with my nose.

15. P (girl, 9):   Roli you stay here. *Tú quédate 'jito con*
                          Suzy.
                          (Stay with Suzy, honey)

Focus.   Here focus refers to the bringing into prominence of a constituent within a sentence, in contrast to *emphasis,* used to apply to the entire sentence. One method of focusing upon a portion of the meaning of a sentence is topicalization. Codeswitched topicalized subjects of the type illustrated in 16 are perhaps used to indicate the ethnicity of the individual who is being discussed.

16. E (boy, 8):   *Este Ernesto,* he's cheating.
                          (This Ernest)

Other examples of focus:

17. J (boy, 7):   *Pegó* right there. (He hit...)
18. C (girl, 7):   Come on give me towel, *la toalla.* (...the towel)

Attention Attraction or Retention.   Within a conversation a child may use a codeswitch as a device to attract or retain the attention of his audience. It seems likely that such codeswitching sometimes serves the same function as a raised voice, address forms, gestures, physical contact, or eye contact.[12]

19. M (girl, 9):   Now let me do it. Put your feets down.
                          ¡Mira! (Look!) It's Leti's turn again.
                          Hi Leti!

Still other cases appear to be a means of avoiding the tedium or insistence caused by multiple repetition. This type of repetition in translation has the impact of a paraphrase, not a repetition and may be used as a device to retain the floor while thinking of what to say next.

20. P (girl, 9):   *A ver, a ver...* let me see, let me see.
                          (Let me see, let me see....)
21. R (girl, 7):   *Éste es el* roof. This the roof. This is the roof.
                          (This is the roof....)

---

[12]It seems that the interjection function mentioned by Gumperz overlaps with that described here.

Parenthesis or Personalization vs. Objectivization. This phenomenon occurred frequently during naration. A child might interrupt a story with a rhetorical request or direct address to the audience. In doing so he switched codes as in:

22. T (boy, 8):   ... *respiran las llantas del tren, y*... That's all
                          I could think.
                          (...the train's tires breathe and...)
                          (This is the last sentence in an all-Spanish
                          story.)

23. H (boy, 9):   *Cayó el reloj que le regaló ella. Y luego—OK,*
                          I will be finished in a minute—*y luego el*
                          otro...
                          (The watch that she gave to him as a present
                          fell.
                          And then...and then the other.)

24. T (boy, 9):   OK. Get off!
                          What for?
                          You said you were gonna go to the mail.
                          I wasted gas for nothing!
                          ¿Qué tiene? (What's the matter with him?)
                          Take me to the party.

25. E (boy, 11):   *El es*—you know—*el hombre que*—

The first two codeswitches represent comments by the narrator about the duration of his performance, the first is also a comment about a performance difficulty. They are entirely outside the realm of statements which can be made in the role of narrator. The second two codeswitches mark a stylistic device whereby the narrator brings the audience closer to the action.

Children also code switch when interrupting a conversation with a self-directed or rhetorical statement:

26. L (girl, 5):   *Mira mi (hi) jito. La leche de tu mamá.*
                          Oh, darn, now what!
                          (Look, honey, Your mom's milk.)

or to indicate the objective truth of a statement as in:

27. J (Anglo researcher): *¿Dónde vive María?*
                          (Where does Maria live?)
    C (girl, 7):   *María vive en mi casa.*
                          (Maria lives in my house.)
                          Really she is

28. Ev (boy, 8):   *Lo pegó aquí.* I saw it.
(He hit him here.)

Topic Shift. Topic is a situational factor affecting code selection, but it does not alone determine it. Consequently, codeswitching may be used stylistically to mark a desired change in topic. An example of this type of codeswitching:

29. T (Chicana researcher):   *Dile que es una casa sin techo.*
(Tell her that it's a house without a roof.)
30. L (girl, 6):   We have a pretty, uh, Christmas tree.

Developmental Trends in Stylistic Codeswitching. Our data do not indicate a uniform developmental sequence in the use of codeswitching as a stylistic device. Some older children do not codeswitch at all for stylistic reasons in our data; some younger children do so frequently. Weeks (1971) found a lot of variability in the degree to which the monolingual children she studied manipulated register and suggested that there may be a greater range in the age in which children master the functional variation in language than in that in which they master its formal properties. Our data support this hypothesis. Nevertheless, there appear to be some patterns. There are only a few examples of emphatic codeswitching by young children; perhaps because most emphatic codeswitches involve commands. In our data there are few examples of commands by young children as most of their recorded interactions were with children older than they, where commands by the younger children were defined as inappropriate. There are no examples of focal codeswitching by children under seven. The latter fact seems strange as sentence expansion or elaboration within a language is a common strategy of young children (vide, e.g., Clark, 1974). One might expect such switching to occur at least going from English into Spanish, the language the young children generally know best. Switching to clarify a meaning by translation appears to be learned quite young. We have many examples from three-year-olds. Likewise, switching to attract or retain attention is learned early. The youngest child for whom we have clear examples of codeswitching to mark parenthesis or personalization vs. objectivization is five. The switch marked a shift from narration to commentary. All our examples of codeswitching to mark topic and addressee shift came from children at least six years old. Disregarding age, the commonest types of stylistic codeswitching were attention attraction and retention followed by emphatic codeswitching. The others were much less common.

Formal Properties of Codeswitching. Two separate linguistic devices appear to be reflected in the children's codeswitching: codechanging and codemixing. *Codechanging,* generally motivated by situational and stylistic factors, is the alternation of languages at the level of the major constituent (e.g., NP, VP, S). The code change is a complete shift to another language system. All function words, morphology, and syntax are abruptly changed as in:

31. I put the forks *en las mesas.* (... on the tables)
32. Let's see *que hay en el dos.* (... what there is on two)

Codemixing, the other type of codeswitching, is the individual's use of opposite language elements which cannot be considered to be borrowed by that individual. It occurs when a person is momentarily unable to access a term for a concept in the language which he is using but can access it in another code, or when he lacks a term in the code he is using which exactly expresses the concept he wishes to convey. Codemixing of color terms by the children studied provides a good example of the former since detailed analysis shows that for these children color terms in Spanish and English have identical referential and affective meanings. The sentence:

33. *No van a aceptar a una mujer que* can't talk business
    (They are not going to accept a woman who...)

is an example of the latter type of codemixing. "Can't talk business" is derived from an idiomatic unit in English which has for the speaker no precise, culturally appropriate Spanish equivalent. Sentences containing codemixes are generally perceived by the children to be sentences of one language containing elements of the other, unlike those containing codechanges which are felt to begin in one language and change to the other.

Codemixing takes place within constituents, and there is usually at some level an indication that the codemixed item is marked for use in a sentence of another code. For example, in 33, the use of *que* instead of *who* to introduce the relative clause suggests that the phrase is a codemix and not a codechange, but in 34.

34. I put the *tenedores* on the table. (forks)

the noun phrase "the *tenedores*" is marked for use in an English sentence by the article "the." The morphology and phonology of *tenedores* (/*tenedor* + es/) is entirely Spanish nonetheless. Consequently, it is unlikely that, among bilinguals, such an occurrence would represent a lexical borrowing. In the sentence:

35. I want a motorcycle *verde*. (green)

we can say that the Spanish adjective *verde* is codemixed into an English sentence. Spanish placement of *verde* indicates it is not a borrowing. The noun phrase "a motorcycle *verde*" is marked by "a" as being an English noun phrase. It could not be used in a Spanish sentence, but "*un* motorcycle *verde*" could, in which case "motorcycle" might be either a borrowed or codemixed noun. Its status is ambiguous because there are no clear morphological or syntactic indicators. Phonology is only one clue in making the status of opposite language elements less ambiguous, because they often contain a mixture of Spanish and English sounds.

Syntactic Constraints on Codeswitching. A codemix may "trigger" a codechange (Clyne, 1967; Valdés-Fallis, 1976; Wentz & McClure, 1977). That may explain why some researchers have concluded that codeswitching is random and others have been led to posit rather complex constraints. Those working with adult bilinguals have posited some general constraints and some which are specific. Included among the former:

1. An immediate constituent or phrase structure boundary constraint (Hasselmo, 1970; Poplack, 1977; Shaffer, 1978) which states that codeswitches occur primarily at phrase structure boundaries and that higher-level constituents have a greater probability of being switched than lower-level ones (Gumperz & Hernandez-Chavez, 1970; Poplack, 1977).
2. A homology or equivalence of structure constraint (Poplack, 1977; Lipski, 1978) stated by Lipski (1978:258) as "Whereas, the portion of a codeswitched utterance that falls before the codeswitch may indeed contain syntactically divergent elements, those portions falling after the switch must be essentially identical syntactically."
3. A frequency constraint which limits the number of code shifts that may be accommodated in a given stretch of discourse (Lipski, 1978).
4. A free morpheme constraint (Poplack, 1977) which rules out codeswitching where the switch is between a free and bound morpheme.

More specific constraints to be found in the literature include:

5. A constraint on switching between pronominal subject[13] or object and verbs (Timm, 1975; Gumperz, 1976; Lipski, 1978).

---

[13]Gumperz (1976) has also stated this conversely as the longer the subject NP the more natural the switch between NP and VP.

6. A constraint on switching the simple adjective (Gumperz, 1976; Lipski, 1978).
7. A constraint on switching between verbs and their infinitive complements (Timm, 1975).
8. A constraint on switching between auxiliaries and verbs (Timm, 1975; Lipski, 1978).
9. A constraint req·iring that a conjunction must be in the same language as the sentence tollowing it (Gumperz, 1976).

Our data on children's codeswitching support all the general constraints (see Wentz & McClure, 1975, 1976, 1977), but they only partially support the more specific constraints. Although we did not observe forms in which a main verb and pronominal subject or object differed in language, there are sufficient occurrences of forms like

36. *estaba* teaching us *en* kinder (she was... in kindergarten)
37. It sounds funny when you're *grabando* (... recording)

to indicate that cases where auxiliary and pronoun differ in language accurately reflect competence and are not just the result of performance factors. (See Wentz & McClure, 1975; Wentz, 1977 for a fuller discussion of this issue.) Furthermore, they and those like

38. '*tá* working *allí* (she was... there)

indicate that main verb and auxiliary do not have to be in the same language at least for the progessive tenses (see also Poplack, 1977; Lipski, 1978). Perhaps this is because of the great degree of structural homology of Spanish and English with respect to these tenses.

We also have many examples of codeswitched adjectives, particularly color adjectives. Adjective placement was in accord with the rule for the language of the adjective. Thus we have sentences like

39. *Yo tengo un* brown *perro.*
    (I have a... dog.)

but not

40. **Yo tengo un perro* brown.

As do Lipski (1978) and Poplack (1977), we have sentences (though few in number) with verbs in English with infinitive complements in Spanish. We have none with the reverse pattern. Perhaps this relates to the structural equivalency principle. A Spanish infinitive has a clear morphological suffix and a switch from Spanish verb to English infinitive would require an equivalent clear morphological suffix which English lacks. On the other hand in English the infinitive marker is the word "to." In a switch from English verb to Spanish infinitive the switch follows the infinitive marker "to." The infinitive suffix of the Spanish verb is ignored. Thus a sentence like

40. He wants to *coserle el cuello*. (... sew his neck)

can exist, but not

42. *Quiere* sew his neck.
    (He) wants

Finally, our data are replete with switches occurring between coordinate sentences. Although the conjunction is usually in the language of the second conjunct, we have found (as has Poplack, 1977) a significant number of instances where the conjunction follows the language of the first conjunct. In our examples this pattern seems to occur when there is an interruption in the flow of speech as for a parenthetical remark:[14]

43. *Yo no se como pero* it was a funny name. (I don't know what but...)

Developmental Patterns in the Syntax of Codeswitching.   In concluding our discussion of the formal properties of the children's codeswitching, we may note a developmental pattern. Like Poplack (1977) and Zentella (1978), we have found that the degree of control of the two language correlates with the type of codeswitching done. Children who do not have equal or almost equal proficiency in Spanish and English codeswitch predominantly at the word level.[15] This was the pattern found by Lindholm and Padilla (1978) for children between the ages of 2:10 and 6:2. Most such switches were of nouns[16]—again paralleling Lindholm and Padilla and Poplack (1977)—but more than a negligible number of interjections and color adjectives may also

---

[14]Shaffer also cites examples where a conjunction occurs in the language of the second conjunct which he attributes to borrowing.

[15]All the children studied began to acquire Spanish before English. Even in homes where siblings speak English, preschool children are addressed primarily in Spanish. A few of the children were proficient in both languages by age five, but the majority were strongly Spanish dominant on kindergarten entry. Their acquisition of English was, however, quite rapid thereafter.

[16]Nouns have generally also been found to be the category of words most frequently borrowed (Ornstein, 1976:84).

TABLE 2
Codemixing and Codechanging by Age and Language

In Spanish Sentences	Informants*			In English Sentences	Informants		
	jr	sr	Total		jr	sr	Total
Nouns							
(Ind Art)s + (N)E	18	10	28	(Ind Art)E† + (N)s	3	0	3
(Def Art)s + (N)E	21	12	33	(Def Art)E + (N)s	3	0	3
(Poss Adj)s + (N)E	21	8	29	(Poss Adj)E + (N)s	2	1	3
(Dem Adj)s + (N)E	3	0	3	(Dem Adj)E + (N)s	1	1	2
(Numeral)s + (N)E	0	3	3	(Numeral)E + (N)s	0	0	0
(Prep)s + (N)E	6	7	13	(Prep)E + (N)s	0	0	0
(Art)s + (Adj)E + (N)E	3	4	7	(Art)E + (Adj)s + (N)s	0	0	0
(Prep)s + (Adj)E + (N)E	0	2	2	(Prep)E + (Adj)s + (N)s	0	0	0
(Adj)s + (N)E	7	2	9	(Adj)E + (N)s	0	0	0
Adjectives							
(Adj)E	9	2	11	(Adj)s	0	1	1
(Adj-color)E	20	8	28	(Adj-color)s	0	0	0
Verbs							
(Verb)E	2	0	2	(Verb)s	1	2	3
Adverbs							
(Adv-place)E	1	3	4	(Adv-place)s	0	1	1
(Adv-time)E	1	2	3	(Adv-time)s	0	2	2
Conjunctions							
(Conj)E	0	0	0	(Conj)s	1	5	6
Others							
(Interjection)E	7	4	11	(Interjection)s	5	4	9
(Epithet)E	1	2	3	(Epithet)s	3	0	3
Total code mixes	138	75	213		22	22	44

*Informants are ranked as junior or senior on the basis of their linguistic maturity. Junior informants are those born after 12/30/66; senior informants were born before 12/31/66. One informant (born 5/14/68) is classified as senior despite his age.

†Nouns occurring with a zero article are classified as neither codemixing nor codechanging since it cannot be determined which they are.

TABLE 3
Codemixing and Codechanging by Age and Language

| | Informants | | | | | | |
| | Junior | | | Senior | | | |
	Sp	Eng	Total	Sp	Eng	Total	Total
Codemixing							
sample	138	22	160	75	22	97	257
percentage	54	9	62	29	9	38	100
Codechanging							
sample	15	10	25*	59	56	115	140
percentage	11	7	18	42	40	82	100

*One junior informant (born 11/3/67) was omitted as her speech differs markedly from that of other junior informants as regards codechanging. She produced 52 codechanges in the material sampled, which changes the junior-senior rates to 40 percent vs. 60 percent instead of 18 percent vs. 82 percent.

be found. Spanish sentences contain such codeswitches far more frequently than do English sentences, as is true also in Lindholm and Padilla's data.[17] The little codechanging done by nonfluent bilinguals is mainly at the sentence level. Perhaps their lack of intrasentential codeswitching relates to the equivalency constraint. Without good control of both languages, one is uncertain about where it is permissible to switch.

Children who are fluent bilinguals (in general the older children[18]) code-switch predominatetly at the constituent level. For them also, however, codechanging is predominantly of sentential-level constituents. Only among the few older siblings and parents of the chlidren in our sample who were fluent bilinguals did intrasentential codechanging occur with the frequency reported in the literature. Perhaps such switching requires a sophistication with respect to syntax which is acquired relatively late. Tables 2 and 3 summarize our data on codeswitching with respect to age.

---

[17]This pattern follows one noted by Bloomfield for borrowing:

In all cases ... it is the lower language which borrows predominantly from the upper (1933:464).

Among the children we studied, it was clear that in certain contexts speaking English carried prestige and that if one could not speak English, codemixing English into Spanish was the next best thing to do.

[18]We should also note that there were children who were competent bilinguals who virtually never code switched and that one young nonfluent bilingual codeswitched incessantly. Thus, it is probable that personal characteristics also affect patterns of codeswitching.

Conclusion. We have demonstrated that just as adult codeswitching has been shown to be governed by functional and grammatical principles, so too is codeswitching by children. Children's codeswitching is neither random nor the result of a linguistic deficit. In fact, the children's codeswitching conveys extralinguistic information about participants, setting, discourse type, and topic. Moreover, as Rayfield (1970) has noted, the ability to codeswitch provides the bilingual with "a double stock of rhetorical devices." In order to mark quotation, addressee specification, emphasis, etc., the bilingual child has not only the resources of each separate language but also the resources of a codeswitching code. Just as the monolingual improves his control over his verbal resources with age, so too does the bilingual. Further, just as there is a developmental pattern in the monolingual's syntactic control of his language, so too may such a pattern be found in the bilingual's control of the syntax of codeswitching, which begins with the mixing of single items from one code into discourse in the other and culminates in the codechanging of even more complex constituents.

REFERENCES

Annamalai, E. Lexical insertion in a mixed language. In *Papers from the Seventh Regional Meeting of the Chicago Linguistic Society.* Chicago: 1971.

Blom, J. P., & Gumperz, J. Social meaning in linguistic structures: Code-switching in Norway. In J. Gumperz & D. Hymes (Eds.), *Directions in sociolinguistics.* New York: Holt, Rinehart & Winston, 1972.

Bloomfield, L. *Language.* New York: Holt, Rinehart & Winston, 1933.

Clark, R. Performing without competence. *Journal of Child Language,* 1974, *1,* 1–10.

Clyne, M. G. *Transference and triggering.* The Hague: Martinus Nijhoff, 1967.

Clyne, M. G. Switching between language systems. *Proceedings of the 10th International Congress of Linguistics,* 1969, *1,* 343–349.

Cornejo, R. The acquisition of lexicon in the speech of bilingual children. In P. Turner (Ed.), *Bilingualism in the Southwest.* Tucson, Aris.: University of Arizona Press, 1975.

Diebold, A. R. Codeswitching in Greek-English bilingual speech. *Georgetown Monograph Series on Languages and Linguistics,* 1963, *15,* 53–62.

Ervin-Tripp, S. An analysis of the interaction of language, topic and listener. *American Anthropologist,* 1964, *66*(6), part 2, 86–102.

Fantini, A. E. *Language acquisition of a bilingual child: A sociolinguistic perspective.* Putney, Vt.: Experiment Press, 1974.

Fantini, A. E. Bilingual behavior and social cues: Case studies of two bilingual children. In M. Paradis (Ed.), *Aspects of bilingualism.* Columbia, S.C.: Hornbeam Press, 1978.

Fisher, J. Social influence in the choice of a linguistic variant. *Word,* 1958, *14,* 47–56.

Genishi, C. *Rules for code-switching in young Spanish-English speakers: An exploratory study of language socialization.* Unpublished doctoral dissertation, University of California, Berkeley, 1976.

Gingrás, R. Problems in the description of Spanish-English intrasentential code-switching. In G. Bills (Ed.), *Southwest areal linguistics.* San Diego, Calif.: Institute for Cultural Pluralism, 1974.

Goodenough, W. Rethinking "Status" and "Role" toward a general model of the cultural organization of social relationships. In S. Tyler (Ed.), *Cognitive anthropology*. New York: Holt, Rinehart & Winston, 1969.

Gumperz, J. J. Linguistic and social interaction in two communities. *American Anthropologist*, 1964, *66*(6), part 2, 137–154.

Gumperz, J. J. On the linguistic markers of bilingual communication. *Journal of Social Issues*, 1967, *23*, 48–57.

Gumperz, J. J. Verbal strategies in multilingual communication. *Georgetown Monograph Series on Languages and Linguistics*, 1970, *23*, 129–148.

Gumperz, J. J. *The sociolinguistic significance of conversational code-switching, Working Paper* 46. University of California, Berkeley, Language Behavior Research Laboratory, 1976.

Gumperz, J. J., & Hernandez-Chavez, E. Bilingualism, bidialectalism and classroom interaction. In C. Cazden, V. John, & D. Hymes (Eds.), *Functions of language in the classroom*. New York: Teachers College Press, 1972.

Hasselmo, N. Code-switching and modes of speaking. In G. G. Gilbert (Ed.), *Texas studies in bilingualism*. Berlin: De Gruyter, 1970.

Haugen, E. *The Norwegian language in America: A study in bilintual behavior*. Philadelphia: University of Pennsylvania Press, 1953.

Haugen, E. *Bilingualism in the Americas: A bibliography and research guide*. American Dialect Society 1956, *26*.

Huerta, A. The acquisition of bilingualism: A code-switching approach, *Sociolinguistic Working Paper* 39. Austin, Texas: Southwest Educational Development Laboratory, 1977.

Kachru, B. Toward structuring the form and function of code-mixing: An Indian perspective. In *Studies in the linguistic sciences* (Vol. 5). Urbana:, Ill.: University of Illinois, Department of Linguistics, 1975.

Lance, D. Spanish-English code-switching. In E. Hernandez-Chavez, A. Cohen, & A. Beltramo (Eds.), *El lenguaje de los Chicanos*. Arlington, Va.: Center for Applied Linguistics, 1975.

Lindholm, K. J., & Padilla, A. M. Language mixing in bilingual children. *Journal of Child Language*, 1978, *5*, 327–335.

Lipski, J. M. Code-switching and the problem of bilingual competence. In M. Paradis (Ed.), *Aspects of bilingualism*. Columbia, S.C.: Hornbeam Press, 1978.

McClure, E. F. *Ethnoanatomy in a multilingual community*. Unpublished doctoral dissertation, University of California, Berkeley, 1972.

McClure, E. F. Aspects of code-switching in the discourse of bilingual Mexican-American children. In M. Saville-Troike (Ed.), *Linguistics and anthropology* (Georgetown University Round Table on Languages and Linguistics). Washington, D.C.: Georgetown University Press, 1977.

McClure, E. F., & McClure, M. Code-switching among Mexican-American children. In H. Sharifi (Ed.), *From meaning to sound*. Lincoln, Neb.: University of Nebraska Press, 1975.

McClure, E. F., & McClure, M. Ethnoreconstruction. *Anthropological Linguistics*, 1977, *19*, 104–110.

McClure, E. F., & Wentz, J. Functions of code-switching among Mexican-American children. In R. Grossman, L. San, & T. Vance (Eds.), *Functionalism*. Chicago: University of Chicago, Department of Linguistics, 1975.

McClure, E. F., & Wentz, J. Code-switching in children's narratives. In F. Ingleman (Ed.), *1975 Mid-American Linguistics Conference Papers*. Lawrence, Kans.: University of Kansas, Linguistics Department, 1976.

Ornstein, J. Sociolinguistic constraints on lexical borrowing in Tarahumara: Explorations in "langue and parole" and "extential bilingualism"—an approximation. *Anthropological Linguistics*, 1976, *18*(2), 70–93.

Pfaff, C. *Syntactic constraints on code-switching: A quantative study of Spanish/English*. Paper presented at the annual meeting of the Linguistic Society of America, 1975.

Pfaff, C. Functional and structural constraints on syntactic variation in code-switching. In *Papers from the parasession on diachronic syntax*. Chicago: University of Chicago, Department of Linguistics, 1976.

Poplack, S. *Quantitative analysis of cosntraints on code-switching, Centro Working Papers.* New York: City University of New York, Centro de Estudios Puertorriqueños, 1977.

Rayfield, J. R. *The languages of a bilingual community.* The Hague: Mouton, 1970.

Rubin, J. Bilingualism in Paraguay. *Anthropological Linguistics,* 1962, *4*(1), 52–58.

Shaffer, D. The place of code-switching in linguistic contacts. In M. Paradis (Ed.), *Aspects of bilingualism.* Columbia, S. C.: Hornbeam Press, 1978.

Swain, M. K. *Bilingualism as a first language.* Unpublished doctoral dissertation, University of California, Irvine, 1972.

Swain, M. K., & Wesche, M. Linguistic interaction: A case study. *Language Sciences,* 1975, *37,* 17–22.

Timm, L. A. Spanish-English code-switching: *El porque y* how-not-to. *Romance Philology,* 1975, *28,* 473–482.

Valdés-Fallis, G. Social interaction and code-switching patterns: A case study of Spanish/English alternation. In G. Keller (Ed.), *Bilingualism in the bicentennial and beyond.* New York: Bilingual Press, 1976.

Weeks, T. Speech registers in young children. *Child Development,* 1971, *42,* 1117–1131.

Weinreich, U. *Languages in contact.* New York: Linguistic Circle of New York, 1953.

Wentz, J. *Some considerations in the development of a syntactic description of code-switching.* Unpublished doctoral dissertation, University of Illinois, 1977.

Wentz, J., & McClure, E. F. Aspects of the syntax of the code-switched discourse of bilingual children. In F. Ingemann (Ed.), *1975 Mid-American Linguistics Conference papers.* Lawrence, Kans.: University of Kansas, Linguistics Department, 1976a.

Wentz, J., & McClure, E. F. Ellipsis in bilingual discourse. In *Papers from the Twelfth Regional Meeting, Chicago Linguistics Society.* Chicago: University of Chicago, Department of Linguistics, 1976b.

Wentz, J., & McClure, E. F. Monolingual codes. In *Papers from the Thirteenth Regional Meeting, Chicago Linguistics Society.* Chicago: University of Chicago, Department of Linguistics, 1977.

Zentella, A. C. Code-switching and interactions among Puerto Rican children, *Sociolinguistic Working Paper* 50. Austin Texas: Southwest Educational Development Laboratory, 1978.

6

Codeswitching as Deliberate Verbal Strategy: A Microanalysis of Direct and Indirect Requests Among Bilingual Chicano Speakers

Guadalupe Valdés
New Mexico State University

Recent interest in the study of bilingualism has led to the increasing examination of a very common language-contact phenomenon known as codeswitching. In essence, *codeswitching* may be defined as the alternating use of two languages at the word, phrase, clause, or sentence level. Such alternation differs from what has technically been called *interference* in that the items introduced by the bilingual speaker avoid interference in the strict sense by a switch between languages, and the result is successive stretches of speech belonging to different systems.

Research in this area has included the study of language alternation in English and German, English and Swedish, English and Greek, English and Italian, English and Spanish, English and Yiddish, two dialects of Norwegian, Hindi, Punjabi, and others; the research has sought to explore the following questions:

1. Is codeswitching random and meaningless?
2. Is social information conveyed by a change in language?
3. Is codeswitching related to the relative proficiency of bilingual speakers in each of their languages?
4. Is codeswitching rule-governed?
5. Are speakers aware that they switch languages?
6. How can different code switching patterns be classified in order to facilitate further study?

and finally,

7. How do personal, as opposed to transactional, factors work to produce the "momentary inclination" which results in specific kinds of socially unpredictable switching.

In essence, whereas early researchers (Espinosa, 1917) spoke of this phenomenon as "speech mixture" and in recent years others (Lance, 1969; Phillips, 1967) have emphasized the seemingly unpredictable nature of the process, it is now evident that codeswitching is neither totally random nor unpredictable. Indeed, it has been demonstrated (Gumperz, 1969, 1970; Blom & Gumperz, 1972) that such language alternation conveys important social information, ranging from reflecting role relationships between speakers to conveying feelings of solidarity, intimacy, etc. Moreover, it is clear from Rayfield's work (1970) that codeswitching occurs not only in response to the social situation but also as a personal rhetorical device which is used both to add color to speech and to emphasize a given statement. Such personal use, as Hasselmo (1956) and Valdés-Fallis (1974) have suggested, is dependent upon the linguistic resources at the disposal of the speaker.

Generalizing broadly, it can be said that to this point research on codeswitching has concentrated on the analysis of two distinct areas: the nature of codeswitching when it occurs in response to a social situation; the nature of codeswitching when it is dependent upon the individual speaker's personal preference, inclination, or need, given that the social situation in question permits either code. This paper is concerned with the second of these two areas, especially with analyzing more specifically a claim which has become central to most discussions of the phenomenon, namely, that some bilinguals "alternate between the two languages for much of the same reasons that monolinguals select among styles of a single language" (Gumperz, 1967:48). Intuitively most researchers have agreed with this claim and, indeed, my own study of codeswitching patterns (Valdés-Fallis, 1976) revealed a number of instances in which language alternation was used for rhetorical or stylistic purposes (for emphasis or contrast) in contexts where one might well conjecture that monolingual speakers would have used other verbal strategies. The problem nevertheless still involves being able to identify concretely some of the "reasons" for which monolinguals choose among different styles or registers. Until we can identify those reasons, or at least some of them, we will not be able to do more than conjecture that language alternation takes place in a parallel fashion.

Recent work in conversational analysis, however, particularly work in the area of requests (Ervin-Tripp, 1976; Labov & Fanshel, 1977) has begun to look closely at the verbal strategies which a speaker uses in order to imply meaning. Most of this work has been done with reference to monolinguals, but the basic principles are clearly applicable to bilingual speech. From this perspective, conversation is essentially seen as a means that people use to deal with one another, and interaction is defined as "action which affects (alters or maintains) the relations of the self and others in face-to-face communication" (Labov & Fanshel, 1977:59).

For the purpose of this study, Labov's recent work on therapeutic discourse served as an ideal starting point for the study of codeswitching as a verbal strategy. His analysis of the processes of both mitigation and aggravation identified *reasons* for which monolingual speakers choose among a number of varying strategies in order to convey desired impressions. These same reasons could then be identified in speech exchanges in which bilingual speakers were seen to be involved in bringing across similar meanings and the strategies utilized in this process analyzed. This paper, then, focuses on codeswitching in one type of speech action, the request, among Mexican-American bilinguals applying the rules for both indirect and direct requests which Labov developed in his work on therapeutic discourse. It will be demonstrated that bilingual speakers used language alternation as a supplementary device in carrying across a number of meanings, most specifically the aggravation and mitigation of requests.

LABOV'S FRAMEWORK OF ANALYSIS:
A BRIEF SUMMARY

Because of the importance of the framework established by Labov to this study, its major points will be reviewed briefly and two major rules of discourse relating to requests will be recalled in their entirety.

For the analysis of therapeutic discourse, Labov and his associates concentrated on four groups of speech acts or verbal interactions. The first of these involves "meta" actions which have to do with the sequencing or regulation of speech itself. In essence, such *metalinguistic actions* encompass what a speaker does when he is doing something other than taking his turn at speaking; i.e., when he is initiating, responding, ending the exchange, etc. The second group includes *representations* which are in fact verbalizations of some state of affairs in the speaker's biography. The third group includes *requests* of various kinds: requests for action, information, attention, confirmation, and the like; pleas and suggestions are classified as mitigated requests, commands and demands are classified as unmitigated or aggravated requests. Finally, the fourth group involves interactional statements which may represent or be interpreted as more personal actions. These statements include challenges (criticism, attacks, denigrations) and statements of support (praise, flattery, etc.). Additionally, these four types of speech actions may be further classified as *direct* or *indirect* depending upon the mode of interaction between the speakers in question.

In order to clarify the relationship between what is said and the immediate interpretation of the actions actually underlying the utterances themselves, Labov developed a number of rules for the interpretation of requests and narratives. His stated purpose was to construct rules which, although using a controlled and limited vocabulary, were written in ordinary language. He emphasized that the application of rules depends upon the researcher's knowledge of the context in question and is based ultimately on the knowledge concerning needs, abilities, rights, and obligations that is shared by the participants.

A summary of Labov's rules for requests, together with the preconditions underlying such requests, follows:

Rule of Requests

If A addresses to B an imperative specifying an action X at a time T_1, and B believes that A believes that

    1a. X should be done (for a purpose Y) (*need for the action*)
     b. B would not do X in the absence of the request (*need for the request*).
    2. B has the *ability* to do X (with an instrument Z).
    3. B has the *obligation* to do X or is willing to do it.
    4. A has the *right* to tell B to do X, then A is heard as making a valid request for action (Labov & Fanshel: 78).

This rule clearly differentiates between an utterance such as *drop dead* and a true direct command. Indeed, in expanding on the preceding rule, Labov makes clear that four conditions must be in evidence before a hearer will interpret a given utterance as a direct request. These four conditions involve needs, abilities, obligations, and rights. When any of these four conditions is not present, an utterance will not be heard as a valid request.

These four conditions are even more important in the interpretation of indirect requests:

Rule for Indirect Requests

If A makes to B a Request for Information or an assertion to B about

    a. the existential status of an action X to be performed by B
    b. the consequences of performing an action X
    c. the time T_1 that an action X might be performed by B
    d. any of the preconditions for a valid request for X as given in the Rule of Requests

and all other preconditions are in effect, then A is heard as making a valid request of B for the action X (Labov & Fanshel: 82).

Essentially an indirect request can be made which refers to any one of the four preconditions. For example, alternative possibilities for the following indirect request: "Wellyou know, w'dy' mind takin' thedustrag an' just dustaround?"

    a.   Existential Status: Have you dusted yet?
                                      You don't seem to have dusted this room yet.

b.	Consequences:	How would it look if you were to dust this room?
		This room would look a lot better if you dusted it.
c.	Time Referents:	When do you plan to dust.
		How long will you let this go on?
d.	Other Preconditions:	
	Need for the Action:	Don't you think the dust is pretty thick?
		This place is really dusty.
	Ability:	Can you grab a dust rag and just dust around?
		You have time enough to dust before you go.
	Willingness:	Would you mind picking up a dust rag?
		I'm sure you wouldn't mind picking up a dust rag and just dusting around.
	Obligation:	Isn't it your turn to dust?
		You ought to do your part in keeping this place clean (Labov & Fanshel: 83).

Indirect requests, because of their indirectness, are generally heard as more "polite" than direct requests. If, however, a speaker chooses the "polite" alternative, he will still retain option of being as gentle as possible or conversely as assertive or even as aggressive as he desires. A wide range of strategies is available. For example, if a speaker wishes to avoid offense and indeed to mitigate or soften his request as much as possible, he can choose a syntactic pattern generally perceived as high on the scale of mitigation, or he may decide to mitigate by the use of specific intonation patterns, or by the selection of references within which he couches his request. In general, references to needs and abilities serve to mitigate requests; references to right and obligations are most likely to be interpreted as aggravating.

Briefly, strategies for both mitigating and aggravating requests may include the choice of syntactic devices, choice of intonational contours, choice of rapid vs. slow speech etc. An illustration of the effect of syntactic devices on mitigation and aggravation can be seen in these examples of Labov's. In this illustration, it is evident that requests for information are higher on the scale of mitigation than are assertions or tag questions.

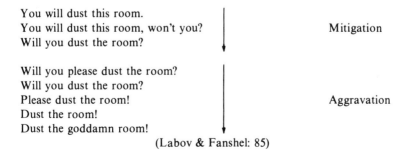

You will dust this room.
You will dust this room, won't you?   Mitigation
Will you dust the room?

Will you please dust the room?
Will you dust the room?
Please dust the room!   Aggravation
Dust the room!
Dust the goddamn room!
(Labov & Fanshel: 85)

The area of mitigation is a particularly interesting one in the study of the use of indirect requests by bilingual speakers. As will be seen, the devices generally employed by monolingual speakers are often supplemented in bilingual speech by a shift in codes.

Labov's work includes a number of other rules which are central to the interpretation of requests as a whole. They are concerned, for example, with how a speaker can put off a request, how an accounting accompanying such a refusal serves to avoid breaking off social relations with the requester, and finally how challenges (requests for information which are actually critical of a person's on-going role) are appropriately reacted to with a defense. Each of these areas lends itself to the examination of bilingual interaction, and especially to the analysis of *how* the bilingual speaker exploits his two languages to criticize, support, blame, mitigate, etc. Because of the limited scope of this paper, however, I shall not expand further on the rules relating to other kinds of requests which were developed by Labov. Instead, the reader is referred to Labov and Fanshel (1977: Chap. 3) for details concerning these areas.

LANGUAGE ALTERNATION IN DIRECT AND INDIRECT REQUESTS

A. Preliminary Considerations

It was hypothesized that the preconditions for the use of codeswitching as a deliberate verbal strategy are:

1. That both participants be bilingual;
2. That both participants be members of the same speech community or be acceptable to one another as persons with whom both languages may be used freely;
3. That both participants have the linguistic resources necessary to carry out the required switches.

B. The Corpus

The tapes examined for this study are part of the New Mexico State University Corpus which I have been collecting since 1973. It now includes over 200 hours of recorded conversations. All recordings have been made by students whose proficiency in each language I had studied in some depth. Each recording involves the student engaged in ordinary, natural conversations (not interviews) with a variety of acquaintances of varying ages, backgrounds, and linguistic strengths. Each conversation has been catalogued according to the characteristics of the speakers involved in the conversation, details of significance relating to the context in which the exchange took place, the underlying relationships between speakers, etc.

For this study, 10 conversations were analyzed which involved speakers categorized as AB according to Valdés-Fallis (1974); i.e., speakers considered to have the linguistic proficiency in both languages sufficient to carry out extended switches in both English and Spanish. Elsewhere (Valdés-Fallis, 1974) I have demonstrated that not all bilinguals have the resources necessary for using the same kinds of patterns of switching in both of their languages.

The 10 tapes which were analyzed had been transcribed for previous studies using standard orthography to indicate such features as rapid, careless speech, pauses, hesitations, and recognized regional and social variations. In the tapes examined, a total of 45 requests was found. Of this number, 16 requests used only one language throughout, and 29 requests involved the use of two languages. For this study, I was concerned exclusively with the dynamics of requests which alternated between two languages.

C. The Use of Two Languages in Direct Requests

Direct requests were defined as those which followed Labov's *Rule of Requests,* essentially those in which an imperative was used. Although overall, direct requests were rare (7 out of 29), and in all cases involved parent/child interaction, they can be said to follow one of two basic patterns.

Pattern 1 (Direct).   If two speakers are momentarily using language A as the base language, a direct request may be emphasized (aggravated or mitigated) by a change to language B for the expression of the imperative itself.

For example, in an exchange involving a mother and a son (about 14), the conversation went as follows:

M. An' then what?
S. Well, we dint really say nothing.. Poncho got on his bike an'went off.
M. Umm..
S. Yeah.. and..
M. Listen, your gum is driving me up a tree.
S. He.. took off.. and.. [Son continues to chew gum noisily.]
M. *Tira el chicle y luego me dices.* (Throw your gum away and then tell me.)

Essentially, an indirect request referring to a need for action (stop chewing gum) is ignored by the son. A direct request is then made but further emphasized by a total change in language. By this switch, the mother alters the relationship maintained in the conversation up to that point. While previously she had acted as a trusted confidante, she now steps back into her role as parent.

A similar strategy was used between a mother and a younger son (10) in which, again, repeated requests went unheard. It is possible that for this specific family, commands given in Spanish are high in the scale of aggravation and might be equivalent to a monolingual English-speaking mother's phrasing request as "Jonathan P. Ellerick, come down this instant!"

> Mother. Who's that going down the street?
> R. That's Dana.
> B. Uh, uh, Dana has blond hair.
> Mother. Leo, *siéntate. Mira lo que estás haciendo. Tas tirando todo el* milkshake. (Leo, sit down. Look at what you are doing. You're spilling all the milkshake.)
> B. Oh, gross.
> Mother. No. No. No. *Agarra algo y límpialo.* (Grab something and clean it.)
> R. *Cochino.* (Dirty)
> Boy (10). *Conchino.* (Dirty)

No examples were found of a change in languages which seemed to mitigate a direct request, but it must be assumed, until it is demonstrated otherwise, that such a change, given the right context, might indeed have that effect.

The second pattern identified for language alternation in direct requests can be stated as follows:

Pattern 2 (Direct). If two speakers are momentarily using language A as the base language and a direct request is then made in that same language, the request can be mitigated by the addition of an accounting (relating to the four preconditions) in language B.

For example:

No toques eso (Don't touch that). I don't want it broken. Hang up right now, *Todavía tienes que acabar con este tiradero.* (You still have to finish with this mess.)

Clearly, this second pattern (mitigating by accounting) is equally available to monolingual speakers. Labov does not dwell on this type of strategy, but in my sample, direct requests seldom occurred without an accompanying softening statement concerning the preconditions previously mentioned: rights, obligations, needs, and abilities. A number of requests which did not change languages involved exactly the same strategy:

Finish it up, Beto. I don't want to have to throw it away.

The direction of the language switch does not seem to be an important factor. That is, switching to English does not necessarily aggravate and

Spanish mitigate. Both can be used to do either, depending upon the base language chosen and the possibilities offered for contrast by switching to the other language. Indeed, it seems that in this area it is precisely the contrast itself which is being exploited, very much the same way that intonational contours are exploited by monolingual speakers.

D. The Use of Two Languages In Indirect Requests

The total number of indirect requests which used two languages was twenty-two. These included indirect requests, requests for information, embedded requests, and reinstated requests. Two predominant patterns were identified.

Pattern 1 (Indirect).   If two speakers are momentarily using language A as the base language, an indirect request may be introduced by a change in language. Such an introductory switch serves to further mitigate the request.

For example, in an exchange involving a young woman who hoped to persuade a coworker to speak in her behalf to their boss, the woman wished to convey the impression that she was uncertain, afraid, and in need of protection. This impression was further accentuated by a change of language.

J. *Pos no sé.* El ya se lo dijo y yo no.. (Well, I don't know. He already told him and I don't..)

M. Well..I..kind of wish.*No cres que si tú le dices otra vez y le explicas*.. (Don't you think that if you tell him again and explain to him.)

In this exchange, M. hoped to persuade J. to intercede in her behalf. Her request, however, given their relationship, could only be an indirect one. For this sample, the steps along the scale of mitigation might be:

No cres que si tú le dices otra vez y le explicas... (Don't you think that if you tell him again and explain to him...)

Pues.. Yo.. como que quisiera.. No cres que si tú le dices otra vez y le explicas..(Well, I kind of would like... Don't you think that if you tell him again and explain to him...)

Well...I...kind of wish...*No cres que si tú le dices otra vez y le explicas*... (Don't you think that if you tell him again and explain to him)

The prefaced remarks in both languages serve to convey an uncertainty by M. concerning J.'s implication that there is nothing to be done. By conveying uncertainty, M. does not question J.'s judgment directly, which she does not want to do. By switching to English for the prefaced remark, M. adds to the impression of uncertainty and confusion which she has sought to convey throughout the interaction. The vacillation, so to speak, between languages is deliberately designed to accentuate the desired effect.

As in the area of direct request, the direction of the language switch for prefaced remarks seemed to make little difference. In all instances, a switch in language was clearly used to soften a request which followed. In a number of cases, however, when English had been sustained as the base language for some time, the switch to Spanish before an indirect request resembled what have been classified elsewhere as identity markers.

>N. I think that's the way it's got to be done.
>B. *Mira mano,* you just have to do it till it's okay and they say it's okay. (Look, man..)

In this particular case, B., as a superior of N.'s but also a Chicano, softened a harsh indirect request (reference to obligations) by reminding N. that he is also a Chicano and therefore on his side. Again, the effect is the mitigation of the request by a prefaced remark, but the effect conveyed is quite different from that conveyed by the first example given.

The second pattern which was identified in the area of indirect requests was similar:

Pattern 2 (Indirect).   If two speakers are momentarily using language A as the base language, an indirect request may be further emphasized (mitigated/aggravated) by a switch to language B for the expression of the entire request.

For example:

>T. Well right now it's not doin' too good.
>N. Why, is it stalling out on you again?
>T. Yeah..especially in the morning.
>N. Maybe you're not letting it warm up enough?
>T. *No, lo que necesita es que alguien que sepa de carros me lo chequié.* (No, what it needs is that someone who knows about cars checks it out for me.)
>N. *Bueno, pos si quieres que le meta mano,* I'll be glad to. (o.k., well if you want me to give it a try,)
>J. *No, pos, ay nomás, dándole. ¿Y tú?* (Well, just going along, and you)
>L. *Batallando con el clase de* sociology *todavía.* (Still struggling with the sociology class.)
>J. *Yo creía que libas* a drop. (I thought you were going to drop it.)
>L. *Sí pero lo decidí que no.* (Yes, but then I decided not to.)
>J. Listen are you going' by Theresa's later on?
>L. Yeah, I guess so, why?
>J. Well, maybe you could drop me by there on your way.

In each of the foregoing examples, the speaker who made the indirect request switched to the opposite language. In both cases the switch served two purposes: to call attention to the speaker's changing the subject; and to couch the request in the right tone. In the first example, a young Chicano further exploited the view that women are helpless in the face of mechanical difficulties by coyly making a very indirect request in Spanish. The same remark in English might have further emphasized her English-language–related qualities of independence and competence. Thus, the request, indirect as it was, might not have met the needs precondition referred to. In any event, T. hoped to emphasize her "need" by playing the role of dependent female. The switch to Spanish added to the desired effect.

In the second example, a young male switched to English to make a sudden request. It is possible that the use of this language seemed to permit a certain kind of relationship with the Chicano in question, not possible for him in the Spanish language context. Indeed, the young man involved prefers to use English with other Chicanos for establishing a friendly, informal mood. He finds it much easier, for example, to joke and kid with young women in English and associates Spanish with highly ritualized family activities.

As illustrated earlier in other types of language switches, the direction of language shift seems again to be unimportant. The bilingual speaker merely uses such shifts as additional devices for emphasizing requests at those points at which monolingual speakers might exploit intonational contours or other syntactic patterns.

LANGUAGE ALTERNATION IN REPORTED REQUESTS

The foregoing analysis of language alternation in both direct and indirect requests has involved samples of statements uttered in the course of actual interaction. It is important to emphasize here that the framework and the analysis used by Labov, which have been cited, were applied specifically to therapeutic discourse, a type of language interaction which involves the patient's recounting a number of speech exchanges held with others. In studying the use of language alternation for the formulation of either direct or indirect requests and specifically the mitigation or aggravation of these requests by a change in language, such "reported" conversations among bilinguals present some difficulties of interpretation.

Examples of speakers relating a past incident which included a request (direct or indirect) made of them by another speaker were many and frequent in the corpus. Such "reported" requests typically took the following form:

Y luego me dijo: (And then he said) "Why don't you ever come to see me, Buddy?"

and:

> *Estabamos así platicando y todo y riéndonse de Sharon y de su hermana.*
> (We were talking in that way and all and laughing about Sharon and her
> sister.) *Y luego me sale con que* (And then he comes out with) "You are
> going to speak to Tino tomorrow aren't you?" *Y pos, ni sabía que decirle.*
> (And well, I didn't know what to say to him.) *Le dije,* "Sure, yeah, I'll talk
> to him." (I told him . . .)

In all such cases, it was difficult to determine whether the speaker was
actually reflecting the language of the original request or whether he was
using the strategy (previously referred to in Valdés-Fallis, 1976) of narrating
in one language and paraphrasing or quoting in another, regardless of the
language of original expression. In any case, it was impossible to determine
whether the original speaker in question might have sought to mitigate or
aggravate by a change in language. Indeed with regard to the study of
language alternation as a strategic device by bilinguals, it may be that
researchers will need to limit themselves to actual rather than reported
interaction.

THE USE OF CODESWITCHING AS AN
INTERACTIONAL STRATEGY

The use of language switching is not limited to the area of direct and indirect
requests. This same device is found in bilingual interaction when speakers are
involved in putting off requests, giving accountings, challenging, and
reinstating requests. Were space not limited here, it would be possible to show
how bilingual speakers use their two languages for each of the categories
established by Labov, to include not only requests in all of their many forms
but also narratives. It *can* be said, however, that his preliminary work
confirms that bilinguals do indeed—as Di Pietro 1976 has suggested—use
their two languages to influence the outcome of their conversations with
others. In the area of requests this mechanism is particularly evident because
they involve actions which are carried out by means of speech.

With regard to codeswitching in both direct and indirect requests, one can
say that such language alternation takes place strategically and serves both to
mitigate and to aggravate requests. Although this same process is carried out
by monolingual speakers by numerous devices also available to the bilingual
(such as change of intonation, pauses, slurring of speech, etc.), the bilingual
can supplement these devices by utilizing other elements in his speech
repertoire. The process of switching languages, then, in direct and indirect
request, may be interpreted as a strategy which is equally deliberate when
used by the bilingual as that used by the monoglingual when he employs the

devices available within his single code. Both are deliberate verbal strategies which contribute to the impact of face-to-face communication between speakers.

REFERENCES

Blom, J. P., & Gumperz, J. J. Social meanings in linguistic structure: Code-switching in Norway. In J. J. Gumperz & D. Hymes (Eds.), *Directions in sociolinguistics*. New York: Holt, Rinehart & Winston, 1972.

De Pietro, R. J. *Code-switching as a verbal strategy among bilinguals*. Paper presented at the Linguistics Symposium, University of Wisconsin-Milwaukee, 1976.

Ervin-Tripp, S. Is Sybil there? The structure of some American English directives. *Language in Society*, 1975, *5*, 26–66.

Espinosa, A. M. Speech mixture in New Mexico. In E. Hernández-Chávez (Ed.), *El lenguaje de los chicanos*. Washington, D.C.: Center for Applied Lingusitics, 1975.

Gumperz, J. J. Verbal strategies in multilingual communication. *Monograph Series in Languages and Linguistics*, 1970, *23*, 129–48.

Gumperz, J. J., & Hernández-Chávez, E. Cognitive aspects of bilingual communciation. *Working Paper 28*, University of California, Berkeley, 1969.

Hasselmo, N. *Bilingualism in the Americas: A bibliography and research guide*. University, Ala.: University of Alabama Press, 1956.

Labov, W., & Fanshel, D. *Therapeutic discourse*. New York: Academic Press, 1977.

Lance, D. M. *A brief study of Spanish-English bilingualism: Final report*. Research Project Orr-Liberal Arts-15504. College Station, Texas, 1969.

Phillips, R. N., Jr. *Los Angeles Spanish: A descriptive analysis*. Unpublished doctoral dissertation, University of Wisconsin, Madison, 1967.

Rayfield, J. R. *The languages of bilingual community*. The Hague: Mouton, 1970.

Valdés–Fallis, G. Code-switching and language dominance: Some initial findings. (Paper presented at the annual meeting of the Linguistic Society of America.) *General Linguistics*,1974, *18*, 90–104.

Valdés-Fallis, G. Social interaction and code-switching patterns: A case study of Spanish/English alternation. In G. Keller et al. (Eds.), *Bilingualism in the bicentennial and beyond*. New York: Bilingual Press, 1976.

7

Tá bien, You Could Answer Me en cualquier idioma: Puerto Rican Codeswitching in Bilingual Classrooms

Ana Celia Zentella
Director, Puerto Rican Studies Hunter College

The ability of bilinguals to alternate between the languages in their linguistic repertoire, generally referred to as *codeswitching,* has been the subject of an increasing number of studies in the last 10 years (Gumperz, 1976; Gumperz & Hernández-Chávez, 1975; Blom & Gumperz, 1972; Valdés-Fallis, 1976; Lance, 1975; Pfaff, 1975; Timm, 1975). A recent manifestation of interest in the area was a conference at ETS on Latino discourse behavior, at which 25 percent of the papers dealt with some aspect of codeswitching.

Adequate comparisons of the studies are severely hampered by differences in definitions, units of analysis, and methodology. Some include loans, others reject them; some work within the boundaries of the sentence, others within one speaker's turn; still others within a conversational episode. In all the approaches, the quantification of intrasentential syntactic constraints rarely complements discourse analysis of conversations. Even if the differences in methodology could be resolved, comparability across speech communities would be limited since the linguistic function and social meaning of codeswitching vary in each bilingual speech community, and among Spanish-English bilinguals in the United States, the majority of the research has been conducted among Mexican-American adults. This research has identified syntactic constraints, (Timm, 1975; Pfaff, 1975) a variety of purposes (Gumperz & Hernández-Chávez, 1975) and at least a dozen patterns of codeswitching (Valdés-Fallis, 1976).

There is as yet scanty knowledge about the development of the communicative competence of bilingual children, but Genishi has documented how six-year-old Mexican-American kindergartners switch situationally with ease, although they were limited in the number of variables on which they were able to focus in the selection of their codes. The language ability and language choice of their addressee were the most significant factors (Genishi, 1976).

McClure found that older children (9–13) of the same background "code changed," i.e., switched completely from one language to the other at major constituent boundaries, more than younger children (2–9), who "code-mixed" more; i.e., they switched for immediate access to an unknown term, usually single nouns (McClure, 1977).

The codeswitching of 2 million United States Puerto Ricans has not been the subject of much research. There are only two studies of Puerto Rican codeswitching to date. The first contrasted one adult's patterns with one ingroup and outgroup interviewer and found that four times as much codeswitching was directed to the ingroup member (Poplack, 1978, and Chapter 10). The other analyzed the syntactic constraints of four adolescents who also only switched to ingroup members, and found that several of the syntactic constraints suggested as universals by Gumperz (1976) were not observed (Marlos & Zentella, 1978). When we turn to the research done with Puerto Rican children, we find only one undergraduate paper (Cohen, 1976), and the work of Shultz (1975). Although the class Shultz studied was predominantly Puerto Rican, his focus was on language choice, and he did not include sentence internal codeswitching. He cites perceived dominance of the addressee, situations, and topics as key factors in determining what language children chose to speak.

In addition, in all the studies of Spanish-English codeswitching by children, the linguistic profile and linguistic performance of the adults who engage the children in conversation have never been incorporated into the analyses, although adult addressees have always included Anglo teachers and/or researchers, or members of other speech communities. The effect of the teachers' and/or researchers' age, sex, speech style, and in- or outgroup membership should be significant in inhibiting or encouraging codeswitching, since the linguistic ability and the language choice of the person who addresses the bilingual child has been recognized as the most significant variable to date in determining the child's language choices. Recent research suggests that even if the teachers and researchers are native or nearly native speakers of the child's mother tongue, but not of the same dialect, codeswitching patterns may be affected. Lavandera (1977) believes that bilinguals may feel uneasy in a monolingual setting in either language, because they are constrained from employing the full range of their linguistic repertoire. Poplack (Chapter 10) and Marlos and Zentella (1978) find that bilinguals are not perfectly comfortable in bilingual settings in which the varieties of the codes spoken are not the same. Some of the literature also reveals that children's interactions with bilinguals who did not speak their dialect may have inhibited their use of Spanish (Shultz, 1975).

Another aspect of language use among bilingual children that has been studied concerns the differential roles assigned to the respective languages in bilingual classrooms. The superior status of English over Spanish was communicated by the teachers in all the classrooms previously studied (Shultz, 1975; Bruck & Shultz, 1977; Cohen, 1976) except one with an avowed maintenance philosophy (Genishi, 1976). In kindergarten to third-grade California classrooms, teachers communicated the powerful role of English by switching to that language for purposes of manipulation 70 percent of the time (Phillips, 1976). The only Chicano teacher in that program switched more than the Anglo teachers, but that study does not discuss the effect of those patterns on the children. On the other hand Bruck and Shultz compared an Anglo teacher to a Mexican teacher and found that the language dominance of the teacher "seemed to determine the linguistic environment of the classroom" (1977:83).

What is the case in those bilingual classrooms where all the participants speak the same varieties of the code(s)? To what extent are the findings about the dominance of English in bilingual classrooms and the limited number and variety of children's switches affected by whether the children identify with the ethnic identity of the teacher and/or the researcher? How do the teacher's own language patterns affect those of the children?

In light of these three problems—namely, the difficulty of comparing the research, the limited information available on the linguistic behavior of United States Puerto Ricans, and the lack of attention paid to the codeswitching patterns among children, teachers, and researchers from the same bilingual speech community—this paper presents data collected by a Puerto Rican researcher among Puerto Rican children and their Puerto Rican teacher in New York bilingual classrooms.[1]

Our research in two New York City bilingual classrooms, one third grade (7–10-year-olds) and one sixth grade (11–13-year-olds), suggests that the organization of speech events provides a fuller picture of the codeswitching of both teachers and students. The investigator was a participant observer for seven days in each class over a period of four months. The data consist of 8½ hours of tape recordings in each classroom at the desks shared by two children and 31 interviews (19 third grade and 12 sixth grade). The interviews were conducted by the investigator in both Spanish and English; the language of the interview was switched unexpectedly in the middle of the interview.

The school, 60 percent Puerto Rican and 40 percent Black, is in a low middle-income area, but most of the children in the bilingual classes live in lower-income public housing, "the projects." English dominates school life.

---

[1]This research would not have been possible without the cooperation of the children and teachers of "3 and 6 bilingual"; *se lo dedico con cariño.*

There are only six bilingual teachers. All substitute and prep teachers are English monolinguals, and the frequent announcements made over the public address system are only in English.

Although the bilingual program has existed for three years, there is still some confusion about its goals. When the teacher of "3 bilingual"—as the bilingual program for third graders is called—was asked whether the program had transitional or maintenance objectives, she replied: "I don't really know, I think it's transitional." Later she remarked: "This class, *ya ahora me recuerdo* (now I remember), you know, talking about it, it comes to me. It's transitional."[2]

THE PARTICIPANTS

There is one bilingual class for each grade, each with an average of 30 students. They have one teacher; no paraprofessionals are in the classroom. Children are placed in the bilingual classes on the basis of their performance on the New York City Language Assessment Battery, developed to comply with the consent decree agreed to in 1974 by the national Puerto Rican agency for educational development, Aspira, and the New York City Board of Education. Those who placed above the 21st percentile in Spanish were to be placed in bilingual classrooms.[3] Table 1, displaying the number of children with different bilingual proficiency profiles for the third and sixth grades, demonstrates that most of the children in "3 bilingual" tested as Spanish dominant, and most children in "6 bilingual"—the sixth-grade bilingual class—tested as English dominant.

The background of the teachers of "3 and 6 bilingual" is representative of two types of Puerto Rican teachers in the New York City public school system. The third-grade teacher, Teresa, was born in Puerto Rico but has lived in the United States since she was three years old. She is a graduate of New York City's public schools and its City University, where she was a Spanish major. Teresa is fluent in both Spanish and English. She is 25 years old and has been teaching for 3 years, all in the same program. The sixth-grade teacher, Eneida, is in her middle forties and has been teaching for the last seven years in New York City. She was born and educated in Puerto Rico, although she finished her college degree in the United states years after beginning it on the island. She speaks fluent English with a Spanish accent. The investigator, a New York Puerto Rican fluent in Spanish and English, was introduced to and first addressed both classes in Spanish, but the children

---

[2]Throughout this paper, translations of English discourse are given in parentheses.

[3]There is widespread dissatisfaction with the exam as an accurate placement tool, and our own work confirmed that many of the children's scores contradicted their performance.

TABLE 1

Number of Children with Various Bilingual Proficiency Profiles in Spanish and English for the Third- and Sixth-grade Bilingual Programs

			Bilingual Profile			
Grade	Bilingual: Above the 21st percentile in both Spanish and English	Spanish-dominant: Above the 21st percentile in Spanish, below that in English	Spanish-dominant: Below the 21st percentile in Spanish, but stronger, in Spanish than English	English-dominant: Above the 21st percentile in English, below that in Spanish	English-dominant: Below the 21st percentile in English, but stronger in English than Spanish	Totals
Third	3	13	7	1	6	30
Sixth	2	4	4	19	0	29

also knew that she spoke English fluently. Her interactions with the third-grade teacher were often mixed, as in discourse segment I.

I. T: *¿Ana, te quedas?*　　　　　(Ana, are you staying?)
　　　I: *Yo voy a subir pá*　　　　(I'm going upstairs to return
　　　　regresarle ehto a ella.　this to her.)
　　　T: OK, I'm so hungry!
　　　I: Yeah! *¿Tú vah a subir*　　(Are you going upstairs to
　　　　a comer o tú vah a salir?　eat or are you going out?)
　　　T: *No, yo salgo afuera.*　　(No, I go out.)
　　　　Maybe if I have time I'll
　　　　go up, but I like to get out.
　　　A: Yeah, it's better.

In contrast, all her conversations with the sixth-grade teacher were in Spanish. No effort was made to speak one language more than another with the students. During classroom activities, the children called out to the investigator in the language of their choice, and this did not always coincide with their perception of her language dominance, as later verified in the interview. Third-grade children most often addressed her in Spanish; most of the sixth graders addressed her in English, reflecting the language dominance of the class members, but the same children would sometimes address her in either language. In individual interviews, however, the children did not follow their own inclination. All the children interviewed, with one exception (30/31), responded in the language of the interviewer. Seventy-four percent (23/31) followed the interviewer's unexpected language switch in the middle of the interview with a switch of their own to the other language without comment; half of that number switched by the investigator. The other half of the children followed suit more slowly after 2–10 questions following the investigator's initial switch. Only eight children never switched; four could not have because they are monolingual English (1) or Spanish speakers (3). Three bilinguals "would rather fight than switch." They included one Ecuadorian sixth grader who is very proud of her ability to speak Spanish and who insisted on continuing in Spanish although she is a fluent English speaker. The other two were English-dominant Puerto Rican boys (one third grader and one sixth grader) who had low scores in Spanish and little confidence in their ability to speak it; they would not switch out of English. These findings agree with those of other researchers that document the willingness and ability of young bilinguals beyond the age of five to speak as they are spoken to, i.e., to "follow the leader." Our data indicate, however, that older children may choose to speak in the language of their preference if they know that their addressee can also speak it. This is true even in an interview setting, which can be characterized as *formal* because of the positional identities invoked in the assymetrical dyad (Seigman & Pope, 1972), and the interviewer's control over topic and turn taking (Irvine, 1978).

Table 2 gives descriptive data on stylistic codeswitching by third and sixth graders during interview sessions between children and the present investigator. Included is information regarding percentage of switches from Spanish to English and vice versa, percentage of switches by location within discourse, and percentage of intrasentential switches which were classified as loans from the other language or loans from the other language involving nouns or noun phrases exclusively. Table 3 displays similar data on codeswitching recorded during discourse among children only in the contexts of bilingual classrooms for third and sixth graders.

Comparison of the entries of Tables 2 and 3 provides us with suggestive information contrasting the characteristics of stylistic codeswitching involving choice of language, sentential vs. intrasentential location of switches, and preference for intrasentential switches involving loans which are nouns or noun phrases, across two different interactional settings involving different interlocutors with children and distinct discourse demands.

We cannot accurately compare the codeswitching statistics shown in Table 2 during interviews with the codeswitching statistics recorded during classes shown in Table 3 because different students are involved for different periods of time. Nevertheless, it is interesting to note that when children spoke to each other at their desks, as shown in Table 3, there was a much lower incidence of codeswitching within the student's turn, and that the majority of it was at sentence boundaries.

The higher percentage of switches involving loans and N/NP's in the interview vs. the classroom setting—i.e., twice as many loans and three times as many N/NP's for both groups occurred in the interview over the classroom setting—may be the result of the interviewer's selecting the topic and leading the speaker into discussions of his/her choice. In order to maintain the language of the interview, the speaker must temporarily change to the other language for an unknown term. The speaker might avoid this switch for a single item in spontaneous conversation by shifting to the other language in anticipation of it, i.e., at the initial boundary of the sentence that includes the term. Only extensive speech samples in interviews and free conversations in which the same speaker switches a particular word or constituent in one situation, but switches before it is reached in another, can substantiate this hypothesis. One example of this occurs in the work that compares the interviews with domino games in which the same children participate (Zentella, 1978).

TABLE 2
Descriptive Data on Stylistic Codeswitching by Third and Sixth Graders during Interview Sessions with the Investigator

| Grade | N^a | Percent of Switches to Each Language | | Percent of Switches at the Sentence Level(s), vs. Intrasententially | | Percent of Intrasentential Switches Involving Loans | |
		Spanish	English	Full S	Intrasentential	All Loans	Loans Involving Nouns (N) or Noun Phrases (NP) Only
Third	61	40	60	7	93	41	41
Sixth	56	19	81	11	89	48	45

N^a represents the total number of stylistic switches observed within child speakers' turns during interviews.

TABLE 3

Descriptive Data on Stylistic Codeswitching by Third and Sixth Graders in Bilingual Classroom Contexts When Speaking Only among Themselves

| Grade | | N^a | Percent of Switches to Each Language | | Percent of Switches at the Sentence Level(s), vs. Intrasententially | | Percent of Intrasentential Switches Involving Loans | |
			Spanish	English	Full S	Intrasentential	All Loans	Loans Involving Nouns (N) or Noun Phrases (NP) Only
	Third	21	58	42	57	43	24	14
	Sixth	46	41	59	63	37	24	13

N^a represents the total number of stylistic switches observed within child speakers' conversational turns while at their desks.

STUDENT-TEACHER INTERACTIONS

In codeswitching between the teacher and students in the classrooms the language choice of the teacher had a clear effect on the language choice of the children in most situations.

Mehan (1977, 1978) and others have demonstrated that when the classroom is viewed in terms of a series of reciprocal events, both teachers and students cooperate in the demarcation of boundaries that separate events, e.g., math class, getting on line, silent reading. The role of teacher in the orchestration of events is crucial, but it must be complemented by the students' interactions.

For successful participation in the classroom, children must not only have the right answer, they must also know when and how to offer it. A correct answer given at the wrong time, e.g., when a teacher pauses to catch her breath but not give up her turn, or in the wrong manner, e.g., by shouting out "yo-teach" or "Misi Gonzalez" instead of quietly raising a hand, may be unacceptable in all or parts of certain classroom events, but acceptable in others. In addition to these rules, the child in the bilingual classroom must also learn the appropriate language for all or parts of various classroom events, i.e., when Spanish, English, or both languages are appropriate. The codeswitching patterns of the children seemed to distinguish between elicitation sequences, controlled by the teacher in group lessons, and the spontaneous conversations they engaged in with the teacher and observer and with each other.

For many of the children, especially the third graders, this was the first year in the bilingual program, and the rules concerning language choice in different classroom events were new to them. Moreover, teachers differ in their norms for appropriate linguistic behavior from one bilingual classroom to the next, although the Aspira decree stipulates that the children "shall receive (a) intensive instruction in English, (b) instruction in subject areas in Spanish, (c) the reinforcement of the pupil's use of Spanish and reading comprehension in Spanish where a need is indicated" (*Bilingual Review,* 1974:I(7):1). The third-grade teacher, Teresa, reported that she followed this procedure, except that she taught math in both languages and was generally plagued by the lack of adequate materials in Spanish. In practice, adherence to the "one language–one lesson" principle demanded by the Board of Education and akin to the one language–one environment theory of Leopold (1949) is often impossible in view of the wide range of linguistic proficiency in both languages that the children in both classes represent. The third-grade bilingual teacher, Teresa, is aware that she switches and condemns switching, but she attributes her switching to the need to communicate with those children who would otherwise not understand:

> When they don't understand something in one language, they'll go to the other, which is easier for them. I know you've noticed that. And like, then sometimes I

have to be bouncing from one language to the other, which is wrong, but that's the only way sometimes they understand.

As in the interview situation, despite the often unpredictable changes in the teachers' language, children in both grades usually responded in the language in which they were addressed during formal sessions, particularly the younger ones. The most typical elicitation sequence is:

Teacher   Student   Teacher

Initiation   Reply   Evaluation or Initiation

Table 4 displays three patterns of language choice found in the study to be recurrent in classroom elicitation sequences of the most typical sort. In Table 4 each pattern of language choice is described by a corresponding heuristic rule which seems to apply. The teacher's choice of language for the initiation is affected by several variables. If the elicitation is a question initially directed to a specific child at the outset, the most significant determinants of language choice appear to be the language dominance of the child and the language in which the lesson is "supposed" to be taught, e.g., English for English language arts, Spanish for Spanish language arts. If the child understands the language of the lesson there is no conflict. This is an example of a Type 1 pattern in Table 4; and as it turns out in our data this was the most recurrent pattern of language choice in teacher-student interactions at lesson time. When the language of the child and the language of the lesson differ, however, the teacher may choose to repeat the question in the other language to the child, or call on another child. This was likely to occur whenever the teacher first

TABLE 4
Observed Patterns of Language Choice in Bilingual Classroom Discourse Between Teachers and Children

Patterns of Language Choice	Teacher Initiation Language*	Student Reply Language	Teacher Evaluation Language
1. Teacher and student:			
"Speak what you are spoken	English	English	English
to" or "Follow the leader"	Spanish	Spanish	Spanish
2. Teacher:	English	Spanish	Spanish
"Follow the child"	Spanish	English	English
3. Teacher:			
"Include the child's	English	Spanish	Code switching
choice and yours"	Spanish	English	Code switching

*The teacher may also code switch for translation during the initiation.

addressed the whole class and then called on a specific child who did not understand the language of the question, as in example II. Teachers' codeswitches for purposes of translation occurred frequently at the beginning of the school year because teachers were still not sure of the language ability of each child. When a child changed the language of the elicitation sequence, this often affected the teachers' choice of language for the evaluative statement and the initiation of the next elicitation sequence as in example III, conforming to a Type 2 pattern of language choice given in Table 4.

II: T: How many tens and how
         many ones in the number
         12? Osvaldo?
     O: *Uno*   (One)
     T: One—*uno que?*   (One what?)
     O: *Uno de a diez*   (One ten)
     T: *Si, uno a diez*   (Yes, one ten)
     O: *y dos de a uno*   (and two ones)
     T: *Si, ta bien*   (Yes, that's right)
         O.K. *y cuan*—oh   (O.K. and how)
         boy—and how many
         tens and how many ones
         in 47, Daisy?

In sequence II, after Teresa switches to Spanish for Osvaldo, who knows very little English, she tries to return to English. She calls on an English-dominant girl but begins by addressing her in Spanish and exasperatedly switches to English. Given the mix of speakers in the classroom, it is surprising that these mid-word switches are not more frequent.

When a child replied in the opposite language, it usually reflected his/her language proficiency and, especially with sixth graders, their degree of linguistic security and language preference as in example III:

III. T: *¿Qué estabas haciendo?*   (What were you doing?)
     C: I was listening but I
         don't understand Spanish
     T: *Eso es muy cómodo de tu parte.*   (That's an easy way
         Quiero oir a Carlos.   out) To class:
                                            (I want to hear Carlos)

         Carlos, put your chair back.
         Ahora, dime el título Carlos.   (Now, tell me the title,
                                            Carlos)

         Quiero oir Carlos.   To class:
                                            (I want to hear Carlos)

Carlos, put your chair back.
Ahora, dime el título Carlos.   (Now tell me the title
Carlos)

Carlos obviously does understand Spanish, or he would not be able to respond to the teacher's questions, but he feels frustrated and uncomfortable during Spanish language lessons. The teacher does not accommodate him by responding in the language he attempts to switch to, because she is determined to keep the Spanish arts lesson in Spanish. She does, however, switch to English for a tangential command concerning his seating behavior, and this selection of both English and Spanish conforms to a Type 3 pattern of language choice as shown in Table 4.

The following is another example of a mixed-code language choice by a teacher, Type 3, including switches for a translation for Spanish monolingual J. and a command as an aside to the class during the initiation:

IV. T: How many tens and how
      many ones in 61? J.?
      ¿Cuántas unidades de diez y   (How many tens and how
      cuántas de uno hay en   many ones in 61)
      sesenta y uno?

      Este es el número 61.   (This is number 61)
      Everybody pay attention
      because you can use this,
      a'right,

      ¿Ahora, J. Cuántas unidades   Now J. how many units
      de a diez tú ves aquí?   of ten do you see here?)
    J: *¡Seis!*   (Six!)
    T: *Ajá, chévere. ¿Cuántas*   (Yes, terrific. How many
      unidades de a uno?   units of one?)
    J: *Uno*   (One)
    T: *¿Entiendes ahora?* O.K.   (Do you understand now?)
      Good. [To class] The next one.

Both teachers responded to the content of the children's reply even if the form, i.e., the language, contradicted the teacher's choice. Even when this occurred during a language lesson, the teachers accepted the content, although they often requested it again in the other language. In an English language lesson in the third grade, the teacher's introduction to a poem about Columbus's voyage included the following interchange, in which the English word "material" eludes the class for a moment:

V. T: What is the sail made out of?
    D: The sail is made of *tela, de tela.**   (Material, of material)
    T: *¿Cómo se dice esa palabra*   (How do you say that
       en inglés?   word in English?)
    K: *Frisa, sábana*   (Blanket, sheet)
    T: *Frisa y sabana son dos*   (Blanket and sheet
       diferentes cosas [sic]   are two different
           things)

    M: A blanket.
    T: Well, not exactly, but what is
       a blanket, pants, shirt
       made out of?
    ?: *¡Tela!*   (Material)
    T: *Sí, tela. ¿Pero cómo se dice*   (Yes, material. But
       tela en inglés? ¿Quién sabe?   how do you say "material"
           in English. Who knows?)

    ?: Material!
    T: Material, right, cloth. I
       like the way you answer me
       sometimes in Spanish when I ask
       you something in English.

---

*Note syntactic correction to keep possessive phrase in same language.

The teacher's evaluation admonishes them to refrain from switching the language of the lesson. The message is conveyed by what Hymes calls the *key*, in this case the sarcastic tone of the evaluation, a more powerful communicator than the content for speakers who share the same interpretation of the components of a speech event (Hymes, 1974). It may well have been lost on many of the Spanish-dominant third graders.

Whereas English lessons pose problems for the third graders, Spanish language lessons are difficult for the 19 sixth graders who are English dominant. Despite the teacher's efforts to keep to the language of the subject, the rules are often broken, and the result is often humorous:

VI. T: *¿Quién me da un diminutivo*   (Who can give me a
        Wilfredo?   diminutive? Wilfredo)
     W: *Pe-rri-to*   (Little dog)
     T: *¿Perrito es el diminutivo*   (Little dog is the diminutive
        de qué?   of what?)
     W: Dog. [class laughter]
     T: *Acuérdate que no estamos*   (Remember we're not in
        en la clase de inglés.   the English class)

¿Perrito es el diminutivo	(Little dog is the diminutive
de qué otra palabra?	of what other word?)
W: *Perro*	(Dog)
T: *Bien*	(Good)

The sixth-grade students seemed more attuned than the third-grade students to the possible comic effect of breaking cooccurrence rules—here the use of English when Spanish was expected; they were quick to laugh at them and took advantage of the possibility of codeswitching morphemes within word boundaries. The following elicitation sequence illustrating this point occurred during the same lesson on diminutives as in example VI:

VII: T: *Lapiz, Lapicito. Tiza—*	(Pencil, little pencil, chalk—)
[awaiting class response]	
[Someone from back of class]: *Chalkita!*	
[Class laughter]	

As already noted, teachers often used codeswitching for asides that momentarily broke with the main focus of the elicitation especially as evaluations of behavior and requests to change it. (See examples III and IV.) In this way, the switch itself seems to represent a softening of the admonition especially when it is into Spanish. Also, a return to the language of the elicitation meant a return to the question at hand as in VIII:

VIII. T: How many tens and how many ones in 41? E.	
E. Ten (in low voice)	
T: *E, cuando te toca hablar*	(E, when it's your turn
no hablas alto, cuando	to talk, you don't talk
no te toca, la voz tuya	loud, when it's not your
se oye XX C'mon!	turn, your voice can be
How many tens and how	heard XX)
many ones?	
Don't tell me you forgot. M?	
[XX here denotes an unintelligible utterance]	

Apparently not all the children in "3 bilingual" had learned by the second month of classes that, in contrast with the language lessons, the correct answer in *either* language was acceptable during the math class:

IX. T: ¿*Cuántas decenas y*   (How many tens and many
cuántas unidades de   units of ones are there
a una hay en el número   in the number 52? [two]
52? [*Dos*] *Miren el*   (look at the number, think
número, piensen del número   of the number.)
[*sic*]
¿*Maria?*

F: *Fi*—[*hesitates*]

T: *Tá* bien, you could answer   (It's ok,
me *en cualquier idioma.*   in any language)

M: Five tens and two ones.

T: OK, *chévere*, the next   (terrific)
one.

Here we have a straightforward communication of the acceptability of codeswitching in the math class, possibly attributable in part to the nature of the subject matter and "get the answer" stress. In addition, the number and variety of Teresa's codeswitches in all classes effectively communicate to her students that codeswitching is an important skill for a fluent bilingual. Teresa switches 127 times during 8 hours of class within her turn at speaking and 42 percent of these switches are intrasentential (see Table 5). Nowhere is the communicative effect of her switches more evident than in her admonitions to the class, in which the switching between English and Spanish occurs within an English framework, and signals constant alternation between an impersonal, New York City school teacher "they" code, and the personal appeals and solidarity of a nurturant Puerto Rican female, conveyed by segments in Spanish, the "we" code. Two examples (X, XI) illustrate these communicative effects of code switching.

X. [A child has just complained that her seven pencils were stolen.]
T: (speaking to the class):
I'd hate to say, "please give me
the pencils back, so and so."
La persona que lo cogió si los   (The person who
devuelve, I forget about it   took it, if he returns
if people return them. Some   them,)
of you were sitting around
here, and Luis, and Johnny,
and Nelida.
(to researcher):
You know some of them *tienen*   (have
malas costumbres and I don't   bad habits)
like that.

TABLE 5

Descriptive Statistics Regarding Language Dominance and Stylistic Code switching by Third- and Sixth-grade Teachers*

Teacher	Grade	Dominant Language	Hours Recorded	Total Number of Code Switches	Percent and Number of Switches to Each Language		Percent of Switches Located at the Sentence Level(s) vs. Intransententially	
					Spanish	English	Full S	Intrasentential
Teresa	Third	English	8	127	51 (65)	49 (62)	58 (74)	42 (53)
Eneida	Sixth	Spanish	8.5	26	41 (10)	59 (16)	50 (13)	50 (13)

*Entries enclosed in parentheses represent number of switches.

125

XI* [There were two fights in the schoolyard]
T: [to class]:
I don't know what the
story was between J. and M.P.
Or the story between
[A], D. y J. I don't wanna know.   (D. and J.)
I don't care   (What you know how to
[B] *Uds. lo que saben hacer*   do is fight, so kill
es pelear, pues mátense.   yourselves)
[C] But I'm not gonna allow
you to do it on my time.
[D] *Todo lo tienen que*   (You have to do everything
hacer con los puños y las   with your fists and
piernas.   legs)
[E] You got problems.   (But you don't XX
[F] *Pero no XX cuando uno*   when you go to fight,
va a pelear, y despues me   and then I feel bad
da lastima a me que me   when you look at me
miren que si un golpe, que   that one got hurt,
si el otro se da un golpe.   that the other one got
Por estar rezando no se van a   hurt. If
dar golpes.   you're praying you
[G] So you better listen and you   don't get hurt.)
better listen good. That goes
for the real troublemakers here.
You know who you are. I'm not
gonna say your names, you know
what I'm talking about. Is
that understood?

Class as a whole: Yeah

(The children give their version
of the fights in Spanish and
English.)
T: O.K. We're gonna start from
scratch.
[H] *Mañana,* whoever comes with   [H] Tomorrow...[I] the
a story   one who brings me the
[I] *el que me traiga el cuento*   tale and the one who
y el que haya llevado   took the punch in the
el puño en la boca y el que   mouth and the one who

se lo dé los dos van a	gives it to him, both
recibir XX Both, I mean	are going to get XX)
that	

---

*XX marks an unintelligible utterance and indicates a long pause. Bracketed capital letters mark points in the discourse which will be discussed.

Although most of her codeswitches in these passages, and in her discourse in general, occur at sentence boundaries, her intrasentential switches include 16 different types of constituents (Table 6). The purposes that trigger particular switches are often difficult to ascertain, but discourse segment XI clearly includes many of those cited by Gumperz (1976) and request patterns suggested by Valdés (1978 and Chapter 6): For person association, as in [A], the switch reflects that persons D. and J. are Spanish monolinguals; persons J. and M.P. are English dominant. For emphasis, as in points [C], [E], and [I] in the discourse and for an aggravated request, as in point [G] in the discourse, the switch is into English, the "they language." In the discourse of XI, for a mitigated sarcastic request at point [B], a mitigated threat, point [H], and

TABLE 6
Distribution of Percentage and Number of Stylistic Codeswitches by
Grammatical Category for Third-and Sixth-grade Teachers

Grammatical Category of Codeswitches	*Third-grade Teacher (Teresa)*	*Sixth-grade Teacher (Eneida)*
Full sentence(s)	58.0 (74)	50.0 (13)
Nouns (N) or		
Noun phrases (NP)	6.0 (7)	23.1 (6)
Adverbial phrases (Adv.)	8.0 (1)	15.0 (4)
Independent clauses	8.0 (10)	3.8 (1)
Adjectives	4.7 (6)	3.8 (1)
Conjunctions and		
dependent clauses	8.0 (10)	3.8 (1)
Conjunctions and		
independent clauses	2.0 (3)	0
Dependent clauses minus		
conjunctions	1.5 (2)	0
Conjunctions	1.5 (2)	0
Prepositional phrases	1.5 (2)	0
Verb or verb phrases	4.0 (5)	0
Relative clauses	1.5 (2)	0
Monomorphemes	1.5 (2)	0
False starts	.8 (1)	0

statements of concern at points [D] and [F], the switch is into Spanish, the "we" language. One is struck by the small number of repetitions, and the dramatic impact of the switches.

As shown in Table 5, in approximately the same length of time during which protocols were sampled for Teresa, the sixth-grade teacher, Eneida, produced only 11 intrasentential codeswitches during 8½ hours of observation, equivalent to 42 percent of her total of 26 stylistic code switches within her turn at speaking. One reason for Eneida's low number of switches is that the linguistic background of her sixth graders is more homogeneous than that of the third graders, and the class is being prepared for participation in monolingual English junior high school classes starting with the seventh grade. Another reason is Eneida's classroom style. As displayed in Table 6, Eneida's switches are more limited in their constituents than are Teresa's switches; 23.1 percent of Eneida's switches involve N's or NP's, most of which are related to school activities; e.g., *Ahora vamos a pasar a* reading, *mañana tenemos* current events (Now we are going on to . . . , tomorrow we have . . .). Her lack of codeswitching within her turn may reflect notions of formality; Eneida's Spanish does reflect such notions; e.g., she usually enunciates intervocalic /d/ and syllable final /s/, which are markers of formality in Puerto Rican Spanish (Ma & Herasimchuk, 1966). Her 26 codeswitches are scattered throughout all the tapes; the only string of codeswitches in her discourse occurred when she attempted to instruct the children on how to fill out an IBM form:

XII*

(1) E: *Donde dice* 'Print your   (where it says)
          name in the boxes provided'
          aquí

(2) E: I want you to be very
          careful. *Pongan arriba*   (put your name above)
          su nombre.

(3)   Student: Last?
          E: Last name first. *¿Me
          estás oyendo* F?   (Are your listening F?)
          El nombre-el appellido   (Your name, your last
          primero.   name first)
          Student: The white thing?
          or the blue?

(4) E: Here! What white thing and
          blue thing: you don't have . . .

(5) E: *Entonces* just put your name   (Then)
          and blacken the letters.
          O.K., *este, En la XX me*   (Um- on the XX put an A
          ponen una A.   for me)

Lucy como tú lo tenías   (Lucy the way you had
está malo.   it is wrong)

---

*XX denotes an unintelligible utterance.

One can account for these switches in part because the IBM form is usually associated with English and because she was forced to switch situationally to respond to the language dominance of two monolinguals in the class. One English monolingual is addressed in (4); one Spanish monolingual, in (3). Obviously, Eneida is not adept at rapidly changing from one code to the other. Enedia's English interferes with her Spanish in the rapid switches; e.g., she began to translate "last name" as *nombre (first name)* but corrected herself, using the correct Spanish term *apellido* in (4). Teresa, on the other hand, can maintain the phonological system of both codes distinct when she switches, but her Spanish shows evidence of English interference; e.g., in the earlier discourse segment IX she incorrectly utters *piensen del número,* which should be *piensen en el número* (think of the number). Also in discourse segment V she incorrectly utters, *son dos diferentes cosas* following English adjectival placement rules instead of the correct Spanish form *dos cosas diferentes* (They are two different things). Since these teachers differ in language dominance, teaching style, and personality variables, it is difficult to attribute the differences in their patterns to anything but a complex configuration of variables.

CONCLUSION

Even if the analysis of classroom interactions could take into account the multiple variables of the teachers' and students' linguistic performance in different settings and interactions, their language proficiency and preferences, degree of linguistic security, and covert norms (Labov, 1972), perceptions of formality and informality (Irvine, 1977), contact with Puerto Rico and Puerto Ricans, and history of family dyads, to name just a few variables, the description would still lack explanatory adequacy and comparability. The latter desirable degree of explanation is only approximated by incorporating the holistic approach characteristic of ethnography, i.e., one that places the patterns found in the classroom in the larger context of those found in the enculturating institutions in the community (Philips, 1972; Hymes, 1976; Heath, 1977). For accurate study of the acquisition of codeswitching, for example, the holistic approach entails participant observation in formal and informal speech events in the community and the analysis of exchanges between bilingual adults and children across a wide range of settings and functions. We need to know, for example, if Puerto Rican parents admonish their children not to codeswitch, but do so themselves, whether we codeswitch when we teach each other at home, when we are in church, watch television, shop in the *bodega* (neighborhood grocery store) or the A & P supermarket, ride in housing project elevators, etc. The assumption is that an awareness of the role of codeswitching in the communicative competence of United States Puerto Rican bilinguals can make an important contribution to classroom methodology and educational success.

Until such an ethnographic approach is undertaken, it seems premature to ban codeswitching from the classroom when we do not know what we are banning along with it, nor is it helpful to say it should be incorporated into the classroom in a mechanistic way, especially by nonnative teachers who do not know its rules. Certainly, the data that exist prove that codeswitching is not an ad hoc mixture but subject to formal constraints, and that for some communities it is precisely the ability to switch that distinguishes fluent bilinguals (Elías-Olivares 1976).

Children who grow up wanting to be a part of their community can be expected to learn to codeswitch well if codeswitching is an identity marker of membership. Indeed, given the important discourse strategies that depend on codeswitching, e.g., persuasion, appeal, and explanation, the child who does not learn how to codeswitch well may be jeopardizing his/her social development. We must decide whether the bilingual schools that many of our community members struggled for and support, and others distrust, should contribute to the development of our linguistic abilities, or whether these schools should prescribe their distribution.

REFERENCES

The Bilingual Review/La Revista Bilingue, 1974, *1*(7). ["Landmark Decision" is theme of the issue.]

Blom, J. P., & Gumperz, J. J. Social meaning in linguistic structures: Code-switching in Norway. In J. J. Gumperz & D. Hymes (Eds.) *The ethnography of communication.* New York: Holt, Rinehart & Winston, 1972.

Bruck, M., & Shultz, J. An ethnographic analysis of the language use of bilingually schooled children. *Working Papers on Bilingualism/Travaux de Bilinguisme,* 1977, *13,* 59–61.

Elías-Olivares, L. *Language use in a Chicano community.* Paper presented at Pan-American College, Edinburg, Texas, February 1976.

Genishi, C. *Rules for code-switching in young Spanish-English speakers: An exploratory study of language socialization.* Unpublished doctoral dissertation, University of California, Berkeley, 1976.

Gumperz, J. J., & Hernandez-Chavez, E. Cognitive aspects of bilingual communication. In E. Hernandez-Chavez, A. Cohen & A. Beltramo (Eds.), *El lenguaje de los Chicanos.* Arlington, Va.: Center for Applied Linguistics, 1975.

Heath, S. *An anthropological perspective on research in education: The view from ethnography.* Paper prepared for Research for Better Schools, Philadelphia, October 1977.

Hymes, D. *Foundations in sociolinguistics: An ethnographic approach.* Philadelphia: University of Pennsylvania Press, 1974.

Hymes, D. *Ethnographic monitoring.* Paper presented at the Symposium on Language Development in a Bilingual Setting, California State Polytechnic University, December 1976.

Irvine, J. T. *Formality and informality in speech events.* Paper presented at the meeting of the American Anthropological Association, Houston, Texas, 1977.

Labov, W. *Sociolinguistic patterns.* Philadelphia: University of Pennsylvania Press, 1972.

Lavandera, B. R. *Code labels for speech events among bilinguals.* Paper presented at the Georgetown University Roundtable in Linguistics, March 17, 1978.

Leopold, W. F. *Speech development of a bilingual child.* Evanston, Ill.: Northwestern University Press, 1949.

Ma, R., & Herasimchuk, E. The linguistic dimensions of a bilingual neighborhood. In J. Fishman et al. (Eds.), *Bilingualism in the Barrio.* Bloomington, Ind.: Indiana University Press, 1971.

Marlos, L., & Zentella, A. C. *A quantitative approach to codeswitching in a Philadelphia Puerto Rican community.* Paper delivered at Nwave, Georgetown University, November 1978. (Also in *Penn Review of Linguistics,* 1978, *3*(1), 41–59.)

McClure, E. Aspects of code switching in the discourse of bilingual Mexican American children. In M. S. Troike (Ed.), *Linguistics and anthropology.* Washington, D.C.: Georgetown University Press, 1977.

Mehan, H. Ethnography for bilingual education. In *Bilingual education: Current perspectives* (Vol. I). Arlington, Va.: Center for Applied Linguistics, 1977.

Mehan, H. Structuring school structure. *Harvard Educational Review,* 1978, *48,* 32–65.

Pfaff, C. *Constraints on code switching: A quantitative study of Spanish/English.* Paper presented at the meeting of the Linguistic Society of America, December 1975.

Philips, S. W. *Participation structures and communicative competence: Warm Springs children in community and classroom.* In J. Cazden, & D. Hymes (Eds.), *Functions of language in the classroom.* New York: Teachers College Press, 1972.

Phillips, J. M. *Code switching in bilingual classrooms.* Unpublished master's thesis, California State University, Northridge, 1976.

Timm, L. A. Spanish-English code switching: *El porque* and how not to. Romance Philology, 1975, *28,* 473–482.

Valdés-Fallis, G. Social interaction and code switching patterns: A case study of Spanish/English alternation. In G. D. Keller, R. V. Teichner, & S. Viera (Eds.), *Bilingualism in the bicentennial and beyond.* Jamaica, N.Y.: Bilingualism Press, 1976.

Zentella, A. C. Code switching and interactions among Puerto Rican children. *Working Papers in Sociolinguistics #50.* Austin, Texas,: SEDL, 1978.

8 Codeswitching in Chicano Six-Year-Olds

Celia Genishi
University of Texas, Austin

INTRODUCTION

Despite the growing interest in codeswitching among linguists and sociolinguistics, there are still few data on how young children develop the ability to codeswitch. The purpose of this observational study was to describe the codeswitching patterns of four Spanish–English-speaking Chicano six-year-olds. My intention was to present case studies of these children, based on talk recorded within a limited period of time in a school setting.

Individual researchers offer a variety of definitions of codeswitching. For the purposes of this study, *codeswitching* is defined as the alternation of languages or dialects to convey social meaning. When a speaker codeswitches, s/he stops speaking Language A and begins to speak language B, or s/he chooses one set of features of language A over another set. These features may be phonological, lexical, or syntactic. According to Blom and Gumperz (1972), there are two general kinds of codeswitching, *situational* and *conversational*. Situational switching involves a change in setting, topic of conversation, or participants; the speaker's perception of the ongoing activity changes. An example is the switch from colloquial Spanish among students to English when a teacher joins the conversation. The activity has changed from an informal chat to a formal conversation.

Conversational switching, on the other hand, occurs within a single activity. Two languages may be mixed in the same sentence to convey a single message. An example from a Spanish-English bilingual in a situation where English is commonly used (e.g., at work) might be:

I just saw Bob, *el pobrecito* (the poor thing). Did you know his car was stolen?

133

The temporary use of Spanish is a deviation from the norm that carries social meaning. Since Spanish is the language of the speaker's ethnic group, it conveys a greater feeling of sympathy than an English equivalent.

The importance of codeswitching lies in its social meaning. Especially in situations of rapid cultural change (e.g., urban areas of the United States), choosing one language over another conveys social information about factors such as speakers' ethnic group membership, values, and relationships of power. The language of an ethnic minority may serve as an identity-marker to maintain a separation between the ingroup and the outgroup.

Bilingualism refers here to intragroup usage of more than one language (Fishman, 1972). A single community or population uses two or more languages for communication within their group. Bilingual speakers are ideally able to speak both languages well, but they are not necessarily "balanced" in both since almost all bilinguals speak one language more of the time or with somewhat greater ease than the other.

With regard to children, learning to codeswitch is part of the child's language socialization. It is an aspect of the development of communicative competence, a speaker's ability to differentiate his or her ways of speaking so that they are appropriate for specific social situations.

The child who speaks more than one language learns to use each according to the requirements of everyday situations. Bilingual children vary in their ability to speak two or more languages, but observation of their use of language in a range of settings may show that they are competent speakers both linguistically and socially.

To see whether selected six-year-olds had developed the ability to use their languages according to sociolinguistic rules and to see how they chose one language rather than the other, the following research questions were asked:

1. Which of the following social and linguistic variables affect the children's choice between languages:
   a. Physical setting (classroom vs. playground)
   b. Activity (free play vs. teacher-structured task)
   c. Features of the addressee (age, ethnicity, linguistic ability)
   d. Topic of conversation (television show, family dog, etc.)
   e. Linguistic intention (requesting help, arguing, etc.)
2. Are the children's rules situational or conversational?
3. How do these six-year-olds' rules of codeswitching differ from adults' rules?

METHOD

An ethnographic approach was used to carry out the study. The four children and their parents were viewed more as informants than as subjects so that what they said about their own speech was treated as part of the data to be analyzed and not as a source of bias. The categories used for analysis were not established ahead of time but were developed after studying the daily activities and conversations of the children in three settings: the kindergarten classroom, the playground, and the day care center.

The Site and the Four Children

The site of the study was a combined day care center–kindergarten for children from three to seven years of age. Twenty of the 50 children in day care also attended the affiliated kindergarten in the mornings. The center was an alternative school, established by a group of Chicano parents in the San Francisco Bay area. The parents and staff valued the maintenance of the Spanish language and their Mexican or Latin-American heritage. Their educational approach was what may be called a "whole child" approach. Teachers were concerned with the cognitive, emotional, and political aspects of education. The kindergartners, for example, heard several lectures on Mexican history and politics during the period of data collection.

All teachers and aides at the site were either bilingual in Spanish and English or monolingual in Spanish. There were two women kindergarten teachers, who spoke both Spanish and English with the children, and one male teacher, who was born in Mexico and spoke only Spanish to the children although he too was bilingual. The woman aide in the kindergarten was a Spanish monolingual from Mexico.

The four children studied were chosen on the basis of (1) my observations in the kindergarten and day care center over a two-month preliminary period and (2) the three kindergarten teachers' rank-ordering of the "most bilingual" kindergartners. My ratings were based on frequency of individual children's talk and frequency of codeswitching, i.e., use of both Spanish and English. The criteria used, then, were based on *production* and not on comprehension. The means of assessment was impressionistic but was justified because of a lack of formal instruments that measure language use outside of testing situations, specifically the child's talkativeness.

Of the 20 kindergartners observed, many were bilingual, but only four were both bilingual and sufficiently talkative to be subjects. The four were bilingual in terms of both comprehension and production and demonstrated their bilingualness by talking relatively often. These features were crucial for collecting enough data for analysis.

Three of the children were boys; one was a girl. They ranged in age from 6:0 to 6:2. The parents of two boys and one girl were not college educated; the parents of one boy were both graduate students. With one exception (an Anglo father), all parents were Mexican or Mexican-American. In interviews with the parents, I found that they all favored the goals of the center to maintain their children's ability to speak Spanish and actively to teach about Mexican/ Chicano culture.

Data Collection

Data were collected in two phases. During the first, or preliminary, phase I familiarized myself with the routines of the children and staff while they became accustomed to me and the use of a tape recorder.

During the second, or recording, phase, either the second observer or I[1] observed, one at a time, for a one- to two-hour period and essentially followed the four children around to audiotape their speech and write a brief record of concurrent behaviors. Data were collected most often in the morning, betwene 9:00 a.m. and 12:00 noon. Although the method of recording was obtrusive, the children became accustomed to it quickly.

Our equipment consisted of a battery-run tape recorder carried in a shoulder bag with a directional microphone attached to the left wrist of the observer. This allowed us to take notes with the free hand. On the coding sheet we identified the speaker, his or her addressee, briefly described the nonlinguistic context, and wrote speech fragments so that the context noted could later be matched with recorded talk.

RESULTS

Categories of Analysis

At the end of 7 weeks, we had recorded 17.5 hours of spontaneous talk during 45 hours of observations, chiefly in the kindergarten building, which was separate from the day care center.[2] Children's speech in the playground, in a nearby park, and in the day care center was also recorded.

The first task of analysis was to identify categories of both nonlinguistic and linguistic features by (a) breaking the talk and activity into segments for analysis, and (b) setting a framework for determining situational vs. conversational switches.

Seven types of nonlinguistic activity settings or group types were isolated:

1. Whole class: teachers usually talked most of the time and children talked very little.
2. Small-group-task: children were engaged in task-oriented activity, e.g., art work or language arts, initiated by the teacher.

---

[1] I am Japanese-American, bilingual in English and Spanish, more proficient or dominant in English. The second observer was a male Anglo, also English dominant. *Anglo* is used here to mean someone who is not a member of an ethnic minority. It is used descriptively, not pejoratively.

[2] Supplementary data, communicative tasks, and interviews with the children and their parents, were also collected. Only the major source of data, the spontaneous talk, is presented in this paper.

3. Small group-game: children themselves chose to play a game with rules.
4. Small group-dramatic play: children assigned roles for fantasy play.
5. Small group-free play: children engaged in unstructured, self-chosen activity, e.g., playing on swings.
6. Small group-eating: snack or lunch time with teachers and other children from kindergarten and the day care center.
7. Dyad: an adult with one of the four children, often one of the observers asking for information about the children's activities.

In order to analyze the kinds of codeswitching that occurred within these activity settings, I transcribed the recorded segments that contained codeswitches for later analysis. All recorded segments were categorized according to linguistic units of three kinds, the *episode,* the *utterance,* and the *subepisode,* by referring to the transcriptions or listening repeatedly to the tapes.

The *episode* was the main unit of analysis, an interactive unit which involved:

1. At least one of the four children talking with at least one other person.
2. A recorded response, either written in our notes if the response was nonverbal, or audiotaped if it was verbal.
3. A point or topic for the interaction that was clear to the coder.
4. A recorded beginning and endpoint, usually marked by a change in participants or in topic of talk.

The episode was also the framework for differentiating between situational and conversational switches. *Situational* switches were defined as occurring between episodes; *conversational* switches occurred within episodes.

An *utterance* was a group of words, expressing a single idea or proposition, and/or was separated from the previous utterance by a pause of one second or more (adapted from Cherry, 1975).

The *subepisode* was a catch-all category for segments of talk which:

1. Did not involve any of the four children.
2. Involved one of the children but had no focus clear to the observer.
3. Were generally inaudible recordings.

A reliability check was done with an assistant who was not involved in the data collection. Using Barker and Wright's percentage of agreement, we found reliability figures were .85 for episodes, .99 for utterances, and .83 for subepisodes (Wright, 1967).

There was a total of 370 episodes for all four children and 187 subepisodes. Episodes lasted from a few seconds to more than half an hour, e.g., when the interactive focus was a game. Using the episode as a framework, we coded 306 examples of situational switches and only 64 conversational switches.

Variables Associated with Codeswitches

In the first research question we asked which of five variables were associated with codeswitches:

1. Physical setting
2. Activity
3. Features of the listener or addressee
4. Topic of conversation
5. Intention of the speaker

Quantitative analysis of the episodes was based on a tabulation of each child's episodes for each variable of interest, according to language used. For activity and two features of the addressee, age and linguistic ability, I figured each child's percentages of episodes in English, Spanish, and both languages, based on the number of episodes within a given category. For example, Gloria spoke Spanish in 36 percent, English in 40 percent, and both languages in 24 percent of 50 recorded episodes in the free play category of activity.

The analysis shows only simple relationships, or main effects, of physical setting on language choice, activity on language choice, etc. Although the five variables were treated as if they were independent, any of the five could have been interrelated. For example, a child's choice of language might have been influenced not by activity alone but by an interaction between the kind of activity and the topic of conversation. Because observations of each child were not random and the number of episodes within categories was not large (e.g., within the seven categories of activity), no statistical test of such interaction was possible.

The observers originally intended to record the four children in all seven activities for approximately equal lengths of time. This was impossible because some activities were associated with more talk than others and because the children had their own preferences. Each child, however, was recorded in all activities except for Gloria, who was not recorded in any of the whole class segments. Arturo was recorded in a total of 97 episodes; Manuel in 89; Gloria in 107; and Kiko in 77. Figures la-ld show the percentage of episodes per child, according to the language used.

A simple tabulation showed that neither the physical setting nor the child's activity, the first two variables listed, was associated with a preference for one language over the other.

Three different features of the addressee (the third variable) were analyzed: age, ethnicity, linguistic ability. Age (adult vs. peer) did not clearly affect

FIGURE 1
Percentage of Observed Episodes according to Language Used

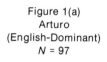

Figure 1(a)
Arturo
(English-Dominant)
N = 97

Figure 1(b)
Manuel
(English-Dominant)
N = 89

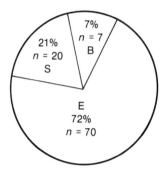

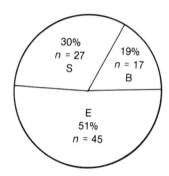

Key:
  N = Total number of episodes observed per child.
  n =Number of episodes per language used.
  S = Spanish used/spoken.
  E = English used/spoken.
  B = Both Spanish and English used within same episode.

Figure 1(c)
Gloria
(Spanish-Dominant)
N = 107

Figure 1(d)
Kiko
(Balanced Bilingual)
N = 77

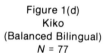

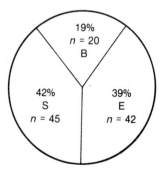

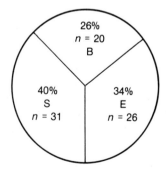

language choice. Similarly, the addressee's ethnicity (Anglo vs. Chicano) did not explain codeswitches. The four children did not have a simple rule, such as "Speak Spanish only to people who appear to be Chicano or Latino."

The only variable that had a clear effect was one feature of the addressee: the listener's linguistic ability. By the end of the recording phase, we had assigned all staff and children to five categories, according to their ability to produce Spanish and English:

1. Spanish monolingual
2. Spanish-dominant bilingual
3. Balanced bilingual
4. English-dominant bilingual
5. English monolingual

Tabulation of episodes in which the identity of the child's listener(s) was known showed that the children generally chose the listener's dominant language. (See Figures 2–5.) The total number of episodes tabulated (413) on the graphs exceeds the number of episodes recorded (370) because in some episodes the child addressed listeners of different abilities. An example of this kind of episode follows. In it one of the four children studied, Arturo[3] (English dominant), talks first to Carlos, an English-dominant child, then to Jorge, a Spanish monolingual child. Their play involves filling a balloon with water and playing with toy astronauts in a sink in the kindergarten classroom. At Utterance 4, Arturo codeswitches to Spanish to address Jorge:

Example 1:

Speaker	Addressee	Utterance
Arturo	Carlos	1. Carlos, I'm going to (unclear) this thing.
Carlos	Arturo	2. Where's the astronaut?
Carlos	Aturo	3. Where's the astronaut?
Arturo	Jorge	4. *Carlos me lo dio.* (Translation: Carlos gave it to me.)
		5. *Yo hallé éste, Jorge.* (I found this one, Jorge.)
Jorge	Arturo	6. *No, este no es tuyo.* (No, this isn't yours.)
Arturo	Jorge	7. *¡Yo lo hallé!* (But I found it!)

The major finding of the study was that these four children were able to choose and maintain the language that their listeners spoke best in both instructional and noninstructional settings. Although there were wide individual variations when they spoke to bilinguals, all four spoke Spanish to Spanish monolinguals and English to English monolinguals between 84

---

[3]Psuedonyms for the children are used.

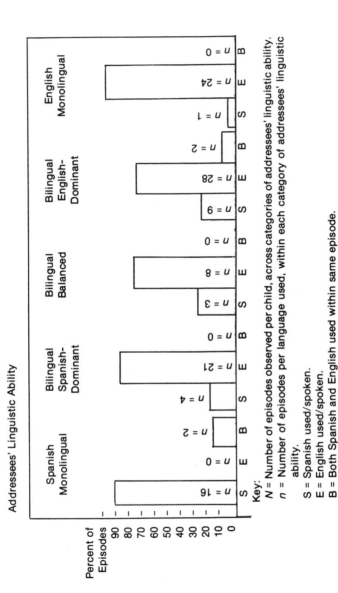

FIGURE 2
Percentage of Observed Episodes according to Language Used with Addressees of Different Linguistic Abilities
(Arturo - English-Dominant)
(N = 118)

Addressees' Linguistic Ability

Key:
N = Number of episodes observed per child, across categories of addressees' linguistic ability.
n = Number of episodes per language used, within each category of addressees' linguistic ability.
S = Spanish used/spoken.
E = English used/spoken.
B = Both Spanish and English used within same episode.

141

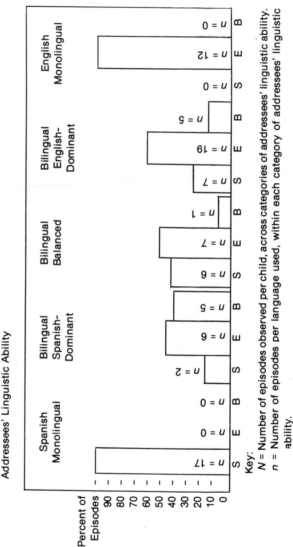

FIGURE 3
Percentage of Observed Episodes according to Language Used with Addressees of Different Linguistic Abilities
(Manuel - English-Dominant)
(N = 87)

Addressees' Linguistic Ability

Key:
N = Number of episodes observed per child, across categories of addressees' linguistic ability.
n = Number of episodes per language used, within each category of addressees' linguistic ability.
S = Spanish used/spoken.
E = English used/spoken.
B = Both Spanish and English used within same episode.

142

FIGURE 4

Percentage of Observed Episodes according to Language Used with Addressees of Different Linguistic Abilities

(Gloria - Spanish-Dominant)

($N = 107$)

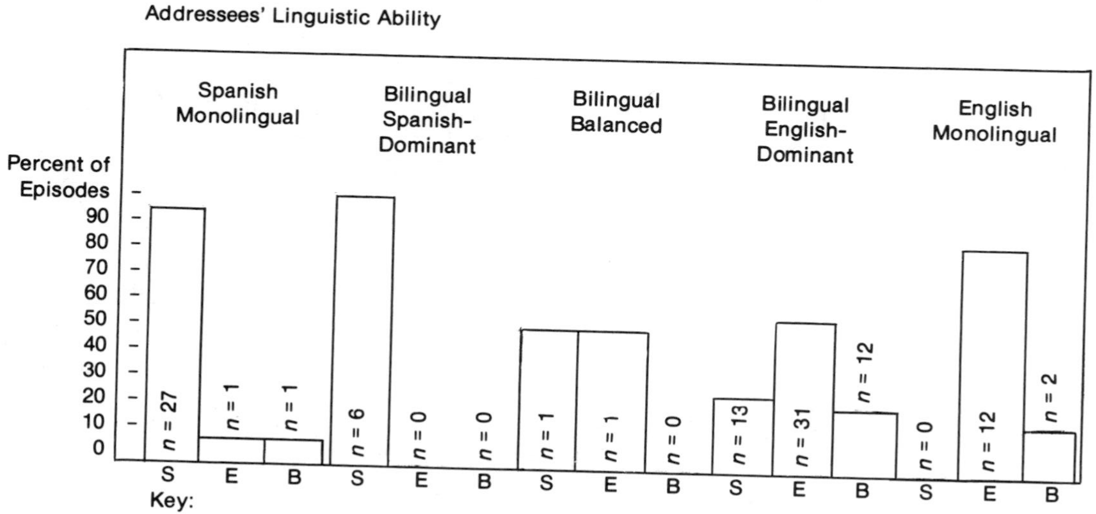

Addressees' Linguistic Ability

Key:

N = Number of episodes observed per child, across categories of addressees' linguistic ability.

n = Number of episodes per language used, within each category of addressees' linguistic ability.

S = Spanish used/spoken.

E = English used/spoken.

B = Both Spanish and English used within same episode.

143

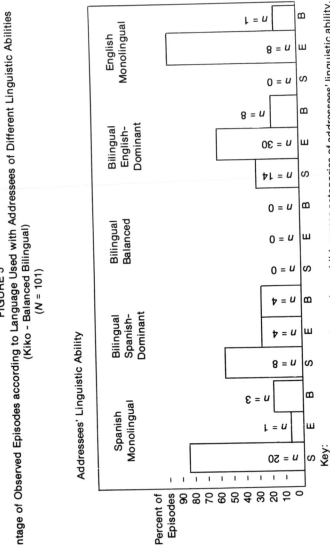

FIGURE 5

Percentage of Observed Episodes according to Language Used with Addressees of Different Linguistic Abilities

(Kiko - Balanced Bilingual)

(*N* = 101)

Key:

N = Number of episodes observed per child, across categories of addressees' linguistic ability.

n = Number of episodes per language used, within each category of addressees' linguistic ability.

S = Spanish used/spoken.

E = English used/spoken.

B = Both Spanish and English used within same episode.

percent and 100 percent of the time. (Since the monolinguals, with one exception, *comprehended* the language they did not speak, the use of that language probably did not lead to gaps in communication.)

Specific cases of the rule the four children applied, "Speak the language your listener speaks best/most," were:

1. Choose the language your monolingual listener speaks:
   a. Choose Spanish when the addressees are Spanish monolinguals.
   b. Choose English when the addressees are English monolinguals.
2. When your listeners are of different linguistic abilities, favor the monolinguals:
   a. Choose Spanish when speaking to an English-dominant and a Spanish monolingual.
   b. Choose English when speaking to the English-dominant and Spanish when speaking to the Spanish monolingual within the same episode.
   c. Choose English when speaking to an English-dominant and an English monolingual.
   d. Choose English when speaking to a Spanish-dominant and an English monolingual, or
   e. Choose Spanish when speaking to the Spanish-dominant and English when speaking to the English monolingual within the same episode.

Another rule that the four children and others in the setting applied was what the second observer termed the *inertial* rule, or "Speak the language in which you were just addressed" (Chambers, 1975). In other words, it was very natural for speakers to respond in Spanish if one spoke to them in Spanish.

The four children's matching of language to addressee, according to the language he or she spoke most, indicates that in general they correctly assessed others' linguistic abilities. Apparently they made an assessment after a small number of verbal enounters with a listener. At least the children seemed to do this with the observers and other newcomers during the data collection period. Based on analysis of these four children's spontaneous talk, the primary finding was that they *could* apply the rules just listed.

TOPIC OF CONVERSATION AND INTENTION OF THE SPEAKER

The last two variables considered were topic of conversation and the intention of the speaker. They were tabulated by episode for each child. There were relatively few topics and intentions that were common to all four children. Those that recurred are presented here.

Topic

Topic was determined by judging that the child was *talking about X*. Since topics varied a great deal among the children, the investigator applied a "criterion of nonuniqueness" (Garvey, 1974). By this criterion a topic was tabulated if at least two children talked about it at least once in different episodes. The five topics that recurred were children's families, television shows or characters, girlfriends/boyfriends, food, and Mexican holidays.

None of the topics was associated with one language, with the exception of Mexican holidays. These were discussed in Spanish in whole class segments while teachers lectured. I expected talk about the family to be in Spanish, since children spoke Spanish with their parents, and that talk about television might be in English. The addressees' linguistic ability again seemed to explain most of the language choices.

Intention of the Speaker

It is possible that part of the bilingual child's communicative competence is the ability to codeswitch when s/her intends to secure the help, affection, or attention of an adult. The relevant categories of intention examined were requesting; currying favor; tattling. Intentions, such as informing, refusing, agreeing, etc., occurred frequently but when tabulated did not seem to be associated with a specific code or with codeswitching.

Children used a large number of requests during the observations but did not seem to have a "language of requests," nor did they consistently codeswitch if a first request did not get them what they wanted.

The only switch common to many of the kindergartners occurred if the initial use of a teacher's name before a request failed to get her attention. One teacher's name was Liz. Children who were Spanish monolinguial or bilinguals called her "Lees" or "Leez" when they spoke Spanish to her. Children switched from Spanish to English phonology ("Lees" to Liz) or vice versa if she did not respond the first time.

The rule to switch if a first utterance was unsuccessful seemed to apply only in special cases. Children seldom repeated unsuccessful requests in the "other" language. Switches did occur in conversations when the child seemed to be reacting to negative feedback, or lack of response, from an addressee.

The activity in which there did seem to be a language of requests was eating. The majority of requests were in Spanish, even in the case of English monolingual speakers. They used Spanish "formulas" to ask for more juice or food, *¡Yo quiero más jugo!* (I want more juice!) or *¡Yo quiero más pan!* (I want more bread!). Repeating the formula in Spanish did not always bring results but seemed to be part of a group activity, often turning into a playful chant or verbal game.

At the beginning of the study, one of the staff told us that some children used Spanish with her, a Spanish-dominant, when they asked for, or 'curried," favors. Very few interactions were recorded between her and the four children, but there were instances in which Arturo and Manuel seemed to use Spanish as an added way of pleasing their adult addressees.

Arturo's currying or coy style with teachers was marked by softness and a nasal quality. He also used this style at home in my presence when speaking Spanish to his parents. He spoke softly and lisped from time to time like a younger child, e.g., "*thi*" instead of *sí* (yes), and "en*the*ñar" for *enseñar* (to show).

Another interesting category of intent was tattling, or "telling on" someone. The example of tattling marked by a codeswitch again involved Arturo and Manuel.

Arturo's example is striking because it follows a series of futile requests for the teacher's services. Arturo does not codeswitch at all during the requesting episodes, A and B, but there is a switch from English to Spanish when he tells the same bilingual teacher about a Spanish monolingual child. The codeswitch is also noteworthy because in most other episodes Arturo used English. In Episode C, he is *talking about* Miguel, a Spanish monolingual, in Spanish, apparently so that Miguel will know he is being "told on."

Example 2

Episode A

Speaker	Addressee	Utterance
Arturo	Teacher	1. I want that other pencil.
Vera	Teacher	2. *Liz, yo quiero una brocha.* (Liz, I want a brush.)
Arturo	Teacher	3. Liz, I want that pencil.
		4. This one's broken.

Episode B:

Arturo	Teacher	1. Leez, get me an eraser.
		2. Leez, an eraser!
Teacher	Arturo	3. Eh?
Arturo	Teacher	4. An eraser. [pause]
Arturo	Teacher	5. I want an eraser! [pause]
Arturo	Teacher	6. Liiiiz, an eraser!!
Teacher	Arturo	7. I can't find one,...,*chulo* (honey). [pause again]
Arturo	Teacher	8. Oh, gimme a new paper.

Episode C:

Arturo	Miguel	1. *Mire, que hicistes.* (Look what you did.)

Arturo	Teacher	2. Leez!
Teacher	Arturo	3. ¿Qué? (What?)
Arturo	Teacher	+4. Lookit, +*que hizo Miguel* (...what Miguel did.)
		5. *El rayó mi papel con la tinta.* (He put lines on my paper with ink.)
Arturo	Miguel	6. Mira, Miguel, que hizo aquí. (Look, Miguel, what you did here.)
Arturo	Teacher	7. ¿*Ves*, Liz? (See Liz?)
		8. Leez, *ven acquí.* (Liz, come here.)
Arturo	Teacher	9. ¡*Ya!* (All right or yeah?)

+Codeswitch

Beginning of Episode D [a short time after Episode C]:
Speaker   Addressee   Utterance
Arturo   Teacher   1. Leez, are we gonna go to the park?

Tattling in this way may be specific to children's interactions. In Episode C, Miguel, the subject of talk, knew Arturo was talking about him. Arturo's desire to include the subject of talk in the conversation differs from polite adults' intentions. Adults might exclude the person by switching to the language he or she does *not* know. Adults discourage tattling in young children, but they generally expect it to be common. Part of the role of adults is to settle arguments among children since they have the authority to do so. Although tattling may be a precursor of adults' attempts to embarrass others, the asymmetry in terms of power between adult and child distinguishes gossip among adult peers from tattling.

In summary, the broad question with regard to intention was whether codeswitching helps a child gain and hold the attention of an adult. Since there were few codeswitches that children may have intended for these purposes, no reliable statements can be made about the four bilinguals' ability for this aspect of sociolinguistic competence. Some examples in the data suggest that codeswitching may be one means of pleasing adults. Other means, used simultaneously, such as lisping or changing loudness and pitch, are also available to monolingual children.

Differences Between Adults and Children

The four children had few episodes containing midepisode, or conversational, switches. Of these 64 conversational switches, only a dozen contained midutterance switches. The answer to the second broad research question, are the children's rules conversational or situational, then, was that they were situational. One specific aspect of the situation, listener's linguistic ability, seemed to determine their language choice. Codeswitches within conversations occurred primarily to accommodate the differing abilities of listeners, so that they conveyed a straightforward message, "I am speaking to X in the language s/he speaks best."

This does not mean that there was no evidence of conversational rules. The children did seem to switch within episodes to specify one addressee when speaking to more than one bilingual (e.g., a Spanish dominant and an English dominant), and to quote another person's speech in the language of the quotation. These are both functions of codeswitching in adult speech (Gumperz, 1975).

The relative lack of conversational switches was the major difference between children's and adult's rules. With respect to the present study, one may cite three possible reasons for this difference:

1. The observers simply did not record conversational codeswitches.
2. Features of the site worked against conversational codeswitching.
3. Developmental differences between young children and adults account for the difference.

The first reason listed is possible but not very likely since the observers recorded the children in a broad range of situations with a variety of speakers. The number of episodes that were evidence of situational rules ($n = 306$) is almost five times larger than the number of episodes containing conversational switches ($n = 64$). The size of the difference makes this explanation even less plausible.

The second reason, that features of the site worked against conversational switching, seems a more likely one. One feature might have been the teachers' and aides' frequent use of Spanish with the children. The adults may have served as "models" for infrequent codeswitching. If, however, the children spoke as adults spoke to them, they should have used more Spanish than they did. In addition, even if the adults in the center were important models, their effects differed according to the individual child. Arturo hardly ever switched during episodes; Gloria and Kiko switched much more often.

The parents of all four children told the investigator that at home their children often codeswitched in the same sentence or conversation, e.g., *Lo voy a poner* out there in that room (I'm going to put it out there in that room). Manuel's mother said her son switched like this when he was being "lazy about his Spanish." The three other children all had older bilingual siblings who spoke English more often than they spoke Spanish, especially with peers, according to their parents. They may have codeswitched often within conversational episodes and influenced the children of the study to do the same.

Another difference between the home and school setting was that although teachers spoke mainly Spanish with Spanish monolinguals and bilingual children, they never required bilinguals to speak Spanish rather than English. The children could choose to speak English or Spanish, depending on their addressee and maintain that code throughout an interaction. At home they might be required or encouraged to speak Spanish. Consequently, they might start utterances in Spanish, find a word easier to express in English, and then switch in midepisode.

The third reason, developmental differences, seems the most probable. Any bilingual needs to make a choice as to which language to speak in each verbal interaction. This study indicates that the children were able to make correct judgments about others' linguistic ability, presumably after a small number of interactions with them. The resulting rule, "Speak the language your listener knows best," is one that adults would take for granted since they control a larger number of codeswitching rules and are more flexible in applying them. They make choices about which language to speak based on features other than the linguistic ability of the addressee.

Gumperz (1975) hypothesizes that codeswitching among adults involves complex semantic processing, below the level of awareness. The six-year-olds did not seem to go through all these simultaneous processes:

1. Make a judgment about what the speaker means. The listener understands what the speaker's intentions are, e.g., "complaining."
2. Apply rules of interpretation, after making a chain of inferences about:
   a. The phonological form of the utterance so that the listener recognizes which language or style is being spoken;
   b. The content of the utterance;
   c. The speaker's background assumptions and knowledge of communicative and social conventions.

The four children were competent in two areas of interpretation: (a) recognizing the language or phonological form of utterances, which led to deciding what a speaker's dominant language was; (b) making inferences about the content of utterances. The children could not carry on conversations without doing this.

The most sophisticated judgments deal with a speaker's intentions and with his or her social/ethnic background and the communicative conventions that signal it. The children in the study did not appear to make these kinds of judgments.

There was some evidence that children were beginning to differentiate among intentions by codeswitching. The data in general did not, however show that children could codeswitch to mark their interpretations about speakers' sociolinguistic background and conventions. The ability to do this would depend on speakers' awareness that they can highlight ethnic differences through choice of the appropriate language. Although one of the children, Manuel, stated that he was ethnically different (Mexican, not American) during his interview, none of the four seemed to mark this kind of awareness by codeswitching.

There were examples in the data of the four children excluding other children from play areas, or "territories." Their way of excluding outgroup members was direct and did not involve codeswitching. For example, Gloria told a younger child from the day care center, "You can't come in!" to inform her that only kindergartners were allowed in the classroom. In addition, we did not observe bilingual children excluding monolingual speakers from conversations by switching to the language the monolingual did not speak.

CONCLUSION

In conclusion, the results of the study challenge the opinion that bilingual children are "deficient" because they speak neither of their languages well. I do not claim that the findings may be extended to young Spanish-English speakers in general because of the small number of children in the study and the unusual social and educational characteristics of the site. When children's linguistic ability is assessed through observation in settings that allow them to talk freely, they may show competence rather than deficits in using language effectively.

In their oral communcations in naturalistic settings, the four children of this study were able to speak both Spanish and English fluently. Although their talk contained some nonstandard forms, it was not "Spanglish," a frequent mixture of both languages that indicates a lack of knowledge of either code. They were able to choose the appropriate language so that they could communicate with peer and adults of different linguistic abilities in a variety of situations. The children did not manipulate their languages to communicate effectively in every situation, but in general, they easily controlled two languages and a range of styles within each language to demonstrate their social and linguistic competencies.

REFERENCES

Blom, J. -P., & Gumperz, J. J. Social meaning in linguistic structures: codeswitching in Norway. In J. J. Gumperz & D. Hymes (Eds.), *Directions in sociolinguistics.* New York: Holt, Rinehart & Winston, 1972.

Chambers, R. An exploration of the effects of bilingualism on referential communication. University of California, Berkeley, 1975.

Cherry, L. The preschool teacher-child dyad: Sex differences in verbal interaction. *Child Development,* 1975, *46,* 532–535.

Fishman, J. A. *Language in sociocultural change.* Stanford, Calif.: Stanford University Press, 1972.

Garvey, C. Some properties of social play. *Merrill-Palmer Quarterly,* 1974, *20,* 163–180.

Gumperz, J. J. The sociolinguistic significance of conversational code-switching. University of California, Berkeley, 1975.

Gumperz, J. J., & Hernández, E. Bilingualism, bidialectalism and classroom interaction. In C. B. Cazden, V. P. John, & D. Hymes (Eds.), *Functions of language in the classroom.* New York: Teachers College Press, 1972.

Wright, H. F. *Recording and analyzing child behavior.* New York: Harper, 1967.

9 Codeswitching: All in the Family

Ana Huerta-Macías
University of Texas, El Paso

INTRODUCTION

There is currently a growing interest in investigating the interrelationships that exist between the two languages of bilingual individuals. Of primary interest in the United States, because of the large population of people of Hispanic origin, has been the contact situation that exists between Spanish and English. The emphasis in this field is now on codeswitching in the bilingual speech community. By codeswitching is meant the use of alternate languages in discourse; within an utterance or between utterances.

The investigation to be described, a case study on Spanish-English codeswitching, was carried out in an effort to further our knowledge of this type of bilingual linguistic behavior. Its primary purpose, therefore, was providing a more extensive description of Spanish-English codeswitching than has been previously available in the literature. To this end, it was decided that a case study done on a single family, as opposed to an anecdotal approach done on a greater number of subjects, would be the more revealing insofar as a description of codeswitching was concerned. That is, a case study would provide a more comprehensive view of codeswitching and would perhaps expose certain speech patterns which become obvious only when a large body of data is gathered from a single source.

PROCEDURE

This case study was done on a bilingual Chicano family living in El Paso, Texas. The data consisted of recordings of informal conversations held among family members in their home. Their conversations, furthermore, were completely natural and uninhibited. They did not know when their speech was actually being recorded; they had previously consented to the use of surreptitious recordings of their conversations by this writer, who is also a member of the family.

These conversations—245, 294, and 305 utterances in length,[1] respectively—were transcribed verbatim and used as the basis for the first part of this study, which involves only the speech of the adult first- and second-generation members of the family.

An additional four hours of recording was used for the second part of this study, which involved the speech of the youngest, third-generation, member of the family, a child still in the process of acquiring his speech. These recordings consisted of short dialogues and utterances produced by the child in talking to, or in the presence of, various adult members of the family.

The subjects, then, included the parents of the family who are in their middle-fifties, three sons and two daughters, all of whom were in the 23–29 year age bracket, and one male child who, at the beginning of the study, was 25 months old.

The data were analyzed for a variety of codeswitching patterns as they occurred in the speech of this family.[2] All codeswitched utterances were first classified by form, or grammatical units. Some of the most frequently occurring units in this classification were sentences, nouns, phrases, adjectives, gerunds and the infinitival complements of verbs.

The social functions of speech were also investigated in this study as they occurred in the bilingual discourse of the family. The speech functions analyzed in the data were the following.[3]

Emphasis-refers to the emphatic nature of speech, often signaled by a rise in pitch.

---

[1]An *utterance* is defined here as the oral linguistic production of a speaker which occurred without a pause. An utterance, however, was preceded and followed by a slight pause which signaled both the end and the beginning of another turn in the conversation. It could then consist of a sentence, a word, a phrase, etc.

[2]For the purpose of this study, any item expressed in a Language 2 in an otherwise Language 1 context was considered to be a codeswitch. The only exceptions to this were single lexical items which were names of particular places or things; i.e., items generally known as proper nouns and/or which did not have an equivalent in the other language. Examples are UTEP and *tortilla*. A code switch was also said to occur when there was a switch in the conversation from predominantly (or all) Spanish to predominantly (or all) English speech, or vice versa. This occurred, for example, across speaker turns and/or with a topic shift in the conversation, as in 7. For further discussion on the definition of codeswitching, see Huerta (1978).

[3]Several broad categories of social speech functions have been identified in the literature on sociolinguistics and it is on these that the included functions were based. Specifically, the emphatic, elaboration, and mode-shift functions are modeled after those of McClure and Wentz (1975: 426–428); the expressive function is from Hymes (1974:204–205). These four categories were quite comprehensive with regard to this particular set of data.

Expressive-speech which is emotive, which involves personal feelings; humor, sarcasm, excitement, frustration, or anger.

Mode-shift refers to a change in the mode of discourse, e.g., from casual to formal, particularly when accompanied by a shift in topic.

Elaboration-where a speaker switches in order to elaborate on something already said or to explain something previously mentioned.

In addition to the preceding analyses, any other frequently occurring characteristics which appeared in the data were also noted. An effort was, therefore, made to identify any patterns which occurred in the bilingual speech of the family and which could provide further insight into the process of codeswitching.

DISCUSSION OF THE RESULTS—I

The following material discusses the results of the analyses which comprised the first part of this study; i.e., it includes only the data gathered from the adult members of the family.

One general observation which was made at the outset of the study was that Spanish was the language of the home for all members of the family. Their codeswitching, therefore, occurred mostly from Spanish to English.[4] The focus of this discussion, then, is on these code-switched utterances in English as they occurred in otherwise Spanish contexts.

First, it was found that codeswitching occurred in approximately one-third of all speech produced by this bilingual family. That is, of the total of 844 utterances which comprised the three conversations, 307 were themselves codeswitched (intersentential codeswitching) or contained within them some codeswitched item(s) (intrasentential codeswitching). This codeswitching, furthermore, was quite consistent across all three conversations, again occurring in approximately one-third of the utterances included in each conversation.

It is pertinent to mention here, however, that four subjects were primarily responsible for most of the speech recorded, as they were the most talkative speakers. These speakers—the mother (M), the eldest son (Mi), and the two

---

[4]A brief explanation concerning the direction and frequency counts of codeswitching as presented in this paper is in order here. Only the initial direction of the switch, as well as the initial switch, were considered to be significant in this study. The utterance "*?Quién está ahí* from the younger ones?" where the speaker continues in Spanish for example, was said to contain only a single switch from Spanish to English rather than two switches, one from Spanish to English and another from English back to Spanish. Likewise, the case where a Spanish item occurred in an otherwise English utterance was counted as having a single switch from English to Spanish. This latter type of switch, however, occurred much less frequently in the data than the former; i.e., than from Spanish to English.

daughters (G and L)—accounted for 285 (92.9 percent) of all the codeswitches occurring in the speech of the family. The greater part of the analysis in this first part of the study, therefore, focused only on the speech of these four speakers, and it is upon their speech that the following description of codeswitching is based.

Most codeswitching in this family consisted of sentences, nouns, and phrases, quantitatively in that order. Adjectives, gerunds, and infinitival complements of verbs also occurred in the data although to a much lesser extent. Examples of these grammatical units, as well as their frequency of occurrence, are as follows: (Frequency counts and percentages, as explained are based on a total of only 285 utterances.)

Sentences[5] (179–62.8 percent)

1. Mi: *Yo no voy a Juarez.* It's not worth it.
   (I'm not going to Juarez.)
   G: *Tengo que ir a visitar a Sunsu, ayer no fui ni la vi.*
   I didn't go to the *Andritsos* yesterday.
   (I have to go visit Sunsu, I didn't go nor did I see her yesterday.)

Nouns (45–15.8 percent)

2. M: *El* pie *está en la heilera.*
   (The pie is in the refrigerator.)
   M: *...y Leti se devolvía a la casa con la* maid *y...*
   (...and Leti would go back home with the maid and...)

Phrases (30–10.6 percent)

3. L: *Lo corrieron,* the board or somebody.
   (They fired him, the board or somebody.)
   M: *Le dan* three weeks.
   (They give him three weeks.)

Adjectives (9–3.2 percent)

4. M: *¿De esas* electric?
   (Those electric ones?)
   M: *¿Los huevos* scrambled *con chorizo?*
   (The eggs scrambled with sausage?)

Gerunds (5–2.0 percent)

5. M: *¿Para qué lo lleva* shopping?
   (Why do you take him shopping?)
   M: *Que trabajando y estudiando y* housekeeping.
   (That she's working and studying and housekeeping.)

---

[5]Parentheses are used here to indicate English translations of Spanish-English utterances and, where appropriate, information relating to the discourse context.

Verbs (3–1.1 percent)
6. M: *Yo me voy a la noche a* babysit.
    (I will go babysit tonight.)
  Mi: *Entonces nos quedamos a* babysit.
    (At that time we will stay and babysit.)

These foregoing units accounted for 271 (95.1 percent) of all the codeswitches found in the data; other miscellaneous units comprised the remaining part of the data.

Of interest here is that most of the intersentential switching was done by only three subjects: Mi (eldest son), G (daughter), and L (daughter); the mother, M, on the other hand, switched intrasententially (usually in the form of nouns) much more frequently. One explanation for this might be that M's Spanish repertoire is more extensive than that of the other three subjects. Thus, M can always continue speaking essentially in Spanish regardless of changes which might occur in the discourse context (as mode-shift changes to be discussed later); Mi, L, and G would, in the same circumstances, find it more comfortable to switch to English. Thus, the other three speakers would be switching intersententially more often than intrasententially; the reverse situation would be the case for M.

Another factor to consider is that M has expressed a positive attitude toward codeswitching; i.e., she finds it quite convenient to be able to draw lexicon from two languages in her speech. One of the other subjects, Mi, has, however, spoken out against "mixing" languages and has criticized the other family members for doing just that. At least for this subject, therefore, one might say that he considers intersentential switching to be a lesser offense, or no offense, whereas switching within utterances is definitely undesirable. Thus, he most often avoids doing the latter and switches only between sentences.

Although it is not within the scope of this paper to discuss grammatical constraints on codeswitching, it is appropriate here to comment briefly on the results of this grammatical analysis with respect to at least two other recent studies which also involve the grammar of codeswitching. Poplock (Chapter 10) found that, except for nouns, those units which appear on a higher-level constituent are switched with greater frequency. Sentences and nouns, therefore, have the greatest probability of being switched.

In her data on codeswitching, Zentella (Chapter 7) found that sentences, nouns, and phrases (in that order) appeared most frequently from her list of grammatical categories. The findings presented herein, therefore, agree with both these studies with respect to the types of grammatical units which are switched most often.

The analysis for the social functions of speech in codeswitching led to the following results. Codeswitching occurred most often with a change in the mode of discourse, and less often with expressive speech, with emphatic speech, and with elaboration, in descending order. Examples and a discussion of the speech functions as they occurred in the data follow.

The mode-shift function most often involved a change from a casual speech to a slightly more formal one. This slight change in formality did not obviously occur because of a change in the situational context (as all the conversations were held at home), but rather, appeared to occur with a change in the topic of discourse. That is, a switch to English cooccurred whenever a topic outside the home domain was discussed, particularly when the topic related to work or school. Notice the following examples, both of which involve an initial switch from predominantly Spanish conversation to predominantly English conversation.

7.   L: *Vi a Betsy con el* doctor.
      G: *¿Está trabajando?*
      L: Mr. Page got fired. [Mr. Page worked with Betsy.]
      G: Mr. Page? Why?
      L: I don't know. She said he was there on a Friday and then on Monday he just didn't come back.
      G: *¡Hijo! ¡Que monjas!*
         (Golly! What nuns!)
      L: *She said that Ann Clare took over with another monja.*
         (She said that Ann Clare took over with another nun.)
      G: *¡Hijo!*
         (Golly!)
      L: She doesn't even know what he did wrong or anything. He just came back one day to clean out his desk.
      M: *¿Qué pasó? ¿Eso fué en* Lamar?
         (What happened? Was that at Lamar?)
      L: *Aha. ¿Se acuerda de* Mr. Page *el que era principal?*
         Lo correrion.   [to M]
         (Yeah. Do you remember Mr. page who was principal? They fired him.)
         The board or somebody. [To G]
      M: *¿Así no más de pronto lo corrieron?*
         (They fired him just like that?)
      G: *Bueno, y* she doesn't like the new administration?
         (Well, and she doesn't like the new adminstration)
      L: No.
      G: And that's why she's quitting.
      L: Oh, it's Ann Clare and Smith and another *monja.*
         (Oh, it's Ann Clare and Smith and another nun.)
      G: Smith?
      L: I knew there was one that was a real winner. The faculty was mad.

8. Mi: *¿Tiene un* Afro? *¿Qué es negrita?*
    Ch: No.
    Mi: *A mi no me gustan* Afros. *Ya hagan el party,* Chito. I'm going to
        leave town and you stay here, get things going and work on the
        paper. I'm not going to leave that book around forever, you
        know. Well, I think I might take it. In case someone asks for it I'll
        give it back to them. If no one asks for it I'll bring it back.
        ¿Entiende?
        (Do you understand?)

This occurrence was consistent in all three conversations and among all
speakers except the parents. It appears that the discussion of a topic which is
not family related, or which deals with a subject outside the home, introduces
more formality into the conversation; perhaps because it is discussed with
somewhat more seriousness than other daily activities within the family. This
type of topic-related mode-shift in the discourse, then cooccurred with a shift
from the home language to English, as in examples 7 and 8.

Notice, however, as in example 7, that the language used, nonetheless, was
dominated primarily by who the listener was and then by the topic or
discourse context. In this example, L switched to Spanish when talking to her
mother, M, even though she was still talking about job-related matters; in fact
the utterance was a translation of what had been previously said. This speaker
then immediately switched back to English when speaking to G. Thus, there
appear to be quite distinct rules operating here with regard to what language
is spoken to whom as well as which factors override each other with respect to
listener and discourse topic.

The expressive function occurred most often when the subject spoke in a
highly emotional tone of voice, as with frustration or anger, or when he
uttered something in a sarcastic or humorous tone. Notice the following, for
example, where Mi sarcastically makes a comment relating to G's previous
utterance about the length of time during which a friend, Gustavo, was
"stuck" in the marines.

9. G: *Y* Gustavo, he's not scheduled to come back to the U.S. until June
       o sabe que.
       (And Gustavo, he's not scheduled to come back to the U.S. until
       June or whatever.)
    Mi: It's only been six years since Joey talked him into joining!
    M: *¡Y Joey anda muy fresco! Se casó. ¡Y el otro pobre anda allá entre
       los pescados!*
       (And Joey's walking around real cool. He got married. And the
       other poor guy is over there among the fish!)

In the following discourse, the conversation has grown into an argument, to a point where G has gotten somewhat frustrated with Mi; hence her statements are not merely emphatic but are rather more emotional in nature.

> 10. Mi: *¿Por qué no estudia aquí?*
>   (Why don't you study here?)
>   G: **I can't! It's impossible!**
>   Mi: *Pero no mas por caprichosa no quiere.*
>   (She just doesn't want to because she's stubborn.)
>   G: **I can't!**

This type of expressive discourse, therefore, was also found to influence codeswitching to English in this family.

Emphatic statements were also often switched to English by the subjects, as a way perhaps of making them stand out more and thereby getting a certain point through to the listener. Examples of this follow:

> 11. Mi: *Yo me voy a ir temprano.*
>   (I'm leaving early tomorrow.)
>   **I can't wait for you to come and type the letter.**
> 12. Mi: Just don't settle for a penny less than two hundred, ***Chito, aunque se esté como mi mamá con el abogado.*** (even if you stay like my mother with the lawyer.)
> 13. M: *Asi como está ahi está* **perfect.**

The following discourse segment is one of the very rare times when M codeswitched to English in speaking to one of her children, in this case Ch. This underscores even more the emphatic nature of her statement, which is also a denial and which overrides the listener factor (which would otherwise call for Spanish).

> 14. Ch: *No mas siguieron viniendo y viniendo. Ya mero chocaban porque mi papá no volteaba para atrás. Ya mero chocaban todito el carro.*
>   (They just kept coming and coming. They almost crashed because my father wouldn't look back. They almost crashed the whole car.)
>   M: **I wasn't backing out that fast!**

Emphasis, therefore, also plays an important role in codeswitching, as seen in the preceding discourse.

Elaboration occurred the least frequently in the data as a speech function relevant to codeswitching. Examples of this are the following:

15. G: *Un cason de cuatro niveles.* It's huge, it's a huge home.
    (A big house with four levels.)
    G: *¿La otra cómo se llamaba?* The one that got pregnant?
    (What was the other one's name?)

It was clearly seen in the data, then, that certain social functions of speech did, to certain extent, influence codeswitching in the discourse of this family.

It is relevant to say here, however, that a large part of the data (approximately 63.5 percent) was found not to manifest any particular social speech function; i.e., these utterances were simply what one would call *informative* with reference to the discourse context. Examples of codeswitching which did not manifest any of the speech functions previously listed are the following:

16. Mi: *Debías de ver los juegos de* chess *que compré ahí.*
    (You should see the chess sets I bought there.)
    L: I saw the boards there.
17. Mi: *¿Cuál?*
    (Which one?)
    G: I don't remember.

Other factors or characteristics in the data did seem to be relevant to codeswitching. Specifically, a large portion of the switching consisted of items previously mentioned in the discourse; i.e., they are actually repetitions, mostly of single lexical times, which had been produced in preceding conversation.

This finding seemed to indicate that a principle of reciprocity, or response matching, may often operate in bilingual discourse and thus partially account for the intersentential codeswitching involved in this type of speech. Notice the following discourse excerpts.

18. Mi: *Llevese a esta muchacha terca.*
    (Take this stubborn girl.)
    G: I'm not *terca!*
19. G: *¡Que monjas!*
    (What nuns!)
    L: She said that Ann Clare took over with another *monja.*
    (She said that Ann Clare took over with another nun.)
    L: Oh, it's Ann Clare and Smith and another *monja.*
    (Oh, its Ann Clare and Smith and another nun.)
20. G: *A la* library.
    (To the library.)
    M: *¿Y a la* library *de UTEP?*
    (And what about the UTEP library?)

Ch: *Siempre yo no voy a la* library.
(I'm not going to the library after all.)
21. Mi: *Bueno, que se quede para el* party.
(Well, let her stay for the party.)
Ch: *¿No van a hacer* party *pues?*
(Aren't you having a party then?)
M: *Bueno, ¿y un* date *para Pepe para el* party?
(Well, and how about a date for Pepe for the party?)
Ch: *Para invitarla al* party.
(To invite her to the party.)
M: *No, no si el* party *ya esta organizado.*
(No, no the party is already organized.)
G: *Pues, su* party *del trabajo de Leti.*
(Well, Leti's party from work.)
Mi: *Ya hagan el* party *Chito.*
(Have the party, Chito.)

In these examples the form of a lexical item, as it is first used, is preserved by other speakers in later discourse without regard to a possible need to switch langauges in order to preserve that form. Note, for instance, that although *terca* in example 18 and *monja* in example 19 did not constitute switching as they were first used they did in following turns, as used by other speakers. "Library" and "party" in examples 20 and 21 constituted a switch from the start and the other speakers reciprocated in the same fashion; i.e., by codeswitching.

It does not seem to be the case, furthermore, that a speaker would repeat a lexical item because a change would be interpreted as a social comment or criticism. This does occur in monolingual or even bilingual speech, but it appears that the item most often involved is some type of stigmatized or nonstandard form, which when changed to a standard form does convey an attitude that one should use "correct" speech. None of the items which were switched in this set of data, however, were nonstandard forms, whether they were in English or in Spanish.

It is also highly unlikely that the listener would interpret the omission of these switches as a criticism not against that one form but against codeswitching in general. This is unlikely because all the speakers in this set of data were themselves codeswitchers, and secondly, because this type of social comment on language usage would not generally occur within the home among family members. Rather, if one member did want to criticize, for example, another member's speech, the former would be much less subtle and, in a much more forthright fashion, would simply tell the other member not to use a certain word or talk in a certain way because he sounded ignorant, vulgar, like a *pachuco,* or some such other more direct comment. Thus, these repetitions might occur as a social criticism in other situations, but this was not the case in this set of speech data.

Reciprocity, especially when a type of characterization is made, as with the adjective *terca* in example 18, may occur rather to preserve just that same characterization in the following utterance. Repetition of *terca* in the second statement in this example assured a reply that in effect said "I'm not exactly what you said I was," whereas the equivalent "I'm not stubborn" might not have necessarily refuted the claim.

The foregoing would be true not only because two different words were in fact used but also because often two terms in English and Spanish which are dictionary equivalents are not so for the native bilingual, for whom use of either term might actually connote subtle differences in meaning. This is particularly true with words involving emotional or behavioral aspects, as in 18. Thus, consistent use of a term in English or Spanish by either speaker becomes important, especially in a case where a lexical item is the main referent in a conversation.

Consistent usage of a word in either English or Spanish not only within a conversation but across conversations, furthermore, also leads to the conclusion that bilinguals habitually, or routinely, use certain words in one or the other language. It is difficult to determine why a word becomes habitual in one or the other language. A factor which may be involved is frequency of exposure to a word, such as "party," for example, which the subjects most often hear in English rather than in Spanish. This leads to more frequent, and eventually, habitual use of a word in either language.

Word associations to either an English or a Spanish-speaking context may also be involved in this type of codeswitching. This would be true especially in cases where counterparts in one and the other language would be identical, i.e., with no denotative or connotative differences. The word "library," which is semantically identical to *biblioteca,* for example, may be always produced in English as it is associated to an educational domain which functions predominantly in that language. Since all the formal education of the subjects who produced "library" as a codeswitch was in English, reference to anything related to their experience in school would be most likely expressed in English. The following examples where "teacher" rather than *maestra* was used provide further support for this claim.

22. M: *Dice Sunsu que le pregunto a la* teacher.
    (Sunsu said she asked the teacher.)
23. M: *La* teacher *y otra hermana.*
    (The teacher and another sister.)

A combination of factors, such as frequency of exposure and/or word associations, may, therefore, be involved in habitually using a word in either

English or Spanish; in some contexts habitual usage may also lead to reciprocity in speech and consequently to codeswitching. This notion of reciprocity in bilingual discourse is also supported by the rare occurrence of cross-language repetition, or translation of an item, in the data, as opposed to the high frequency of occurrence of simple repetition.

DISCUSSION OF RESULTS—II

The second part of this study involved the speech of a child who has been raised in the type of bilingual speech environment exemplified; one where codeswitching is the norm. The male subject, C, aged 25 to 34 months during the time of this study. At the beginning of the study, C appeared to be at a stage in his speech where he was moving from one-word utterances to two- and three-word utterances, commonly referred to as *telegraphic speech*. He had acquired at this time active as well as passive knowledge of both English and Spanish. He was, therefore, also producing English, Spanish, and code-switched utterances in his speech. Utterances recorded at the 2:1–2:4 stage included the following:

1. C: ¿*eto ceme?*   (*esto*...; pointing to a bottle of lotion)
   (this creme?)

2. C: me *ten*   (...*tren;* uttered on different
   me train   occasions: while pointing to a train,
                          while pulling a train, while unraveling
                          the string on a train.)

3. C: ¿*ota* boot?   (*otra*...?; pointing to one of
   (other boot)   two boots)

4. C: *oto* piece   (*otro*...; asking for another
   (other piece)   piece of candy)

5. C: (me *ota* cookie)   (...*otra*...; asking for another
   (me other cookie)   cookie)

6. C: me *capé* too   (...*café*...; while drinking his
   (me coffee too)   coffee)
   and minutes later:

7. C: coffee   (pointing to a cup of coffee)

At this stage the subject has acquired both English "me" and Spanish *otro, otra* as pivot-type words which he uses with either English or Spanish nouns (see 2–6). His codeswitched utterances, furthermore, show that he has internalized grammatical rules of both Spanish and English. Notice in examples 3 and 4, for instance, that there is gender agreement between the article and the noun, where the nouns (*la*) *bota* and (*el*) *pedazo* are feminine and masculine, respectively, and thus the corresponding *ota* (*otra*) and *oto* (*otro*) feminine and masculine forms which modify them are made to agree in gender. The subject is, therefore, able to apply these rules cross linguistically in cases where the Spanish noun is also in his vocabulary; not violating any language-specific rules even in his bilingual speech.

At this point, however, most of C's vocabulary is available to him in only one or the other language so that his bilingualism is to a great extent complementary. His codeswitched utterances, therefore, are unlike those of the adult bilingual, where the use of English and/or Spanish is often socially meaningful, as discussed in the first part of this study.

Later utterances recorded between the ages of 2:4 and 2:6 continue to show not only codeswitching but also English and Spanish speech.

8. C: go *ousay* play ball   (... outside ...; taking G by the hand)

9. C: me mell pepper   (... smell ...; trying to smell some black pepper which is mother is showing him)

10. C: *muchos niños*   (as sees children walking home from (many children)   school)

11. C: *no tá ocuro*   (... *está obscuro;* after G has (it's not dark)   just told him it is too dark to go outside)

12. C: Huky *quita* my coke   (handing G his coke and telling (Husky takes away   her that the dog, Husky, will my coke)   take it away)

13. C: me *no veo, me entes*   (... *lentes* ...; while watching (me can't see, me   TV) glasses

14. (At the lake waiting for the ducks to swim by)
   C: *¿Ita hay patos?*   (... *ahorita* ...)
      (soon there are ducks?)
   F: *Ahorita. Vamos a esperar.*
      (Soon. Let's wait.)
   C: *¿Ita sale patos? ¿Ita*   (... *ahorita* ...)
      sale ducks?
      (Soon the ducks will come out?)

The subject has also always maintained, as in example 12, correct word order and used appropriate lexicon even in these bilingual utterances. *Quita* in this example is not only syntactically and morphologically appropriate but is also semantically appropriate, as the single verb *quitar* corresponds to "take away" in English; thus producing "Husky takes away my coke" with no redundant or duplicated forms.

Bilingual referentiality, where the speaker produces Spanish/English counterparts, also occurred more often in C's speech at this stage. His vocabulary in either language had increased so that he now produced alternate forms for a larger number of words, even within the same speech event, as in example 14.

Utterances recorded in the stage from 2:7 to 2:10 continued to provide evidence that the subject was continuing to develop not only his English and Spanish speech but his codeswitching as well.[6]

15. C: me wan go wit you   [Taking G by the hand]
16. C: wha you writing?   [as G is taking notes on his speech]
17. C: *quí tá bolsa*   (*aquí está...*; when asked to
       (here is bag)   put his hat in a bag]
18. C: *no hay tuenos*   [... *truenos...;* looking outside
       (there is no   after a rainstorm]
       thunder)
19. C: *ahora martes* coming   [talking to his mother]
       garbage truck
       (today, Tuesday, garbage truck is coming)
20. C: *no hay* ducks, *pura*   [looking at a picture in a
       water   book]
       (there are no ducks, only
       water)
21. C: no tie my *cinta*   [as his mother is trying to
       (don't tie my   tie his shoelace]
       shoelace)

The subject, then, continued to produce new and varied codeswitching patterns in his speech. Of interest at this stage was that some of his utterances, despite their Spanish-English composition, reflect the syntax of Spanish. This is seen, for example, in 19 where the temporal adverb phrase *ahora martes* is placed in sentence initial position and where the subject "garbage truck" is placed after the verb "coming." This post-posed subject word order is common in Spanish, although ungrammatical in English.

This utterance, nonetheless, is well formed; given that codeswitched utterances obey the constraints of either English or Spanish. A constraint which appears to operate in Spanish is that if an adverb phrase is in initial position in a sentence with an intransitive verb with nothing following it, the subject noun phrase, if expressed, must follow the verb. Because *ahora martes* was in initial position in this type of structure, therefore, and because the verb *venir* (to come) is intransitive, the subject had to be postponed. This

---

[6]The utterances in each of the examples 18–21 do not necessarily represent continuous dialog.

constraint was thus being adhered to in example 19, and as such it was a well-formed utterance which was in agreement with the syntactic constraints of Spanish.

Furthermore grammatical analysis of these data is again beyond the scope of this paper. Suffice it to say, then, that this child continued to codeswitch to a large extent in his speech, his utterances always being well-formed in one language or the other. At the same time, his exclusively English and Spanish speech appeared to also be following a normal rate and order of development (see Huerta, 1977).

CONCLUSIONS

This study has provided a description of Spanish-English codeswitching as it occurs in conversation among members of a bilingual family. The first part of this investigation, which focused on the speech of the adult members of the family, led to the following conclusions.

First, Spanish was the language of the home for this family. They did, however, codeswitch extensively in their speech; approximately one-third of all their utterances contained codeswitching.

An analysis of the types of grammatical units that were switched revealed that most codeswitching consisted of sentences, followed by nouns and phrases. There was also a difference in the bilingual speech of the mother, as opposed to that of her daughters and son, in that the former switched intrasententially most often; the latter switched intersententially most of the time. Mi, L, and G thus codeswitched and spoke basically in English much more frequently than did their mother. This switch to English, furthermore, often occurred when the topic of conversation was one outside the home.

An examination of the social speech functions in the bilingual discourse of this family showed that codeswitching often occurred with a shift in the mode of discourse, with expressive speech, and to a lesser extent, with emphatic speech and with elaboration in speech. The mode-shift function was frequently accounted for by shifts in the topic of discourse which also led to slightly more formality in the conversations.

Finally, it was found in the first part of the study that, very frequently, the same items were codeswitched throughout and across conversations. This indicated that a type of reciprocity existed in the family's bilingual speech, that certain words were associated to English-speaking contexts and were thus expressed in English, and/or that certain words were habitually expressed in English by these speakers.

The second part of the study concerned a third-generation member of the family who was still in the process of acquiring his speech. This analysis revealed that this subject was developing his English as well as his Spanish speech. He also codeswitched to a large extent; his bilingual utterances being well formed not only in that they had the correct word order of either English or Spanish but also in that they contained no redundant or duplicated forms.

In sum, the data recorded from this speaker seem to show that codeswitching may be one approach to the acquisition of bilingualism, and a very viable one, especially in the Southwest where, because of the very nature of the bilingual atmosphere, it is nearly impossible to keep the languages apart.

Codeswitching is in fact not only relevant to the acquisition of bilingualism but also to language maintenance among bilinguals. A language is maintained only if it is used. Because codeswitching, therefore, involves the use of two languages, it becomes also a very viable means of maintaining a language. This would again be true in particular in a community where an alternate language is not functional in any other way.

Finally, whereas speculation about the future may lead some to think that extensive codeswitching may instead lead to some type of linguistic convergence this would not necessarily be the case. Codeswitching, where it serves certain social or other speech functions, actually depends on the separateness of the languages for its effectiveness, so that the tendency might instead be for codeswitching itself to perpetuate two distinct languages as such, rather than to bring about their convergence.

REFERENCES

Fantini, A. *Language acquisition of a bilingual child: A sociolinguistic perspective.* Putney, Vt.: Experiment Press, 1974.

Gumperz, J. J. The sociolinguistic significance of conversational codeswitching, *Working Paper 46,* 1974b. University of California, Language Behavior Research Laboratory, 1974b.

Huerta, A. *Codeswitching among Spanish-English bilinguals: A sociolinguistic perspective.* Unpublished doctoral dissertation, University of Texas, Austin, 1978.

Huerta, A. The acquisition of bilingualism: A codeswitching approach. *Working Papers in Sociolinguistics,* Number 39. Austin, Texas Southwest Educational Development Laboratory, 1977.

Hymes, D. H. The ethnography of speaking. In B. G. Blout (Ed.), *Language, culture and society: A book of readings.* Cambridge, Mass.: Winthrop Publishers, 1974.

McClure, E. Aspects of code-switching in the discourse of Mexican-American children. In M. S. Troike (Ed.), *Linguistics and anthropology,* Washington D.C.: Georgetown University Press, 1977.

McClure, E., & Wentz, J. Functions of codeswitching among Mexican-American children, *Chicago Linguistic Society Parasession on Functionalism,* 1975, 421–432.

Padilla, A. M., & Liebman, E. Language acquisition in the bilingual child. *The Bilingual Review,* 1975, *1,* 34–55.

10 Syntactic Structure and Social Function of Codeswitching[1]

Shana Poplack
Center for Puerto Rican Studies
City University of New York

Long-term ethnographic observation of a block in El Barrio, one of the oldest continuous Puerto Rican communities in the United States, has suggested that residents can be divided into networks whose membership is defined, among other things, by their public use of language (Pedraza, 1978). Some of these networks are observed to use predominantly Spanish; others, predominantly English; and still others, a mixture of the two, codeswitching.

Codeswitching constitutes an integral part of community discourse norms on 102d Street: everybody appears to do it to some extent, although it is so rare in the speech of some speakers that it escapes observation altogether and can be located only through painstaking transcription of recorded speech. On the other hand, it is so frequent in the speech of others that the observer's impression is that it is a constant phenomenon. The occurrence of codeswitching depends, among other things, on the norms or perceived norms of the speech situation, the bilingual ability or perceived bilingual ability of the speaker and the hearer, and as I will demonstrate, on the ethnicity or group membership of the interlocutor.

This study describes the linguistic configuration of codeswitching and suggests a framework which relates its occurrence to a well-documented (e.g.,

[1]This study is a result of many discussions with the Language Policy Task Force of the Center for Puerto Rican Studies. My thanks to Pedro Pedraza and Felix Toledo, who participated in the data collection and transcription; and especially to John Attinasi for comments and suggestions from the earliest stages of this work. This paper has also benefited greatly from comments by Bill Labov, Don Hindle, and Susan Thomas.

169

Gumperz, 1971, Valdés-Fallis, 1976) function of switching: that of an ethnic identity marker.

Gumperz (1970:136) has suggested that as a behavioral strategy, codeswitching is similar to the use of polite and familiar address pronouns in that Spanish forms used among members convey secondary meanings of solidarity and confidentiality. This study investigates empirically both differential frequencies of codeswitching with a member of the same ethnic group and a nonmember, and different configurations of the switches in these two situations.

CODESWITCHING

There is some disagreement in the literature as to what constitutes a "true" instance of code-switching. For the purposes of this study, I define a *switch* according to degree of adaptation to the other language. At one èxtreme is complete adaptation of items from one language (L_1) to the phonology and morphology of the other (L_2). Examples of items I am considering fully integrated into L_2 can be found in 1:

1a. *Vendré* **straight** [ʔ tɾe] *del trabajo pa'l bloque.* (I'll come straight to the block from work.) (Bla, 137)[2]

1b. *Yo* **jangueo** [haŋ'geo] *en la ciento quince.* (I hang out on 115th Street.) (B5b, 50)

1c. *Tabanos una nota bien* **jevi** [he'βi]. (We were into a heavy vibe) (Bla, 336)

If these forms followed only Puerto Rican Spanish phonological patterns (as in *straight,* which follows the attested Caribbean process of glottalization most common in word-internal position: [es'tre → tre]), morphological patterns (as in *jangueo*), or syntactic patterns (as in *jevi* which follows Spanish rules of adjective placement) they were not here considered instances of codeswitching, nor included in the present analysis. At the other extreme is the complete lack of adaptation of patterns from one language to the patterns of the other, which I am calling *codeswitching,* as in 2.

2. You didn't have to worry *que somebody te iba a tirar con cerveza o una botella* or something like that. (You didn't have to worry that somebody was going to throw beer or a bottle at you or something like that.) (C17, 49)

---

[2]Items in parentheses refer to tape and switch number.

At the discourse level, instances in which the speaker simultaneously switched codes at a turn boundary while participants and social setting remained constant, were also included in the analysis, and considered as switches in the code of the discourse.

Not all varieties of Latino codeswitching are structurally equivalent however. As Pfaff (1976) has suggested for the Chicano speech community, there appear to be several types of switching behaviors which may be characterized by use of differential proportions of switchable categories, and whose occurrence is presumably constrained by the presence of certain extralinguistic factors.

One type of codeswitching that can be found on 102d Street is apparently related to degree of control of L_2: the less knowledge the speaker has of the other language, the less structurally integrated into the discourse will be his switches into that language. Preliminary comparison of language attitudes of block residents with their recorded speech reveals, understandably enough, that those who claim Spanish as "the language they feel most comfortable in," and also evidence positive attitudes toward its use and maintenance, tend to switch into English primarily through use of tags, frozen forms, and idiomatic expressions. Thus 82 percent of the English switches transcribed for Juan, a key Spanish-dominant figure on the block, were of this type: e.g., "right," "you know."

Another type of codeswitching can be characterized by high proportions of what I call *noun switching*: switches of a single noun in an otherwise L_1 utterance, as exemplified in 3 below:

3a. We'll go to the *sala*. (We'll go to the living room.) (B6a, 1)
3b. All those *viejas* that sit in the *banca* all day spending their welfare checks playing numbers. (All those old ladies that sit in the numbers parlor all day spending their welfare checks playing numbers.) (C17, 31)

Yet another type may be characterized by higher proportions of intrasentential switches, as in 2, than in either of the latter types.

I shall demonstrate that both frequency and type of switching within the stream of discourse (i.e., preference for intrasentential over single-noun or tag switching) varies with the ethnicity of the interlocutor.

Lola

One speaker was selected as an informant for this exploratory study, since on the basis of both ethnographic observation and comparison of her taped speech with that of others on the block, she appears to be the most skilled codeswitcher in the community. Lola switches frequently and smoothly: only a small percentage of her switches is preceded by hesitations, false starts, or other repair mechanisms which might mark a shift in code. Her Spanish is not influenced by contact with English. Variation in key Puerto Rican Spanish phonological variables corresponds to that of monolingual speakers. An analysis of her use of Spanish tense and mood reveals that these also cluster in the same areas found for monolinguals. Nor were any instances of syntactic irregularity noted. Likewise, Lola's English is rarely affected by Puerto Rican Spanish phonology. When it is, it can be considered part of her repertoire range, as she also controls vernacular and corrected New York City English, as well as Black English vernacular. Her English is also unaffected by contact with Spanish at other linguistic levels.

Lola was born in Humacao, Puerto Rico, 35 years ago, migrated to El Barrio at the age of five, and has lived there ever since. She is a member of a network of housewives and mothers on the block, and functions as a link between them and a subgroup of single women. She is able to participate in both groups because she is both a mother and a single woman, and she was born in Puerto Rico and raised there until the age of five, as were most of the other Spanish-speaking housewives on the block. Having lived in New York City since the age of five is a characteristic she shares with the single women born or raised in New York City. That she was raised in El Barrio when most residents were recent monolingual arrivals from Puerto Rico (the 1940s), as well as her having completed high school in New York, explains her linguistic ability in both Spanish and English.

Her use of codeswitching as a mode of communication is more extensive than that of most other members of this network, who generally revert to monolingual speech outside of the group setting. Lola, in contrast, extends this behavior to other settings, such as the home.

Lola evinces very positive attitudes toward bilingualism. She denies that Puerto Ricans in New York are creating a new language, Spanglish, although she does admit that some members of the speech community mix Spanish and English together.[3]

Although Lola has lived in El Barrio ever since she moved to New York, she expresses uniformly negative attitudes toward her relationship to Puerto Rican ethnicity. For example, when asked how the neighborhood had changed since she moved in, she responded:

> When I came to my block—to 102d Street—it was a joy! It was beautiful! There were very few Puerto Ricans, and less... blacks. It was mostly *griegos, italianos* (Greeks, Italians). In my building there were only one—two Puerto Rican families. The fa—the other ones *eran polacos* (were Polish). (C14, 47)

---

[3]The foregoing information about Lola has been excerpted from Pedraza's ethnographic diary of 102d Street.

Methodology

The research design included recording sessions with Lola on separate occasions by Pedraza, an ingroup member who has a long-standing relationship with the informant, and the author, a nongroup member. When setting up an appointment for me to interview Lola, Pedraza specifically described me as a person who was not Puerto Rican but who could speak fluent Spanish anyway. Lola immediately assured him that this was no problem since she could speak English. English, parenthetically, is the language claimed by Lola to be the one she "feels most comfortable in," and in fact was the "base" language used with both Pedraza and me. The majority of the material discussed below refers to switches into Spanish.

The data I report on here consist of 4 hours and 15 minutes of taperecorded speech collected in four different recording sessions with Lola:

1. A "formal" interview session in which she responded orally to a questionnaire about language attitudes, ethnicity, bilingual education, etc.;
2. An open-ended "informal" session with minimal input from the interviewer during which Lola basically directed the conversation toward topics of interest to her (e.g., a childhood illness, life in El Barrio);
3. A session in the street with no directing input from the interviewer during which Lola was accompanied while doing her errands, and chatting with passersby, which we will refer to as *vernacular*.

All these were collected by Pedraza, the ingroup member. A fourth segment of speech may be designated as *informal* by the preceding criteria, but was recorded by the author, a nongroup member. The first half of this interview was directed by Lola toward general, ethnically neutral topics of interest to women: men, sex, child rearing. During the second half of the interview, I concentrated on introducing ethnically specific topics, such as recipes for Puerto Rican dishes, Puerto Rican childhood games, etc. Ethnically neutral items were considered to be those with a low degree of cultural specificity, or those which could be easily translated from L_1 to L_2 (Hasselmo, 1969), e.g., *pan* (bread), *casa* (house). Ethnically specific items were those which were highly culturally specific, or located in a low position on a translatability scale, e.g., *gandinga* (a Puerto Rican dish), *culantrillo* (maidenhair fern (an herb used in making rice and beans)).

On the basis of the study of switching behavior of a single speaker, highly skilled in two languages, and close to the so-called ideal bilingual, I suggest a framework which can be used in a community-wide study of codeswitching, including speakers at different stages of bilingual ability.

THE LINGUISTIC CONFIGURATION OF
CODESWITCHING

Although in some of the earlier literature (e.g., Lance, 1975: 143) it was felt that codeswitching was a random phenomenon, most investigators today appear to agree that it is not random but rule-governed. There is, however, no present agreement on the precise nature of the rules which govern codeswitching. It seems clear that some of the constraints on its occurrence are extralinguistic. Other factors constraining the occurrence of codeswitching are linguistic, or internal to the discourse. I suggest that these factors covary, such that there will be higher proportions of certain types of switches in the presence or absence of certain extralinguistic factors.

In order to describe linguistically the different types of codeswitches, we must first define the total population of possible forms: are there elements in discourse which cannot be switched? Are there environments in discourse where switches cannot occur?

A comparison of some of the syntactic constraints on codeswitching suggested in the literature with our own data revealed counterexamples, some of which are listed in 4:

4a. Proposed Constraint: Switching is restricted between pronominal subjects or objects and verbs. (Gumperz, 1970:158; Timm, 1975:477.)

Counterexample: You *estas diciendole la pregunta* in the wrong person. (You are asking the question to the wrong person.) (B9b, 43.)

4b. Proposed Constraint: Switching is blocked between finite verbs and their infinitive complements. (Timm, 1975:748.)

Counterexample: There's an old Spanish saying that it goes, you have to *dar de l'ala pa' comer de la pechuga.* (There's an old Spanish saying that, it goes, you have to give from the wing to get to the breast.) (B6a, 9)

4c. Proposed Constraint: Switching does not occur between auxiliaries and verbs. (Timm, 1975:478.)

Counterexample: So you take the ham . . . as they're *ablandando, ya que está* un poquito hirviendo, tu le echas el güeso del jamón. (So you take the ham . . . as they're softening, as they're boiling a little, you throw in the ham bone.) (B7b, 56.)

4d. Proposed Constraint: The conjunction must be in the same code as the conjoined sentence. (Gumperz, 1976:34)

Counterexample: *es mía* . . . because *ellas son puertorriqueñas* to the core. (It's mine . . . because they are Puerto Rican to the core.) (B9b, 23.)

4e. Proposed Constraint: Switching phrases in which the [main] verb is not repeated (gapping) is only marginally acceptable. (Gumperz, 1976:34).

Counterexample: There's a lot of them that are working very hard out there and struggling and *adelant ándose,* okay? (There's a lot of them that are working very hard out there and struggling and getting ahead, okay?) (B9b, 62)

4f. Proposed Constraint: A lone determiner cannot be switched. (Wentz, 1977:142)

Counterexample: Where are they, *los* language things (Where are they, the language things?) (003)[4]

Counterexamples to many of these constraints were also found by Pfaff (1975, 1976) in her study of Chicano codeswitching performance.

Analysis of performance data suggests two linguistic constraints on codeswitching:

The Free Morpheme Constraint.   A switch may occur at any point of the discourse at which it is possible to make a surface constituent cut and still retain a free morpheme.[5] According to this constraint, it is possible to switch full sentences (including conjoined sentences, repetitions equaling full sentences, and interjections) as well as any constituent within the sentences, provided that the constituent consists of at least one free morpheme.

Wentz and McClure (n.d.) have also suggested a constraint for the Chicano speech community on the "bicodal word": "no words with morphology from both languages can exist without first having the stem integrated into the language of the suffix phonologically and semantically" (p. 245).

The Equivalence Constraint. A second syntactic constraint operates simultaneously with the first. It states that codes will tend to be switched at points where juxtaposition of English and Spanish elements does not violate a syntactic rule of either language, i.e., at points where the surface structures of the languages map onto each other. Consider example 5:

5a.   E I/told him/ that/ so that/ he would bring it/ fast.
5b.   CS I told him that *pa' que la trajera ligero.* (C4, 3)
5c.   S (*yo*) le dije eso pa' que la trajera ligero.

---

[4]The 00 series refers to switches collected from our built-in data source: the researchers at the Center for Puerto Rican Studies, many of whom are codeswitchers.

[5]Included under this constraint are idiomatic expressions or frozen forms, which are not broken up.

According to the free morpheme constraint a codeswitch could take place after any free morpheme in 5. There are, however, some differences in English and Spanish morpho-syntax which limit these choices. For one thing, both the main and subordinate clause contain an indirect pronominal object, which in Spanish precedes the verb, and in English follows it. Because of surface discrepancy, or nonequivalent word orders of Spanish and English, the probability of a switch between verb and object in either clause is lower, so in our data there were no occurrences like those listed in 6:

6. *told *le, le* told, him *dije, dije* him
    bring *la, la* bring, it *trajera, trajera* it.

In the embedded sentence, whereas English marks tense and mood on the modal auxiliary, "would," Spanish marks the same categories morphologically on the main verb itself, *trajera*. Here again there is no overlap between the surface structures of L_1 and L_2. (There is an option in Spanish of marking tense and mood on the auxiliary as well: *pudiera traer*. Had it been chosen, the probability of a switch between auxiliary and verb would be greater, as these two surface structures are equivalent.) The speaker actually opted to switch at a higher node, 5b, producing the entire main clause in English, and the entire embedded sentence in Spanish. Switching an entire higher-level constituent when the equivalence constraint is not met at a lower node is a device which Lola appears to use frequently. This can be seen by the higher proportions of major constituent switches than of switches of the elements within them (Table 1). Points at which these constraints predict possible occurrences of codeswitches are indicated by the slashes in 5a.

The free morpheme and equivalence constraints are exemplified in example 7, which lists the major switch types found in the data:

7a. Full Sentence:
    ella canta canciones insultando a los hombres. That's why you never heard of her. (She sings songs insulting men. That's why you never heard of her.) (B6b, 36)

7b. Conjoined Sentence:
    yo voy por to' esos sitios y I was in 7th Avenue and Broadway. (I go to all those places and I was in 7th Avenue and Broadway.) (B9b, 51)

7c. Interjection
    There should be a stop with these kids where there should be sta-discipline. *¡contra!* You know, open classrooms... (There should be a stop with these kids where there should be sta- discipline. Darn! You know, open classrooms...) (B9b, 61)

7d. Between Major Noun Phrase and Verb Phrase: Years ago people *se iban a trabajar.* (Years ago people would go to work.) (B6a, 62)

7e. Between Verb Phrase and Object Noun Phrase:
What ruined this people is la *vagancia de no 'cer na."*(What ruined this people is the laziness of not doing anything.) (B6a, 61)

7f. Between Verb Phrase and Prepositional Phrase:
tu quieres meter mano wid a man, that's your business. (You want to fool around wid a man, that's your business.) (C17, 85)

7g. Between Verb and Adverb:
Un americano me puede preguntar very nicely *"hace tiempo que yo te estoy viendo así y perdona que te pregunte."* (An American can ask me very nicely "I've been seeing you like this for some time and excuse me for asking you.") (B9b, 41)

7h. Between Noun and Adjective:
cojo mi garlic *puro.* (I take my garlic pure.) (C17, 103)

7i. Between Determiner and Noun:
Because if you smash it with the *pilón* and spray it, you don't get that burning sensation. (Because if you smash it with the pestle and spray it, you don't get that burning sensation.) (B7b, 53)

7j. Between Auxiliary and Verb:
So...you take the ham...as they're *ablandando, ya que está un poquito hirviendo, tu le echas el güeso del jamón.* (So...you take the ham...as they're softening, as they're boiling a little, you throw in the ham bone.) (B7b, 227)

Furthermore, as can be seen in Table 1, it appears that the higher the syntactic level of constituent, the greater the probability that it will be switched.

Full sentence types together constitute nearly half the switches. Major constituent boundaries within the sentence, such as those between noun phrase and verb phrase, verb phrase and object noun phrase, verb phrase and prepositional phrase, follow full sentence types as favorable switch points, with about 6 percent of the total number of switches occurring at each. Smaller-sized elements within these constituents such as those which modify the noun and the verb follow, whereas a switch within the verb itself accounts for only 1 percent of the data ($N = 4$). There is one exception, the noun, which at 34 percent is the single most frequently switched category in the corpus. We return to the noun in the next section.

We can also see the equivalence constraint operating through the behavior of adjectival switches in the data. English and Spanish have different rules of adjective placement. In English, attributive adjectives typically precede the nouns they modify, whereas in Spanish, they typically follow them. A closed set of Spanish adjectives (e.g., *grande/gran; bueno/buen*) may also precede the noun, although their use entails some change in semantic referent. Switching an adjective within the noun phrase by following either English or Spanish adjective placement for adjectives other than those in the closed set,

TABLE 1
Percentage of Occurrence of Switches at Different
Surface Constituents

Switched Segment	Percent
At Major Constituent Boundaries	
Full sentence	13
Conjoined sentence	15
Interjection	11
Repetition	4
Between noun phrase and verb phrase	6
Between verb phrase and object noun phrase	6
Between verb phrase and prepositional phrase	5
Within Major Constituents	
Noun	34
Adjective	3
Adverb	1
Within verb	1

$N = 400$

appears to result in a construction which would be judged unacceptable by, for example, Timm's informants (1975:479), and which occurred only once in the data. Instead, when switching adjectives, the data indicated an overwhelming preference for a rule of predicate adjective formation which exists in both Spanish and English. This is exemplified in 8:

8a. S *A mi mamá le gusta el arroz amogollado.*
8b. E My mother likes her rice sticky.
8c. CS My mother likes her rice *amogollado.* (B6b, 84)

These constraints also explain the unacceptability of certain other constructions cited by Timm. For example, she claims that negating elements in each language must correspond in code to the verbs undergoing negation, so that a sentence such as 9 is judged unacceptable.

9. *I don't *quiero* (Timm, 1975:479).

According to the free morpheme constraint, a switch could occur at any point in the sentence except after *do,* given that the contracted form of *not* is a bound morpheme. Operation of the equivalence constraint, however, prevents this from taking place. English requires the dummy morpheme *do* or a modal auxiliary for negative support, whereas Spanish negates by inserting the negative particle immediately before the verb. These two rules do not overlap, and switching is therefore avoided in negative constructions. Timm also cites as unacceptable a switch between finite verb and infinitive complement:

10. *(they) want *a venir;* want *a* come; *quieren* to come;
    *(I'm) going *a decidir;* going *a* decide; *voy* to decide; *voy a* decide
    (Timm, 1975:478).

I suggest that the "unacceptable" constructions can be explained by the free morpheme constraint, which excludes switches from occurring at bound morphemes. That *want to, going to, have to,* are often perceived as single modals is supported by their most frequent phonological realization in spoken language: ['wanə, 'gɔnə, 'hæftə]. So although there are no occurrences of constructions like "going + *a decidir"* in our corpus, there were examples like "have to + *dar"* with the switch occurring after the finite verb. That the Spanish counterparts of these verbs are perceived in the same way is evidenced in counterexamples to Timm's constraint provided by Pfaff's Chicano data:

11. *fui a* + cash *su cheque.* (I went to cash her check.)
    no van a + bring it up. (They're not going to bring it up.) (Pfaff, 1975:11).

Within the framework of the free morpheme and equivalence constraints, I analyzed 400 switches occurring in Lola's speech in three different speech styles, ranging from formal to vernacular, and with two different participants, an ingroup member and a nonmember.

Relationship of Ethnicity
to Codeswitching Configuration

In comparing the data collected from these four recording sessions there appears to be some correlation between formality of speech style and raw frequency of codeswitching as indicated in Table 2.

Table 2 is highly suggestive even though these measurements were derived by dividing total time of the interview involving two interlocutors by the total number of Lola's codeswitches, rather than by what would be a truer measure, i.e., dividing the total time of Lola's speech by the total number of codeswitches she produced. As can be seen, even from this rough measure, switching occurs much more frequently in informal speech styles than in formal speech styles. What is more, frequency of codeswitching is also constrained by the group membership of Lola's interlocutor: it occurs as infrequently with the nonmember in an informal speech style as it does in

TABLE 2
Average Number of Code Switches per Minute by Speech Style and Group
Membership

Speech Style	Number of Code switches	Number of Conversation (minutes)	Average Number of Code switches (per minute)
Formal	87	90	1
Informal (nongroup)	107	120	1
Informal	152	30	5
Vernacular	54	15	4

$N = 400$

formal speech—the least favorable environment for switching with the group member. These results add empirical support to Gumperz's hypothesis of ethnic identity.

Apart from actual frequency of codeswitching shown in Table 2, when the participant was held constant there did not appear to be any differences in the type of codeswitching in the formal, informal, and vernacular speech styles that could not be explained by the nature of the speech event. For example, there were more interjections in the vernacular data (19 percent) than in the remainder of the data combined (11 percent). This is due to the sort of interaction Lola was engaged in at the time of recording (yelling at her daughter, exchanging greetings, etc.). When the participant was changed from an ingroup to a nongroup member, there were qualitative differences in the configuration of the switches, as can be seen in Table 3. For the remainder of the analysis, therefore, the data from the three "in-group" sessions will be considered together and compared with the "nongroup" session.

Table 3 indicates that the configuration of the switches used with a group member is substantively different from that used with a nonmember. For one thing, although we have seen in Table 1 that noun switches (i.e., switches of a

TABLE 3
Distribution of Noun Switches by Raw Frequency and Ethnic
Specificity with Ingroup and Nongroup Member

Noun Switches	Participant	
	Ingroup (%)	Nongroup (%)
Nouns out of Total	24	65
Number of Code Switches	($n = 70/292$)	($n = 70/180$)
[+ Ethnic] Nouns	49	89
	($n = 34/70$)	($n = 62/70$)

single noun in an otherwise L_1 sentence) are the most switchable category at 34 percent, noun switches account for a disproportionate amount of the switches when interacting with the nongroup member. On the other hand, they account for less than one-fourth of the switches with the group member. Furthermore, a full 89 percent of the noun switches with the nonmember are used for ethnically specific terms, or items low on the scale of translatability, whereas when interacting with a group member, the speaker is about as likely to switch for items not ethnically specific.

The noun has been found to be the most frequently switched element by several scholars (e.g., Wentz, 1977; Timm, 1975). Many, however, do not consider the presence of an L_2 noun in an otherwise L_1 sentence to represent a true instance of codeswitching (Wentz, 1977; Gingràs, 1975; Gumperz, 1971). Gumperz (1971:139) believes the introduction of such an element to be part of the speaker's monolingual style. Similarly, Wentz's (1977:142) approach regards noun phrases containing switches between determiner and noun as monolingual constituents. Such switches were included in the present study by reason of our initial definition of a switch as any L_1 item which is unadapted phonologically, morphologically or syntactically into L_2 discourse. Although it is clear that noun switches are different in nature from intrasentential or even sentential switches, it is also clear that they can be used as a discourse strategy. Their inclusion has permitted differentiation of the type of switching used with a group member and a nonmember. Switching with a group member allows for a wider latitude of possible switch points, as can be seen in Table 4.

TABLE 4
Distribution of Major Switch Types with Ingroup and
Nongroup Member

	Participant	
	Ingroup	*Nongroup*
Switch Type	*(%)*	*(%)*
Full sentence	45	23
Intrasentential	31	12
Noun	24	65

Table 4 shows that intrasentential switches, those which all investigators agree to be "true" instances of codeswitching, constitute nearly one-third of Lola's codeswitches with the group member, whereas with the nonmember, they account for only 12 percent.

DISCUSSION

To identify these different codeswitching configurations it was necessary to define constraints on switching which would account for our own data and, if possible, for the Chicano data on which the majority of the literature is based. We cannot rule out the possibility that different sets of discourse rules obtain for Chicano and Latino switching behavior. But given that neither the Spanish dialects nor the English dialects with which they came in contact differ significantly in a structural way, as well as that empirical studies of actual performance are beginning to show important areas of convergence (Pfaff, 1975; 1976; Wentz & McClure, n.d.),[6] it would not be surprising if codeswitching in the two speech communities were governed by at least the same set of linguistic rules. Ongoing variable rule studies of Hispanic dialects (Cedergren, 1973; Terrell, 1975; Poplack, 1977) are beginning to show that these dialects may all be described by similar sets of constraints, which function in different proportions. There seems to be no reason why a similar framework could not account for different varieties of codeswitching.

There are two major issues in the study of codeswitching: (1) why it occurs (functional or pragmatic constraints); (2) where it occurs (formal or syntactic constraints). These have traditionally been treated separately, although all scholars agree that the two constraints interact. It has been pointed out that we cannot predict where a switch will occur any more than we can predict when a speaker will opt to produce an embedded sentence.[7] Our results suggest that it is possible to predict where switching is *more likely* to occur. We can also predict where it will not occur.

If we treat the constraints proposed in this study as rules whose probability of application will vary in the presence of well-defined extralinguistic factors, such as the ethnic identity factor, we should be able to account for different types of codeswitches in terms of different probabilities of rule application.

Weighting of constraints should account for several points raised in this paper, although at this point any hierarchy would be speculative at best. The free morpheme (and constituent size) constraint might explain the fact that occurrences of the counterexamples listed in example 4 are rare enough to have led investigators to posit constraints against them. The equivalence constraint should account for speakers' different bilingual abilities. We might expect that equivalence (or well-formedness) will apply in lower proportions for less-skilled bilinguals, or as appears to be the case in the Puerto Rican community, that switch points which are "risky" in terms of syntactic well-formedness, will tend to be avoided altogether. (Hence, the preponderance of

---

[6]For example, these three scholars and the author have all independently posited a constraint similar to the "free morpheme" constraint. Wentz and McClure's (1977) constraint on the bicodal word is discussed on page 175. Pfaff (1976) found that stems of borrowed verbs are adapted to Spanish phonology when inflected with Spanish morphology.

[7]Beatriz Lavandera, personal communication.

tag switching cited for Juan earlier.) Further studies of codeswitching performance between both typologically similar and dissimilar languages would provide invaluable data to test this constraint further. The interaction of both constraints with pragmatic factors (e.g., display of ethnic identity, norms of the speech situation) which might be specific to different speech communities should show differential switching configurations which could be accounted for by the same framework.

Quantitative analysis has uncovered two syntactic constraints which function simultaneously. Together they are general enough to account for all the instances of switching in the Latino data under consideration as well as some Chicano data we have examined, yet they do not seem strong enough to generate instances of nonoccurring switches. The first constraint states that it is possible to switch any constituent in discourse, provided that it is a free morpheme. Moreover, it appears that the more major the constituent the greater the probability of a switch, with the exception of nouns which are the most frequently switched category. This constraint interacts with the equivalence constraint which states that codeswitching will tend to occur in those areas where surface structure representations in the two codes are equivalent.

The equivalence constraint suggests that the codeswitching mode proceeds from that area of the bilingual's grammar where the surface structures of L_1 and L_2 overlap, whereas the outer areas where there is no equivalence will tend to be reserved for monolingual segments of discourse. The hatched portion in Figure 1 below represents the area in which surface structures are equivalent in two languages.

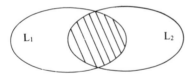

FIG. 1.   Representation of Codeswitching Grammar

The most striking evidence in favor of this hypothesis, however, comes from Lola's data: only one example of the 400 investigated did not satisfy either English or Spanish surface structure constraints. The remaining 399 were well-formed utterances by both English and Spanish standards.

This is additional evidence that codeswitching, rather than arising from insufficient control of L_2, can be a highly developed skill requiring competence in two languages, a skill which is governed by rules common to both.[8]

[8]Since the work reported in this paper was completed (1978), further studies (Poplack in press, Sankoff and Poplack 1980) have confirmed the validity of the codeswitching constraints on a wider sample of speakers, and investigated their implications for a formal account of bilingual syntax.

REFERENCES

Cedergren, H. *The interplay of social and linguistic factors in Panama.* Unpublished doctoral dissertation, Cornell University, 1973.

Gingràs, R. Problems in the description of Spanish-English intra-sentential codeswitching. In G. Bills (Ed.), *Southwest areal linguistics.* San Diego, Calif.: Institute for Cultural Pluralism, 1974.

Gumperz, J. J. *Language in social groups.* Stanford, Calif.: Stanford University Press, 1971.

Gumperz, J. J. The sociolinguistic significance of conversational codeswitching, *Working Paper* 46. University of California, Berkeley, Language Behavior Research Laboratory, 1976.

Gumperz, J. J. & Hernandez-Chavez, E. Cognitive aspects of bilingual communication. In E. Hernandez-Chavez et al. (Eds.), *El lenguaje de los Chicanos.* Arlington, Va.: Center for Applied Linguistics, 1970.

Hasselmo, N. On diversity in American Swedish. *Svenska Landsmal Och Svenskt Folksliv,* 1969.

Lance, D. 1975. Spanish-English code-switching. In E. Hernandez-Chavez et al. (Eds.) *El lenguaje de los Chicanos.*

McClure, E. The acquisition of communicative competence in a bicultural setting. NIE Grant NE-G-00-e-0147 final report, undated.

Pedraza, P. 1978. Ethnographic observations of language use in El Barrio. Unpublished ms.

Pfaff, C. *Syntactic constraints on codeswitching: a quantitative study of Spanish/English.* Paper presented at the LSA annual meeting, 1975.

Pfaff, C. Functional and structural constraints on syntactic variation in codeswitching. *Papers from the parasession on diachronic syntax.* Chicago: Chicago Linguistic Society, 1976.

Poplack, S. 1980. The notion of the plural in Puerto Rican Spanish: Competing constraints on /s/ deletion. In W. Labov (Ed.), *Locating language in time and space.* New York. Academic Press.

Poplack, S. in press. "Sometimes I'll start a sentence in Spanish *y termino en espanol":* Toward a typology of code-switching. *Linguistics 18:7/8.*

Sankoff, D. & Poplack, S. A formal grammar for code-switching. Working paper no. 8. New York: Center for Puerto Rican Studies, 1980.

Timm, L. A. Spanish-English codeswitching: el porqué y how-not-to. *Romance Philology, 28,* 1975.

Terrell, T. 1975. Functional constraints on deletion of word-final /s/ in Cuban Spanish. Berkeley Linguistic Society, *1.* Berkeley: University of California, 1975.

Valdés-Fallis, G. Social interaction and codeswitching patterns: A case study of Spanish/English alternation." In G. Keller et al. (Eds.), *Bilingualism in the bicentennial and beyond.* New York: Bilingual Press, 1976.

Wentz, J. *Some considerations in the development of a syntactic description of codeswitching.* Unpublished doctoral dissertation, University of Illinois at Urbana-Champaign , 1977.

II LATINO LANGUAGE, COMMUNICATION, AND COGNITION IN HOME, COMMUNITY, AND SCHOOL SETTINGS

11 Culture, Language, and Communicative Behavior: The Psychiatric Examination of Spanish-Americans

Luis R. Marcos, M.D., Med. Sc. D.
*New York University School of Medicine,
and New York City Health and
Hospitals Corporation, New York City*

Manuel Trujillo, M.D.
*Columbia University College of Physicians and Surgeons and South
Beach Psychiatric Center, Staten Island, New York.*

Language and communicative behavior are powerful mediators in the individual's adaptation to the environment. In many urban areas of this country a major portion of the psychiatric population, already a casualty of adaptation, includes individuals whose dominant language is not English. Specifically, in New York's Gouverneur Hospital and Washington Heights Community Service, two institutions affiliated with New York University and Columbia University respectively, approximately 50 percent of the mentally disabled patients are primarily Spanish-speaking.

For the past nine years, at New York University School of Medicine, the effects of interview language on the psychiatric assessment of bilingual Spanish-American patients have been the subject of several studies. As part of this program of research, we have used discrete linguistic dimensions of bilingualism (i.e., language dominance, language independence, and language attitude) and have attempted to evaluate their effect upon the expression of psychopathology (Marcos, 1976a). A consistent finding in these studies has been that the clinicians' frame of reference applicable to the Anglo-American patient is not equally appropriate for the evaluation of the communicative behavior of patients who are affected by cross-language and cross-cultural factors. In effect, the psychiatric examinations of a group of Spanish (Marcos, Alpert, Urcuyo, & Kesselman, 1973). These patients, all subordinate bilinguals,[1] were found to exhibit higher levels of somatic concern, motor tension, mannerisms, anxiety, hostility, depressive mood, and emotional withdrawal. Although several factors may have been responsible for the results (e.g., clinicians' negative or positive prejudice, the language barrier, cultural misunderstanding, or a combination of all), subsequent studies have shown that the switch in the language of the interview had a significant effect on the content, paralinguistic, and motor components of the patients' communicative behavior (Marcos, Urcuyo, Kesselman, & Alpert, 1973; Marcos, 1976b).

The purpose of this paper is to consider the effects of the patient's bilingual condition on the specific areas of the Mental Status Examination. The discussion will focus on major bilingual dimensions, such as the *language barrier*, or linguistic deficit in the nondominant language, the *language independence,* or bilinguals' capacity to maintain two alternate experiential inner worlds associate with the languages, and the *language attitude* or bilinguals' evaluation of their languages as either additive to, or subtractive from, their image and social status.

THE MENTAL STATUS EXAMINATION

The *Mental Status Examination* is a systematic record of current findings in a range of areas of the patient's behavior relevant to the assessment of psychopathological states. These data must be gathered by direct examination on the basis of the patient's spontaneous behavior as well as the patient's responses to the specific questions of the clinician. The Mental Status Examination includes the descriptive evaluation of the patient's appearance, motor behavior, speech, cognitive functioning, affect, and the patient's attitude throughout the examination as well as the reactions evoked by the patient in the examiner.

The Mental Status Examination constitutes the foundation of the psychiatric diagnostic process. In assessing a patient's mental status, the clinician's responsibilities go beyond assigning the patient's disorder to one or another diagnostic category. Clinicians must consider alternative diagnoses, make judgment about the reliability of the information obtained, and recommend therapeutic procedures necessary to assure the patients' safety and to restore their health. For the patient, the Mental Status Examination frequently represents the entry point to the psychiatric care system and imposes an additional burden to his/her already failing coping ability.

---

[1]Subordinate bilinguals are persons whose linguistic performance shows a differential competence in the two languages. In comparison with their dominant language, in their nondominant language these bilinguals reveal lexical, syntactic, and phonetic deficit.

The following constitute the major areas of the Mental Status Examination which are most commonly affected by the Spanish-American bilingual condition:

Patient Attitude

This component of the Mental Status includes a range of behavioral dimensions, such as patients' cooperativeness, responsiveness, alertness, and attention. We have observed that Spanish-American patients who struggle with the language barrier tend to behave rather passively and submissively in psychiatric interviews. This complaint attitude is, then, paradoxically interpreted by the interviewer as an indication of uncooperativeness and guarded behavior in the sense of "unwillingness" to give sufficient information.

Apart from the patient's culturally "preset" unfavorable expectation of the English-speaking examiner (Marcos, 1974), closer to the linguistic realm, there are a number of nondominant language behaviors which can create the impression of slow and reluctant participation in the interview process. Thus, in a comparative content analysis of the speech of Spanish-American schizophrenic patients whose dominant language was Spanish and who had been interviewed in both English and Spanish, one found a striking tendency of the patients to answer English questions with short sentences, a word, or even a silent pause. In fact, when interviewed in English, these patients produced a significantly higher number of expressions, such as "I don't know"; "I don't think so"; "no, Sir,"—all easily interpreted by the clinicians as defensive reluctance to communicate.

The patient's attitude about the language of the interview may easily permeate his/her attitude toward the interviewing clinician. In general, Spanish-American patients with Spanish as their dominant language, show a clear preference to be interviewed in Spanish. This may be consonant with the concept of "language loyalty" proposed by Weinreich (1953) as a form of ethnocentrism. In the course of our work, however, we have studied situations in which a primarily Spanish-speaking patient has refused to speak in Spanish while expressing his preference to communicate in English. This reaction may be related to the additive-subtractive dimension of bilingualism (Lambert, 1973), and the values and attributes associated with the particular language (Marcos, Eisma, & Guimon, 1977).

Motor Behavior

In clinical psychiatry, the evaluation of the patient's motor activity has always been considered a fundamental part of the Mental Status assessment. By conceiving body movements as an expressive behavior clinicians may interpret them as a reflection of the patient's affect (e.g., motor retardation and depression), or the patient's thinking (mannerisms and autism). Clinicians may also utilize the patient's motor behavior to make inferences about the quality of the interview interaction. As we have indicated before, Spanish-American schizophrenic patients, when interviewed in English, were evaluated by clinicians as exhibiting more motor tensions and more mannerisms (Marcos et al., 1973). Recent studies, however, have shown that when subordinate bilinguals communicate in their nondominant language, they produce more hand movement activity (Grand, Marcos, Freedman, & Barroso, 1977; Marcos, 1978). This extra nonverbal activity has been considered by a group of investigators to have a facilitatory function in the process of verbalization (Freedman, 1972). In light of these findings, the clinician assessing the motor behavior of Spanish-American subordinate bilingual patients faces a difficult discriminatory task. Unaware of the motoric component of the verbalization process, clinicians may interpret some of these verbalization-related movements as reflecting tension, anxiety, mannerisms, or hyperactivity; thus, ascribing to bilingual patients-psychopathology what belongs to the adaptive task of compensating for a verbalization handicap.

Speech

The evaluation of the patient's speech and stream of associations constitutes a fundamental component of the Mental Status. Dimensions, such as tone and rate of speech, grammatical and semantic congruency, and concatenation of ideas, are evaluated from the verbal productions of the patient. As with other components of the Mental Status, however, the valid interpretation of these characteristics of the patient's thinking is significantly hampered by linguistic productions which are a result of the patient's bilingual condition.

Thus, in a recent experiment we demonstrated that subordinate bilingual patients, with Spanish as their primary language, when interviewed in English produced a significantly higher frequency of speech disturbances—i.e., sentence correction, sentence incompletion, stuttering, repetition, omission, incoherent sound, tongue-slip, and Ah sound—(Marcos, et al., 1973). Since these speech disturbances have been suggested to be indicators of anxiety in monolingual patients (Mahl, 1959), it is possible that English-speaking clinicians may interpret them as such without taking into account that these disturbances may be a consequence of the effort to verbalize in a nondominant language.

Spanish-American patients, when interviewed in English, show a lower speech rate and longer silent pauses than when the interview is conducted in Spanish (Marcos et al., 1973). Thus, it appears that speaking in a second language may have a low activation effect on speech similar to what has been described in depression (Alpert, Frosh, & Fisher, 1967). If the English-speaking clinician is not aware of this, he may interpret these vocal cues as indicators of the patient's depression although the patient may be manifesting nondominant-language–related signs.

Another related issue is the occurrence of "language mixing" during the English language interviews of Spanish-American patients (Marcos et al., 1973). Thus, a majority of patients utilize Spanish words during their English interviews. This language intrusion made their stream of thought sound less logical and more confused.

We see, then, a number of vocal and paralinguistic aspects of verbal behavior which may be interpreted as having clinical significance, whereas they derive from the special problems posed for patients when they are interviewed across the language barrier.

Thought

The evaluation of patients' thought content includes the assessment of the patient's present ideation and beliefs, the responsiveness of this ideation to both internal and environmental cues, its congruence with the cultural system, and the richness of the associations.

In the content analysis of the psychiatric interviews of Spanish-American patients, we found that on numerous occasions the patients gave different responses to the same question in English and Spanish. Most often the English response suggested greater psychopathology (Marcos et al., 1973). A critical issue in the interpretation of these findings is whether the greater pathology in the English language is real or based on the interview conditions? One might wonder which interview reflects the "true" condition of the patient. It seems reasonable, however, to assume that the interview demands contribute to the manifest level of psychopathology and that under the lower linguistic demands of the Spanish-language interview patients are in fact less sick.

Beyond the linguistic problems, the psychiatric evaluation of thought content involves the assessment of culturally bound attitudes and beliefs which permeate the patient's emotional experience and behavior. In this regard, the Spanish-American population is characterized by a diversity of cultural values which are often misunderstood or misdiagnosed by clinicians who are unfamiliar with the Spanish culture (Marcos, 1974). Some of these attitudes include the concepts of "spiritualism," "santeria," "machismo," "respeto," "dignidad," "ataque," "black magic," "visiones," and other culturally bound attitudes, such as the disposition toward authority, time notion, male dominance, the idealized female role, and the mother-son relationship. We may, then, conclude that a valid evaluation of thought content in Spanish-American patients requires both familiarity with the effect of bilingualism and knowledge of the culture.

Affect

Affect is the feeling tone or emotion that accompanies an idea. The clinician's task in evaluating the patient's affect is to assess the patient's articulation into words of his/her internal world. Often, however, patients suffering from psychiatric conditions are unable to verbalize their overwhelming experiences. At those times, facial expressions and other nonverbal behavior may convey to the clinician the patient's emotional state.

In general, Spanish-American subordinate bilingual patients are found by clinicians to be more anxious, more depressed and emotionally withdrawn when the interview is conducted in English than when it is in Spanish (Marcos et al., 1973; Marcos, 1976b). Apart from the changes in the patients' stream of thought, secondary to the verbalization in a nondominant language (e.g., longer silent pauses, lower speech rate, etc.) which are often interpreted by clinicians as indicators of depression or anxiety, we contend that the process of verbalization in a nondominant language may constitute an impediment for the emotional involvement of the patient. Thus, the extra cognitive demands placed on subordinate bilinguals when speaking across the language barrier determine a deflection of affect into the task of encoding itself. In fact, these patients tend to invest the affect in *how* they say things and not in *what* they are saying. Frequently the patient manifests this tendency by verbalizing emotionally charged material without displaying the expected emotion.

Another source of distortions in the evaluation of Spanish-American bilingual patients' affect is the language-independence condition of some bilinguals. In effect, some bilinguals do not simply have a duplex set of words to refer to experiences; they may have alternate and not necessarily congruent experiential inner worlds linked to each of the languages. When a patient's significant experience is verbalized in the language in which it did not take place, the patient may report it and not show the appropriate involvement (Marcos & Alpert, 1976).

CONCLUSIONS AND RECOMMENDATIONS

It is crucial that clinicians conducting a Mental Status Examination of Spanish-American bilingual patients be sensitized to the significance of linguistic factors, such as the language dominance of the patient, the language-independence pheomenon, and the patient's attitude toward the language of the interview. A clinician who is unfamiliar with the effects of these bilingual dimensions on the experience and expression of psychopathology could easily misevaluate the patient's mental status by neglecting the consideration of some communicative cues as nondominant-language related.

When a patient must be interviewed in a language in which he is less competent, the clinician must make every effort to assure that the patient understands what is being expected. The clinician should introduce redundancy to facilitate communication, and he ought not accept laconic responses as evidence of depression or emotional withdrawal. Furthermore, cues residing in the patient's motor activity or in the vocal channel of communication should be carefully evaluated before considering them indicators of psychopathology. In addition, clinicans evaluating Spanish-American patients should be familiar with the cultural-bound attitudes and beliefs of this population.

Clinicians should be aware that the language barrier of Spanish-American bilinguals often interferes with their ability to understand and derive meaning from the interviewer's use of paralinguistic cues, such as voice intonation, pauses, and emotional tone. This effect tends to minimize the patient's capacity for involvement in the interview interaction and, thus, his/her motivation. Also, a patient who speaks in a poorly commanded language poses additional demands for clinicans. Apart from possible misunderstanding of the patient's verbalizations, the clinician faces the difficult task of deciding which of the patient's verbal cues are relevant and which are mere consequences of the language deficit. This demand on the clinician may give rise to feelings of frustration, uncertainty about the diagnostic process, and even rejection of the patient.

REFERENCES

Alpert, M., Frosh, W. A., & Fisher, S. H. Teaching the perception of expressive aspects of vocal communication. *American Journal of Psychiatry,* 1967, *124,* 202–211.

Freedman, N. The analysis of movement behavior during the clinical interview. In A. Siegman & B. Pope (Eds.), *Studies in dyadic communication.* New York: Pergamon, 1972.

Grand, S., Marcos, L. R., Freedman, N., & Barroso, F. Relation of psychopathology and bilingualism to kinesic aspects of interview behavior in schizophrenia. *Journal of Abnormal Psychology,* 1977, *5,* 492–500.

Lambert, W. E. *Culture and language as factors in learning and education.* Paper presented at the Fifth Annual Learning Symposium. Western Washington State College, Bellingham, Wash. 1973.

Mahl, G. F. Measuring the patient's anxiety during interviews from "expressive" aspects of his speech. *Transactions of the New York Academy of Science,* 1959. *21,* 249–257.

Marcos, L. R. On the assessment of psychopathology in the Puerto Rican patient. *Research in Education,* 1974, *9,* 20.

Marcos, L. R. The linguistic dimensions in the bilingual patient. *American Journal of Psychoanalysis,* 1976a, *36,* 347–354.

Marcos, L. R. Bilinguals in psychotherapy: Language as an emotional barrier. *The American Journal of Psychotherapy,* 1976b, *30,* 552–560.

Marcos, L. R. Hand movements in relation to the encoding process in bilinguals. *Dissertation Abstracts International,* 1978, *38,* 11.

12 Preparing to Leave: Interaction at a Mexican-American Family Gathering[1]

Maryellen Garcia
National Center for Bilingual Research
Southwest Regional Laboratory for
Educational Research Development

This study analyzes communicative interaction in an informal social setting, investigating how the social task of leave-taking organizes the interaction into a cohesive discourse. The data is taken from the last five minutes of a half-hour tape recording made during one Mexican-American family's Christmas gathering,[2] the relevant section involving the preparing for leave-taking of one group of guests, from which the discourse emerges. The discussion is divided into two parts: the first orients the study to an ethnographic framework, the basis on which the component parts of the interaction will be considered; the second examines the interaction more closely, analyzing the interactional structure of the discourse, its relationship to conversational closings, and its illustration of Mexican-American ethnicity.

1.0 ETHNOGRAPHIC FRAMEWORK

Speech Community.   First the discourse must be situated within the social unit of its speakers, which Hymes (1972) calls the *speech community.* In this study, the speech community represented is that of Americans of Mexican

---

[1]I take this opportunity to give heartfelt thanks to Marilyn Merritt and Bruce Osborne for their invaluable guidance and encouragement. Both saw me through rough drafts of this paper. Many insights and interpretations of the data would not have been possible without their help.

[2]I taperecorded my own family's Christmas celebration in 1970. Then a graduate student in Hispanic linguistics, my only goal was to get unmonitored speech; I was not sure how the resulting recording would be used. I was a natural participant in the interaction and was not aware of my cassette recorder at the time of this interaction.

descent living in the United States. Presently this is a very broad and diverse group; more specifically the family in this study belongs to that subgroup of second- and third-generation Mexican-Americans living in suburban communities in Southern California.

Speech Situation.   The discourse is also situated within a speech situation, which provides a context for the verbal interaction but is not governed by its own set of rules for the use of speech. In this study, the speech situation is that of a party, the family's Christmas day gathering.

Speech Event/Interactional Segment.   The speech event is the next unit of analysis, "... restricted to activities, or aspects of activities, that are directly governed by rules or norms for the use of speech" (Hymes, 1972:56). A speech event may consist of one speech act or several, according to Hymes; it is not clear, however, whether the discourse under consideration here comprises only one speech event. The activity involves not only many speech acts, but also many different kinds of speech acts which accomplish several kinds of "social business." In view of these complexities, we shall refer to the entire discourse by the term, *interactional segment,*[3] as it circumcribes a segment of human interaction within a social frame, in this case, leave-taking activity. The component aspects of speech events as outlined by Hymes (1972:58-65) will also be relevant to the description of the interactional segment and will be discussed later.

Speech Acts.   Functionally, a speech act is an utterance which accomplishes a type of verbal act by the very fact of its utterance, e.g., a promise, as in, "I promise to mow the lawn today." Its form can be that of an entire narrative or a one-word utterance, and so is not identifiable as any one level of grammar. Here we are concerned with the function of the speech acts in this discourse, looking to the specific context of the speech situation to understand the social norms for their use and interpretation.

1.1   SPEECH EVENT COMPONENTS

Speech events are made up of various component parts, many of which are also applicable to the description of the interactional segment. Briefly, the components of speech events are setting, participants, ends, act-sequence, key, instrumentalities, norms of interaction, and genre. (The first letter of each is easily remembered as contained in the word, "speaking.")

---

[3]The term, *segment,* was suggested to me by Marilyn Merritt to describe this type of interactional unit. It was suggested to her by Erving Goffman for use in her own work.

Descriptive Components.   The descriptive components—setting, participants, and instrumentalities—situate the discourse in the physical world.

The discourse takes place in the dining room of a Mexican-American home, a modest tract house in a suburb of Los Angeles. The central location of the dining area where the tape recorder is set up—adjacent to the kitchen and not separate from the living room—makes it a good place for capturing much verbal interaction. The social scene is that of a family gathering on Christmas day—very informal, no "best behavior" required. The event is characterized by lively, sometimes boisterous, multifocused interaction. The taperecorder which has been set up on the dining table has already been noticed and commented on by the guests in its immediate area, and then has been forgotten. Not all the participants in the leave-taking segment are within range of the microphone previous to that activity, but the adults within range, predominantly women, converse about topics of general interest and family gossip; children can be heard to be playing in the background. The room is very noisy, with the sound of children's piano playing in the next room, and the television in the living room.[4]

The participants are all related in the context of one three-generational nuclear family. The matriarch, aged 69, is the first generation in the United States, having immigrated from Mexico before 1920. (She will be referred to as *Mamá* or *Mom* in the discussion.) The party is at the home of one of her daughters; the guests are also her daughters and sons-in-law, and their children—her grandchildren. The second generation, *Mamá*'s daughters and their husbands, range in age from 34 to 51. Their children are third-generation Mexican-Americans, ranging from preschool age to age 23. The situational roles in the speech situation include hostess, co-hostess, host, and guests. These roles are relevant to the interaction but subordinate to the familial relationships, as an individual has only a temporary role in the speech situation but a permanent role in the speech community. The significance of these relationships to the interaction may be discussed further as relevant to the analysis of the data.

The relevant instrumentality here is speech. Paralinguistic features, such as body language, facial expression, and the like, are also relevant to the analysis of human interactions. Because these data are taken from a taperecording, the analysis does not include any nonaudible channel of communication. At some points in the interaction when simultaneous interchanges obscure the linguistic message, suprasegmental cues, e.g., pitch, intonation, etc., suggest

---

[4]Although much of the noise has died down by the time the leave-taking sequence occurs, interaction that one would like to attend to on the tape is often lost because of the multilayering of speech in the situation. Only my status as a participant and member of this family group allowed me to pick out relevant utterances after repeated listenings. For these reasons and to avoid an unduly long presentation, no transcript of the entire five-minute interaction is given here.

how the message was intended, even though the actual content cannot be decoded.

The languages used are English and Spanish, with a much greater part of the discourse taking place in English than in Spanish. *Mamá* is usually addressed in Spanish and speaks it exclusively, although she understands almost all the English spoken around her. Her daughters and sons-in-law usually speak Spanish to *Mamá*, and occasionally with each other, although they prefer English and almost always use it with their children. The children address everyone in English, except for an occasional word or phrase in Spanish.[5]

Interpretive Components.   The remaining components of this analysis relate more closely to the social frame of the interaction and call for the subjective interpretation of the analyst.

The genre of speech found in this discourse is that of lighthearted "social talk," and is very much tied to the type of social occasion that this is. The fact that all the participants are closely related and are intimate observers of each others' lives allows for the topics to become very personal, but unselfconsciously so.

The key of the individual speech events ". . . provides for the tone, manner, or spirit in which an act is done" (Hymes, 1972:62). Finding one key is not easily done here, since the discourse in this study is comprised of many speech acts within speech events which occur over a six-minute time period. Rather, there are several keys in evidence, as the various moods and attitudes of the participants are not repressed as they might be in a nonfamilial context. This may be discussed with regard to individual interchanges later where relevant to the analysis.

Act-sequence is the term used to deal with the message form and message content of speech acts. It refers to the close interrelationship between how an act is accomplished (e.g., singing, praying, etc.) and the meaning it conveys. Both form and content are central to the analysis of how a speech act communicates; what the speech acts accomplish will, however, be of more interest than how they do what they do, so the act-sequence of speech acts will not be central to the analysis.

The norms of interaction for participants in the leave-taking segments are, in the main, those of the speech situation. In this Mexican-American family gathering, any participant may address any other at virtually any time and may respond to anyone else's verbal contribution whether addressed or not. The familiarity of the participants and the looseness of the involvement

---

[5]The informal family setting, the participants' ingroup status (members of one closely knit family, sharing the same social and linguistic background), would all seem to make extended use of Spanish or codeswitching appropriate, yet the preferred language here is English: no codeswitching style is in evidence.

structure[6] for this social occasion allows for this high degree of conversational accessibility among the participants.[7] Thus, the verbal interaction within this speech situation consists of many conversations, with a rapid turnover of topics and participants. Speakers may address each other in varying levels of volume depending on the speech act they wish to perform or the noise level of the room at the time of speaking. Other interactional norms are relevant only to the frame provided by the leave-taking activity. Later in the analysis, leave-taking emerges as structured interaction and suggests its own norms of appropriate behavior to be superimposed on those of the speech situation.

The norms of interpretation are shared by the participants in this speech situation because of their close familiar relationship and frequent social interaction. This discourse exhibits no misunderstandings which could be the result of two groups of persons having different social interpretations of the constituent speech acts.

The goal of the guests in initiating the interaction is to take their leave of the occasion in a manner that is respectful of both the social relationships involved and the nature of the occasion itself. The logical ends of the interactional segment are served: those of the participants, since the departing guests succeed in leaving the family gathering in a socially acceptable manner, and those set up as the expectations of the leave-taking, for the same reason.

2.0 GOALS OF ANALYSIS

The primary goal of this discussion is to analyze the structure of the interactional segment in terms of the functions of the interchanges, or speech acts, which make up the discourse. To do so, the author of the present study draws upon personal knowledge of the people and the speech situation, offering her unique perspective as a member of the family group and a natural participant in the interaction. Secondary goals will be to relate aspects of the leave-taking segment to closing sections of conversations, as discussed by Sacks and Schegloff (1973) and to illustrate how the discourse manifests the ethnicity of this group. The latter will be discussed after the analysis of the data.

---

[6]"Looseness" and "tightness" are terms which Goffman prefers to "informal" and "formal" in describing social gatherings. He explains his terms as a way of talking about the involvement structure of a social occasion: "... there may be one overall continuum or axis along which the social life in situations varies, depending on how disciplined the individual is obliged to be ..." (with regard to the appropriate behavior for the social situation). For a more complete discussion see Goffman (1966:199).

[7]Marilyn Merritt suggested to me that easy conversational accessibility accounted for much of the verbal interaction in my data. She discusses the related notion of transactional accessibility in her dissertation (Merritt, 1976).

2.1 ANALYSIS OF DISCOURSE STRUCTURE

The discourse begins when one of the participants informs one of her group that they will be leaving. This announcement opens the way for a single focus of attention in the speech situation; the participants, whose main activity up to this point has been social conversation on a variety of topics, now direct their attention to the activity of the departing guests. The interaction itself is still multifocused[8] in that two or more people may begin their own conversations. Often, however, the conversation relates to or contributes to the leave-taking rituals which are now the focus of the speech situation.

The nature of the interactional segment called "leave-taking" is a series of interchanges which the participants engage in to conduct *social business*—everything from negotiating the decision to leave to the offering of assistance in leave-taking preparations. These interchanges are comprised of speech acts classifiable as *levels* within the interaction. This term emphasizes their function in the overall activity, several levels providing the paradigmatic structure of the entire interactional segment. The syntagmatic aspect of the speech acts in the discourse is also undeniably important; the sequential appropriateness of certain types of speech acts near the beginning, middle, or at the end can, however, be accounted for in terms of the function they serve in the activity. In leave-taking, the sequential ordering of classes of speech acts may be seen as a corollary operation of their functional classification, although their division into stages is not so neat in this real data. Thus, level is more important to this analysis as a functional classification rather than a sequential one.

Level 1: Initiation of Leave-Taking

It is early evening (5 or 6 o'clock) on Christmas Day when the leave-taking is initiated. The group about to take their leave is comprised of Helen, her husband, Manuel, and their immediate family, Valerie and Annette.[9] They have brought Helen's mother, the matriarch of the family group, to the Christmas gathering, and so are responsible for taking her home. She is also the mother of Connie, Concha, and Lucy, all married with children of their

---

[8]"Focused interaction" is a term which Goffman proposes which deals with "... the kind of interaction that occurs when persons gather close together and openly cooperate to sustain a single focus of attention, typically by taking turns at talking" (1966:24). This suggests that a conversation is a single-focused event. A party may have many such ongoing conversations, and would constitute what Goffman calls a *multifocused gathering* (1966:91). In this paper I adopt Goffman's distinctions, but I also use focus in its common meaning in saying that the leave-taking activity provies a common focus for the participants involved.

[9]Those named in the text either participate, or are referred to, in the interaction as reported by means of the examples. They are not the only people present at the family gathering.

own. The party is at Lucy's house, making her the hostess, her husband, John, the host, and daughter Maryellen, the co-hostess.

This is one of a well-established tradition of family gatherings held on the occasion of religious or secular holidays, or rite-of-passage celebrations, such as birthdays, baptisms, etc. Normally, guests stay until mid-evening, occasionally until late evening. Helen's family group will be the first to leave, signaling the beginning of the termination of the yearly Christmas celebration. Moreover, her leaving will mean the departure of *Mamá*, whose presence is one of the requisite components of the occasion.

The leave-taking segment is initiated by Helen's informing her mother that they will be leaving shortly. She accomplishes this by saying in a low conversational tone, (1) "*¿Ya nos vamos a ir,* Mom?" (000),[10] roughly equivalent to saying, "We're going now, Mom. Okay?" This statement has the effect of announcing her plan of leaving to the group in general, although she directs it only to one of the persons who will be leaving with her. Due to the high degree of conversational accessibility in the speech situation, the rest of the group is free to respond to it as well, which they quickly do.

It is evident that Helen creates a state of tension by her announcement. The other participants in the interaction, her sisters, try to induce her to stay. In the following examples, both familial roles and situational roles are pertinent to the interpretation and effectiveness of the objections of the participants. (Extraneous comments are not represented in these examples, although they may intervene; this exchange occurs within a very short span of time. Addressees are indicated except where obvious.)

(2)   Helen: (To her mother) *¿Ya nos vamos a ir,* Mom?(000) (We're goin now, Mom. Okay?)
TELEPHONE RINGS LOUDLY (001)

    Connie: (To Helen) *¿Ya se van tan pronto?* (002) (You're going so soon?)

    Concha: (To general audience) Gee, just when the party was getting good. (002.5)

    Connie: (To Helen) Really? *¿De Veras? ¿Se Van?* (003) (Really? Truly, You're going?)

    Concha: (To general audience) Just when the party was getting charming. (004.5)

---

[10]The numbers after the examples refer to counter numbers on the Hitachi Auto Shop Cassette Recorder TRQ-341. Each count of 10 represents 35 seconds to tape, each digit, approximately 3.5 seconds. For subsequent examples, double parentheses (( )) indicate undecipherable speech; the same double parentheses enclosing a word indicate what was probably said. The double slash // indicates that the utterance is overlapped at that point by the subsequent utterance or noise, as indicated on the typescript. CAPS indicate an audible activity on the tape relevant to the interaction.

Concha: Just when I was// (005.5)
Helen: (To Valerie) Valerie, we're going. (006)
Concha: Just when I was losing my depression. (007)

Here, Connie expresses genuine surprise and disappointment at the announcement, since the hour is so early. Concha, however, objects because she evaluates the party as "getting good" and "getting charming," and is reluctant to have anyone leave, thereby signaling the end of the social occasion. The end of the party will mean the end of her good time as a guest, a situational role in which she has been forgetting about her depression.

(3) Concha: (To general audience) Just when I was getting ov// (011)
MOMENTARY DIN
Concha: Just when I was getting over my conflicting emotions! (012)
Helen: Well, it doesn't take very, you very . . . , very much to get over your conflicting emotions! (013–4).

Helen dismisses her objection, indicating that Concha couldn't have been so upset if a family gathering could alleviate her problems.

Concha's repetition of the theme of her depression functions to elicit a response. A supportive response from one of her sisters would indicate that her problems were cause for familial concern, but Concha's semi-joking key and persistence in recycling bids for attention undermine the serious content of her objections, and contribute to her receiving a nonsupportive response. When Helen alludes to the social occasion in minimizing her sister's alleged inner turmoil, she also minimizes the social occasion which, in turn, serves to diminish the importance of her decision to leave.

Whereas Concha's joking tone and series of apparent bids for attention belie her words, the sincerity of Connie's objections are evidenced in the rise in pitch of her voice and her persistent reiterations of them, both to Helen and to *Mamá.*

(4) Connie: (To Helen) How come you're going so early? (014)
Concha: (To Mom) Do you have to go, *Mamá?* (015)
Connie: (To Helen) Do you have to go? (016)
Helen: Huh? (016.5)
Connie: Do you have to go? (017)
Helen: Yes, (( )) (017.5) 'Cause we don't live in Pico Rivera, we live over there. (018) (Imitates Connie's distressed high-pitched tone and intonation.)
Helen: (To Connie) We stayed up real late, and we went// (021)
Connie: Probably not, not later than we did. (022)

In this example, Helen's mocking tone shows that she is aware of her sister's distress and is amused by it, but her decision stands firm. She tries to excuse herself by offering the fact of having stayed up late, but she is only countered by Connie's saying that she did, too. A brief interchange ensues, where Connie explains the circumstances of her late Christmas Eve. Thus, the objection is deflected without Helen's having to argue for it as a valid reason for leaving.

We can infer from the strength of Connie's objection that the hour is unusually early for anyone to leave the family party. In doing so, Helen is violating a situational rule regarding the appropriate hour for leaving, which, in turn, is apparently overruled by the looseness of the involvement structure for this type of family party. It is this looseness which allows her to leave when she wants. As we can see, Connie's strong objections are the price that must be paid for breaking the rule and standing by the decision to leave.

Meanwhile, Lucy has reacted in her role of hostess by offering what to her seem attractive inducements to stay.

(5) Lucy: (To Helen) You don't, you don't want to . . . you don't want to stay and listen to// (009)
OTHER INTERACTION
Lucy: (To Helen) You don't want to stay and listen to Tom Jones? I mean, to hear . . . to see Tom Jones in color? (010)
NONRELATED INTERACTION
Lucy: (To Helen) I have a Tom Jones record from Maryellen for ((Christmas)). (015)

Helen, however, ignores this, for she is busy attending to Connie's objections. That Lucy makes her offers in a conversational tone, in contrast to Connie's high-pitched insistences, could be a reason for nonattention.[11]

Helen has opened the leave-taking segment by acting on a decision to leave, presumably made jointly with her husband earlier. Immediately following the announcement of their plan, there has occurred a period of feedback wherein other guests in the situation have voiced their objections. Helen's indirect announcement of her decision to leave as a *fait accompli* shows that she does not feel that she needs to negotiate with the other guests as to whether her own family's participation in the social occasion will end or not. But since her announcement is met with much resistance, this period of feedback is crucial as a test of her determination to leave, and so serves as a period of negotiation

---

[11]Much later in the interaction, Maryellen apparently offers another inducement to stay by saying to Helen: "You're gonna miss the pie" (073). This however, delivered in a resigned tone and a broadly joking foreign accent, and Helen replies jokingly in kind, "No, thanks. I've got to go on a diet," effectively deflecting the offer as a serious reason for her stay.

among the participants in which they determine the subsequent nature of the occasion.[12]

At the end of the interchanges between Helen and her sisters, the tension created by the initial announcement is resolved, and some social business has been accomplished. It has been established as a plan of action that Helen and her entourage will leave; this has divided the social occasion into two groups, one which will be leaving and one which will be staying. That the character of the party is being altered subsequently affects the verbal interaction of the group at large.

Level 2: Leave-Taking Preparation

In another type of interchange, participants attend to the physical and social concerns occasioned by the imminent leave-taking. For the departing guests, this means notifying their own family group, gathering up belongings and storing them in the car, and so on. Helen's first utterance in the leave-taking segment. "*¿Ya nos vamos a ir,* Mom?" is the first step in carrying out the decision to leave. It can properly be classified in two levels of the interaction. Soon afterwards, she informs another family member of the decision, with: (6) "Valerie, we're going now (006)." (See example 2 for context.) It is interesting that Helen's announcement to Valerie has the same informational content as her initial utterance to her mother, yet does not have the same impact on the group because of its noninitial slot in the flow of interaction. Both utterances are propositionally the same, but the first has two perlocutionary effects whereas the second has only one.

Mamá is the first to begin gathering things together by directly soliciting help from the hostess as she asks for: (7) ... *un paquetito para poner esto* (024) (A little bag to put this in). Her request is made early on, while the decision to leave is being negotiated by Helen and her sisters. By beginning her preparations, she—as the family figurehead—indicates her acceptance of the decision, although she wields no real authority over it because of her acquiscent nature and her dependence on her daughter for a ride home.

Later, when Manuel starts to ask about his things, it is an indication that the decision to leave is irreversible. Respect for and compliance with his wishes are due to his status as a male and therefore the acknowledged head of his household. His physical preparations include finding lost objects and gathering things together. An important social duty to be performed first is to say goodbye to the host, his brother-in-law, John.

---

[12]A means of negotiation is also found in the closing sections of telephone conversations, where the two parties need to determine the subsequent nature of the speech event, i.e., whether it will terminate or not. See Sacks and Schegloff (1973:295-298) for discussion of how an adjacency pair suspends transitional relevance especially 298.

(8)   Manuel: (To general audience) I don't know where John is. (051)
        Manuel: (To unknown adressee) Huh? So I can go. (052)
        Connie: (Over the din, to Lucy) ¿Ónde// está Juan? (053) (Where is John?)

(9)   Manuel: (In response to an undistinguishable question.) Wher**ev**er you hide clothes. (053)
    Maryellen: (To Manuel) What are you looking for? (053.5)
        Manuel: (To Maryellen) My// (( )) (inaudible due to overlap) (054)
         Helen: (To Maryellen, almost simultaneously) (( )) jacket. (054)
    Maryellen: Oh—(sustained falling intonation) I understand. (055)

(10)   Manuel: (In response to an undistinguishable question) **Yes** it **is**. (To unknown addressee) Where are you hiding my son? (059)
        Connie: (To Manuel) Your family are...They're all in there. (059.4)// Val's in there with them. (060) Where **is** Val? (061)
        Manuel: (To unknown addressee) (( )) hiding my son? (060)

(11) Maryellen: (To Manuel) Your hunting jacket. (061.5) (While offering it; an announcement that it has been found.)

First, Manuel, then Helen engages the help of the group in general, establishing a period of transition from the guests' passive acceptance for the group's leave-taking to their active participation in it. Whereas previously the participants, Connie in particular, had objected strongly to their leaving, now they are allied in a cooperative effort to expedite it. They have apparently given up their objections to breaking up the party, which they had raised in their roles as guests, and are now acting as concerned family relations helping each other out. The speech community, exemplified by the long-standing relationships within the family, resumes its primacy, and the apparent break between the two groups within the speech situation is repaired.

These interchanges show that it is the force of speech acts such as Manuel's which is responded to in situations like this, rather than the presuppositions which the utterances convey. This is due to the key of the interaction, which Manuel intends as good-natured joking. He makes a statement about "clothes," with the jocular presupposition that someone has hidden them. Maryellen determines that "clothes" refers to his jacket, and soon presents it to him. Manuel demands to know where someone had "hidden" his son in an utterance with the illocutionary force of a question with a presupposed accusation which is intended humorously. Connie responds with helpful information, ignoring the accusation and responding to the real force of the utterance. He is effective in eliciting help and facilitating the progress toward his leave-taking by making his indirect pleas for help in a manner appropriate to the light-hearted spirit of the social occasion.

Helen, having been the one to initiate her family's leave-taking with a great deal of resistence from her sisters, feels free to call on them in helping her collect her things for departure. The initial tension has been fleeting, because her assertiveness in leaving is her prerogative as their eldest sister, and because this family's norm of interpretation for such disagreements is that they are minor and not disruptive of family harmony. Examples 12 and 14 show Helen soliciting help from her sisters, but members of her immediate family are better able to supply the information. Example 13 shows her daughter also finding the immediate family more helpful in leave-taking preparations.

(12)   Helen: (To unknown addressee) Oh, oh. Oh, really. (057) (To general group) Where, where is my...where are my...ah...my gifts? (054)

(13)   Annette: (To her mother, Helen) Where did you put it? (063.5)
         Helen: Ask Daddy. I told Daddy to, to keep (( )). (064)

(14)   Helen: (Probably to hostess, Lucy) Where's our box of gifts? I told you I'd take those. (068) (In a joking tone.)
         Manuel: (To Valerie) Did you put them in the car? (069)
         Helen: Huh? (069.5)
         Valerie: (To Helen) I put them in the car. (070)
         Helen: Oh. (071)[13]

This last example is important because it underscores the integrity of the immediate family group within the social unit of the extended family. This integrity is demonstrated by the personal obligations assumed by the family members as well as by the discourse obligations assumed by them. Evidently, responsibility for the gifts has been taken by another of Helen's immediate

---

[13]The interchange among the immediate family members continues with the following:

> Manuel: (To Valerie) ((You didn't tell me.)) Did you? (i.e., Did you put them in the car?) (072)
> Valerie: ((Yeah)) (072.5)
> Manuel: Oh. (073)

It is clear from the tape that Valerie has addressed her answer in example 14 to Helen and that it resolves Helen's question about the whereabouts of the gifts. The tape also registers the peripherally related and overlapping verbal interaction and extraneous background noise of the situation, so it is understandable that Manuel might not have heard Valerie's response to his question. (Although it was directed at Helen, it would have been conversationally accessible to Manuel had the room not been so noisy.) As indicated by the double parentheses parts of this last exchange between Manuel and Valerie are not clearly audible on the tape, but those clearly audible portions, along with the suprasegmentals of the partially obscured portions, invite this reconstruction.

family. The discourse shows that the topic of *gifts* is one that only the immediate family has information on, Manuel readdressing a more specific question about the gifts to a member of his and Helen's immediate family group. It is that person who answers Helen's question, doing so because of Manuel's question to her and, interestingly, providing a response which is pragmatically more appropriate to Helen's need for information.

Leave-taking preparations, as shown in examples 7–14 foreshadow the actual leave-taking of the guests in much the same way that preclosings[14] in telephone conversations foreshadow the end of the conversation. Within the context of the family party, preclosings are accomplished by the activity of leave-taking preparations and by the speech acts associated with them.

Sacks and Schegloff (p. 301) find that the main function of foreshadowing is to leave the option open for inserting new items into the conversation, which they call "mentionables," items which could not have been fitted naturally into the conversation at a previous point in the discourse. The leave-taking preparations of the departing guests signal a similar opportunity to bring up mentionables addressed to people who are leaving the party, which take the form of speech acts which were not performed previously during the social occasion.

One guest thanks her mother for bringing the sweater that she had forgotten.

(15)　　Concha: (To her mother) Thank you for finding my sweater, Mom. (026)

　　　　　Mamá: (To Concha) *O, si. Cómo no... Pos, no... Esta memoria de esta muchacha no me ayuda.* (027) (Oh, yes. Certainly. Well, it doesn't... This girl's memory doesn't help me.)

We see that Concha also takes advantage of leave-taking preparation time to attempt to elicit another verbal "stroke," this time from the departing Valerie, as to the acceptability of her Christmas gift.

(16)　　Concha: (To Valerie) Do you like your record box, Val? (034)

　　　　　Valerie: (To Concha) Sure. (034.5) (In a noncommital tone)

　　　　　Concha: Well, you better. (035)

Once again, she does not succeed in getting the stroke, perhaps because it is an obvious solicitation of praise.

---

[14]Sacks and Schegloff suggest a category of utterances as possible preclosings, things such as, "Well...," "Okay...," "So-oo...," etc. (with downward intonation contours) as the entire utterance. In a two-party conversation, a preclosing takes a speaker's turn without speaking to the topic or indicating a new one, giving a free turn to the other person, who can introduce a new topic (pp 303–305).

This exchange occurs in the middle of the leave-taking segment, but Concha calls attention to another gift very near the end, after the first "goodbye" is said. This interchange seems out of place in the discourse, seeming to create a structural flaw in the interaction. It requests an activity which might take longer to comply with than the time available. Only a few seconds after this, the adults in the group finish their leave-taking and move toward the door.

(17)   Concha: (To Annette) Show Auntie Connie the, the, show Auntie Connie the towel I got you. (097.5) (To Connie) Did you see the towel// I got her? (098)
Manuel: **Towel**? (098.5)
Connie: No, I didn't see the towel. (099)

Sacks and Schegloff point out that when new items are inserted into the closing section of a conversation, especially activities usually performed in another section of the conversation, they are usually "marked" as having been misplaced. This is accomplished linguistically by a word or phrase, or by intonation, which indicates that its user is oriented to the proper sequential organizational character of the conversation (p. 320). Although she does not mark it as such, Concha's final bid for a supportive exchange seems to be "misplaced," as it does not pertain to the imminent leave-taking of the guests, and yet occurs immediately before it. The speaker is either not aware of violating a norm of interaction in terms of the sequential progression of the leave-taking, or because of the norm of looseness in the situation founded in the close familiarity of the participants, she feels free to suspend the displacement marker that might properly accompany such a request, e.g., "I know you're leaving, but could you show...?"[15]

Near the end of the segment, Lucy, the hostess, and Maryellen, her daughter and co-hostess, both work in concert in their situational and familial roles to assure the smooth departure of their guests. As illustrated in the following example, they are oriented to the holiday that is the occasion of the family gathering as they continue the gift-giving ritual characteristic of the day.

(18)   Lucy: (To Maryellen) *María Elena.* (087). Do you have anything that's, uh, anything that's here for my mom? (088)
Maryellen: (To Manuel) Will you see Anna Marie before long? (091)

---

[15]The lack of such a marker may also be accounted for by an adult's addressing a much young niece, who is outranked in terms of age and kinship status and is therefore not normally given such linguistic deference.

Lucy's speech act is taken as a request for action, and so the slot for a response to her question is filled by the activity of looking through the pile of undistributed gifts. The question to Manuel is relevant to that activity because Maryellen finds one gift there for his granddaughter, Anna Marie, which might be given over to him for delivery. In directing the question to Manuel, Maryellen has assumed Lucy's responsibility for the proper distribution of belongings to the guests, appropriate not only to their roles in the social situation, but daughter being supportive of mother because of their interpersonal relationship.

Within this level of the interactional segment there appear to be two subclasses of speech acts: one which foreshadows the leave-taking by dealing with the concerns of the departing guests, and another which introduces mentionables, much as Sacks and Schegloff have found in the closing sections of conversations. The departing group—Helen, Manuel, *Mamá*, Valerie, and Annette—carry out the decision to leave by gathering belongings, finding people, and looking for things with the help of their relatives. Other participants orient to the foreshadowing by taking advantage of the period to introduce mentionables reflective of the season, e.g., soliciting praise for gifts, as well as the family setting, e.g., thanks for a sweater that was forgotten on a previous visit.

Level 3: Final Joking Interchanges

In this level of the interactional segment, the tone becomes very lighthearted as allusions are made to "next time." These interchanges are final opportunities to engage in the type of interaction that characterizes this type of gathering—good-natured joking and teasing.

(19)   Helen: (To Maryellen and Concha) Aren't you, aren't you invited to Billy's and Christie's young adults? (043) (( )) young adults? (044)

Maryellen: They didn't tell **us** about it. I don't think we're invited. (045)

Helen: You, you were taking about . . . about how// (045.5)

Concha: No, just didn't make it. (046)

Helen: . . . about how you guys (( )) young adults. (048)

This topic then leads to much joking about the appropriateness of the term, *young adult,* for one of the participants.

Another exchange, clearly initiated in a jocular tone, turns attention to the certainty of another family party such as the one that is ending. That this type of gathering is customary for this family group is reflected in the presupposition in example 20.

(20)   Manuel: (To general audience) All right. Where's the next party
                gonna be? (077)
        Concha: Down at your house. (078)
        Manuel: **Again?** (078.5)
                LAUGHTER (079)
        Helen: See what you get? (079)

This exchange opens the floor to much joking about the would-be party. One guest says, "Expect us." Another interjects, "Well, we don't smoke or drink," and the interaction continues in a similar vein for a short period.

The topics introduced in these examples, which refer to future parties, seem to have very little to do with leave-taking at first glance. If they are new topics in the interaction, they may be related to what Sacks and Schegloff report for conversations, "... topics may be improvised for insertion into a closing sequence to extend the time available for such pre-leave-taking preparations, as when visitors gather their belongings before departure (p. 323)." In our data, Helen seems to be using the time afforded by the rest of her group's leave-taking preparations to introduce the topic of another party, although she does not do so in order to lengthen the time for them. But it is not properly a new topic, since she relates it to a previous conversation when she says, "You, you were talking about..." This could be related to what Sacks and Schegloff call *topic shading,* ... the fitting of differently focused but related talk to some last utterance in a topic's development (p. 305)

By relating this topic to one discussed before the initiation of leave-taking, Helen recalls the previous nature of the party, creating an overlap between two ideally sequential stages of the social gathering. Example 19 seems to perform the function of shading one level of interaction, i.e., "party conversation," into another, i.e., leave-taking, much as topic shading provides a transition between topics in a conversation.

Leave-taking preparations having been completed, Manuel introduces the final topic for group interaction by saying, "All right. Where's the next party gonna be?" Thus, he reaffirms the unity of the whole family group by looking forward to the next family gathering, although it is his group's early departure that has perhaps precipitated the end of the present gathering. The general joking conversation which follows is the last focused interaction in which the whole group takes part.

Manuel's introduction of the "next party" as a final topic serves as a "signature," calling to mind the type of social occasion that is ending. Sacks and Schegloff use the term, *signature,* to refer to one possible component part of the closing section of a conversation which displays a recognition of the type of conversation that is terminating. Goffman's description of what a "goodbye" does also seems to describe the function of the next party topic in example 20: "... the goodbye brings the encounter for the relationship, and bolsters the relationship for the anticipated period of no contact" (1972:79).

Its sequential placement shortly before the goodbye ritual makes it perhaps interactionally more a part of the final leave-taking than merely a final opportunity for socializing within the interactional frame.

Level 4: Final Leave-Taking

The final leave-taking is accomplished by a final terminal exchange, i.e., a goodbye ritual which serves to cut off new topics of interaction with the departing guests. During the joking about the next party, Helen offers her first "goodbye" to the hostess, saying simply, "Bye, Lucy." Although this is ignored at the time, possibly due to general participation in the joking, it is significant that it is Helen, the initiator of the leave-taking, who is the one to attempt the first terminal exchange. Her singleness of purpose leads her to disregard her husband's need to find the host to say goodbye to, a situational obligation which must be accomplished before they can leave in a socially appropriate manner.

In Manuel's initial attmept to locate John, Connie came to his aid, asking the hostess where he was. The next time Manuel asks about John, it is done quickly and quizzically, and Connie once again offers help. Helen's final leave-taking prompts Manuel to raise the volume of his voice and to express exasperation in his intonation upon making his final direct request to learn John's whereabouts:

(21)   Manuel: (To general audience) Where's John? (100)
         Connie: ((I saw him)) Outside a while ago.
                 SEVERAL SECONDS ELAPSE.
          Helen: Well, we're gonna go, Lucy. Thanks for ev//erything.
                 (102)
         Manuel: **Where is John?** (102)

Obviously he, unlike his wife, feels that he cannot properly leave the family gathering unless he takes leave of the host as well as the hostess.[16]

Unfortunately, we never do find out where John is or whether Manuel finds him before he goes, because Manuel's exasperated voice is the last one we hear on the tape before it ends. Nevertheless, the social interaction can be seen to have come to a logical end with the proffering of a final leave-taking ritual from Helen. Manuel has shown proper and serious concern for his social

---

[16]This obligation may be more strongly felt by Manuel than his wife because traditionally the men interact more with each other than with the women at these occasions. That the men's membership in the family is due to marriage rather than blood and upbringing contributes to their self-exclusion from the activity of sisterly gossip during the gathering.

obligations by expressing his frustration at not finding the host to take leave of; thus, he can be said to have completed his obligation in spirit.

The terminal exchange properly signals the end of the departing guests' involvement in the social event, and the end of the leave-taking segment. In these data, however, the terminal exchange is not accomplished by an adjacency pair as it is strictly defined. Rather, what we see here is a terminal exchange ritual which is recycled by one departing guest to ensure the attention of the hostess. The host's physical absence from the scene would necessitate a goodbye to be conveyed by proxy; yet, such a leave-taking cannot be as satisfactory as a face-to-face ritual which would bolster the relationship for the time during which they will not see each other. All other guests present may informally take leave of the departing guests after the host and/or hostess do. Unlike the terminal exchange in a two-party conversation, which ends the speech event, the final leave-taking of some of the guests does not necessarily end the social occasion if there are other groups of guests still present.

2.2 SUMMARY OF ANALYSIS

In the analysis of the data, we have considered Helen's utterance, "¿*Ya Nos vamos a ir,* Mom? (We're going now, Mom. Okay?), to have initiated the interactional segment of leave-taking. We have seen that the structure of this interaction is representable in four levels, ideally sequential, but in fact overlapping.

Level 1: Initiation of leave-taking
Level 2: Leave-taking preparations
Level 3: Final joking interaction
Level 4: Final leave-taking

Throughout the five-minute segment during which leave-taking activity is the prime focus of attention, no one conversation has been sustained. Here, however, we have shown that many interchanges involving different participants achieve an overall coherence in light of their focus on the leave-taking activity. This coherence allows for our interpretation of this interaction as a discourse.

3.0 ETHNICITY

This has been a microstudy of a segment of human social interaction situated in a Mexican-American home which is reflective of the social and linguistic behaviors of one Mexican-American family in the greater Los Angeles area.

In some respects, the interaction examined here is reflective of human interaction in general; in some others, it is reflective of a broader American culture context; in yet others it is uniquely Mexican-American. Here we discuss how Mexican ethnicity in some of the components of this interactional segment contributes to the nature of this particular interaction, and at the end of the discussion, we present suggested areas of future research.

The Mexican ethnicity of the group becomes evident in the themes which underlie the discourse and in the situational characteristics of the scene. The closeness and importance of the family is a cultural theme of many ethnic groups, and in this situation underlies much of the interaction: for example, *Mamá's* leaving changes the status of the party; the family helps the departing guests to find their things, the next family party is mentioned, and so on. The male as the more important of the sexes is another theme which is manifested, as it is the only male in the interaction who provides authority for the decision to leave and rallies everyone to his aid.

One of the cultural characteristics of the interaction is the great commotion in the background, obscuring the discourse at several points. This is not a quiet leave-taking—everyone is conversationally accessible to everyone else, there is much overlapping in interchanges, and voices often rise in pitch and volume, all of which indicate that noise, verbal overlapping, simultaneous interchanges, and free emotional expression are interactional norms for family social events in Hispanic communities.

The use of Spanish and English, with evidence of certain nonstandard features in each, mark the interaction as Mexican-American. For example, Connie switches from English to Spanish in: Really? *¿De Veras? ¿Se Van?,* and when she asks about the host, she says, *¿Ónde está Juan?* using the nonstandard, *ónde* (where), but more significantly, asking in Spanish rather than English. Although the group is English-dominant, save for *Mamá*, there is some phonological interference in some of the English in the data, e.g., Connie: "Do you have to go?" [du you hef to gow?]. There is also an occasional lexical inappropriateness, e.g., Concha: "Just when I was losing my depression." ("Getting over" might have been more appropriate.) There is even a pragmatically odd-sounding offer, e.g., Lucy: "You don't want to stay and listen to Tom Jones?" Another phenomenon is the changeover within the family from Spanish names to English names. Thus, *Elena* is Helen, *Consuelo* is Connie, and so on. Even *Manuel* is called /Mǽnyel/ instead of /Manwél/. Spanish names are used to evoke the intimacy of family ties, as illustrated when Lucy (*Luz*) directly addresses her daughter as "*Mari Elena*" in example 18, whereas in example 5 she had been referred to as *Maryellen*.

Unfortunately, the scope of this paper permits only brief mention of the ethnicity of the interaction; these are only a few of the themes and characteristics which are manifested in it. We hope to have shown that this group's membership in a Mexican-American Speech community is very much a part of the character of the discourse.

It would be fruitful for future research in this area to investigate in greater depth the ethnic aspects of conversational interaction. The particular interaction investigated here was representative of an English-dominant, second-generation, acculturating working-class group, in the context of a social situation which is common to both the Mexican-American and American mainstream cultures. If the data had been collected at a party in Mexico, there undoubtedly would have been differences in the character of the components of the interaction aside from the use of Spanish as the primary language. In Mexico, different social norms would have been operative, altering the nature of the speech situation and the rules for the communicative interaction. It would be speculative to suggest here exactly how they would be different; this type of comparative study with a Mexican family of the same class in Mexico would be one avenue for further research. Or, future research could focus on other Hispanic speech communities in the United States, changing, for example, the variables of locality, length of time of the group in the United States, language dominance of the participants, social class of the family, degree of contact with a non-Spanish-speaking greater community, in an effort to characterize what is common in communicative interaction across groups of Mexicans and other Hispanics, and what is particular to specific Hispanic speech communities in different locales. This type of work, the investigation of ethnicity in the context of social, communicative interaction, can contribute to providing empirical evidence for questions of Hispanic identity, culture, and ethnicity, important to the characterization of the group as a distinct, cultural entity in the United States.

4.0 CONCLUSION

In this paper we have used data from the leave-taking activity of one group of guests at a Mexican-American family gathering to analyze the structure of the discourse and its social functions. We have looked at the data in terms of the ethnography of communication, utilizing the term, *interactional segment,* not included as one of Hymes' levels of speech, to designate an activity analyzable in the social frame of "leave-taking." We have analyzed the interaction which makes up the discourse, and have shown that it is comprised of four levels, which constitute the structure of the interactional segment. We have also compared some aspects of the leave-taking sequence with the characteristics of the closing sections of conversations, and have found some similarities, such as a period for introducing mentionables, the occurrence of structurally "misplaced" material, interactional shading related to conversational topic shading, and a verbal signature which recalls the type of event that is ending. Finally, we have indicated how the cultural heritage of the Mexican-American interactants provides, in part, for the character of the discourse.

Future studies would profit from investigating how social interaction organizes discourse and from considering the interaction from the perspective of group ethnicity.

REFERENCES

Goffman, E. *Behavior in public places.* New York: Free Press 1966 (Originally published, 1963).

Goffman, E. *Relations in public.* New York: Harper Colophon Books, 1972.

Hymes, D. Models of the interaction of language and social life. In J. Gumperz & D. Hymes, (Eds.), *Directions in sociolinguistics.* New York: Holt, Rinehart & Winston, 1972.

Merritt, M. *Resources for saying.* Unpublished doctoral dissertation, University of Pennsylvania, 1976.

Reisman, D., Potter, R. J., & Watson, J. The vanishing host, *Human Organization* (Sp. 1960), *19,* 17–27.

Schegloff, E. A., & Sacks, H. Opening up closings, *Semiotica* 1973, *8,* 289–327.

13 Language Attitudes and the Speech of Spanish-English Bilingual Pupils

Arnulfo G. Ramírez
State University of New York at Albany

With the advent of bilingual education in this country, investigations of various problems facing Mexican-American and other linguistic minority children in the classroom have been undertaken. Foremost in the study of the language of the Mexican-American child are the following: his/her linguistic performance in Spanish or English; the standard and nonstandard linguistic features present; language variability, including codeswitching; language attitudes and their impact on the child's self-concept and cross-ethnic relationships; and teacher and student language attitudes and their relationship to achievement among bilingual students. This study will attempt to examine

1. The meaning of language attitudes and the language of the classroom
2. Teacher attitudes toward speech variation
3. Bilingual pupils' attitudes toward speech variation—elementary and secondary school setting
4. Language attitudes—implications for the teacher and the learner
5. Attempts at changing teachers' attitudes about language variation.

LANGUAGE ATTITUDES AND CLASSROOM LANGUAGE

Although traditionally the study of attitudes has fallen into the realm of social psychology, attitudes toward language have recently become a topic of sociolinguistic studies. Sociolinguists have adopted the term *language attitudes* (Fishman, 1975), which can be defined as evaluative reactions or feelings toward language use. Thus, each of the following could be subsumed under language attitudes, broadly defined as feelings toward a language (e.g., "French is more pleasant to the ear than the harsh sounds of German"); reactions toward the use of a specific variety of a language under certain circumstances (e.g., emotional responses to hearing someone with a strong Southern accent present the national news on nationwide television); and attitudes toward a language as a specific group connotation ("Russian is spoken by Communists"). In the classroom, language is used to convey information and, at the same time, maintain and confirm the social identity and relationship of the participants who are speaking or writing to one another (Barnes, 1973). In most situations, the language variety used for instruction is the formal standard variety. Holmes (1978:135) points out that the

> ...use of a relatively formal code in educational institutions seems to characterize a wide range of speech communities, whether monolingual, bilingual or multilingual... There is no convincing evidence to suggest that such instruction cannot be adequately carried out in a nonstandard dialect, a minority group language, or even in a less formal style of a language. The use of formal varieties in the school can be seen then as a reflection of social features of the situation, monolinguistic constraints which in turn reflect the values and beliefs of the soceity concerning education and the ways in which it is appropriately transmitted.

TEACHER ATTITUDES TOWARD SPEECH VARIATION

In an extensive survey of research on teacher/student interactional patterns and student performance, Brophy and Good (1974) found that individual student differences (e.g., personality, physical attractiveness, and speech characteristics) led teachers to form different attitudes and expectations, which, in turn, resulted in differential treatment of students within the same classroom. In terms of speech characteristics, they noted that students who did not speak standard English were likely to engender negative attitudes and low expectations among teachers.

Although teachers may frequently be unaware of their expectations and attitudes regarding students, Brophy and Good reported that their perceptions about pupil performance and behavior might depend on only a few days of contact in the classroom. Within the first week of school, students were usually assigned to reading or study groups by teachers who were basing their decision on very little information.

Seligman et al. (1972) demonstrated experimentally that speech style or dialect, among other pupil characteristics, had a strong impact on teacher expectations and attitudes. Student teachers attending a teachers' college in Montreal were asked to evaluate eight hypothetical third-grade boys basing their judgments on the stimulus material presented (photograph, taperecorded voice, drawing, and composition). The subjects were also asked to make an overall evaluation of each of the students based on a list of six characteristics (e.g., intelligent, self-confident), using 7-point rating scales.

The results of the study showed that speech style was a significant factor in teachers' evaluations of students. Students with good voices were evaluated more favorably than students with poor voices. These differential judgments were in terms of such characteristics as intelligence, well-behaved student, privileged, enthusiastic, self-confident, and gentle. Based on the photographs, students who looked intelligent were judged as more self-confident. Those students who had written a good composition and had made a good drawing were also considered more self-confident. A "good" or "poor" photograph did not have a significant effect on teachers' evaluations of students' self-confidence if these photographs were presented with a good drawing as well as a good composition. Also, the type of photograph did not affect teachers' judgments when presented together with a good voice. If a child had a good composition, an attractive and alert face, but a lower-class speech style, he would be regarded as limited in intelligence and academic ability. Thus teachers' judgments about students' academic abilities were made on the *basis of speech* and *physical appearance* rather than on objective, pertinent information (e.g., artistic drawing or written composition).

Williams and his associates (1976) conducted a series of studies in which Anglo, Black, and Mexican-American teachers from elementary schools in the central Texas area were asked to evaluate the language (e.g., ethnicity—nonstandard) and personality (e.g., confidence—passive eagerness) of Anglo, Black and Mexican-American children. They used a matched-guise technique in which videotapes of the children were paired with audiotapes in various combinations so that both visual and vocal features were controlled. Their findings, for the most part, showed a correlation between the characteristics of the speakers and those of the teachers. In the first place, teachers gave different evaluations to Anglo, Black, and Mexican-American children; Anglos received higher ratings (e.g., more confident, less ethnic-sounding) than the rest and Mexican-Americans received lower ratings than the other two groups. Secondly, they found teachers' ethnicity to be related to their judgments in two interesting ways. On the attitude scales related to language (ethnicity and standardness), teachers of all backgrounds evaluated Black and Mexican-American students more negatively than Anglo students, but Black teachers were more positive than white teachers in their evaluations of both Black and Mexican-American children. Mexican-American teachers rated Mexican-American children as having better capabilities than Anglo counterparts on unrelated language arts assignments (music, arts, physical education); Anglo teachers rated Anglo children more favorably. Ratings also varied according to the social class of the speakers. For example, among middle-class youngsters of all three ethnic backgrounds, Mexican-Americans were judged to be least confident and eager. The ethnicity-standardness ratings for the low- and middle-class groups were lower for both Mexican-Americans and Blacks than for Anglos of either class.

Williams's findings indicate that teacher attitudes toward pupils' patterns of speech can be broken down into two clusters that form judgmental dimensions. One cluster (made up of such adjective pairs as standard American–marked ethnic style, whitelike–nonwhitelike, low social status–high social status, and disadvantaged–advantaged) was grouped by Williams under the heading, "ethnicity and nonstandardness." The other cluster (made up of such adjective pairs as unsure-confident, active-passive, reticent-eager, hesitant-enthusiastic, and like talking–dislike talking) was interpreted by Williams as indicating an overall evaluation of a child's confidence-eagerness. Probably the latter factor is associated with the prophecy of failure which establishes in the teacher's mind this causal link: nonstandard speech + lack of eagerness ⇒ low achievement.

Frender and Lambert (1973:246) have concluded that "speech characteristics can influence the evaluations that a listener makes about a speaker," and particularly, "speech characteristics of lower-class speakers prompt relatively unfavorable perceptions of their overall competence." Rist's (1970) detailed observation of a kindergarten class provides evidence that teachers' expectations about the academic potential of a student are determined primarily by a series of subjectively interpreted attributes and characteristics. The successful attributes include ease of interaction with adults, a high degree of verbalization in Standard American English, ability to become a leader, and ability to participate effectively as a member of a group.

Ramírez et al. (1978) studied the relationship of language attitudes and the achievement of bilingual pupils in grades 4 and 5 in San Jose, California. The matched-guise technique was used to assess teacher attitudes toward four different speech varieties: Guise I—standard English; Guise II-standard English with phonological and morphological deviations; Guise III—standard English with phonological, morphological, and syntactical deviations; Guise IV—English/Spanish codeswitching. (See Appendix.) The teachers were asked to listen to each speech sample (4 speakers × 4 guises = 16 total number of passages) and react to its (1) *appropriateness for school*, (2) its *correctness*, (3) the speaker's *likelihood of achievement in school*. The score for each of the scales had a potential range of 4 (a score 1-4 for each speaker) to 16. The higher the score, the more favorable the teacher's attitude.

On the dimension of *correctness* (degree of conformity to the speech variety generally accepted by teachers in a school environment) all teachers ($N = 18$) gave standard English (Guise I) the highest rating over the other three guises.

The teachers (Group II, $N = 9$) who were participating in a Title I project rated speakers of Guise IV (Spanish/English codeswitching) higher on the *likelihood of achievement* scale than speakers of Guise III (ungrammatical English). The other group of teachers (Group I, $N = 9$) that attended two workshop sessions, designed to stress sociolinguistic concepts (e.g., linguistic and communicative competence, codeswitching, bilingualism), tended to rate speakers of Guise IV as less likely to achieve than speakers of Guise III.

The study indicated that teachers' attitudes regarding the "likelihood of successs" of codeswitching bilingual pupils were directly related to pupils' grades as well as to their relative reading gains as shown by an objective test. To investigate this relationship, three different scores on the *likelihood-of-achievement* attitude dimension were computed for each teacher: the evaluation of Guise I minus, respectively, the evaluations of Guises II, III, and IV. The rationale behind this procedure is that the magnitude of the difference score can be assumed to be proportional to the teacher's negative attitude toward Guise II, III, or IV relative to standard English.

Each of the three teacher difference scores was then correlated with these three measures of pupil achievement: relative reading gain score for the class, mean pupil grades in reading, and mean pupil grades in English. The resulting correlations were largely negative: "Guise I minus Guise IV, Grade in English," was large (-.50) and statistically significant. This single result gives a rather clear indication that teachers' negative attitudes toward codeswitching (and correspondingly strong positive attitudes toward standard English) generate low assessments of their pupils' language abilities and performance and lead to low grades in English. Table 1 presents relationships between these scores, i.e., between teacher attitude and pupil achievement.

TABLE 1

Correlations between Mean Teacher Difference Scores on Likelihood of Achievement and Three Class Achievement Measures

Source of Teacher Difference Scores	Correlations with		
	Relative Gain Score in Reading (N = 17 teachers)	Grade in Reading (N = 18 teachers)	Grade in English (N = 18 teachers)
I–II	.01	–.16	–.33
I–III	.08	.03	–.05
I–IV	–.24	–.21	–.50*

*$p < .05$.

NOTE: Guise I: Standard English
Guise II: Standard English with phonological and morphological deviations.
Guise III: Standard English with phonological, morphological, and syntactical deviations.
Guise IV: English/Spanish codeswitching.

BILINGUAL PUPILS' ATTITUDES TOWARD
SPEECH VARIATIONS—STUDIES IN
ELEMENTARY SCHOOL SETTINGS

A study by Politzer and Ramírez (1973) of Mexican-American (N = 17) and Anglo children (N = 10) in the third grade attempted to determine whether children who had taken part in a Spanish/English bilingual program had different attitudes toward four speech varieties than children who had been exposed solely to a monolingual (English) program. The four varieties included three guises spoken by four speakers (Guise I-English with Spanish proper names pronounced in Spanish, Guise II-English with Anglicized Spanish proper names; Guise III-colloquial Southwest Spanish) and a single guise of four different speakers (Guise IV) who spoke English with a marked Spanish accent. The children were asked to react to the recorded voices on semantic differential scales (1–4 points) which included eight characteristics (e.g., nice, handsome, happy, smart). A score for each guise was computed by adding the reactions to the eight characteristics for each of the four speakers (a score of 4–16 for each adjective) which had a potential range of 32–128.

Anglo children in both bilingual and monolingual programs in Redwood City, California, gave higher ratings to the first two guises; Mexican-American children in bilingual programs gave Guise III the highest ratings. Guise IV was given the lowest rating by most children included in the study.

In another study conducted in San Jose, California, by Ramírez et al. (1978), students in grades 4 and 5 evaluated five guises in terms of appropriateness for school, correctness, and likelihood of achievement in school by the speakers. The guises included Guise I—Standard English, Guise II—standard English with phonological and morphological deviations, Guise III—standard English with phonological, morphological, and syntactical deviations; Guise IV—English/Spanish codeswitching: Guise IV—Standard Spanish. (See Appendix.) On the *dimension of correctness,* the students rated Guise III (English with Spanish influence in phonology, morphology, and syntax) as the least favorable. Pupils' evaluative judgments with regard to *appropriateness* and *likelihood-of-achievement* were similar. In both cases, the guises with hispanized English were given the lowest ratings. Even though the students do not downgrade codeswitching to the same degree that they do accented English, they share the teachers' attitudes that codeswitchers are "less likely to achieve" in school than Standard English speakers. On the *appropriateness* dimension, standard Spanish speakers are judged differently from Standard English speakers. This evaluation by the students reflects their perceptions of Spanish speakers as potential "achievers" in bilingual schools, but this could not be confirmed because all the pupils were attending a monolingual (English) school.

To examine the relation of pupil language attitudes to pupil achievement, four pupil difference scores (Guise I minus, respectively, the evaluations of

Guises II, III, IV, and VII) on the *likelihood-of-achievement* attitude scale were correlated with seven measures of actual pupil achievement (see Table 2). The difference scores comparing Guise I (standard English) and Guises II, III, and IV (all "nonstandard" varieties) all have a significant positive relation to the pupils' performance on the *Multiple-Choice Test in English Grammar.* This relationship is not surprising, since to some extent the evaluation of the nonstandard guises and the multiple-choice test involve similar tasks: i.e., the recognition of standard as opposed to nonstandard English speech. The positive correlation between the grade in reading and the pupil difference score (Guise I–Guise III) can be explained in much the same way: both the reading grade and the evaluation of different guises are likely to involve an ability to distinguish between standard and nonstandard speech varieties. Somewhat surprisingly, all the achievement measures are positively related to the degree to which pupils downgrade codeswitching in comparison with Standard English (Guise I–IV), though only two correlations are significant. These findings suggest that pupils' grades and actual reading achievement may have some relation to the congruence of pupils' attitudes with teachers' attitudes.

BILINGUAL PUPILS' ATTITUDES TOWARD SPEECH VARIATION IN SECONDARY SCHOOL SETTINGS

A study by Politzer and Ramirez (1975) of Mexican-American and Anglo pupils in grades 3, 6, 9, and 12 in Redwood City and San Jose, California, investigated student attitudes toward four speech varieties: Guise I—English with Spanish proper names pronounced in Spanish; Guise II—English with Anglicized Spanish proper names; Guise III—colloquial Southwest Spanish; and Guise IV—hispanized English. Students were asked to react to the recorded voices (4 guises × 4 speakers = 16 passages) on semantic differential scales ranging from 1 to 4 points on eight characteristics (e.g., nice, handsome, clean, smart). A score for each guise was computed by adding the reactions to the eight characteristics for each of the four speakers (a possible score of 4–16 for each adjective) which had a potential range of 32–128. Accented (hispanized) English—Guise IV—was downgraded by all subjects in comparison to other varieties. There was comparatively little upgrading of Guises I, II, or III in relation to Guise IV by the Mexican-American pupils. The heaviest upgrading occurred among the third- and especially the sixth-grade Anglos, who upgraded English guises over Spanish. Ninth- and twelfth-grade Anglos, however, did not follow the same pattern.

Analysis of the subjects' judgments concerning the same speech variety indicates that the main difference was in their reaction to Spanish (Guise III), which was perceived more favorably by Mexican-Americans, females, and students in the upper grades. The absence of any pronounced upgrading of

TABLE 2

Correlations of Pupil Difference Scores on the Likelihood-of-Achievement Dimension with Pupil Achievement Measures

Source of Pupil Difference Scores	Relative Gains in Reading (N = 35)	Grade in Reading (N = 73)	Grade in English (N = 73)	Spanish Multiple Choice* (N = 67)	English Multiple Choice* (N = 68)	Spanish Production* (N = 17)	English Production* (N = 23)
I-II	.13	-.05	.09	.03	.24†	.33	-.04
I-III	.20	.26‡	.14	.04	.25†	.23	.09
I-IV	.38‡	.12	.17	.13	.22†	.02	.17
I-VII	.05	-.04	-.16	-.11	-.12	.00	.11

*These four measures of achievement in grammar are subtests of the *Stanford Dominance Test*.

†$p < .05$

‡$p < .01$

NOTE: Guise   I: Standard English
Guise II: Standard English with phonological and morphological deviations.
Guise III: Standard English with phonological, morphological, and syntactical deviations.
Guise IV: English/Spanish code switching.
Guise VII: Standard Spanish.

English over Spanish by Anglos in the ninth and twelfth grades, as well as the generally more favorable reaction to Spanish among these students, may have the following explanation. The ninth and twelfth graders came from different school environments than the third and sixth graders, especially since Mexican-Americans actually constituted the majority of the enrollment at the school attended by the ninth and twelfth graders. The more positive evaluation of Spanish in the upper grades, especially among Mexican-Americans, may also reflect these subjects' conscious assertion of their heritage.

Mora's (1975) study of Santa Cruz high school students revealed that recent Mexican immigrants had a more negative attitude toward the use of *pochismos* than those students who had resided in the United States for a longer period. Attitudes toward the use of *pochismos* (hispanized English words: dime ⇒ daime, lunch ⇒ lonch, to watch ⇒ wachar) were elicited in relation to context (appropriate setting for the use of the word—classroom, home, neighborhood) and participants (persons with whom the use of term would be appropriate-children, teenagers, parents, teachers). In terms of codeswitching (use of both Spanish and English in the same sentence), she noted three basic attitudes: (1) a negative attitude among students who were familiar with the phenomenon but would never use it; (2) a benevolent attitude among those students whose friends used it but who would not use it themselves; (3) a favorable attitude among those who used the strategy as part of their normal speech patterns.

Ryan and Carranza (1975) asked Anglo, Black, and Mexican-American female high school students in Chicago to rate the personality of male speakers of standard English and hispanized English in two contexts (home and school) with two sets of rating scales (status-stressing and solidarity-stressing). Standard English speakers were assigned more positive ratings on all the scales used in both contexts; differences were significantly greater in the school context than in the home domain and on status-stressing scales than on solidarity-stressing dimensions. Anglo pupils rated speakers of accented (hispanized) English significantly lower on status scales than did either Mexican-American or Black students.

LANGUAGE ATTITUDES—SOME IMPLICATIONS FOR THE TEACHER AND LEARNER

The role that language attitudes play in the schooling of Spanish-English bilinguals is often differentiated by the type of instructional program. Some students, because of limited English proficiency, attend bilingual schools in which Spanish is used to establish initial literacy and as the primary medium of instruction to teach such subjects as math and social studies. Other students attend monolingual schools where standard English is used as the medium of instruction and speech varieties such as codeswitching are covertly or overtly rejected by the teachers.

The Spanish and English that the bilingual child brings to school may not be the standard language used by textbooks or by the teacher. A child acquires the particular variety of a language s/he learns at home. The variety of Spanish spoken at home, marked regionally and socially, is the one the child will learn. If the family also speaks English at home and the variety of English is strongly influenced by Spanish pronunciation or grammar, the child acquires that particular variety.

Codeswitching is a common phenomenon among Spanish/English bilingual pupils. It has a significant influence on teachers' expectations and therefore on the child's learning environment. The teacher in a culturally diverse classroom should understand that codeswitching is not a random mixing of English and Spanish words.

In terms of the role of language attitudes in monolingual school settings, a relationship has been found to exist between the positive attitudes of bilingual pupils toward Standard English and their achievement in language learning (Ramírez et al., 1978). Bilingual students who rank the achievement potential of standard English speakers higher than that of speakers of nonstandard varieties, including codeswitching, appear to have greater gains in English language arts and reading. Furthermore, the relative gain made in reading by one group of Mexican-American students appeared to have been influenced by the teachers' attitudes toward the codeswitching speech variety (i.e., the intermixing of two languages in a controlled manner) of the students: the more negative the teachers' attitudes toward the pupils' speech variety, the lower the relative gains of the pupils in reading.

In the case of learning a second language, Richard (1978) notes that individual variables such as age, attitudes, and learning styles account for differences in levels of achievement. From the learner's point of view, the individual acquiring a second language may have to adopt various aspects of behavior that characterize values of the second linguistic group, and the learner's ethnocentric tendencies and attitudes toward this second group will consequently influence success in learning the language (Lambert et al., 1966). This could cause the Spanish-speaking child to adopt a negative attitude toward Spanish and the persons who speak it.

In the process of learning English, the child could say "choe" for "shoe" and "I not have it" for "I don't have it." If the teacher is unaware of the nature of interference (Spanish) in acquiring English as a second language or the creative role that "errors" play in language learning (Richards, 1978; Gingras, 1978), s/he may create a barrier to learning.

In terms of achievement in Spanish language arts within a bilingual program, Shultz (1975) speculates in his study that the variety of Spanish used by the teacher may indeed affect the pupils' performance. Shultz notes:

The teachers when they used Spanish in the classroom used a more "standard" variety than the one the children were used to. The variety of Spanish spoken in the classroom was not the variety of Spanish the children used at home. This is another reason why the children may not have spoken very much Spanish: they may have been made to feel that somehow the variety of Spanish they spoke was "inferior," and that therefore they shouldn't speak it (p. 17).

He also noted that the language used by the teachers conveyed the attitude that English was the "natural" language to use in the classroom whereas Spanish was always used in a "marked" way:

Arithmetic, science and English language arts were all taught in English, and the only subject which was actually taught in Spanish was Spanish language arts. However, even during the Spanish language arts lesson... the teachers would frequently revert to English to give directions or to reprimand someone... The "hidden agenda" of this classroom, then, was that it was disadvantageous to use Spanish (p. 18).

The nature of teachers' attitudes toward the speech of bilingual pupils could also be explored through an examination of the dynamics of classroom discourse. Within the framework of the exchange (Sinclair & Coulthard, 1975), which consists of (1) the teacher asking a question, (2) a pupil responding, (3) the teacher providing evaluative feedback, one could study the type of language that is demanded by teachers in different content areas (e.g., Spanish language arts/social studies). By analyzing the teacher's reaction (evaluation/feedback) to a pupils' response, one could investigate the relation of language attitudes to knowledge of the subject (Barnes, 1969; Stubbs, 1976): what counts as knowledge—"good" grammar or the correct content? The following examples illustrate the behavior of two teachers engaged in Spanish reading instruction (Ramírez, 1978):

Example 1

Student 1: ...*interrumpio la garza.* (...the heron interrupted.)
Teacher: *¿Qué quiere decir eso? Antonia.* (What does that mean? Antonia.)
Student 2: *es como si, si una maestra está hablando y luego una nina le está hablando—le está interrumpiendo.* (It's as if, if a teacher is talking and later a girl is talking to her—she [the girl] is interrupting her.)
Teacher: *Ajá.* (Uh ha.)
Student 3: *¡No! Está metiendo la cuchara.* (No! She "is putting in the spoon" [butting in].)

Teacher: *esta metiendo la churara—otro modo si—La cuchara quiere decir más o menos*... (She is putting in the spoon" [butting in]—another way yes—the spoon means that more or less.)

Student 3: *¿Qué está interrumpiendo?* (What is she interrupting?)

Example 2

Teacher: *¿Qué, qué quiere ese (sic) garza? Quiere tender las plumas de todos los colores... vamos a ver...* (What, what, what does that heron want? She wants to have her feathers in every color... let's see...)

Student 1: *No quiere ser garza.* (She doesn't want to be a heron.)

Teacher: *No quiere ser garza, ese garza... Alejandro no vamos (sic) a seguir—aqui... asi...* (She doesn't want to be a heron, that heron... Alexander we are not going to continue—here... that way.)

Student 1: *Asi, se di... cia... (That's the way you would say it...)*

Student 2: *Decía* (Used to say it.)

Student 1: *Decia.* (Used to say it.)

Teacher: *Decía, si...* (Used to say it, *yes.*)

The teacher in Example 1 is primarily concerned with meaning. Student 2 interprets the meaning of *interrumpio la garza* (the heron interrupted) as *como si una maestra esta hablando y luego una niña le esta... interrumpiendo* (if a teacher is talking and later a girl is interrupting her). The teacher acknowledges this interpretation *aja* (uh ha) and also allows Student 3 to explain the meaning metaphorically *esta metiendo la cuchara* (butting in) using colloquial Spanish. The teacher in Example 2, on the other hand, appears to be more concerned with standard pronunciation—*decía* (used to say it) instead of nonstandard *dicia*—rather than the answer to the question *¿Que queria la garza?* It is interesting to note that although the teacher twice produced ungrammatical Spanish *ese garza* (that heron), he would agree with Student 2 not to allow Student 1 to pronounce the word *decia* according to his own dialect *dicia*.

CHANGING TEACHERS' LANGUAGE ATTITUDES

Within a monolingual (English) instructional setting, teachers and bilingual pupils appear to have well-defined and largely similar attitudes toward specific speech varieties found in a Spanish/English bilingual environment. Ramírez et al. (1978) found that teachers and bilingual pupils in grades 4 and 5 rated Standard English higher than nonstandard speech varieties on correctness, appropriateness for the classroom, and likelihood-of-achievement in school by the speaker. Teachers and pupils also agreed in rating Standard English significantly higher than codeswitching.

Workshops (2 sessions, each lasting two and a half hours) conducted for one group of teachers did not result in changes in language attitudes in the desired direction. After the workshops, the teachers tended to rate codeswitching lower than even ungrammatical English in terms of likelihood-of-achievement in school by the speaker. Although the workshop presentation stressed, among other sociolinguistic facts the naturalness of codeswitching as a legitimate and expressive form of communication among bilinguals, postworkshop attitude measures indicated a further deterioration of teacher attitudes toward codeswitching, compared to other hispanized and ungrammatical English. The results suggest that relatively short in-service workshops may be an unsuitable vehicle for bringing about predictable attitudinal changes on the part of teachers. Tuckman et al. (1969) found that information about classroom conduct by itself was not as effective in changing teacher behavior as when it was accompanied by details about the teachers' specific behaviors in their own classrooms. This study did not examine changes in teaching behaviors or patterns of interaction with codeswitching pupils.

The language attitudes of teachers and pupils in bilingual instructional contexts remain almost totally unexplored. As reported before, Politzer and Ramírez (1973) found Mexican-American children, after attending a bilingual program for three years, rated colloquial Spanish higher than three other varieties of English. The examples of two teachers engaged in Spanish reading instruction (Ramírez, 1978) suggest that the concern for Standard Spanish rather than meaning (comprehension of the text) could affect not only the content of the lesson but the degree of pupil participation and achievement potential.

The view of teaching from a linguistic perspective seems to provide a broader framework to study the role of language attitudes in relation to classroom and communication problems encountered by students from different ethno-linguistic backgrounds.

The NIE Conference on Studies in Teaching, Panel 5—*Teaching as a Linguistic Process in a Cultural Setting* (Gage, 1974)—offers procedures for analyzing various aspects of classroom discourse as well as a number of methods for changing teaching behaviors through the use of self-analysis. A number of hypotheses are presented to improve teaching and thereby learning on the basis of knowledge about linguistic processes in the classroom. Of the six hypotheses that are proposed, Hypotheses D, E, and F (Gage, 1974:24–25) are directly relevant to teachers of bilingual pupils, whether they attend a bilingual or monolingual school:

Hypothesis D: If teachers are led to analyze films and tape recordings of pupils' verbal behavior outside the classroom in such situations as conversations with parents, with friends, in street groups, etc., they will become aware of the range of communicative abilities that such children already possess, and will be more likely to look for the source of miscommunication in the patterns of classroom interaction rather than in deficiencies in the children.

Hypothesis E: If teachers have the opportunity to study tapes and transcripts of children which draw attention to features of what is regarded as nonstandard language in such a way that they are required to determine the grammatical rules themselves, they will develop more positive attitudes toward the dialect in question and, as a result, toward the speakers as well.

There is no expectation that teachers will learn to speak another variety of Engish. Moreover, the approach embodied in this hypothesis contrasts markedly with attempts simply to persuade teachers that they *ought* to have different attitudes toward the speech of their pupils.

Hypothesis F: Teachers' modifications of interaction patterns in the classroom lead to changes in pupil behavior—for example, changes in attitudes toward the classroom, the teacher, achievement, and so on. Such modifications also result in changes in the teacher's perceptions of, and attitudes toward, the pupils.

CONCLUSION

Language plays a unique role in classroom settings. It is the means by which teachers transmit school knowledge and the vehicle through which social identity and role relationships are maintained among the various participants in the classroom. Studies by Seligman, Tucker, and Lambert (1972), Frender and Lambert (1973), Williams (1976), and Ramírez, Arce-Torres, and Politzer (1978) have demonstrated that speech style or dialect, among other pupil characteristics, has a strong impact on teacher expectations and attitudes about a pupil's language and his academic potential.

A number of hypotheses have been advanced by the NIE Conference on Studies in Teaching, Panel 5— *Teaching as a Linguistic Process in a Cultural Setting*— as means for changing teaching behaviors through the use of self-analysis. In the process of modifying teacher attitudes about speech varieties, one needs to examine more closely the linguistic mission of schools and cultural attitudes about language, including accented speech. It is unlikely that schools will use the child's home language (nonstandard) variety for instruction. One of the major functions of schools is extending the child's linguistic repertoire by "teaching" in the standard dialect. Gonzalez (1979:126) argues

> Although the use of the child's Spanish dialect-variety is encouraged, this form should not be the only variety the child is exposed to. As the student progresses in language development and as horizons continue to expand, the student should be made aware of other varieties of Spanish such as the standard form. To deny the child this exposure is to limit communication skills and to hamper the ability to communicate in Spanish beyond the limits of the child's *barrio* or *colonia.*

In terms of societal attitudes toward the accented English speech of the Chicano bilingual, Gonzalez (1977:57) makes these observations:

> It is a fact of life in the Chicano community that those who achieve the highest degree of success in the dominant Anglo society are those that have the least amount of Spanish "accent" in their English speech. I would be hard pressed to name even *one* successful Chicano who has a noticeable accent...

Pedagogically this would mean that "we should focus more on pronunciation toward the end of the child's public school career, as his encounter with the job market and other realities draws near."

REFERENCES

Barnes, D. Language in the secondary classsroom. In D. Barnes, J. Britton, H. Rosen, & the L.A.T.E., *Language, the learner, and the school.* Harmondsworth: Penguin Books, 1969.

Barnes, D. *Language in the classroom.* Bletchley: The Open University Press, 1973.

Brophy, J. E., & Good, T. L. *Teacher-student relationships: Causes and consequences.* New York: Holt, Rinehart & Winston, 1974.

Fishman, J. A. Language attitudes, *International Journal of the Sociology of Language,* 1975, *1* (3), 1–14.

Frender, R., Lambert, W. E. Speech style and scholastic success: The tentative relationships and possible implications for lower social class children. In Roger Shuy (Ed.), *Linguistics and language study* (23rd Round Table Meeting), Washington, D.C.: Georgetown University Press, 1972.

Gage, N. L. (Ed.). *Teaching as a linguistic process in a cultural setting.* (NIE Conference on studies in Teaching—Panel 5). Washington, D.C.: National Institute of Education, 1974.

Gingras, R. C. *Second-language acquisition and foreign language teaching.* Arlington, Va.: Center for Applied Linguistics, 1978.

Gonzalez, G. Teaching bilingual children. *Bilingual Education: Current Perspectives* (vol. 2). Arlington, Virginia: Center for Applied Linguistics, 1977.

Gonzalez, G. The development of curriculum in L1 and L2 in a maintenance bilingual program. *Language Development in a Bilingual Setting.* Los Angeles: National Dissemination and Assessment Center, California State University, Los Angeles, 1979.

Holmes, J. Sociolinguistic competence in the classroom. In J. C. Richards (Ed.), *Understanding second and foreign language learning.* Rowley, Mass.: Newbury House, 1978.

Lambert, W. E., Frankel, H., Tucker, G. R. Judging personality through speech: A French-Canadian example, *Journal of Communication,* 1966, *16,* 305–321.

Mora, J. *Spanish language attitudes of high school students.* Unpublished paper, Santa Cruz University, 1975.

Politzer, R. L., & Ramírez, A. G. *Judging personality from speech: A pilot study of the effects of bilingual education on attitudes toward ethnic groups. Research and Development Memorandum No. 106.* U.S., Educational Resources Information Center, 1973 ERIC. Document ED 076 278).

Politzer, R. L., & Ramírez, A. G. Judging personality from speech: A pilot study of attitudes toward ethnic groups, *California Journal of Educational Research.* 1975, *26,* 16–26.

Ramírez, A. G. *Teaching reading in Spanish: A study of teacher effectiveness.* Stanford, Calif.: Stanford University, CERAS, March 1978.

Ramírez, A. G., et al. *The CERAS bilingual attitude measure.* Los Angeles: National Dissemination and Assessment Center, in press.

Ramírez, A. G., Arce-Torres, E. & Politzer, R. L. Language attitudes and the achievement of bilingual pupils in English language arts, *The Bilingual Review/La revista bilingüe,* 1978, *5,* 190–206.

Richards, J. C. *Understanding second and foreign language learning.* Rowley, Mass.: Newbury House, 1978.

Rist, R. C. Student social class and teacher expectations: The self-fulfilling prophecy in ghetto education. *Harvard Educational Review,* 1970, *40,* 411–451.

Ryan, E. B., & Carranza, M. A. Evaluative reactions of adolescents toward speakers of standard English and Mexican American accented English, *Journal of Personality and Social Psychology,* 1975, *31,* 855–863.

Seligman, C. R., Tucker, G. R. & Lambert, W. E. The effects of speech style and other attributes on teacher's attitudes toward pupils, *Language and Society,* 1972, *1,* 131–142.

Sinclair, J. McH., & Coulthard, R. M. *Towards an analysis of discourse.* London: Oxford 1975.

Shultz, J. Language use in bilingual classrooms, Paper presented at the TESOL Conference, Los Angeles, 1975.

Stubbs, M. *Language, schools and classrooms.* London: Methuen, 1976.

Tuckman, B. W., et al. The modification of teacher behavior: Effects of dissonance and coded feedback. *American Educational Research Journal,* 1969, *6,* 607–619.

Williams, B. W., et al. Explorations of the linguistic attitudes of teachers. Rowley, Mass.: Newbury House, 1976.

APPENDIX

CERAS BILINGUAL ATTITUDE MEASURE:
ATTITUDES TOWARD VARIETIES OF
ENGLISH AND SPANISH*

Guise I: Standard English

Ann is thirteen years old. She likes to play with her brother Richard who is eight years old. Ann's mother brought her a red shawl for her birthday. When Ann was going to put on her shawl, she couldn't find it because Richard had hidden it under some boxes. Ann was very angry, but her mother told her not to be upset because her brother was only playing a game.

Guise II: Standard English with Phonological and Morphological Deviations

Ann is *th*irteen[4] years old. *She*[1] likes to play with her brother Richard who *is*[2] eight years old. Ann's mother bring[6] her a red *sh*awl[1] for her birthday. When Ann was going to p*ut*[3] on her *sh*awl,[1] *she*[1] couldn't find *it*[2] because Richard had hidden *it*[2] under some boxes. Ann *is*[2,6] very angry, but her mother told her not to be upset because her brother was only playing a game.

---

*The *CERAS Bilingual Attitude Measure* (in press) is a matched-guise instrument consisting of 28 passages recorded on tape. The passages are based on four paragraphs written in seven guises (4 × 7 = 28 passages). The key to the phonological, morphological, and syntactical variations follows at the end of the Appendix.

Guise III: Standard English with Phonological, Morphological, and Syntactical Deviations

Ann___[7] *thi*rteen[4] year[5] old. *She*[1] likes to play with her brother Richard who *is*[2] eight year[5] old. Ann's mother *bring*[6] her a red *sh*awl[1] for her birthday. When Ann was going to pu*t*[3] on *his*[8] shawl,[1] *she*[1] no[10] could find *it*[2] because[9] had hidden *it*[2] under some box[5]. Ann *is*[2,6] very angry, but her mother told her *no*[10] upset because her brother was only playing a game.

Guise IV: English/Spanish Codeswitching

Ana tiene thirteen years. She likes to play *con su hermano* Richard *que tiene* eight years. Ana's mother *le trajo un* red shawl *para su* birthday. When Ana *se fue a poner su* shawl, she couldn't find it *porque* Richard *lo había escondido* under some boxes. Ana was very angry, *pero su madre le dijo* not to be upset *porque su hermano* was only playing a game.

Guise V: Standard Spanish with Phonological, Morphological, and Syntactical Deviations

Ana tene[18] *trece años. A e'a,*[12] *le gusta jugar con su hermano Ricardo, quien tene*[18] *ocho*[11] *años. L'*[15] [14] *amá de Ana le trujo*[17] *a e'a'*[12] *un rojo*[19] *rebozo para su cumpleaños. Cuando Ana jue*[13] *a ponerse su*[20] *rebozo, no lo pudo encontrar porque Ricardo lo había escondido debajo de una* [16] *cajas. Ana estaba furiosa, per su'*[14] *amá le dijo que no'*[14] *nojara porque su hermano sólo estaba jugando.*

Guise VI: Standard Spanish with Phonological Morphological Deviations

Ana tene[18] *trece años. A e'a'*[12] *le gusta jugar con su hermano Ricardo, quien tene*[18] *ocho*[11] *años. L'*[15] [14] *amá de Ana le trujo*[17] *ae'a'*[12] *un rebozo rojo para su cumpleaños. Cuando Ana jue*[13] *a ponerse el rebozo, no lo pudo encontrar porque Ricardo lo había escondido debajo de unas cajas. Ana estaba furiosa, pero su'*[14] *amá le dijo que no se enojara porque su hermano sólo estaba jugando.*

Guise VII: Standard Spanish

Ana tiene trece años. A ella le gusta jugar con su hermano Ricardo, quien tiene ocho años. La mamá de Ana le trajo a ella un rebozo rojo para su cumpleaños. Cuando Ana fue a ponerse ell rebozo, no lo pudo encontrar porque Ricardo lo había escondido debajo de unas cajas. Ana estaba furiosa, pero su mamá le dijo que no se enojara porque se hermano sólo estaba jugando.

KEY TO PHONOLOGICAL, MORPHOLOGICAL, AND SYNTACTICAL VARIATIONS

English

Phonological Variations

1. /"sh"/—/"ch"/ confusion.
2. /I/—/i/ confusion.
3. /u/—/U/ confusion.
4. /θ/ → /t/.

Morphological Variations

5. Misuse of pluralization rules.
6. Incorrect simple past tense.

Syntactical Variations

7. Omission of a form of the auxiliary "be."
8. Confusion in use of the possessive pronoun.
9. Misuse or omission of third-person pronoun.
10. Incorrect negation.

Spanish

Phonological Variations

11. /"ch"/—/"sh"/ confusion
12. The weakening of the intervocalic (y).
13. /f/ → /X/.
14. *Apheresis* (loss of initial sound or syllable).
15. Elision.

Morphological Variations

16. Gender or number disagreement.
17. Archaism.
18. Regularization of irregular verbs.

Syntactical Variations

19. Adjective-noun word disorder
20. Possessive redundance.

14 Aspects of Bilingual Students' Communicative Competence in the Classroom: A Case Study

Robert L. Carrasco,*
Arthur Vera,
Courtney B. Cazden
Harvard University

We present a narrative account with discussion of a bilingual Chicana student , Veronica, engaged in peer-teaching. In this case study, our aim is to describe the strategies with which Veronica communicates the information her tutee, Alberto, needs to do the task, and the strategies with which she manages the interpersonal relationships inherent in the teaching role. Such strategies are part of children's communicative competence, or sociolinguistic repertoire. That broader competence, that repertoire of ways of doing things with words and without, is the focus of this analysis; not narrower structural features of the children's linguistic competence except as they are means to these functional ends.

Teaching can be construed, by definition, as a speech event with two interpenetrating aspects: communication of information that the teacher knows and the learner does not; and the management of interpersonal aspects of the teacher-student relationship which, temporarily at least, is an asymmetrical relationship of more or less power. Teaching is an achieved role; not only in the static sense of achieved, via education, certification, or employment, but also in the dynamic and emergent sense of a performance that requires the complementary performance of at least one other person who is willing to be taught. Teaching, therefore, is a role that must be interactionally maintained. Teaching role behaviors are obvious when a child teacher stands while the tutee sits; uses a pen while tutees use pencils; or holds a paper close to the chest lest the tutee gain independent access to the tutor's special knowledge. We are interested in additional and more subtle interactional strategies that the children may use for creating and maintaining the teaching role.

---

*Robert Carrasco's present affiliation is Arizona State University.

In addition to this performance demand on all teachers, our child tutor had an additional problem. Both tutor and tutee were members of a single classroom peer group, with its own concepts of rights and obligations built up during this school year (and for some children, in previous years as well). We have no independent measures of their patterns of friendship, nor of their understanding of what rights and obligations peer relationships and friendships entail. Because the role of teacher is here enacted by children, we also cannot take as given any prevailing definition of the teacher-student relationship. We have only videotapes in which to find evidence of children relating as peers, and as teacher and student. Because the instructional chain as a speech event brought these two sets of role relationships (of peers and of teacher-student) into conflict, it brought them into the foreground of talk. When reality must be reframed, one way that reframing is accomplished is through talk. In Veronica's words, *Te voy a decir que hagas esto. No lo sabes hacer.* (I'm going to tell you to do this. You don't know how to do it.) In this peer scene, we see and hear two children constructing one social definition of the situation or another, and we try to understand how they do it.

Veronica's peer-teaching situation was captured on videotape and used for this descriptive analysis. This tape is part of a larger corpus of videotapes of classroom interaction collected in a multigrade/multiethnic classroom in San Diego, 1974–1975. Cazden, on leave from Harvard University, was the full-time classroom teacher; Hugh Mehan of the University of California at San Diego was the collaborating researcher. Although there was no bilingual education program in the school, there was a bilingual coteacher in this particular classroom and the use of Spanish was actively encouraged.

Because wireless microphones and transmitters were available, videotapes made in the classroom during the 1974–1975 year include interactions among the children as well as more formal teacher-led lessons. As an extended part of this peer interaction, *instructional chains* were also recorded in which the adult teacher taught a task to one child who then was asked to teach it to one or more peers. In language research, instructional chains are one kind of corpus extension technique. In the instructional chain (IC) analyzed here, the task was an English spelling lesson.

An IC has, in its most complete form, four episodes:

1. Teacher teaches a task to the focal child;
2. The focal child rehearses back to the teacher, what s/he is going to do;
3. The focal child is publicly designated as teacher for that particular lesson, and teaches one or more peers while the teacher is busy elsewhere in the classroom;
4. Finally, in a post-task evaluation, the focal child gives an account to the teacher about what happened and how the teaching had gone.

In education, ICs are another name for what is usually called *peer-* or *cross-age tutoring.* There has been considerable interest (whch we share) in such tutoring as a learning environment for tutor as well as tutee. But most of the research looks only at learning outcomes. We did not attempt to measure such outcomes, but focused instead on the instructional chain as a setting for investigating children's language use and interactional strategies.

Our interest in ICs is twofold. In the interest of both instruction and research, we want to find or create speech events that we call *concentrated encounters:* encounters that permit naturally occurring patterns of speech, but are structured to stimulate particular kinds of speech in denser, more concentrated amounts. Concentrated encounters contrast, on a continuum, with more *contrived encounters,* such as tests, in which the possibilities for normally contextualized speech is severely limited. An instructional chain is one kind of concentrated encounter.

In the multigrade classroom, informal child-teaching initiated by the children frequently took place. For the ICs, that teaching was structured by the assignment of tutor, tutee(s), task, and time. But a great deal of freedom remained to the children to impose their own interactional style on the speech event.

We are also interested in the IC as a hybrid of informal teaching and the two-person communication game used in a generation of experimental studies of referential communication. In the experimental and more contrived situation, one person tells another person how to select a picture or make a construction across an opaque screen. In our classroom version, there was no screen and no constraints on the children's talk; but we are still interested in how the tutor communicates referential information about the assigned task. In the IC, comparison can be made among the versions of the instructions given in each of the four episodes from the teacher's initial teaching to the tutor's post-task account.

PARTICIPANTS

Veronica, our child tutor, is a bilingual Spanish-dominant first-grader who at the time of the taping was repeating the first grade because of "weak" English language skills. Language dominance was assessed by the teacher. Veronica was also at this time attending English as a Second Language classes (ESL) but eventually dropped out; she refused to attend them. Alberto, the tutee, is a younger bilingual Spanish-dominant first-grader who at the time of taping was also attending ESL classes.

THE TASK

The English spelling lesson which Veronica learns from the teacher and is asked to teach has two parts: spelling by manipulating paper letters (task one) and spelling by writing (task two). This lesson could also be classified as a

FIGURE 1
The Spelling/Phonics Task Worksheet

A T	T I P	A
S A T	S I P	T
S A P	S I T	P
T A P	I T	S
		I

lesson in phonetics, concentrating on short vowel sounds and beginning and ending consonants. Figure 1 shows the worksheet with a list of eight words to be spelled and a set of five letters which are to be cut out.

SEGMENTATION OF VIDEOTAPE

Figure 2 illustrates how the taped activity—the IC—is segmented into events (level one) and subevents (level two) for analysis. These events and subevents were given common labels intuitively arrived at by repeated viewing: Teacher instructs students; Practice; Veronica instructs Alberto, etc. We refer to these labels in the subsequent pages to locate where an event fits into the larger picture. Numbers below level two give real time in minutes and seconds put on the videotape by a time date generator at the time of analysis. (For a detailed description of the methodology used in this segmentation analysis, see Erickson and Shultz, 1976). We discuss these events in turn, starting at the end of the teacher's instructions to Veronica. We present descriptive analyses and discussion of Set-up and Task One, followed by a discussion in which Task Two will be referred to more briefly.

TEACHER INSTRUCTS STUDENTS:
RECAPITULATION

After the teacher instructs six students in English how to do the two related spelling tasks, she asks Veronica to recapitulate the instructions for the task that she will teach Alberto. That is, Veronica is asked by the teacher to "restate" what she is going to do.

   9:10 V: He has to make words in here.
          T: And then...
          V: And then write the words right here.

The teacher probes for further clarification and finally accepts Veronica's recapitulation:

      V: *At, Sat, Sap,* I saying this and sh- and he is write it.

FIGURE 2
Segmentation of Instructional Chain Event
(Two Levels, One and Two)

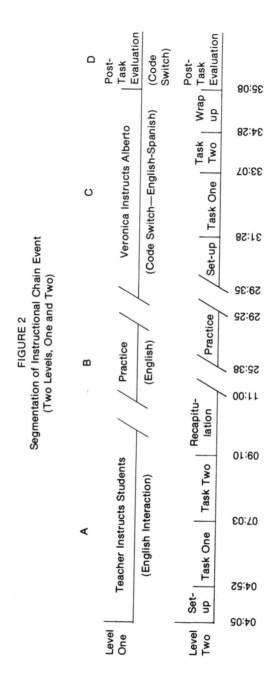

241

PRACTICE

When the teacher finishes her formulation of instructions to the tutor group and seems satisfied that its members are ready to teach the task, she then shifts the group's direction into a math lesson about number lines. (This lesson accounts for the time break between A and B in Diagram 1.) Immediately after the math lesson, Veronica, left without assigned work, walks over to one of the learning centers, selects a manipulable word-recognition exercise, brings it to her table, and begins to read the different words aloud. We label this part of the event *Practice* because it paralleled the task she was about to teach to Alberto. This short event in the tape is of interest because it further exemplifies what some students do "out-of-teacher awareness." As already mentioned, Veronica is a Spanish-dominant bilingual child who refused to attend ESL classes. Yet, this particular event shows her serious atittude toward learning English by self-practice.

>   25:38 V: Sun. Fun. Gun. Run. Bun.
>   V: Top. Pop. Stop. Cop. Drop. Hop. Mop.
>   V: Pig. Fig. Dig. Wig. Big.

Immediately apparent in seeing and hearing Veronica pronounce these exercise words is her crisp exaggerated pronunication of the English sounds, stressing the consonants and vowels as would a teacher teaching listening and pronunciation skills. Similarly crisp, even exaggerated, pronunciation of English consonants characterized the teaching of one of the Black tutees (Cazden, et al., 1979). Both examples show how situationally specific children's communicative performance can be.

VERONICA INSTRUCTS ALBERTO

Veronica begins by cutting out from the worksheet the letters to be manipulated by Alberto in Task One. All her instruction to Alberto is in Spanish, confirming other research findings that the speaker speaks the language that the listener knows best (Bruck & Shultz, 1977; Genishi, 1976). The IC ends when Veronica returns to the teacher to report the completion of the task:

>   35:09: V: She, he finish, he finish. She do all right. Look.
>   T: He did all right...Oh, and you wrote *good*! Very good, very good.
>   T: Um, tell me, how did it work? Did he do, did he...
>   V: Sh-I say the words and she, and he write it.

The last statement by Veronica is strikingly similar to her earlier recapitulation statement to the teacher: "I saying this and sh-and he is write it." From these pre- and post-task statements, which carry minimal information, one might easily underestimate Veronica's intellectual and interactional competence. For example, Veronica's meager report to her teacher about what went on during the peer-teaching episode might be mistaken for a lack of intellectual capacity; and her uncertainty about pronoun gender might be taken as evidence of lack of linguistic proficiency.

We next present a descriptive analysis and discussion of two portions of the IC: the portions between these pre- and post-task statements. Each of the two portions, Set-up and Task One, is presented in two forms: (1) a transcription that includes English translation (in parentheses) and information on nonverbal behavior (in square brackets); (2) a narrative description.

Set-Up. We begin with the subevent we label *Set-up,* because it is here that Veronica prepares the task materials and begins to negotiate her role as "teacher." Before having been designated tutor and tutee, Veronica and Alberto maintained a social relationship between them of "equal status" students. This relationship must now be temporarily altered to accommodate their newly designated roles.

Set-up[1]

Veronica	Alberto
(2) [To Alberto from across table] Ok. *Vente, Vente aqui.* (Ok. Come. Come here.)	(1) [Sitting opposite Veronica, head facedown on table]
(4) [With an accentuated command and looking at Alberto] *Ven.* (Come)	(3) [Still in same position as (1) and no response—verbal or nonverbal]
(6) *Ay, asi cres como tonto.* (Wow, how stupid you're acting.)	(5) [Still in same position as (1) and no response]
(8) [Not looking at Alberto, and with a weaker command] *Ven.* (Come.)	(7) [On the word *Tonto* (stupid) Alberto looks up at Veronica in a crouched position.]
(10) [Her pencil rolls off table to floor; trying to find it] *Te voy a decir que hagas esto.* (I'm going to tell you to do this.)	(9) [Still looking at Veronica, no response, and still in a crouched position]
(12) [Standing up still looking for pencil] *No lo sabes hacer.* (You don't know how to do it.)	(11) [Crouched position] *Yo lo hago solo.* (I'll do it alone.)
(14) [Still looking for pencil] *No lo sabes.* (You do not.)	(13) [Crouched position] *Si* lo sabo hacer. (I **do** know how to do it.)
(16) [Standing and still looking for pencil] *Si quieres...* (If you want ...) [Utterance interrupted by discovery of pencil, goes down on floor to pick it up, moves to chair next to Alberto]	(15) [Rises from crouched position to upright position looking up at ceiling.]
	(17) [Returns to crouched position looking away from her.]

---

[1]The transcripts of event dialogues preserve grammatical and morphological errors made by children.

Sitting opposite each other, while Veronica is cutting the letters from the worksheet, Alberto shows no reaction to Veronica's activity, sitting with his head resting on the table, his arms helping to hide his face (1). After Veronica completes her cutting, she tells Alberto to come sit next to her (2). Alberto continues to ignore Veronica by keeping his position (3). Receiving no response, Veronica uses an accentuated command to convey to Alberto, "Come over here *now!*" (4) Alberto maintains his position (5); Veronica, with a tone of frustration then tells Alberto how "stupid" (*tonto*) he's acting (6); and Alberto looks up at precisely the moment when *tonto* was said (7). Veronica preoccupied with gathering the task material, repeats the command to come but in a weaker tone than before (8), while Alberto maintains his crouched position and does not respond in any manner (9).

Veronica's pencil rolls off the table and while she's looking for it, she tells Alberto what she intends to do (and implicitly what he has to do) (10). Alberto responds that he wants to do it alone (11). Still involved in pencil searching, Veronica flatly replies that he doesn't know *how* to do it (12); Alberto emphatically states that he does know how to do it (13); and Veronica quickly insists that he doesn't (14). Alberto rises from the crouched to an upright position (15) as Veronica prepares to join him at his side of the table (16). Alberto responds to her move by returning to the crouched position and looking away (17).

Even though Veronica was persistent in trying to establish her role, this series of exchanges show Alberto's reluctance to accept Veronica's new role as teacher and his own complementary role as tutee. The Set-up ends with Veronica trying to establish her teaching position proxemically by sitting next to her tutee. But the negotiation process does not end in this particular segment. It continues throughout the entire task as Veronica, never calling on the adult teacher, employed both verbal and nonverbal strategies to get Alberto to do the assigned task.

Task One. How does Veronica formulate what she has learned into instructions so that Alberto can understand what his task will be? This is an important question because Veronica, a Spanish-dominant bilingual, received the original instructions from her teacher in her weaker language. Given that her pre-task recapitulation was so minimal: does she really understand what she was asked to do?

Task One

Veronica	Alberto
(1) [*Sits beside Alberto, places and arranges letters in front of him.*] *Tienes que hacer estas palabras.* (You have to abras. (You have to make these words.)	(2) [Crouched position, looking away from her; no response, verbal or nonverbal.]
(3) [*Leans toward Alberto.*] *Tienes que hacer las palabras aquí.* (You have to make the words here.) [*Picks up her word list.*] *Laque te digan aquí.* (The ones I tell you here.) [*Hits Alberto on the arm.*]	(3a) [Same as (2).]
	(4) [Responds by slowly turning head, looks at her, still in crouched position.]
	(6) [Same position as (4) and with no response.]
	(8) [Same position as (4) with no response]
(5) [With pencil, points to words on list.] *Las que te digan aquí de todas estas, las*	(10) [Same as (4), no response.]
	(12) [Same as (4), no response.]

vas hacer aquí (con) cinco letras. (The ones that I will tell you from all these [on word list] you will make them here (with) five letters.)

(7) [Lifts word list to hide its content] *Tonces, At. At.* (Now, *At. At.*)

(9) [Looking down at him, pointing at the letters.] *At. At. At.*

(11) [Looks down at table.] *Haz at.* (Make *at.*)

(13) [Straightens up and looks at Alberto.] *!Hala!* (Make it!)

(15) [Looking at word list] *La at. La palabra at. At.* (*At.* The word *at. At.*)

(17) *Sat...Sap, sap, sap.*

(19) *Tip, Tip.*

(20) [Extends arm and moves one letter.] *Sip. Sip. No, esta se queda aquí.* (No, this one stays here.)

(21) *Sit. Sit.*

(22) *It. It.*

(14) [Same position as (4) with response.] *¿Qué?* (What?]

(16) [Rises to upright position, makes the word, returns to crouched position.]

(17a) [Again to upright position, makes word, holding position.]

(18a) [Same as (17a)]

(19a) [Same as (17a)]

(20a) [Same as (17a)]

(21a) [Same as (17a)]

(22a) [Same as (17a)]

This subevent begins as Veronica sits beside Alberto, places and arranges the letters in front of him, and tells him that he must make the words (1). Ignored by Alberto (2), Veronica, leaning in his direction, repeats her initial statement and simultaneously picks up her word list and quickly tells him that she will say them (the words) from the list. Still being ignored by Alberto (3a), she gently hits him on the arm (3) to which he slowly reacts by looking at her (4). Veronica immediately points to the word list and begins to formulate the instructions—how to use the five letters (5). Looking at her in a head-resting, crouched position, he refuses to respond (6). Lifting her word list to hide the words, she attempt to start the task by stating the first word, "at," twice (7), to which Alberto (holding his position) does not react (8). This time she looks down at his face, points to the letters and repeats the same words (9). Still no reaction (10). She commands him to "make *at*" (11), but Alberto still firmly holds his position (12). Veronica then straightens up, looks directly at him, and emphatically insists that "he make it!" (13). Finally, Alberto responds by asking *¿Qué?* (What word are you talking about? (14). Being informed which word he must make (15), Alberto "rises" to the occasion, makes the word, then returns to his crouched position (still looking in her direction and in the direction of the task materials (16). Succeeding in finally getting him to perform, she quickly states the next word three times (17) while Alberto simultaneously rises again to make the word (17a). In a quick series of saying-the-word and making-the-word exchanges, Alberto sustains his upright position, actively accomplishing the first part of the task (18–22).

DISCUSSION

Four aspects of this case study merit particular discussion: the directives with which Veronica established her role as teacher; the relationship between instruction and role management in Task One; the significance of videotapes for the analysis; and the importance of seeing and hearing children—especially bilingual children—in a wide variety of interactional settings.

Directives.   In acting to establish her role as teacher and thus to control the interaction with Alberto, Veronica uses three series of directives that become increasingly emphatic—both verbally and nonverbally—as Alberto fails to respond.

From *Set-up:*
Vente. Vente aquí. (Come. Come here.)
Ven. (in more emphatic tone) (Come)
Ay, así cres como tonto. (Wow, how stupid you're acting.)
From *Task one:*
Tienes que hacer estas palabras. (You have to make these words.)
Tienes que hacer las palabras aquí. (leaning toward Alberto).
(You have to make these words here.)
Las que se digan aquí... (and hits Alberto on one arm).
(The ones I will tell you here...)

'Tonces, At. At. (Now, *At, At.*)
At. At. (rising a little, looking down at him and pointing at the letters)
Haz at. (a gentle directive) (Make *at.*)
¡Hala! (more emphatic command, accompanied by straightening up further and looking directly at him) (***Make it.***)

In these sequences, Veronica's directives to Alberto become more aggravated in response to Alberto's refusal to move to her side of the table and then to do the first task. A contrasting sequence of increasingly mitigated requests occurred in another IC in which the tutee requests the tutor to help with the task (Cazden, et al., 1979):

Before the children move to the work table:
"You gonna help me do it?"
"See, help me, then we can go to Miss Blethen's at the same time."[request justified with a reason why the requested action is in the interest of the hearer as well as the speaker]
Later, at the table:
"You gonna help me?"
"Leola, help me" [in a pleading tone].

Many researchers have noted that the selection of directive forms is a device for expressing social rank and have contrasted mitigated and aggravated requests (e.g., Labov & Fanshel, 1977; for adults; Shatz & Gleman, 1973, for children as young as four). It seems from these ICs, including Veronica's, that not only the initial directive, but the change within sequences of repeated directives, is influenced by perceived status.

We know of no sociolinguistic analyses of the distribution and social meaning of Spanish directives other than the word of Valdés included in this book. Our analysis of this aspect of Veronica's repertoire is therefore a suggested interpretation to be confirmed by further research.

We are tempted to consider Veronica's use of *'Tonces* at the beginning of the spelling words in Task One (turn 7 in the transcription) as another marker of control. In English, *now* is reported to be an indicator of teacher speech, and more generally of the speech of someone in control (Ervin-Tripp & Mitchell-Kernan, 1977: 11; Cazden et al., 1979, note its use by one of the Black child tutors). We intuitively feel that *'tonces* also also not only announces a shift to a new situation or topic, but that it would be used only by a speaker who assumed the right to make the shift. As with the directives, however, we can merely suggest this interpretation and hope for further sociolinguistic research on Spanish usage.

Instruction and Interpersonal Relationships. It is important to note how Veronica's formulation of the instructions becomes more elaborated in response to Alberto's noncompliance.

Tienes que hacer estas palabras. (You have to make these words.) *Tienes que hacer las palabras aquí.* (You have to make these words here.) *Las que digan aquí de todas estas, las vas hacer aquí (con) cinco letras.* (The ones that I will tell you from all these (on word list) you will make them here (with) five letters.)

Labov, in commenting on a conflict in one of the Black tutor ICs (personal communication, April 1978), has speculated on the cognitive learning that can take place in conflict situations such as this. Veronica must have learned to do the task through the direct experience of doing it with the adult teacher, but she was pressed to formulate it in more and more fully explicit Spanish in the service of intensified action. In this respect, we see the interpenetration of the referential and the interpersonal aspects of teaching.

The Importance of Videotape. Accomplishing the second part of the task (Task Two), in which Alberto must write each of the eight spelling words, becomes complicated when they are joined by a bilingual third-grader, Miguel. Veronica's instructions get interrupted by side-sequences led by Miguel about a possible boy-girl relationship between Veronica and Alberto. One aspect of the eventful instructions indicates how critical videotape can be. If one listed only to the audiotape, one would hear Veronica say only *Sap, Tip, Sit,* and *It* (words 3, 5, 7, 8) and probably infer that Miguel's presence has confused her and diminished her teaching competence. The videotape presents evidence for a radically different interpretation.

While Veronica was distracted by Miguel, Alberto glanced at Veronica's word list and copied *At* and *Sap.* Veronica, noticing this, lifted her word list to hide the words; appropriately, she starts her lesson with the third word. When Miguel again diverts Veronica's attention, Alberto copies the fourth word and later the sixth. Each time, Veronica monitors Alberto's actions, successfully "time-sharing" her involvement in two agendas—the instructional task with Alberto and the side-sequence with Miguel—and finally completes the teaching task.

Videotape is thus important not just for showing cooccurring nonverbal action—as in the nonverbal accompaniments of verbal escalation in the sequence of directives. More importantly, it can be essential to the interpretation of the talk that does occur.

Toward More Adequate Description of a
Child's Communicative Competence

It is clear from this case history that anyone, teacher or researcher, would have seriously underestimated Veronica's communicative competence without access to her behavior—out of sight of the teacher—in the particular peer interaction of this IC. We are convinced this is not an isolated example, and that the "moral of the story" is not limited to the assessment of bilingual children by monolingual adults.

Carrasco (1978) has analyzed the behavior of another bilingual child, Lupita, in a kindergarten class in Santa Barbara. Unlike Veronica, Lupita is in a bilingual program with a bilingual Chicana teacher. But like Veronica, Lupita is a well-behaved little girl who never becomes visible to the teacher as "behavior-problem" children often do. For example, when during Task Two the teacher approaches the table to remove Miguel from the IC scene, Veronica leans way down, focusing on Alberto's paper and repeats the word "sit" three times. Veronica's action can be interpreted as "looking busy" as the teacher approached, because she had already said "sit" earlier and Alberto had already written it at that time. And like Veronica, in peer interaction out of the teacher's view but "on camera," Lupita demonstrates greater cognitive and intellectual competence than the teacher otherwise realized she had.

Even more generally, the staff of a large project on "Children's Functional Language and Education in the Early Years" at the Center for Applied Linguistics reports:

> ...a number of teachers were astounded when watching videotapes of their classrooms to see certain children behave in a certain way. Some of these behaviors that were not overtly displayed to the teachers would possibly have received negative evaluations from them but by no means all. In fact, the majority of the "discoveries" made by the teachers when viewing the tapes were of positive attributes that they didn't know their children had. One third grade

teacher for example was amazed when a third grade student believed to be timid and "mousy" orchestrated the interaction at the table where she was sitting (Griffin & Shuy, 1978).

From these three examples, we wonder whether the underestimation of "good" children's competence occurs disproportionately for girls, and especially for Latina girls, because of socialization patterns at home and later at school.

Most previous classroom ethnographic studies have focused on children's inappropriate behavior, with the underlying assumption that teachers use these behaviors as a basis for negatively assessing the social and intellectual competence of children. In his analysis of videotapes in Veronica's classroom, Mehan says:

> As we study classroom interaction from the student's perspective, we are finding that the alignment of behavior and situation is a significant skill in the repertoire of the "competent student." It appears that the raw number of appropriate and inappropriate behavior does not vary across students in the classroom. But those students whom the teacher independently rates as "good students" are those who are able to keep their appropriate behavior in the eyes of the teacher, and their inappropriate behavior out of sight. The students who are not rated as "good students" have not made that distinction. They indiscriminately perform inappropriate action both in the teacher's gaze and out of it (Mehan, 1976:9).

Although we agree with Mehan, we recommend that teachers as well as researchers not only focus their attention on inappropriate behaviors by children, but also investigate what "inappropriately behaved" children do outside of the teacher's gaze.

REFERENCES

Bruck, M., & Shultz, J. An ethnographic analysis of the language use patterns of bilingually schooled children. *Working Papers on Bilingualism,* No. 13, May 1977. Ontario Institute for Studies in Education.

Carrasco, R. L. Expanded awareness of student performance: A case study in applied ethnographic monitoring in a bilingual classroom. In H. T. Treuba, G. P. Guthrie, & K. H. Au (Eds.), *Culture and the bilingual-bicultural classroom.* Rowley, Mass.: Newbury House, in press.

Cazden, C. B., et al. You all gonna hafta listen: Peer teaching in a primary classroom. In W. A. Collins (Ed.), *Children's language and communication.* 12th Annual Minnesota Symposium on Child Psychology. Hillsboro, N.J.: Erlbaum, 1977.

Erickson, F., & Shultz, J. When is a context: Some issues and methods in the analysis of social competence. *Quarterly Newsletter of the Institute for Comparative Human Development,* Rockefeller University, 1977, *1*(2).

Ervin-Tripp, S., & Mitchell-Kernan, C. (Eds.). *Child discourse.* New York: Academic Press, 1977.

Genishi, C. S. *Rules for code-switching in young Spanish-English speakers: An exploratory study of language socialization.* Unpublished doctoral dissertation, University of California, Berkeley, 1976.

Griffin, P., & Shuy, R. *Children's functional language and education in the early years.* Final report to the Carnegie Corporation of New York. Washington, D.C.: Center for Applied Linguistics, 1978.

Labov, W., & Fanshel, D. *Therapeutic discourse: Psychotherapy as conversation.* New York: Academic Press, 1977.

Mehan, H. 1976. Students' interactional competence in the classroom. *Quarterly Newsletter of the Institute of Comparative Human Development.* Rockefeller University, 1976, *1* (1).

Shatz, M., & Gelman, R. The development of communication skills: Modifications in the speech of young children as a function of listener. *Monographs of the Society for Research in Child Development,* 1973, *38*(5)

15

An Analysis of Bilingual Mother-Child Discourse

Eugene E. Garcia
Robert L. Carrasco
Arizona State University

INTRODUCTION

Recently, much attention has been centered on the multifaceted nature of early childhood bilingualism. This phenomenon occurs in young children who inhabit bilingual home environments and whose functioning in those environments depends on ability to either understand and/or speak both languages within this social network. The present investigation is an exploratory study that attempts to provide an analysis of a set of taperecorded mother-child interactions, in Spanish and English, of participants who come from Spanish-English home environments. Of specific interest will be the instructional characteristics of these interactions as they relate to the languages themselves. That is, what aspects of these interactions are similar to previous conceptual treatments of teacher-student interactions during formal "instruction time" (lessons) at microinteractional levels (Mehan et al., 1976). First, it will be necessary to determine whether these mothers are involved in an overt instructional process. Secondly, the analysis will attempt to establish interactional differences in mother-child verbal interactions across languages (English and Spanish); i.e., are there any style differences from one language context to the other?

With respect to the first empirical determination, whether mothers are engaged in a teaching situation related to one of two languages, four separate preinvestigatory considerations strongly suggest an affirmative response:

1. All mothers and children were part of a voluntary preschool bilingual/bicultural effort. Therefore, it was clear that mothers were very much interested in their children's learning both languages.

2. All mothers served on a cooperative basis as instructors at the preschool. Their duties included both curriculum development and implementation in both Spanish and English. Therefore, although professional guidance was provided, all mothers served as teachers in the school.

3. All recordings were obtained at the preschool. Although these were done individually with each mother-child pair, and only instructions concerning the interactive nature for these sessions were given, it is very likely that the teaching format experienced at the preschool influenced the nature of the recorded mother-child interactions. The influence was most probably in the direction of perceiving this interaction as another teaching situation.

4. Previous detailed linguistic analysis of Spanish interactions combined with a parallel set of English mother-child interactions for these pairs indicated the dominance of English speech for each of the children. This is not to say that children did not "know" or use Spanish, but their recorded English was much further advanced linguistically than their recorded Spanish.

It is these preconditions which strongly suggest that mothers were involved in an instructional process during the mother-child interactions forming the data for the current study.

In performing an empirical evaluation of this hypothesis on our converational data, we used the Mehan interactional analysis model for analyzing the sequential oganization of speech acts within classroom lessons. This model concentrates on the sequential characteristics of teacher initiations, followed by student responses, and teacher evaluations, where, in our study, the role of teachers was replaced by that of mothers. In so doing, this form of interaction analysis attempts to provide a qualitative analysis of interaction style, taking into consideration both the individual content and illocutionary force of teacher and student utterances and topic selection and conversational management in turntaking. It was hypothesized that the original Mehan model of instructional interaction sequencing would describe the present mother-child interactions. Some modification of the original Mehan model was necessary to accommodate the conversational data we actually encountered in our transcripts.

The current investigation is one of the few attempts to deal with the interactional nature of bilingual mother-child pairs. It also tries to analyze these interactions as they relate to unbalanced bilingual situations in early childhood. Recent surveys have indicated that the majority of the estimated 2–4 million Spanish-English bilingual children in this country are characterized by dominance of one language. Therefore, the nature of the present mother-child interaction corpus should be generalizable to a very large segment of the presently recognized bilingual population. Also, if one is concerned with bilingual instruction, might it not be important to consider how the mother goes about this process since children readily identify mother and teacher in initial schooling? We believe our form of sequential analysis of discourse between mother and children would be helpful in understanding formal bilingual instruction which does not make use of the mother as a formal instructor, but in the most socially and culturally sensitive approaches attempts to consider the relevance of nonschool interactions of children. Lastly, in the current study, we also attempted to explore interactional codeswitching (when a switch in language is observed from one speaker to the next) in each of the two language contexts we analyzed. Although certainly not all-encompassing, the current investigation provides important exploratory information concerning mother-child interaction of instructional relevance.

Subjects

Four dyads were selected for this study. They were Spanish-English bilingual mother-child pairs, Chicanos, from Salt Lake City, Utah. The children were informally identified by mothers, fathers, and the preschool staff as English-dominant bilinguals, approximately 3½ years old; the mothers were informally assessed by the staff to be fairly equally bilingual (balanced) and ranged in age from 23 to 29 years of age. These dyads participated in a bilingual/bicultural, voluntary cooperative preschool program.

Setting

All mother-child discourse took place in an experimental room located at the preschool in which a concealed audiorecorder recorded all utterances which were later transcribed. Two interactions per month (15-minute duration) across a nine-month span were recorded. Before each of the two monthly sessions, the mothers were instructed to speak only in Spanish for one session and only in English for the other (each session took place on different days). Thus, we have equal number of sessions in both language contexts. The mother was given a picture of a circus (ETS Test: Circus, Production Test 10C) to serve as stimulus for discussion during these sessions. It contained several items which could be discussed, e.g., animals, balls, clowns, etc.

Utterances

Briefly, the utterances were reliably transcribed from the cassette recordings by two bilingual observers with an utterance defined as any word (English or Spanish) or set of words separated from one another by a 2-second time interval of silence or by the occurrence of an utterance by a second speaker. This two-second interval of silence was extremely useful when investigating silence as a message form.

Data Source

For this exploratory study, three consecutive months of mother-child interactions were selected (January, February, March, 1976) which were in the middle of the nine-months corpus of taped interactions.

Methodology

Initial review of the selected transcripts representing our data coupled with a general understanding of the Mehan interaction analysis system for coding classroom teacher-student dialogues resulted in some necessary modifications of the Mehan typology. While keeping Mehan's sequential model of initiation, reply and evaluation intact, we renamed these latter modes of conversing to reflect the social relations in dyadic discourse between a mother and child: Mother initiations, Child replies, and Mother replies. The subcategories of speech acts underlying each of these three speech modes in the Mehan system were also similarly modified to reflect a mother-child relationship (see Table 1-A for the Mehan Modified System). The major addition in this modified model were Child Repetitions and Mother Repetitions; no parallel speech forms were present in the Mehan account of teacher-student interactions during "instruction time." This addition was necessary because initial review of the transcripts revealed many repetitions by both participants (especially in the Spanish transcripts).

After a trial test of the modified model and subsequent refinement of the system, two bilingual investigators independently coded each of the 24 transcripts (12 English and 12 Spanish) and each disagreement was jointly resolved.

As mentioned earlier, each utterance was defined as any word or set of words separated by a 2-second interval. Most commonly many sentences or words were found to occur in utterances. In coding, each utterance was categorized as an instance of a speech act represented in our conversational model with the 2-second interval between utterances coded. *No Reply* was scored whenever the child did not reply to a mother elicitation.

RESULTS

Using the modified Mehan model, an analysis of mother-child interactions according to language (Spanish or English) produced comparative differences. For each of the three speech modes of an interactional sequence

TABLE 1-A

Definition of Interactional Characteristics for the Modified System

I. Mother Initiation
  A. Elicitations
    1. Choice: An elicitation act in which the initiator provides responses in elicitation itself. ("Is it blue or green?")
    2. Product: An elicitation act to which the respondent is to provide factual response. ("What is this?")
    3. Process: An elicitation act which asks the respondent for opinions and interpretations. ("What's he doing?")
    4. Metaprocess: An elicitation act which asks the respondent to be reflective on the process of reasoning itself. ("Why does he?")
  B. Directives: These are preparatory exchanges designed to have respondents take specific actions. ("Look here.")
  C. Informatives: Acts which pass on information, facts, opinions, or ideas ("This girl's dress is blue.")
II. Child Reply
  A. No reply: Child does not answer initiation acts; silence for a 2 sec. period.
  B. Topic-relevant Reply
    1. Choice: Choice response relevant to the initiator's topic ("blue")
    2. Product: Product response relevant to the initiator's topic. ("car")
    3. Process: Process response relevant to the initiator's topic. ("Playing with a dog.")
    4. Metaprocess: Metaprocess response relevant to the initiator's topic (" 'cause he's not scared.")
(These responses were also scored: 1, if irrelevant to initiator's topic; 2, if relevant to the initiator's previous topic.)
  C. Bid: These constitute statements which attempt to gain the floor, i.e., change the topic. These can be considered as initiation by the child. ("What is this?")
  D. Reaction: Negative acts taken in response to a directive. ("I don't want to.")
  E. Repetition: Child repeats the previous mother statement: (1) partially, (2) exactly, (3) expanded.
  F. Don't Understand: Child indicates he did not understand initiator. ("What?")
III. Mother Reply
  A. Repetition: Mother repeats previous child utterance: (1) partially, (2) exactly, (3) expanded.
  B. Evaluation: Mother (1) accepts (positive) or (2) rejects (negative) previous child utterance. ("O.K., that's good"; "not that way.")
  C. Prompts: Statements given in response to incorrect, incomplete or misunderstood replies. ("There are three.")
  D. Child Topic Initiator: Initiating statements in response to initiations by the child. (These were earlier designated as Child Bids.) ("There are two tigers.")

(mother initiation, child reply, mother reply), the relative frequency or percentage of occurrence of various subcategories of speech within each mode shown in Table 1-A was computed. Thus, for example, the number of coded mother product elicitations over the total number of statements coded as mother initiations was computed and contrasted across the Spanish interactions and the English interactions.

TABLE 1
Mother Elicitations (percentages)

Elicitation Type	Language Context	
	Spanish	English
Product	51.6	32.3
Choice	1.6	19.7
Process	6.9	19.3
Informatives	26.3	22.5
Directives	13.6	6.2
Mother-determined	92.9	81.3
Child'determined	7.1	18.7

Mother Elicitations: Spanish vs. English (Table 1)

In the Spanish discourse we found that the mother used slightly more product elicitations (56.1 percent) than in the English (32.3 percent). *Product elicitations* were defined as elicitation acts to which the respondent is to provide a factual response. A typical example in English is, "What's this?" In Spanish, *¿Cómo se llama esto?* (What's this called?). The higher percentage of product elicitations in the Spanish interaction and the nature of the product elicitations were found to coincide with the teaching of Spanish pronunciation and/or translation from English to Spanish. For example:

Mother: *¿Qué es eso?*	(What is that?)
Child: *Casa*	(House)
Mother: *Una casa, muy bien.*	(A house, very good.)

In this typical example, the mother asks a product type of question and receives a product response (*casa*). In the Spanish utterances, it was typical for the mother to request identification of an item in Spanish. Additionally, the mother was likely to restate the child product response (and sometimes expand on it) possibly indicating that the pronunciation was being reinforced.

In the English discourse context, the product elicitations may have been typified as similar to the Spanish context except that pronunciation (or translation) was not important. That is, few child product responses were restated by the mother. In the Spanish context, the child seemed to be cued to pronunciation by stressed terms in the mother's elicitations. This did not occur in the English interactions. An example of this situation in Spanish follows:

Mother: *Hay **Dos escaleras**.*	(There are **two ladders.**)
Child: *Dos escaleras.*	(Two ladders.)

The percentage of choice category elicitation utterances for mothers revealed major differences across languages. Very few choice elicitations occurred in the Spanish context (1.6 percent) as compared to the English (19.7 percent). A choice elicitation occurred when the mother provided the child's response as part of an otherwise product category elicitation (e.g., "Is it blue or green?").

Process elicitations were defined as speech acts which request opinions and interpretations from an interlocutor (e.g., "What's he doing?"). In the English context, 19.3 percent of the total mother elicitations were of this process type; only 6.9 percent occurred in the Spanish context. This interesting finding along with the finding for choice elicitations seems to reinforce a conjecture that the mother knows that the child is linguistically incapable of grammatically stringing words in the Spanish language (necessary for replying to process questions but not necessary for identifying a correct choice). Informatives and directives were generally similar in relative frequency of occurrence in both language contexts, although directive elicitations in Spanish were twice as likely as directive elicitations in English.

Child Replies: Spanish vs. English (Table 2)

Major differences in relative frequency of occurrence of child replies across Spanish and English contexts were found for three subcategories of child reply: choice reply, process reply, and repetition reply. There were no choice replies by the children in response to mother's choice elicitations in the Spanish interactions; in the English interactions, 18.3 percent of replies by children were to the choice type. This could be expected, given that in a

TABLE 2
Child Reply (percentages)

| | Language Context | |
Reply Type	Spanish	English
Product	22.4	27.1
Choice	0.0	18.3
Process	9.1	28.5
Repetition	42.3	4.1
No reply	16.7	4.1
Don't understand	0.7	1.6
Irrelevant reply	0.2	0.6
Bid	8.6	15.7
Successful	4.0	12.7
Unsuccessful	4.6	3.0

Spanish context the mother asked very few choice questions (1.6 percent), whereas in an English context, the mother asked more questions (19.7 percent). The few process responses of children in reply to mother's elicitations compared to the English (28.5 percent) can also be accounted for by the relatively few process elicitations by the mother in Spanish vs. English. The majority of child replies in the Spanish context were in the form of repetitions (42.3 percent); in the English context, only 4.1 percent of child replies were repetitions. In the Spanish interactions, child repetitions involved phonetic pronunciation activities as evidenced by mother stating or stressing a word, the child repeating, then the mother repeating the same word, etc. For example:

> Mother: *Sonrisa*   (Smile)
> Child: *Sonrisa*
> Mother: *Sonrisa*
> Child: *Sonrisa*

Child bid replies (or child initiations), were almost twice as frequent in English (15.7 percent) as in Spanish (8.6 percent). Child bids in Spanish and English were also coded as successful or unsuccessful in interrupting the mother or initiating a new topic. In the English interactions, the great majority of child bids (81.5 percent) were successful with the child gaining control of the conversational topic, whereas slightly more than half of the Spanish context bids of the child were successful in this regard. In the discussion of conversational codeswitching, later, this difference will be addressed.

Bids are coded successful if the mother accepted the child initiations, and the topic of discussion raised in an initiation became the topic for further discourse. This coding of child bids is how we determined child-determined and mother-determined elicitations shown in Table 1. Inspection of Table 1 shows that a child was about two and one half times as likely to gain control of conversation in English as in Spanish, though the mother clearly dominated the topic of conversation in both languages.

Mother Replies: Spanish vs. English (Table 3)

The majority of all mother replies in the Spanish interactions were in the form of repetitions (39.3 percent). Again, this seems possibly to reflect the mother's reinforcement of the child's Spanish pronunciation. Although evaluation replies occurred roughly at the same level of relative frequency in Spanish and English contexts, the affective reinforcing character of evaluations, positive or negative differed in relative frequency across language contexts. The Spanish context's positive and negative evaluations occurred with about the

TABLE 3
Mother Reply (percentages)

Reply Type	Evaluation Type	Language Context	
		Spanish	English
Repetition		39.3	24.2
Evaluation		33.9	27.9
	Positive	18.3	22.6
	Negative	15.6	5.3
Prompt		26.8	47.9

same relative frequency, but in English positive evaluations were about four times more frequent than negative evaluations.

Prompting in mother replies was defined as statements in response to incorrect, incomplete or misunderstood replies by a child (e.g., as in the mother stating, "There are **three**!" when a child replied incorrectly). The majority of all mother replies in the English context were prompts (47.9 percent). The nature of these interactions (in English, the stronger language for the child) was such that the mother and the child were continually building on each other's statements, the mother usually completing or adding where the child left off. The Spanish interaction prompts of mothers were usually in the form of correcting the child's incorrect Spanish pronunciation or asking the child to reply in Spanish and not English.

INTERACTION ANALYSIS

Using the quantitative measures and qualitative structure of the mother-child interactions discussed, we have developed different interaction models for Spanish vs. English dialogues. In uncovering the different interaction models for each language, we first generated a general interactional model for interactions in both languages as shown in Figure 1, then we looked at the

FIGURE 1
General Interactional Model

Mother Elicitation	1st Order
Child Reply	2nd Order
Mother Reply	3rd Order

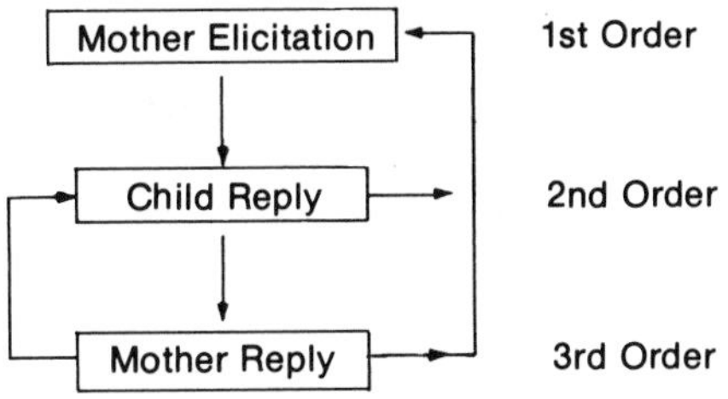

nature of the interactions around topic lengths. This process of analysis led us to the models for each language. The general interaction model we first worked with corresponds to our earlier discussion of the Modified Mehan model of classroom conversation with the teacher replaced by the mother, etc. This model is depicted by a flow chart in Figure 1 showing the various forms of sequencing possible in speech acts between a mother and child. Using the General Interaction Model of Figure 1, we further determined interactional length during which a single topic of discourse was maintained into first order, second order, third order or fourth-(or more) order interactions. First-order length is defined as mother-initiated topic elicitation with the child either ignoring the topic by not replying or by changing the topic by bidding; or in another instance by the mother changing the topic after failing to elicit a response from the child. This latter case is shown by the following example:

Mother: *¿En dónde estan los niños?* (Where are the children?)
  Child: **No reply**
(Change topic)
Mother: *¿Qúe trae puesto la niña? ¿Qúe es eso?*
     (What is the girl wearing? What is that?)

Interactions coded as first-oder and representing a mother's simple elicitation are not "true" interactions; they are attempts to start them. Second-order–length interactions were typified by mother initiation of topic, the child replying, but with no mother reply regarding the same topic:

Mother: *¿Cómo se llama todo esto? Esta es una foto, un retrato de mucha gente.*
     (What is all this called? This is a picture, a picture of many people.)
  Child: *Azul* (Blue)
                        End of topic
Mother: *El está jugando con las pelotas.*
     (He is playing with the balls.)
  Child: *Pelotas* (Balls)
                        End of topic
Mother: *¿Eso qúe es?* (What is that?)
  Child: *Boca* (Mouth)
                        End of topic

Third-order interactions included three part sequences during which a topic of conversation is maintained.

Mother: *¿De qúe color son los elefantes?*
     (What color are the elephants?)

Child: *Verde* (Green)
Mother: *Verdes*(Green)

End of topic

Fourth-order–length interactions were made up of four part sequences in which the mother's topic of conversation was maintained or the child succeeded in bidding for a new topic for discussion. The following example illustrated a fourth-order form involving a single topic:

Mother: ¿ *Qúe es?* (What is it?)
  Child: *Una silla* (A chair)
Mother: *Silla del dentista* (A dentist's chair)
  Child: Yeah

Interactions of length greater than fourth order involved maintenance of the same basis patterns of child reply, followed by mother reply followed by child reply.

Table 4 shows the percentage of mother-child discourse in each language falling into each of the four order categories of interactional length. We found that the highest percentage of the English language interactions were of the second-order form (53.8 percent): The mother initiates a topic, the child replies, and the mother moves to a new topic. Spanish language interactions used more third-order interaction sequences. This is possibly accounted for by high incidence of the mother's repeating the child reply (as found in the higher percentage of mother repetition replies, 39.3 percent).

Spanish Interaction Model (Figure 2)

The Spanish interaction model we proposed to describe the relative frequency of occurrence of interactions of different orders in Spanish is shown in Figure 2. This model can be seen as a qualification on the chances that various links in the general model of interaction will be realized.

In the Spanish model, the mother elicits a topic, the child repeats, then the mother replies. This sequence is followed by new mother elicitation (new

TABLE 4
Interaction Length Percent

Order	Spanish	English
1	11.6	14.9
2	36.3	53.8
3	36.1	12.7
4	16.0	18.6

FIGURE 2
Spanish and English Interactional Models*

Spanish Interaction Model

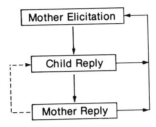

English Interaction Model

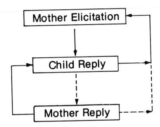

*Dotted lines indicate a more infrequent course of responding.

topic). Therefore, it is categorized primarily as a third-order form; or, the mother elicits, child replies, then mother elicits a new topic yielding a second-order form. The broken line in the illustration of the Spanish interaction model of Figure 2 means that more infrequently the child builds onto the mother reply usually with a new topic (child initiation).

English Interaction Model (Figure 2)

The model we propose for English language interactions is shown at the bottom of Figure 2. This model differs qualitatively from the Spanish model in two ways: (1) most interactions are of the second-order type (Table 4); (2) child replies and mother replies in four or more order forms tend to be void of repetition (Tables 2 and 3). The broken lines in this model refer to the least-used path of mother elicitation: (1) mother reply; (2) mother initiation after mother reply. Here the two models differ. Recall that in Spanish, mothers were more apt to reply (i.e., produce more third-order interactions and initiate new topic interactions after their reply). This difference seems to indicate that instruction is taking place in the Spanish interaction and not in the English since the Spanish interaction pattern seems closely to follow the

TABLE 5
Spanish and English Qualitative Model Comparison

	Spanish	*English*
Mother Elicitations	*Mostly Product* ◄┐ Informatives Directives	Product ◄┐ Process Choice Informatives
Child Reply	*Mostly Repetitions* Product	Process ──┐ Product ◄ Choice Bids
Mother Reply	*Mostly Repetitions*┘ Evaluations Pos/Neg Prompts	└*Mostly Prompts* Repetitions Positive evaluations

classic Mehan sequence of instruction: Teacher initiation—Student reply—Teacher reply.

Qualitatively, the Spanish interaction model seems to reveal not only a teaching strategy by the mothers but also that the mothers were aware of inappropriate strategies (as evidenced by the tendency to avoid process elicitations which require linguistically advanced Spanish). In general, the English interaction model is congruent with a more informal conversational model of interaction in which interaction either moves from topic to topic or builds on to a single topic without repetition or evaluation.

INTERACTIONAL CODESWITCHING

Interactional codeswitching was defined as a switch in language observed from one speaker to the next. The following is an attempt to analyze this phenomenon for the interactions under study. In coding the transcripts, interactional code switches were classified in two ways: (1) full codeswitch; (2) mixed codeswitch. A *mixed* codeswitch occurred when participants switched into another language (another code) within one identifiable statement (or utterance). For example:

> I was in the classroom yesterday, sitting down minding my own business *cuando entró el director*. Then he started to yell at me *por nada*.
> (... When the director entered ... for no reason.)

Mixed codeswitching occurred in either language context, i.e., in either Spanish or English interactions. Full codeswitching depended on the language context. For example, if the interaction was in English, the participants would have to switch into Spanish; and if the context was in Spanish, they would have to switch into English to be coded as codeswitch. In general, very little codeswitching occurred in the English interactions. Thus the thrust of the current analysis and discussion will deal mainly with the Spanish interactions.

Spanish Interactional Codeswitching (Table 6)

The interactional codeswitching to be discussed took place during Spanish language sessions. As mentioned earlier during these Spanish sessions, mothers were instructed to speak to their children only in Spanish. As might well be expected, children (English dominant) codeswitched most often when the replies required more than single word utterances.

As mentioned previously, 7.1 percent of the mother elicitations were child determined (see Table 1) when Spanish was the primary language of conversation. This may be accounted for by the fact that 65.2 percent of all

TABLE 6
Percentage of Speech Act Types (Major Categories) and
Accompanying Percentage of Codeswitching (within Each
Type) Spanish Interactions

	Category	Code Switch
Mother Elicitations		
Product	51.6	5.9
Choice	1.6	8.6
Process	6.9	18.1
Informatives	26.3	19.3
Directives	13.6	10.1
Child Reply		
*Product	22.4	43.9
Choice	0.0	0.0
*Process	9.1	85.6
		(14/19)
Repititions	42.3	11.3
Don't understand	0.7	16.0
		(2/10)
*Child bids	8.6	65.2
Mother Reply		
Repetitions	39.3	16.1
Evaluations	33.9	8.2
Positive	18.3	2.1
Negative	15.6	23.7
Prompts	26.8	3.6

child initiations (child bids) were in the form of codeswitches (mostly of the full type-English) and nearly all of these were successful bids. Some examples:

> (Previous Spanish Statement by Mother)
> Child: Isn't that his tail there, huh? That's his tail there, huh?
> Mother: *¿Cómo se dice* tail *en español? Una cola.*
> (How do you say "tail" in Spanish? *Una cola.*)
> (Previous Spanish Statement by Mother)
> Child: Look at this.
> Mother: *¿Qúe es eso?* (What is that?)
> Child: *Casa* (House)
> Mother: *Una casa, muy bien.* (A house, very good.)
> (Previous Spanish Statement by Mother)
> Child: What does *rojo* mean?
> Mother: *Rojo* is red.
> Child: Red
> Mother: *En inglés es* red. *En español es rojo.*
> (In English it's red. In Spanish it's *rojo.*)
> Child: *Españ*ol (Spanish)
> Mother: . . . *es rojo.* (. . . it's red.)
> Child: *Es rojo.* (It's red.)

This analysis indicates that most child elicitations during Spanish interactions were in English. This finding seems to account for the broken line path in the Spanish interactional model. (See Figure 2.) That is, few child elicitations occurred during Spanish mother-child interactions. Coincidentally, this path is the same occurring during English interactions. The following illustrates this point:

Mother elicitation	(Previous topic)
Child Reply Bid:	What does *rojo* mean?
Mother reply	*Rojo* is red
Child Reply	Red.
Mother Elicitation	*En inglés es* red. *En Español es rojo.*
	In English it's *red.* In Spanish it's *rojo.*)
Child Reply	. . . *es rojo* (It's red.)

Following the interactional "flow" in the preceding example and applying it to the English Interaction Model and to the Spanish Interaction Model shown in Figure 2, the cyclical nature of the interaction clearly corresponds to the English interaction mode. But this correspondence may have implication or interpretations not made explicit in the interaction models posited for each language. First, it may be that if the child had more knowledge of Spanish and thus was able to use more than one-word utterances, the models for both Spanish and English interactions might be similar. Secondly, it could be that the child was reverting to "English rules for interaction," rules that are more familiar and comfortable to him (given that he is English dominant). In any case, the ability of the child (and mother) to codeswitch during the interaction tended to increase the length of a topic-specific interaction.

Qualitatively, negative evaluations and process elicitations seem to have induced child codeswitches. At least half (27 of 46) of the mother negative evaluations (Spanish context) were directly followed by codeswitched child responses.

Example:

(Wrong reply)	Child:	*Tres, cuatro, cinco* (Three, four, five)
(Negative) evaluation)	Mother:	*¡No! No te pregunté qúe tantos.* *¿Qúe estan haciendo?* (What are they doing?) *¿Qúe estan haciendo?* (No! I did not ask how many. What are they doing?)
Codeswitch	Child:	Holding hands
	Mother:	*Deteniéndose las manos, mijo* (Holding hands, son)
	Child:	Yeah, *manos* (Yeah, hands)

This suggests that negative evaluations lead to the child's returning to his or her dominant language in the quest for the right answer (and positive evaluation). Thirty-six of the total 53 mother process elicitations also preceded child codeswitched replies.

Example:

(Process elicitation)	Mother:	*Tambien* (Glossed Translation: And this? what's happening here?)
Codeswitch	Child:	He's swinging.
	Mother:	*Se está columpiando, columpiando.* (He's swinging, swinging.)
	Child:	*Columpiando.* (Swinging.)

This finding further suggests that although the child did understand the question in Spanish, he was not linguistically advanced or secure enough to

TABLE 7
Percent Codeswitches into Spanish
(By Statement Type)

Mother: full	17.5
Mother: mixed	83.5
Child: full	72.6
Child: mixed	28.4

give a process answer in the Spanish language. *But he did answer!* The child's process replies were mostly of the full (English) type of codeswitching.

Codeswitching (By Mixed or Full Type)

Interestingly for the Spanish interactions, 83.5 percent of all codeswitchings by the mother were of the mixed type, i.e., mixing Spanish and English in single statements (e.g., Jail, *cárcel donde ponen los prisioneros.*) In contrast, the child codeswitched mostly into the full type (English), relying on English for more difficult replies (Table 7). This hesitancy for children to use intrautterance language switches has been noted elsewhere (Garcia, 1979; Padilla & Liebman, 1979).

DISCUSSION

The present study has attempted to provide a preliminary analysis of bilingual mother-child discourse. It is important to emphasize that the children involved in this study were each perceived by both mothers and preschool instructional staff as English dominant. Yet, they all resided in bilingual, Spanish-English home environments. Both parents spoke Spanish and English but reportedly (self-report) spoke more Spanish than English to these children. Home interaction data presented elsewhere for these children (Garcia, 1978) substantiate this self-report information.

This analysis first centered on the nature of this discourse as it related to previous investigations of "teaching" discourse (Mehan, et al., 1976). What has always been an interesting question is how parents go about teaching two languages to their children (Leopold, 1939, 1947, 1949a, 1949b). Do parents have a strategy for ensuring that a child will be bilingual? A study by Padilla (1974) found that the majority of Spanish/English bilingual parents in this country wanted their preschool children to speak Spanish in addition to English. He found that few of the parents, however, had an explicit strategy for implementing bilingualism. Parents relied only on the child's exposure to two languages in the home and maintained that this was sufficient for their children to become proficient speakers of Spanish and English. Mere passive exposure to two languages without active speaking practice in two languages accounts for the widely reported notion that children are not balanced bilinguals in the sense of being equally competent in both languages. The mothers in this study exposed their children to both languages at home, but they (like many bilingual parents) probably did not insist that their children speak in both languages. It is not uncommon to observe a parent communicate to his or her child in Spanish and have the child reply in English.

What seems to have surfaced in this study is that there may be an explicit teaching strategy parents use in teaching their children two languages. In the current study, however, this strategy may have surfaced so noticeably because the mothers were in a school setting, considered themselves as teachers, and believed in the aims of the bilingual/bicultural program which they helped to develop and implement. That is to say, in the school context, status and role requirements of acting as teacher/mother may have contributed to reliance on discourse involving teaching strategies not usually exercised so emphatically in nonschool settings. Regardless of such possibilities, it is important to know something about the various strategies parents use in teaching their children two languages and this exploratory study only begins to provide such analyses. Additionally, more focused studies in bilingual mother-child interactions are needed to investigate in detail various strategies parents use in teaching preschool children two languages—in school settings as well as in the home. These strategies may help teachers in bilingual/bicultural programs to be more effective in the classroom and may also open the school doors to parents allowing them potentially, to play a major role as formal instructors in these programs.

A second concern of this investigation centered on the nature of interactional codeswitching in schooling contexts where mothers enacted teacherlike roles. The question posed was what might the nature of codeswitching in these contexts tell us about interactional strategies and the subsequent sequencing of speech acts in mother-child discourse? Analysis of our discourse data indicated that interactional codeswitching in the present subject population occurred at predictable points of interaction: primarily at those points where the child's linguistic ability did not match the linguistic requirements imposed by a successful response to the mother. More technically, children tended to switch codes (languages) after process elicitations by the mother and after evaluation by the mother. In addition, they tended to switch topics at these same interactional junctures. (In a majority of cases they were successful in changing the topic.) This interactional strategy is not surprising, given the less well-established linguistic "ability" in the language which the child switched from.

This codeswitching style is not an interaction style characteristic of adult bilinguals (Lance, 1975). It seems that the mother-child strategies of this study are adapted to the linguistic abilities of the children and the possible language-teaching intent of the mothers (as previously discussed). Further research in this area should consider these present preliminary findings and expand its search for other "representative" styles of codeswitching with other populations of bilinguals. This type of research should add significantly to our present limited knowledge of mother-child bilingual discourse.

REFERENCES

Garcia, E. *Final Report: Bilingual Preschool Research Project.* Report submitted to HEW, Office of Child Development, Washington, D.C., 1978.

Garcia, E. Language switching in bilingual mother child interactions. *TESOL Quarterly,* in press, 1979.

Genishi, C. S. *Rules for codeswitching in young Spanish-English speakers: An exploratory study of language socialization.* Unpublished doctoral dissertation, University of California, Berkeley, 1977.

Gumperz, J. J.   On the linguistic markers of bilingual communication. *The Journal of Social Issues,* 1967, *23*(2); 48–57.

Gumperz, J. J., & Hernandez, E. Cognitive aspects of bilingual communication. In E. Hernandez et al. (Eds.) *El lenguaje de los Chicanos.* Arlington, Va.: Center for Applied Linguistics, 1975.

Lance, D.   Spanish-English codeswitching. In E. Hernandez et al. (Eds.), *El lenguaje de los Chicanos.* Arlington, Va.: Center for Applied Linguistics, 1975.

Leopold, W. F. *Speech development of a bilingual child: A linguist's record.* Vol. I, Vocabulary Growth in the first two years. Evanston, Ill.: Northwestern University Press, 1939.

Leopold, W. F. *Speech development of a bilingual child: A linguist's record.* Vol. II, Sound learning in the first two years. Evanston, Ill.: Northwestern University Press, 1947.

Leopold, W. F. *Speech development of a bilingual child: A linguist's record.* Vol. III, Grammars and general problems in the first two years. Evanston, Ill.: Northwestern University Press, 1949a.

Leopold, W. F. *Speech development of a bilingual child: A linguist's record, Vol. IV. Diary from age two.* Evanston, Ill.: Northwestern University Press, 1949b.

Lindholm, K., & Padilla, A. Language mixing in bilingual children. *Journal of Child Language, 5,* 327–335.

Mehan, H., Cazden, C., Coles, L., Fisher, S., & Maroules, N. *The social organization of classroom lessons,* Center for Human Information Processing Report, December 1976, University of California, San Diego, 1976.

Padilla, A. *Child bilingualism: A study of some Spanish-English bilingual children.* A paper presented at the XV Congreso Interamericano de Psicologia Bogota, Colombia, December 1974. (Paper available through the Department of Psychology UCLA.)

Schultz, J. Language use in bilingual classrooms. Annual Convention of Teachers of English to Speakers of Other Languages (TESOL), Los Angeles, 1975.

Weinrick, U. *Languages in contact.* New York: Linguistic Circle of New York, 1953.

16

Socialization Via Communication: Language Interaction Patterns Used by Hispanic Mothers and Children In Mastery Skill Communication[1]

Kathryn J. Lindholm
Amado M. Padilla
University of California, Los Angeles

From the moment infants are born they are introduced to a social structure in which they must eventually learn to survive. The infant needs to acquire the communicative sophistication necessary to interact within society's rules and to conform to cultural expectations. Communicative competence and socialization will evolve as the child begins to assimilate social, cognitive, linguistic, and contextual information based on social experience. Prerequisite to the child's assimilation of the necessary information for rule integration and application is development of a "set of 'interpretive procedures,' a set of taken-for-granted assumptions that enables the member to see the rules in the first place" (Cook, 1973:331).

During the early years of a child's development, the burden of relaying these interpretive procedures and social rules to children rests within the family unit, especially the parents. Teaching of the pertinent social, cognitive, and linguistic information is largely accomplished through parent-child communication. Recent sociolinguistic research has provided information on

[1]The research reported on here was supported by Research Grant OHD 90-C-905 from the Agency for Children, Youth, and Families. We would like to extend appreciation to the research assistants—Maria Gabriela Alvarez, Hortensia Amaro, Leticia Cuecuecha Lopez—who collected the data and who collaborated with the authors in the development of the coding system. In addition, we are grateful to the staff researchers—Elena Cardona, Ana Maria Garreton, Gloria Monteros, Beatriz Zamudio—who helped to refine the coding system and who coded the data. Also, we wish to thank the secretaries—Dolores Campos, Marisa Campos-Reyes, Cecilia Torres—who transcribed the tapes. Finally, our appreciation is extended to Arturo Romero who located the families and to the families who welcomed us into their homes and shared their familial communication with us.

parent-child interaction (Bloom, 1970; Gleason, 1973; Holzman, 1972; Nelson, 1973). The results indicate that as high a proportion as 33 percent of mothers' speech to their children consists of interrogatives, thus illustrating the importance of the mother's teaching role (Holzman, 1972). Gleason (1973) describes the communication parents direct at their young children as a "teaching language," because it is full of social and conversational rules as well as cognitive and affective information.

A variable which reportedly affects children's socialization and communicative competence is the familial network. Bernstein (1971) discriminates between two types of familial structure: (1) positional, where the decision making is contingent upon the member's "formal status" (age, sex, authority figure); (2) person-oriented, where the decision making is a function of the psychological attributes of a person. In the positional type, the communication system is restricted whereas in person-oriented families the communication system is very open. Essentially, these types of familial patterns and their corresponding communication systems have important socializing and linguistic consequences. Thus according to Bernstein, role definition within the family structure determines in part the familial communication patterns. Furthermore, he notes that the literature strongly suggests that working-class families operate within a positional role network.

Bernstein (1971:125) also distinguishes between two types of communication codes: elaborated and restricted. He defines them

> on a linguistic level, in terms of the probability of predicting for any one speaker which syntactic elements will be used to organize meaning across a representative range of speech. In the case of an elaborated code, the speaker will select from a relatively extensive range of alternatives and the probability of predicting the organizing elements is considerably reduced. In the case of a restricted code the number of these alternatives is often severely limited and the probability of predicting the elements is greatly increased.

Bernstein and his colleagues (Bernstein, 1962, 1971; Bernstein & Brandis, 1970; Bernstein & Henderson, 1973; Henderson, 1973) have investigated the relationship of social class and communication patterns largely in terms of restricted and elaborated codes. Basically, the studies have demonstrated that middle-class mothers tend to use elaborated codes with their children, whereas working-class mothers use restricted codes with their children. Identical results have been obtained when maternal teaching strategies are studied (Bee, Van Egeren, Streissguth, Nyman, & Leckie, 1969; Olim, Hess, & Shipman, 1967). Thus, type of familial role network and mother's language style are associated with socioeconomic status.

One should note that the subject populations in the studies cited have been limited to Black and white working- and middle-class families. An important question at this point is what communication patterns do Mexican-American parents use to socialize their children? This question is important because in many Mexican-American families two cultures and two languages are taught. The available literature does not address the communication patterns of Mexican-American parents, in fact, Padilla and Ruiz (1973) indicate that there is no research which pertains to the socialization practices of Mexican-American parents and only a few studies which are tangentially related to the socialization of the Mexican-American child. A review of the limited research available points out that there are differences in child-rearing attitudes and practices between Mexican-American, Anglo, and Afro-American parents (Durrett, O'Bryant, & Pennebaker, 1975). For example, Mexican-American mothers provide less assistance than Anglo mothers in teaching three-year-old children sorting and motor-skill tasks since they feel teaching is the responsibility of the school (Steward & Steward, 1973; 1974). As a result of differing child-rearing practices, cognitive styles differ for Anglo and Mexican American children (Buriel, 1975; Ramirez & Castañeda, 1974; Ramirez & Price-Williams, 1974). Also, Mexican-American children tend to demonstrate more cooperative behavior than Anglo children (Kagan & Madsen, 1971; Madsen & Shapira, 1970). As might be expected, Mexican-American children with high academic potential come from home environments that offer a greater variety of stimulating experiences than are available to children in a low-potential group (Henderson & Merritt, 1968).

The research relevant to the socialization of Mexican-American children is fragmented and has neglected to control for significant variables, such as generation of family or the influence of other family members, such as siblings, on the child and total family unit. In addition, the majority of studies conducted on socialization practices or communication patterns among family members has been limited to contrived quasi-laboratory settings or to questionnaire data which were obtained either in short periods of time or at one point in time. Considering the preceding methodological limitations, we know very little about the socialization process in Mexican-American families.

The present study proposed to investigate the socialization practices of first-generation immigrant and third-generation Mexican-American parents. Its underlying premise was that socialization is in part a communication process. Thus, focus was on the communcation patterns that occur between parents and children, between other significant adults and children, and between siblings and peers.

Our assumption was that a multitude of sociolinguistic interactions can be categorized into a number of mastery skills where *mastery skills* comprise the behaviors and underlying knowledge usually implied when we speak of *socialization practices*. By categorizing our dependent variable (i.e., sociolinguistic interactions between mother-child, father-child, etc.) into varying types of mastery skills we were able to specify the language patterns used by parents, siblings, or peers in socialization communication. This analysis allows for an understanding of the reciprocal transaction that occurs between interactants in the process of socialization.

Mastery skills are one set of skills primarily acquired through communication which are critical to the child's socialization. They are prerequisite to successful school entrance and adjustment both in terms of the child's self-perceptions and in turn of the teacher's and peers' perceptions of the child. Mastery skills were categorized by the domains of skills and knowledge they represent as follows: adaptive, academic, social, cognitive, language, and moral skills. *Adaptive skills* were defined as the kind of behavioral competencies or knowledge which assist the child in meeting physical and environmental demands (e.g., eating, health care). *Academic* skills referred to those skills and knowledge that pertain primarily to classroom-learning or teaching activities (e.g., knowledge of numbers or colors). *Social* skills were those skills that assist the child in meeting and accepting interpersonal demands (e.g., politeness, sex role expectations). *Cognitive* skills were defined as skills which the child manifests through higher-order processing which is a function of past experience and developmental processes (e.g., memory, conceptualizing time). *Language* skills referred to the knowledge children have about language structure and use including skills that enable the child to learn language more proficiently (e.g., syntax, semantics). *Moral* skills related to the child's internalization of adherence to authority and judgment of proper conduct (e.g., definition of right/wrong).

The present study addressed the following questions:

1. What are the communication strategies that mothers use to teach their children mastery skills?
2. Do these strategies differ for the various categories of mastery skills?
3. Which categories of mastery skill information do mothers emphasize in their communication to children as part of their child-rearing practice?
4. What language strategies do children use in communicating with their siblings that contain mastery skill information?
5. Are the mastery skill communication strategies that children use the same as those used by mothers?

METHOD

Subjects

Twelve Mexican-American families residing in the greater Los Angeles are participated in the study. Eight of the families were first generation; four were third generation. *First generation* is defined as both parents being born in Mexico but now residing in the United States. In the third-generation families, the grandparents of the parents were born in Mexico and immigrated to the United States. The families were chosen in accordance with the following criteria:

1. Generation;
2. That the family consist of four members; a father, mother and two children;
3. That the family members reside together;
4. That the children be between two- and five-years-old;
5. That the older child not yet attend school, but that school attendance begin the following year;
6. That the family be willing to participate weekly for a two-year period.

From the 12 families, we selected six to report on here, representing 42 hours of taped conversation. Three of the families were first generation and three were third generation; sex of children within the six families studied was not used as a criteria for family selection. Further, sex differences in communication strategies between mothers and children were not analyzed for in the current study. All the families selected for study were members of the working class.

A brief description of the six families follows; roman numerals followed by a number indicate generation and family identification number within generation.

I:1 is a first-generation family in which the older child (OC) is male. The data reported on here were collected during the period when the child was 4:10–5:1 years of age. THe younger child (YC) was 3:10–4:1 and a male.

I:2 is a first generation family with two female children. The older child was 4:4–4:7; the younger, 3:2–3:5 years of age.

I:3 is a first-generation family in which OC was a female; 3:9–4:4; YC was male, 2:7–3:2 years of age.

III:1 is a third-generation family in which the male OC was 4:0–4:2; the female YC was 1:7–1:9.

III:2 is a third-generation family with two male children. The older child was 4:9–5.1; the younger, 2:0–2:4.

III:3 is a third-generation family in which the female OC was 4:10–5:5 and the male YC, 3:3–3:10.

Equipment and Recording

Sony cassette taperecorders, TC-205, with Scotch C90 minute tapes, were used to collect the language samples. Books and toys were also taken to the children's homes at times to stimulate the children's spontaneous speech.

Procedure

Each family was visited weekly by a bilingual female experimenter. At this time, the experimenter either taperecorded the parent-child and/or child-child interactions or collected a tape from the parent who had taperecorded the interactions during the week. The parents were encouraged to taperecord the interactions to provide more varied and naturalistic communication. Each family was visited by the same experimenter throughout the duration of the study and was paid $5.00 per visit/tape.

The language sample consisted of interaction between the older child and either the mother, father, younger child, friend, experimenter, or any combination of speakers, with the focus on the interaction of the older child and others.

Tapes were transcribed either by the experimenter or by a bilingual transcriber, in the language(s) in which the interaction occurred. The unit of speech was the *utterance,* which was operationally defined in an earlier study by Padilla and Lindholm (1976):

> (1) a complete thought process; (2) a grammatical phrase; (3) an incomplete phrase due to the child's shift in attention, e.g., "the boy was..." (child stops talking and becomes interested in something else); (4) a one word utterance (e.g., dog or *perro*); and, (5) a repetition of an utterance, elicited by huh?, *¿cómo?* (how?), or *¿qué?* (what?) on the part of another individual, which differs from the initially produced utterance (pp. 123–124).

Every attempt was made to transcribe each word on the tape, but whenever it was impossible to understand what was being said, a (u)/(U) was typed: (u) signified that one word could not be understood, and (U) meant that several words or a whole sentence was unintelligible. In addition, wherever possible, notes of context were included.

Coding

The transcripts were coded with a coding system that integrates a psycholinguistic and sociolinguistic approach to language analysis. More specifically, each utterance in the transcript was coded according to: (1) situational context; (2) the language mode; (3) turntaking; (4) converser; (5) recipient; (6) grammatical form of the utterance; (7) social function of utterance; (8) mastery skills.

Situational context classifies the context in terms of the type of activity that is occurring during the taping. *Language mode* pertains to whether the utterance is in Spanish or English, or if it is mixed or contains a borrowing. *Turn-taking* refers to the flow of discourse and to the allocation of turns to persons in a conversation. Furthermore, for our purposes here we divide turntaking into either the maintenance of a topic or a change in topics with the new allocation to speak. The converser and recipient refer to who is talking and to whom the conversation is directed. *Gramamtical form* categorizes the utterance according to whether it is a declarative statement, question, exclamation, etc., and further breaks these categories down. False starts and overgeneralizations are also included under grammatical form. The *social function* abstracts the intention of the utterance—whether its purpose is to inform, direct behavior, teach, clarify previous utterances, correct, etc. In all, 62 subcategories of mastery skill information were derived from the six categories mentioned earlier (i.e., adaptive, social, academic, language, cognitive, moral) and were used to code conversational content.

RESULTS AND DISCUSSION

The first analysis involved determining what percentage of the mothers' speech was mastery skill communication (MSC), i.e., what percentage of their communication contained mastery skill information. To obtain the percentage of mastery skill information in conversation, the general formula used was:

$$\text{Percent MSC} = \frac{\text{number of utterances containing mastery skill information}}{\text{total number of utterances}}$$

Using this formula it is possible to obtain the mean percentage of the mothers' MSC which is the total number of utterances containing mastery skills directed to the older and/or younger child for the six mothers (i.e., 1917 utterances) divided by the six mothers' total number of utterances directed to the older and/or younger child (i.e., 6330 utterances). The result is a mean percentage of 30, indicating that overall mastery skill information comprised 30 percent of the speech mothers directed to their children. Next, this computational procedure was used to specify each mother's individual percentage of MSC as well as to categorize what percentage of such communication was directed to the older child and what percentage to the younger child. Similarly, the older and younger children's speech was analyzed to determine the mean percentage of MSC between siblings and for each child and the mother.

Table 1 presents the breakdown of MSC between mothers and their children as well as between siblings. Attention to the means presented in Table 1 discovers that overall the mothers produced slightly more speech containing mastery skill information (30 percent) than the older children (28 percent) who in turn engaged in more MSC than the younger children (24 percent). Furthermore, mothers tended to direct more MSC to their older children (32 percent) than to their younger children (25 percent). Both older

TABLE 1
Percentage of Mothers' and Children's Mastery Skill Communication (MSC) Categorized
according to Converser-Recipient Family Relationships*

Converser-Recipient Relationship	Families						Mean % MSC
	I:1	I:2	I:3	III:1	III:2	III:3	
M (mother) total % MSC	30	25	36	20	28	30	30
% MSC M ⟶ OC†	24	15	41	18	30	32	32
% MSC M ⟶ YC	16	35	27	16	9	29	25
OC (older child) total % MSC	20	38	26	17	36	32	28
% MSC OC ⟶ M	24	37	26	18	36	37	31
% MSC OC ⟶ YC	17	42	19	11	13	11	18
YC (younger child) total % MSC	11	27	28	0	0	32	24
% MSC YC ⟶ M	14	28	27	0	0	39	27
% MSC YC ⟶ OC	8	22	32	0	0	15	15

*The converser's total percentage of MSC is not necessarily the addition of the percentage of MSC directed at the two recipients individually. The total percentage of MSC was computed using the utterances directed at both recipients simultaneously as well as those directed at each recipient individually.

†Arrows represent the direction of communication from converser to recipient.

and younger children directed more MSC to their mother (31 percent and 27 percent, respectively) than to their sibling (18 percent and 15 percent respectively). Both older and younger children directed about as much MSC to their mother (31 percent and 27 percent respectively as their mother directed to them (32 percent and 25 percent respectively). Similarly, older and younger siblings produced about the same amount of MSC with each other (18 percent and 15 percent, respectively).

Close inspection of Table 1 also finds that the families differed individually in MSC. For example, the mother in family I:3 produced a much larger percentage of MSC than the other mothers. Most mothers directed more of such communication to their older children, but the mother from family I:2 communicated mastery skill information much more often to her younger child than to her older child. Similarly, the older child from family I:2 also directed a larger proportion of such communication to her sibling than the other older children did.

Although differences existed between families, there did not appear to be any clear differences that could be attributed to generation. For the three first-generation families, the mean percentage of MSC was 32 percent for the mothers, 26 percent for the older children, and 21 percent for the younger children. The three third-generation families produced mean MSC percentages of 28 percent for the mothers, 31 percent for the older children, and 29 percent for the younger children. Thus, generally the first-generation mothers produced slightly more MSC than the third-generation mothers and both the older and the younger third-generation children produced more of such communication than the first-generation children. This variance between the two generations appears to be related to the differential use of MSC among the individual families rather than to any differential patterns of usage among the two generations. For example, family III:1 deflated the percentages of MSC for the third-generation families. In addition, the age of the children varied, with two of the younger children in the third-generation families at the transition stage between preverbal and verbal communication which lessened the amount of communication between the mother and the younger child and between the siblings. It is clear that the differences that did emerge between generations can be attributed to the individual families.

Approximately one-third of all mother-child interactions involves MSC. The most obvious question at this point is: what is the relative frequency of the various categories of mastery skill information that are contained in MSC? To determine which categories of mastery skills were focused on in the mothers' and children's communication, the mastery skills were divided into the six categories defined earlier (i.e., adaptive, social, academic, language, moral, cognitive). Then the computational procedure described was used to classify the percentage of speech containing information relevant to the exercise of each of the six types of mastery skills. Thus, the number of utterances containing adaptive mastery skill information was divided by the total number of utterances for each mother, older child, and younger child in each family. In addition, the mean percentage of each category of mastery skill information for the mothers, older and younger children was obtained. Table 2 presents the percentages of MSC classified according to family, converser, and category of mastery skill.

Table 2 depicts the amount of communication devoted to each category of skill. Obviously, each of the categories of skills separately does not comprise a great portion of conversations between mothers and their children. Academic skills are discussed in more of the mothers' utterances than any other category of skill, but they reflect only 14 percent of the mothers' speech. Academic skills, however, represent 55 percent of the mothers' MSC. Table 3 presents the mean relative percentages of the appearance of the six categories of skills in the mothers', older children's and younger children's communication.

Inspection of Table 3 indicates that more mastery skill information was devoted to academic skills than to any other category of skill regardless of

TABLE 2
Percentage of Mothers' and Children's Mastery Skill Communication (MSC) Classified
According to Category of Mastery Skill

Category of Mastery Skill		Families						Mean % MSC
		I:1	I:2	I:3	III:1	III:2	III:3	
Adaptive: Mother	(M)	1	2	1	8	.7	1	1
Older child	(OC)	5	1	.5	0	1	4	.6
Younger child	(YC)	1	2	.6	0	0	1	.8
Social:	M	.5	0	1	3	1	2	1.5
	OC	1	.3	1	2	1.7	.3	1
	YC	0	1	.3	0	0	.6	.4
Academic:	M	14	11	22	7	7	12	14
	OC	7	25	13	8	11	9	11.3
	YC	8	15	19	0	0	17	12
Language:	M	.4	.1	.5	.8	.3	.1	3
	OC	1	0	.1	0	.1	0	.2
	YC	0	0	0	0	0	0	0
Moral:	M	.6	2	.2	3	2	1	1
	OC	.3	0	0	1	.3	0	.1
	YC	0	.2	0	0	0	0	.1
Cognitive:	M	4	9	6	2	8.5	12	7.5
	OC	9	9	28	4	13	16.5	9
	YC	2	9	4	0	0	9	6

converser. Cognitive skills are the second most discussed category of skill. The remaining categories of skills are referred to much less frequently. In fact, each category made up only 6 percent of mastery skill communication which means they received only 1.5 percent or less discussion in general speech.

The remaining analyses yield results which are largely observational rather than quantitative. First, we wanted to determine which subclasses of skills comprising each category of mothers' and children's MSC appeared frequently. A criterion of three out of six families for the mothers, and two out of six families for the children referring to that particular skill was established. Table 4 presents the classification of the most frequently discussed individual skills for each of the six categories of mastery skills.

Attention to Table 4 indicates that for the adaptive skills, the mothers concentrated on health care, use of money, and personal reference (e.g., name, address). The children discussed personal reference, family reference (e.g., naming grandma/abuelita, mother) and use of money the most. In terms of social skills, the mothers directed their attention to argument settlement, politeness, and sharing; the children were more interested in sex differentiation, sex role expectations, and ethnicity as well as sharing and helping behaviors. With the academic skills, mothers focused on object

TABLE 3
Mean Relative Percentages of the Six Categories of
Mastery Skill Communication (MSC)

Category of Mastery Skill		Mean % MSC
Adaptive: Mother	(M)	4
Older Children	(OC)	2.5
Younger Children	(YC)	4.4
Social:	M	6
	OC	5
	YC	2
Academic:	M	55
	OC	50.5
	YC	64.3
Language:	M	1
	OC	1
	YC	0
Moral:	M	4
	OC	1
	YC	.3
Cognitive:	M	30
	OC	40
	YC	29

identification, numbers, and storytelling. The children also concentrated on object identification the most, and the older children additionally discussed, in decreasing importance, numbers, and animals, the younger children, animals and colors.

The younger children did not meet the criterion for language or moral skills, but mothers centered on phonology and lexicon in language skill communication and adherence to authority for moral skill communication. For the older children, reference to second language was the most frequent language skill discussed and reference to authority was the most frequent moral skill discussed. In terms of cognitive skills, mothers and children focused on reasoning or inferring and descriptive conceptualization; mothers only communicated numerical conceptualization to their children. The younger children referred to spatial conceptualization and the older children to creative representation as well. Overall, the most common mastery skills referred to in conversation involved object identification (an academic skill) and object description (a cognitive skill).

What follows are several conversational interactions which exemplify particular instances of MSC. Other mastery skill components of conversation were coded from these interactions, but each interaction exemplifies and is mostly devoted to one particular mastery skill. The first interaction is taken from family III:3 and involves the mother (M), and older child (OC) and the

TABLE 4

Classification of Most Frequently Discussed Individual Skills for Each of the Six Categories of Mastery Skill Communication (MSC)

Converser	Relative Frequency	Adaptive	Social	Academic	Language	Moral	Cognitive
					MSC Category		
M	1	Health Care	Argument Settlement	Object Identification	Phonology	Adherence to Authority	Reasoning/Inferring
	2	Currency	Politeness	Numbers	Lexicon	0	Description
	3	Personal Reference	Sharing	Storytelling	0	0	Classifying Quantity
OC	1	Personal Reference	Sex Differentation	Object Identification	Reference to Second Language	Adherence to Authority	Reasoning/Inferring
	2	Family Reference	Helping Behaviors	Numbers	0	0	Description
	3	Currency	Sharing	Animals	0	0	Creativity/Symbolizing
YC	1	Family Reference	Sex Role Expectations	Object Identification	0	0	Description
	2	Personal Reference	Ethnicity	Animals	0	0	Reasoning/Inferring
	3	Currency	0	Colors	0	0	Classifying Space

younger child (YC). (The children's names are replaced by their corresponding codes of OC or YC to protect the family's right to privacy). This communication is primarily centered around the social skill of argument settlement:

   M: Go put his cars away OC.
OC: He said I could play with them.
YC: I did not.
OC: You did too.
  M: Heh... did you say she could play with them YC?
YC: (Shakes head).
OC: You did too.
  M: She wouldn't have taken them if you didn't say she could.
YC: She did take them.
  M: Did you say she could play with them?
YC: No!
  M: YC... did you say she could play with them?
YC: I said no.
  M: Are you sure?
OC: He did say yes.
  M: (To YC) Okay... look into my eyes. Open your eyes. Look into my eyes. Did you say she could play with them?
YC: No I didn't.
  M: (To OC) Well then you better go put them away.
OC: He said I could. He did too.
  M: She said that you said she could, did you?
YC: I don't know.
OC: Then I said... I said he really did let me.

The next example was obtained from family I:2 where the mother is teaching the older child academic mastery skill information pertaining to the subcategory of alphabet:

  M: *¿Qué letras son éstas?*
     (What letters are these?)
OC: *U... la U.*
  M: No, *no es la U. Es la P.*
     (No, it's not U. It's P.)
OC: *La P.* (Imitation)
OC: *¿Y éste?*
     (And this one?)
  M: *Es la A.*
     (It's A.)

OC: *La cuatro.*
  (Four)
M: *Se parece un cuatro pero es una A.*
  (It looks like a four but it's an A.)
OC: *Ah...¿y éste?*
  (Oh...and this one?)
M: *La P.*
OC: *La P.* (imitation)...*¿Y éste?*
  (And this one?)

The adaptive mastery skill pertaining to the subcategory personal reference is evident in the following exchange between the mother and younger child of family III:3:

M: His name is David just like yours.
YC: I was named Davy...I'm named Davy.
M: Your real name's David.
YC: His name is David.
M: What's your whole name?
YC: (provides his nickname).
M: What's your whole name? (Pause) David.
YC: Davis.

Moral mastery skills are seen in the next interaction in which the mother of family III:2 teaches the older child about the importance of prayer:

M: We have to pray before we do anything else, all right?
OC: Hmm? (what?)
M: We have to pray. Would you pray?
OC: Let me turn on the TV.
M: TV makes too much noise while we're eating dinner. Let's pray. Dear Lord, thank you for this day. Thank you for our food, Lord.
OC: No, I do it.
M: Okay.
OC: Thank you for (Unintelligible).
M: I can't hear you.
OC: Okay. Thank you God, thank you for Daddy and thank you (U)...
M: Louder, I can't hear you. OC, start again now. Come on.
OC: (Unintelligible word) Daddy and Momma. God love us, uh, let us (Unintelligible), always be good and don't fight, and Amen.
M: Amen. Thank you OC. That's good.

Language skills are evident in the following examples from families I:3, III:2 and III:1:

I:3: OC: El tolefono.

      M: *Te-lé-fono* (corrects pronunciation)

III:2: M: Okay, how do you say "horse" in Spanish?

      OC: *Caballo.*

      M: Caballo, okay.

III:1 OC: I know how to count in English.

      M: Okay, let's hear you count.

      OC: *Uno.*

      M: That's in Spanish. *Uno.*

      OC: *Uno.*

      M: What else?

      OC: *Des.*

      M: *Dos* (corrects pronunciation).

      OC: *Dos, tes.*

      M: *Tres* (corrects pronunciation).

A large portion of the mastery skill communication contained reference to more than one mastery skill. The majority of these interactions addressed cognitive and academic skills simultaneously. The following interaction from family III:1 pertained primarily to both colors, an academic mastery skill, and class inclusion, a cognitive mastery skill:

    OC: See a dark blue, huh.

    M: What's that one?

    OC: That's a blue blue.

    M: How 'bout a light blue.

       A blue blue (laughs).

    OC: (U) a dark blue.

       Cause this is how blues be... dark.

Mothers also spent much time communicating academic information (e.g., as in story telling), which included communication regarding other academic skills (e.g., animals), cognitive skills (e.g., problem solving) or language skills. The following example, from family I:1, contains a number of references to mastery skill information, concerning storytelling, exposure to second language, translation, and classifying of time skills:

    M: *Aquí se lee primero.*

       (Here, we'll read this first.)

    OC: *Sí, otra vez.*

       (Yeah, again.)

    M: *Ya*... Snow White and the seven dwarfs. Okay... *dice:* Once upon a time in a far far land.

OC: *A ver...*
   (Let's see...)
 M: Yeah...Once upon a time in a far away land a lovely queen sat by
   window...(continues reading story)...
   ¿Oístes lo que te dije?
   (Did you hear what I said?)
OC: *¿Qué?*
   (What?)
 M: *Que ésta era la reina de de un país* muy lejos...y...
   (That this one was a queen from a country very far away...and...)

The mother continued to translate the story into Spanish. Occasionally, she
switched back to reading in English, but then she would translate it into
Spanish, especially when the older child asked her to:

 M: As the year passed Snow White grew more and more beautiful and
   her sweet nature made everyone love her.
OC: (Interrupts) *!En español!*
   (In Spanish!)
 M: *!Pos está en inglés mijo!*
   (But it's in English son)
   ¿Cómo te voy a decir en español?
   (How am I going to say it in Spanish?)
OC: *Quiero en español.*
   (I want it in Spanish)
   ¿Oqué?
   (Okay?)
 M: Um...*con-cuando los años pasaron Blanca Nieves creció muy
   grande y muy hermosa y como era tan hermosa, todo el mundo la
   quería...*
   (Um...as the years passed Snow White grew very tall and very
   beautiful and since she was so beautiful, everyone loved her...)

Thus, a number of utterances referred to more than one mastery skill. Most
of the multiple MSC contained reference to a cognitive skill combined with
reference to information from one or more other categories of mastery skills.
   Context of an utterance or the general activity surrounding a conversation
in part determines the category of mastery skill and even the individual
subcategories of mastery skills that will be discussed. Although the parents
were instructed that we wanted naturalistic conversation, a large number of
the tapes contained contexts in which the mother is reading the child a story.
Conseqently, the academic skills are frequently discussed, especially the skills
of storytelling and object identification. The majority of contexts are simple
conversations where interaction between speakers is the only activity

occurring. Within this conversational context, one finds object description (a kind of cognitive skill) as well as an array of other skills, such as adherence to authority (a kind of moral skill). For game playing activities, the most frequent skill discussed is directions, an academic mastery skill, helping behavior, a social mastery skill; for paper-and-pencil tasks, the most common specific skills were numbers (an academic mastery skill) and spatial conceptualizing (a cognitive mastery skill). There are several taped conversations of children bathing or during meal times. The mastery skill conveyed in communications in these tapes clustered around cleanliness and health care for bathing situations and around eating for contexts involving meal times. The cognitive mastery skills of reasoning, inferring, and problem solving as the referents of conversation seemed to recur independently of situational context. In sum, as one would have expected, contexts which were academically related (reading, paper and pencil tasks, game playing) tended to produce more communication containing reference to academic mastery skills, and contexts pertaining to adaptive situations (bathing, eating) provoked mention of adaptive mastery skill information. Informal conversational contexts tended to include reference to academic or related cognitive mastery skills.

We now address the remaining communication patterns pertaining to the language environment, grammatical form, and social functions used in MSC. First and most obvious, choice of either Spanish or English differed as a function of generation; the first-generation families communicated almost exclusively in Spanish whereas the third-generation families interacted almost entirely in English. Second, an analysis of the grammatical form of MSC demonstrated that all conversers, regardless of whom the recipient was, most frequently communicated their information with declaratives. There were far fewer questions than we had thought there would be. In fact, in view of Corsaro's (1979) findings that 38.7 percent of the mother's speech to her child consists of interrogatives, many of which were not specifically seeking information, we expected that mothers would "test" their children with questions while teaching them mastery skills. Results revealed that a large number of the mothers' MSC contained questions of the Wh-K/D form (e.g., why, where, etc., in English and *qué, dónde,* etc., in Spanish) or questions requiring a simple yes or no answer. Nonetheless, the majority of utterances consisted of declaratives. Additionally, it was hypothesized that children would ask their mothers many questions during MSC, but the data indicated the children's more frequent use of declaratives. The declaratives of the mothers and older children usually contained more words than the younger children's declaratives; however, the use of shorter vs. longer declaratives seemed to be associated with who the recipient was. Both older and younger children produced more declaratives consisting of one or two words than the mothers. But both older and younger children tended to use these shorter declaratives much more frequently with their mothers whereas they used longer declaratives with their siblings.

Mothers produced more Wh-K/D type questions than yes-*sí*/no questions. Also, questions were more frequent during academic MSC than any other category of mastery skill, followed by cognitive MSC. Imperatives appeared much more often when social skills were being communicated than with any of the remaining categories of mastery skills.

The *social function* of an utterance refers to the illocutionary, perlocutionary, or other purposes of an utterance in context and it consists predominantly of speech acts involving relaying of information, requesting information, and directive statements. As with grammatical form, the social function of utterances was found to covary with the occurrences of the various categories of MSC. For social and moral MSC, mothers used predominantly the directive and personal events/activities social functions. The absolute information social function, which involves relaying factual, descriptive, or characteristic information about objects, people, or events, was used more frequently, especially for academic, language and cognitive MSC. Children evidenced more absolute information social functions overall, even for social and moral skills where the mothers in contrast used directives and personal events/activities social functions. Older children, however, also used the personal thoughts information function for social MSC.

For our purpose here the social function labeled *teaching* is defined as a speech act where the purpose is to teach a word or concept (e.g., this color is red.). Mothers frequently used the teaching function combined with the absolute information function, especially for academic and cognitive MSC. In fact, approximately a quarter of the academic MSC, consisting of absolute information was combined with the social function of teaching, except in the case of children who rarely utilized the teaching social functions altogether. In addition, mothers used the correction social function in communicating language skills to their children. When older children referred to language skills in their speech, they often relied on the imitation social function. For the adaptive, academic, and cognitive skills, the children relied primarily on the absolute information social function, although they also tended to use the personal information with the adaptive skills category. Mothers were seen to use directives often, but their children rarely used the directive form in mastery skill communication.

To determine the most frequent communication pattern for the grammatical and social functions, for purposes of analysis of mastery skill content, utterances were first examined to establish which grammatical functions were consistently used with which social functions. The data indicated that the most common pattern consisted of a declarative grammatical function plus an absolute information social function. This pattern occurred most frequently when the content of communication concerned academic and cognitive mastery skills. In the communication of adaptive, social, and moral mastery skill information, the most common functional communication pattern was an imperative grammatical function plus a directive social function, although declaratives and the various categories of information social functions were also noted. Mothers were never observed to use directives with questions of any kind; in almost every speech act studied, directives were grammatically structured as declaratives or imperatives.

For all the categories of MSC there were many combinations of grammatical plus social functions within which such communications were embedded. The consistency of certain patterns seemed to differ according to individual families. For example, the mother in family I:3 produced a much greater variety of such combinations than the other families. The older child of this family followed suit in producing a greater variety of combinations of grammatical plus social functions, as did the older child in family III:3. Whatever the variety of patterns observed across families, enough frequent communication patterns emerged so that one could propose a rule for the most frequently occurring communication patterns that were observed in the mothers' as well as the children's MSC.

Before actually proposing such a rule, however, another dimension of communication must be discussed. This dimension concerns topic maintenance or change following turntaking in conversation. Mothers and children referred to information pertaining to the categories of mastery skills in different ways which influenced the topic of discourse. Adaptive, social, moral, and language skill information was for the most part, referred to but not discussed as a topic of discourse. That is, references to these skills were interspersed throughout communication in general, but these skills were not discussed as topics of conversation. Similarly, cognitive skills did not comprise conversation topics, but they appeared regularly in interactions. In contrast are the academic skills which did appear as discourse topics. Mothers and children engaged in conversations about animals, numbers, or colors, but rarely did they talk about, for example, sex role expectations. Thus, the integration of mastery skill information into conversation differed depending on whether the topic of communication was directed at academic vs. other mastery skills. This difference in integration of mastery skill information was not, however, reflected in the overall flow of conversation from turn to turn. The discourse topic was maintained even when there was a switch from regular communication to communication of mastery skill information. Academic skill information was almost the only exception to this, and even when an academic skill formed the discourse topic, the flow of discourse was usually maintained because the more general topic of conversation largely concerned academic skills.

A general rule is offered for incorporating results obtained from topic maintenance, turntaking, language environment, converser-recipient relationships, grammatical form, social function, and categories of mastery skills. The rule which is depicted in Figure 1 accounts for communication of

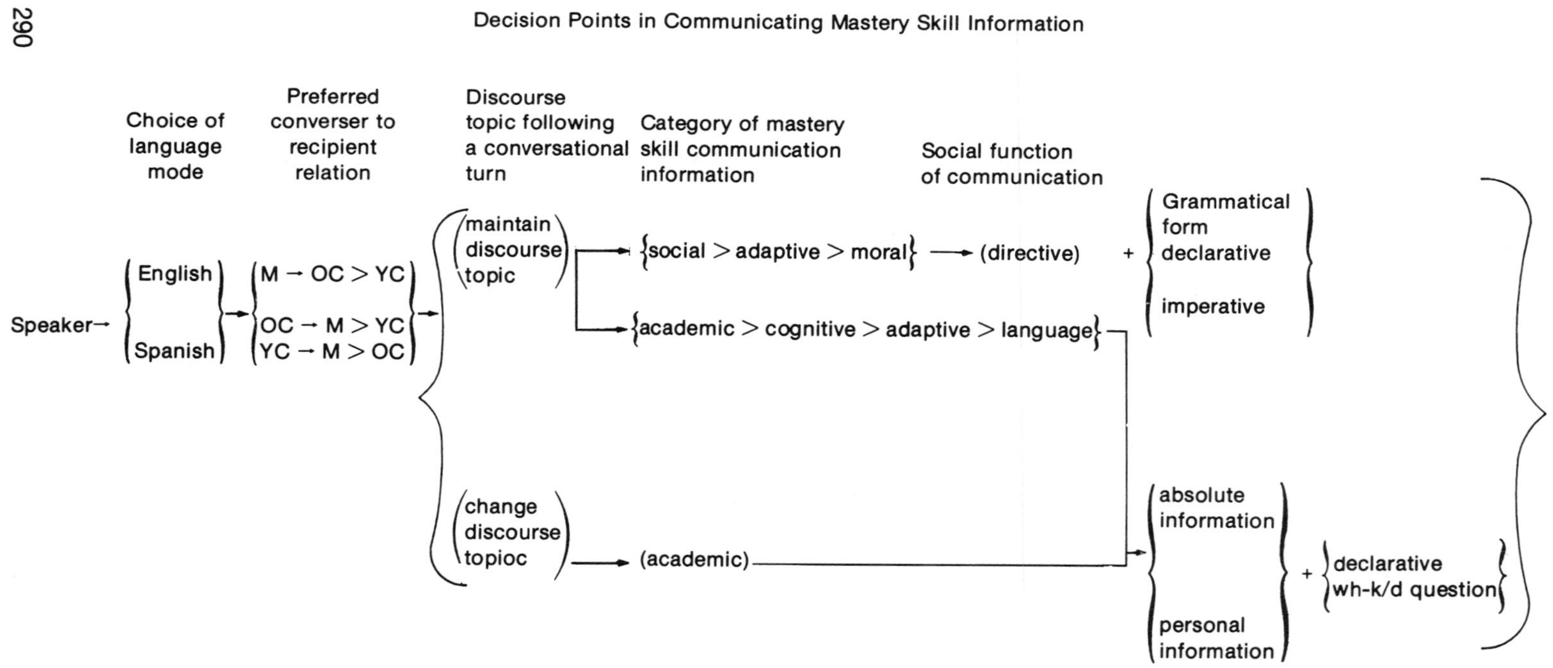

Figure 1. Mastery skill communication rule integrating choice of language mode, converser-recipient relationships, selecting of discourse topic, accompanying turntaking, categories of mastery skills and their relative possibilities of appearance, social functions, and grammatical form of the speech utterance.

mastery skill information. Reading Figure 1 from left to right shows major decision points and alternatives that speakers must consider in communicating mastery skill information.[2] This rule explains a large portion of the mother-child and sibling communication in the current study pertaining to mastery skills. It specifies that a language mode (English or Spanish) will be chosen and signifies the possibilities of converser-recipient relationships and indicates the greater likelihood of one recipient over another; for example, $M \rightarrow OC > YC$ indicates that a mother (M) is more likely to communicate mastery skill information to an older child (OC) than to a younger child (YC). Next, it shows that any converser, regardless of recipient, may change or maintain a discourse topic. Across conversational turns if the topic is changed, the new topic is usually concerned with academic skill information and the social function is most frequently information of an absolute or personal nature and the grammatical form of utterances is a declarative or a Wh-K/D or a yes or no question. Finally, if the converser maintains the topic, the relative order of mastery skill categories about which the conversation focuses is shown in Figure 1 along with the social and grammatical forms corresponding to the mastery skill in question.

For the most part sibling interaction was very similar to mother-child communication. That is, children seemed to use the same communication patterns in their MSC with each other as the mothers produced with the children. The only notable differences occurred with grammatical forms of utterances and their social functions. For grammatical form, the children produced more complete sentences with each other than they did with their mother. Even younger children who frequently used one- to two-word utterances would produce longer utterances in communicating with their older sibling. Mothers quite often would directly teach a skill, especially academic skills usually combining the teaching social function with another social function, such as absolute information. Children rarely used the teaching function.

In sum, mother-child and sibling MSC is very similar and for the most part follows the rule presented in Figure 1. Socialization as we have defined it here comprises almost one-third of the communication between the mothers and their children. This high frequency of communicative socialization conforms to Gleason's (1973) description of mother-child language as a "teaching language," especially with such a large number of utterances classified as providing information. Consequently, we disagree with the laboratory studies that have been conducted with working-class families suggesting that working-class mothers use some sort of restricted communication code in their maternal teaching strategies (Bee, Van Egeren, Streissguth, Nyman, &

---

[2]The operation of the rule as a cognitive and linguistic activity need not occur, in real time, exactly in the order indicated. The intent of the rule is rather to show the interdependence of different decisions that are made in communicating mastery skill information.

Leckie, 1969; Olim, Hess, & Shipman, 1967). On the contrary, our working-class mothers' communication is loaded with the direct and indirect teaching of mastery skills.

Further data analyses will determine the authenticity of the MSC rule we have extracted from our current data and future augmentation of this rule will incorporate other aspects, such as other familial converser-recipient relationships (e.g., father–older child) not considered in our present study.

Note that experimental bias operates to some extent in the language interactions. Perhaps academic skills were emphasized because the parents felt this was what was wanted in the way of taping conversations, even though, they were repeatedly informed that we wanted naturalistic speech. In addition, the older child was the focus of the project and perhaps more language was directed at him/her than usual. Further, the bulk of social, moral, and adaptive skills are transmitted sporadically throughout the day and recording a small segment of conversation in any week represents only a minuscule sample of such interaction. Yet, we think that the data reported here are representative of the type of communication that occurs between parents and children, despite the limited sampling of naturalistic speech in any week and despite parents' initial beliefs of what we as experimenter were seeking in the recordings.

In conclusion, we have shown that much of what occurs in the process of socialization can be studied through an analysis of the patterns of communication between mothers and their offspring. Mastery skill communication as observed in our study follows an orderly course that enables description according to a coding system that distinguishes between types of mastery skill information, social function of the communication, and the grammatical form taken by the speaker to communicate a skill. Further, our study was undertaken with working-class families, yet it illustrates the richness of communication strategies among the mothers and children studied. These data document that elaborate communication strategies are not confined to middle-class families as Bernstein and Henderson (1973) argue. Future studies of the type reported on here will enrich our understanding of the socialization of children from Hispanic working-class families. An important consideration in such studies not discussed in the current study should be the way in which bilingualism determines how mastery skill information is communicated.

REFERENCES

Bee, H. L., Van Egeren, L. F., Streissguth, A. P., Nyman, B. A., & Leckie, M. S. Social class differences in maternal teaching strategies and speech patterns. *Developmental Psychology,* 1959, *1,* 726–734.

Bernstein, B. Social class, linguistic codes and grammatical elements. *Language and speech,* 1962, *5,* 31–46.

Bernstein, B. *Class, codes and control.* Vol. 2, *Theoretical studies towards a sociology of language.* London: Routledge & Kegan Paul, 1971.

Bernstein, B., & Brandis, W. Social class differences in communication and control. In W. Brandis & D. Henderson (Eds.), *Social class, language and communication.* London: Routledge & Kegan Paul, 1970.

Bernstein, B., & Henderson, D. Social class differences in the relevance of language to socialization. In B. Bernstein (Ed.), *Class, codes and control.* Vol. 2, *Applied studies towards a sociology of language.* London: Routledge & Kegan Paul, 1973.

Bloom, L. *Language development: Form and function in emerging grammars.* Cambridge, Mass.: MIT Press, 1970.

Buriel, R. Cognitive styles among three generations of Mexican American children. *Journal of Cross-Cultural Psychology, 1975, 6,* 417–429.

Cook, J. Language and socialization: A critical view. In B. Bernstein (Ed.), *Class, codes and control.* Vol. 2: Applied studies toward a sociology of language. London: Routledge & Kegan Paul, 1973.

Corsaro, W. A. Sociolinguistic patterns in adult-child interaction. In E. Ochs & B. B. Schieffelin (Eds.), *Developmental pragmatics.* New York: Academic Press, 1979.

Durrett, M. E., O'Bryant, S., & Pennebaker, J. W. Child-rearing report of black, white, and Mexican American families. *Developmental Psychology,1975, 11,* 871.

Gleason, J. B. Codeswitching in children's language. In T. Moore (Ed.), *Cognitive development and the acquisition of language.* New York: Academic Press, 1973.

Henderson, D. Contextual specificity, discretion and cognitive socialization: with special reference to language. In B. Bernstein (Ed.), *Class, codes and control. Volume 2, Applied studies towards a sociology of language.* London: Routledge Kegan Paul, 1973.

Henderson, R. W., & Merritt, C. B. Environmental backgrounds of Mexican American children with different potentials for school success. *Journal of Social Psychology,* 1968, *75,* 101–106.

Holzman, M. The use of interrogative forms in the verbal interaction of three mothers and their children. *Journal of Psycholinguistic Research,* 1972, *1,* 311–336.

Kagan, S., & Madsen, M. C. Cooperation and competition of Mexican, Mexican-American, and Anglo-American children of two ages under four instructional sets. *Developmental Psychology,* 1971, *5,* 32–39.

Madsen, M. C., & Shapira, A. Cooperative and competitive behavior of urban Afro-American, Anglo-American, Mexican-American, and Mexican village children. *Developmental Psychology,* 1970, *3,* 16–20.

Nelson, C. Structure and strategy in learning to talk. *A Monograph of the Society for Research in Child Development,* 1973, *149*(38), Nos. 1–2.

Olim, E. G., Hess, R. D., & Shipman, V. C. Role of mothers' language styles in mediating their preschool children's cognitive development. *School Review,* 1967, *75,* 414–424.

Padilla, A. M., & Lindholm, K. J. Development of interrogative, negative and possessive forms in the speech of young Spanish/Engish bilinguals. *The Bilingual Review/La Revista Bilingüe,* 1976, *3,* 122–152.

Padilla, A. M., & Ruiz, R. A. *Latino mental health: A review of literature.* Washington, D.C.: Government Printing Office, 1973.

Ramirez, M., & Castañeda, A. *Cultural democracy, bicognitive development, and education.* New York: Academic Press, 1974.

Ramirez, M., & Price-Williams, D. R. Cognitive styles of children of three ethnic groups in the United States. *Journal of Cross-Cultural Psychology,1974, 5,* 212–219.

Steward, M., & Steward, D. The observation of Anglo, Mexican and Chinese-American mothers teaching their young sons. *Child Development,* 1973, *44,* 329–337.

Steward, M., & Steward, D. Effects of social distance on teaching strategies of Anglo-American and Mexican-American mothers. *Developmental Psychology,* 1974, *10,* 797–807.

17 Maternal Teaching Strategies and Cognitive Styles in Chicano Families*

Luis M. Laosa
Educational Testing Service

Hypotheses, derived from field-dependence theory, were tested concerning (a) the role that cognitive styles play in determining maternal teaching strategies, (b) the role of these strategies in children's development of cognitive style, and (c) the emergence of cognitive styles in Chicano children. Forty-three Chicano mothers were observed teaching their own 5-year-old children. Relatively field-independent mothers used inquiry and praise as teaching strategies, and field-dependent mothers used modeling. Trends suggest that the teaching strategies to which the child is exposed may influence which cognitive style the child develops. The data provide evidence of construct validity for Chicano women and suggest that at age 5, field dependence—field independence begins to emerge as a coherent construct in Chicano children.

Considering the apparent differences in modes of interaction between people with different cognitive styles (Witkin & Goodenough, 1977), one would expect parents with contrasting cognitive styles to differ in the approaches

*Reprinted from *Journal of Educational Psychology,* 1980, *72,* 45–54. (Copyright American Psychological Association.)

This study was supported in part by a Spencer Foundation faculty research grant through the University of California, Los Angeles, Graduate School of Education and in part by Grant RR05729-02 from the Biomedical Research Support Grant Program, Division of Research Resources, National Institutes of Health, through Educational Testing Service.

Appreciation is expressed to Dorothy Torres, Perla Pflaster, Luiza Amodeo, Luis Moll, Roberto Rueda, Denise Minden, Tina Rueda, and Patricia Conry-Oseguera for research assistance, to Jack Krakower and Janet Allen for assistance in data processing, and to Jessie Cryer for assistance in manuscript preparation. The author is grateful to Herman A. Witkin and Walter Emmerich for helpful comments on a previous draft of the article.

Requests for reprints should be sent to Luis M. Laosa, Educational Testing Service, Princeton, New Jersey 08541.

that they take in teaching their own children. Conversely, it is reasonable to expect, as cognitive style theory predicts (Goodenough & Witkin, Note 1), that certain patterns of parental teaching behavior influence children's development of cognitive styles.

In the most recent formulation of field-dependence theory (Witkin & Goodenough, Note 2), the designations of field-dependent and field-independent cognitive styles are applied to the contrasting tendencies to rely primarily either on external referents or on the self. The theory further assumes that the degree of autonomy from external referents will have two important consequences. First, it may affect the manner of processing information from the field. A person who functions less autonomously would tend to adhere to the dominant properties of the field as given. A more autonomous individual would more likely restructure the field by using internal referents as mediators; that is, he or she would "go beyond the information given" or "act on the field." Second, primary reliance on external referents is likely to increase the frequency of opportunities for developing interpersonal competencies; hence, field-dependent people are likely to develop greater interpersonal competence. The field dependence–field independence cognitive style dimension is conceived as bipolar and neutral with regard to value, with each pole having adaptive value in particular situations (Witkin & Goodenough, Note 2; Witkin, Goodenough, & Oltman, Note 3).

Three sets of questions are addressed in this study. One set centers on the role that cognitive styles play in determining individual differences in maternal teaching strategies. A second set of questions focuses on the role of maternal teaching strategies as mediators of children's development of cognitive styles. A third focuses on the emergence of cognitive styles as a coherent construct among Chicanos.[1]

Maternal Teaching Strategies and Cognitive Styles

Are maternal teaching strategies selected, organized, and controlled as a function of field-dependent and field-independent cognitive styles? If that is the case, what strategies do relatively field-dependent and field-independent mothers use to teach their own young children? Field-dependence theory provides the basis for making general predictions regarding how people with

---

[1]The term *Chicano,* as used in this study, refers to persons who were born in Mexico and now hold United States citizenship or otherwise live in the United States or whose parents or more remote ancestors immigrated to the United States from Mexico. It also refers to persons who trace their lineage to Hispanic or Indo-Hispanic forebears who resided within Spanish or Mexican territory that is now part of the southwestern United States.

a field-dependent or a field-independent cognitive style will behave in certain specific role relationships, such as that between teachers and students in the classroom and that between therapists and their clients (Witkin, Moore, Goodenough, & Cox, 1977); and it seems that how individual differences in cognitive styles find expression varies as a function of the specific role relationships. Field-dependence theory, in its present stage of evolution, does not provide precise hypotheses regarding the role that cognitive styles play in determining maternal teaching strategies. At least three different predictions are possible; they need not be mutually exclusive, however. First, one may hypothesize that mothers will exhibit teaching behaviors that reflect their own cognitive styles. Thus, in teaching their own children, field-independent mothers may restructure the field and act autonomously of external referents.

A second possible type of prediction is that mothers will adopt teaching strategies that are likely to foster in their children the development of a particular cognitive style. Thus mothers, regardless of their own cognitive styles, may encourage sex typing in their children's development of cognitive style. The field-independent cognitive style carries with it characteristics that are traditionally associated with the male role, and males tend to be more field-independent than females (Witkin & Berry, 1975). Hence, mothers may more frequently adopt with girls than with boys strategies that "demand" from the child reliance on external referents and acceptance of the field as given, thereby encouraging girls to develop a field-dependent cognitive style. Or, considering that there appears to be a tendency for people of similar cognitive styles to feel greater attraction toward each other and perhaps to achieve greater progress in the goals of their interactions than persons mismatched on cognitive style (Witkin et al., 1977), one could predict that each mother, regardless of the child's sex, will adopt teaching strategies that stimulate her child's development of a cognitive style similar to her own.

A third possible prediction is that mothers will adopt the teaching strategies that better meet the learning needs that emanate from each child's cognitive style (Witkin et al., 1977). For example, we know that field-dependent children tend to perform less well on learning tasks that lack clear structure (Goodenough, 1976; Shapson, 1977). Hence, whatever their own cognitive styles, mothers may use with field-dependent children teaching strategies that help to structure the field.

Maternal Teaching Strategies as Mediators of Children's Development of Cognitive Styles

Do certain maternal teaching strategies influence children's development of field dependence-field independence? Which teaching strategies seem most likely to foster the development of each cognitive style in children? For these questions, precise predictions can be derived from field-dependence theory. Results of early exploratory studies (Dyk & Witkin, 1965; Witkin, Dyk, Faterson, Goodenough, & Karp, 1962/1974) led to the hypothesis that child-rearing practices that encourage autonomous functioning foster the development of a field-independent cognitive style. In contrast, child-rearing practices that stress dominant control, conformance to authority, and harsh punishment are likely to encourage a more field-dependent cognitive style. More recent studies have added confirmatory evidence for this hypothesis (see Goodenough & Witkin, Note 1, for a review), although a few did not conform to it (Hoppe, Kagan, & Zahn, 1977; Goodenough & Witkin, Note 1). Therefore, it is hypothesized that mothers' use of maternal teaching strategies that encourage autonomous functioning, on the one hand, or dominant control, conformance to authority, and harsh punishment, on the other, will foster the development of a relatively field-independent or field-dependent cognitive style, respectively, in children.

Emergence of Cognitive Styles

The third focus of the study is on the age at which field dependence–field independence appears as a coherent cluster of behaviors in Chicano children and on the presence of such a cluster in adult Chicano females like that commonly found in adult Anglo-American females and males as well. Numerous studies over a wide variety of cultures indicate that field dependence–field independence is evident as a coherent cluster of measures as early as 6 to 7 years of age (Holtzman et al., 1975; Witkin & Berry, 1975). However, the evidence on whether field dependence–field independence is firmly established in children *younger* than 6 years is scanty, although it suggests two conclusions (Kogan, 1976): (a) At 4 to 5 years the various indicators of field dependence-field independence do not yet comprise a coherent cluster, and (b) the cluster emerges slightly earlier in girls than in boys. The present study examines (a) whether the field dependence-field independence dimension has emerged as a coherent cluster of measures in Chicano children by 5 years of age, (b) whether the dimension is firmly established as a coherent cluster of measures in adult Chicano females, and (c) whether the finding that cognitive styles emerge earlier in girls than in boys can be generalized cross-subculturally to Chicanos.

The reason for selecting Chicanos as subjects for the study is to test the generalizability of field-dependence theory to Chicanos, an issue that has become a focus of much interest in psychology and education (Hoppe et al., 1977; Laosa, 1977; Ramirez & Castañeda, 1974).

METHOD

Subjects

The subjects were 43 Chicano mother-child dyads (20 boys, 23 girls). The children were in kindergarten in either of two public schools in Los Angeles. The mean age of the children was 69.81 months, SD = 4.36, the mean age of the mothers was 33.79 years, SD = 6.46. The fathers' occupational statuses ranged from service workers other than in private households to professional and technical (M = 4.37, SD = 1.33).[2] The mothers' occupational statuses ranged from housewives not employed outside the home (67%), to service workers other than in private households to professional and technical (M = 1.67, SD = 2.65). All but one of the families were intact.

From the children in the two schools whose parents volunteered to participate, the sample was selected to be as representative as possible of Chicano families in the United States with regard to socioeconomic status. The families were informed that the study was designed to increase our knowledge about how children learn and about the conditions surrounding children's learning.

Procedure

To assess maternal teaching strategies, the maternal teaching observation technique (Laosa, Note 4) was used. Nine different dimensions of maternal teaching strategy are measured by this technique. To examine the questions addressed here, these dimensions may be classified according to (a) the cognitive style characteristics that they reflect on the mother's part in her role as a teacher; (b) the type of cognitive demand that they are likely to make on the child as a learner; or (c) their relative emphasis on dominant control, conformance to authority, and harsh punishment. Thus, inquiry as a maternal teaching strategy is likely to involve cognitive restructuring on the mother's part. Inquiry is also likely to involve a "demand" on the child to engage in cognitive restructuring. Similarly, the use of praise, in the context of

---

[2]Occupational statuses of the fathers were measured using the following scale, which was adapted from that used by the US Bureau of the Census: 1 = private household workers; 2 = service workers except in private household; 3 = laborers and farmers; 4 = equipment operators; 5 = craftsmen, foremen, and kindred persons; 6 = sales, clerical, and kindred workers; 7 = small business owners, managers, or administrators; 8 = professional and technical; 9 = large business owners or managers. The same scale with an additional point (0 = housewife, does not work outside the home) was used to measure mothers' usual occupational statuses.

the tasks used here, is likely to reflect cognitive restructuring on the mother's part and to encourage the child to "act on the field." Modeling, on the other hand, an enactive, concrete form of instruction, is likely to reflect a relatively low degree of self-nonself segregation; moreover, by using modeling as a teaching tool, she probably is encouraging her child to rely on others as sources of information in ambiguous situations. When she uses visual cues as a teaching strategy, the mother organizes the material to be learned in such a manner that structuring is not particularly called for in the child. With regard to the relative emphasis of a given teaching strategy on dominant control, reliance on parental authority, and harsh punishment, the use of negative physical control certainly reflects such an emphasis, and it contrasts in this sense with such strategies as physical affection and positive physical control.

Three dimensions of the maternal teaching observation technique were excluded from the study for the following reasons. Negative verbal feedback or disapproval and directives appeared to be too multifaceted to allow unambiguous classification by the previously described criteria. Each may include in its domain acts of speech that reflect harsh punishment and dominant control, as well as specific feedback that encourages the child to engage in cognitive restructuring. Another variable, physical affection, yielded a very low frequency and therefore was excluded from the analyses.

The maternal teaching observation technique was administered in the subjects' homes, using the subjects' home language, by two Chicano, English-Spanish bilingual, female university students. They began collecting data after achieving exact interobserver agreement to within one frequency point on every variable. The hypotheses of the study were not discussed with the observers; subjects were randomly assigned to observers.

Each subject was administered parallel Forms A and B of the technique. The interval between administrations of the two forms was approximately ten minutes. A description of the technique follows. The mother is given an assembled Tinkertoy model and all of the disassembled parts necessary for making an identical model. (The disassembled parts are "worked" in and out prior to using them with the subjects until none is unusually difficult for a child to fit into any other part.) The mother is asked "to teach" her child "how to make" a model like the one already assembled.[3] The observer manually records the frequency of each maternal behavior from the following six categories.

---

[3]In pilot testing of the procedures, it was found that *enseñar*, in the Spanish version of the instructions, was interpreted to mean *to show* and elicited slightly different maternal teaching strategies than did the English *to teach* instructions. *"Hoy quiero que Ud. haga que____(niño) aprenda a hacer"* and "Today I would like you to teach ____ (child) how to make" did not elicit different teaching strategies and therefore were used in the Spanish and English versions of the instructions, respectively.

1. *Inquiry*. The mother asks the child a question or otherwise directs a verbal inquiry to the child.

2. *Praise*. The mother praises or otherwise verbally expresses approval of the child or the child's activity or product.

3. *Modeling*. The mother works on the model, and the child observes. A behavior unit is considered complete (and a frequency point is recorded) every time the mother fastens together or unfastens two parts.

4. *Visual cue*. The mother attempts to direct the child's attention toward a given aspect of the task by providing a visual cue. This category is limited to attempts to direct the child's attention by sliding, pushing, or lifting a part or portion of the model being assembled (but short of fastening or unfastening any parts). The behavior unit is considered complete (and a frequency point is recorded) when the mother releases the part or portion of the model or otherwise moves her hand away from it. (More subtle visual cues, such as merely touching a part or pointing, were included initially as additional categories but are not included in this study because of relatively low interobserver agreement.)

5. *Positive physical control*. The mother manually controls the child's motor behavior to facilitate the child's solution of the task, for example, turning the child's body toward the task or restraining the child as the child tries to leave the task area.

6. *Negative physical control*. This category includes two classes of nonverbal behavior, both displaying mother's disapproval of the child's activity on the task or product: (a) an action that generally would be interpreted as physical punishment, for example, slapping the child's hand; or (b) manually restraining or controlling the child's motor activity as the child works on the task, to keep him or her from pursuing what the mother apparently perceives as action not conducive to learning or solving the task or not appropriate for that particular time, for example, she takes or pushes the child's hand away from the task material, or she holds the child's arm as the child begins to reach for a Tinkertoy part.

For each parallel form, the observation is discontinued either 5 minutes after the mother is signaled to begin teaching or when the task is completed, whichever occurs first. The observation time in seconds is recorded. Ratio scores are computed by dividing raw frequencies by observation time. These ratio scores are summed across the two parallel forms to yield summed-ratio scores.

The two parallel forms differ from one another only in the Tinkertoy models used. Form A uses the Robot and Form B, the Jet Airplane (Questor Education Products, 1972). Both are of approximately equal difficulty. The criterion for selecting these tasks and their difficulty levels was that maternal teaching behaviors would be elicited from the entire range of subjects by materials and activities of approximately equal familiarity to all of the subjects. (See the later section on Prior Exposure Effect.)

Reliability. Spearman rank correlations were computed between the raw frequencies that were obtained simultaneously but independently by the two observers on each of 10 mother-child dyads selected at random intervals during data collection. These coefficients of interobserver agreement during data collection, which were computed separately for each of the two parallel forms, were highly significant ($p < .001$ for five coefficients and $p < .01$ for four coefficients, one-tail tests, $n = 10$). The median coefficient was .88. Rho coefficients were not computed for the remaining variables because both observers obtained zero frequencies; their agreement for these variables was 100%.

To determine the parallel form consistency, Spearman rank correlations were computed for each variable between the raw frequencies obtained on Form A and Form B. These rho coefficients were also highly significant ($p < .001$, $n = 43$, one-tail tests: .75 for inquiry, .83 for modeling, .69 for praise, and .70 for visual cue). Because of very low frequency, rho coefficients were not computed for the two remaining variables; nevertheless, the parallel-form consistency was high also for these variables, as reflected in the mean frequencies, which were highly similar across forms. These results indicate that each measure of the maternal teaching observation technique is at least a moderately stable attribute of maternal behavior.

Prior Exposure Effect. Prior to the administration of the maternal teaching observation technique, there was a Tinkertoy set in eight of the homes. To determine whether such prior exposure to the task had an effect on the observed behaviors, point biserial correlations were computed between summed-ratio scores on the maternal teaching observation technique and on whether there was a Tinkertoy set in the home prior to the administration. The coefficients were near-zero and not significant ($n = 43$, $p > .05$, one-tailed). There was no evidence, then, of any effect as a result of prior exposure to the task materials.

Field Dependence–Field Independence Measures

As measures of field dependence-field independence, the Embedded Figures Test and the Block Design subtest of the Wechsler Adult Intelligence Scale were administered to the mothers, and the Children's Embedded Figures Test, the Block Design subtest of the Wechsler Intelligence Scale for Children, and a human figure drawing test were administered to the children. Successful performance on these tests is assumed to involve cognitive restructuring of the perceptual field, a major component of field independence; as such, they represent measures of the individual's relative position along the field dependence–field independence cognitive style dimension (Witkin & Goodenough, Note 2; Witkin, Goodenough, & Oltman, Note 3). The tests were individually administered by bilingual (English-

Spanish) trained examiners, using each subject's home language. The hypotheses of the study were not discussed with the examiners; subjects were randomly assigned to examiners.

Embedded Figures Test.   Parallel Form A was used. For each item the task is to locate the outline of a simple figure that is embedded in a complex geometric design. The scores are the mean solution time per item and the number of incorrect solutions. Higher scores indicate greater field dependence (Witkin, Oltman, Raskin, & Karp, 1971).

Children's Embedded Figures Test.   For each item the subject is asked to locate the shape of a simple form that is embedded in a complex design that represents a recognizable object. A score of 1 is given for a correct response on the first attempt. No time limit is imposed. Higher scores represent greater field independence (Witkin et al., 1971).

Block Design.   The task is to copy, within an alloted time period, geometric designs of increasing complexity by the appropriate arrangement of multicolored blocks (Wechsler, 1955, 1949). Raw scores were used in the analyses. Higher scores indicate greater field independence.

Human Figure Drawings.   The human figure drawings were scored according to the Goodenough-Harris scoring system (Harris, 1963; Laosa, Swartz, & Diaz-Guerrero, 1974). Because of the high Pearson product-moment correlation between raw scores on the male and female figures ($r = .89$), raw scores on only one figure (the male) were selected for use in subsequent analyses. Higher scores indicate greater field independence.

RESULTS

Because the distribution of scores like those used here may at times not conform closely to the assumptions underlying the Pearson product-moment correlation, distribution-free methods were used as the principal form of statistical analysis. Table 1 presents Spearman rank correlations of the maternal teaching strategy variables with the three measures of maternal field dependence–field independence. As can be seen, the pattern of significant correlations is highly consistent across the different measures of field dependence–field independence and also is similar for mother-son and mother-daughter dyads. Because the level of education has been found to be related to teaching behavior (Laosa, 1978) and to field dependence (Witkin & Berry, 1975), partial correlations were computed between maternal teaching strategy variables and maternal measures of field dependence–field

TABLE 1
Spearman Rank Correlations of Summed-Ratio Scores on the Maternal
Teaching Observation Technique With Measures of Mothers' Field
Dependence-Field Independence in Chicano Families

Maternal teaching strategy and dyad structure	EFT		
	Solution time	Incorrect solutions	BD
Inquiry			
Mother-son dyads	−.75***	−.43*	.49*
Mother-daughter dyads	−.35*	−.46*	.39*
All	−.50***	−.47***	.44**
Praise			
Mother-son dyads	−.80***	−.43*	.44*
Mother-daughter dyads	−.44*	−.48**	.50**
All	−.59***	−.46***	.43**
Modeling			
Mother-son dyads	.46*	.62**	−.27
Mother-daughter dyads	.50**	.33	−.40*
All	.46***	.50***	−.31*
Visual cue			
Mother-son dyads	.03	.06	.17
Mother-daughter dyads	.12	.24	−.10
All	.03	.12	.04
Positive physical control			
Mother-son dyads	.18	.04	−.08
Mother-daughter dyads	.12	.38*	.14
All	.17	.22	.01
Negative physical control			
Mother-son dyads	.07	.30	.00
Mother-daughter dyads	.04	−.08	.04
All	.09	.11	−.07

NOTE. EFT = Embedded Figures Test; BD = Block Design; n = 20 and 23 for mother-son and mother-daughter dyads, respectively.

*$p < .05$, one-tailed test.
**$p < .01$, one-tailed test.
***$p < .001$, one-tailed test.

independence, partialing out mothers' education. The matrix of partial correlations showed the same pattern as that in Table 1, although, as expected, the partial coefficients were lower in magnitude.

Table 2 presents Spearman rank correlations of the maternal teaching strategy variables with the three measures of children's field dependence–field independence. As can be seen, the correlations are generally low, and the patterns of significant correlations are not, in general, highly consistent across the different measures of children's field dependence–field independence.

TABLE 2
Spearman Rank Correlations of Summed-Ratio Scores on the
Maternal Teaching Observation Technique With Measures
of Field-Dependence-Field Independence
for Chicano Boys and Girls

Maternal teaching strategy and group	CEFT	BD	HFD
Inquiry			
Boys	.06	.10	−.07
Girls	.34	.29	.13
All	.26*	.21	.07
Praise			
Boys	.00	−.07	−.19
Girls	.43*	.18	−.03
All	.23	.00	−.06
Modeling			
Boys	−.24	.10	.01
Girls	−.32	.14	−.16
All	−.26*	.12	−.11
Visual cue			
Boys	−.40*	−.46*	−.14
Girls	−.17	−.20	−.19
All	−.28*	−.32*	−.18
Positive physical control			
Boys	.28	.28	.12
Girls	.19	.20	.19
All	.12	.19	.11
Negative physical control			
Boys	−.31	.02	−.30
Girls	−.36*	−.01	−.21
All	−.31**	−.02	−.22

NOTE. CEFT = Children's Embedded Figures Test: BD = Block Design; HFD = human figure drawing test; n = 20 and 23 for boys and girls, respectively.
*$p < .05$, one-tailed test.
**$p < .01$, one-tailed test.

Spearman rank correlations (n = 43) among the three maternal measures of field dependence–field independence are as follows: .50, $p < .001$, for solution time with errors on the Embedded Figures Test; −.72, $p < .001$, for solution time on the Embedded Figures Test with Block Design; and −.44, $p < .002$, for errors on the Embedded Figures Test with Block Design.

The intercorrelations among the children's measures of field dependence–field independence are shown in Table 3. As shown in Table 3, for two out of three intercorrelations, the magnitude of the coefficients is slightly higher for girls than for boys.

TABLE 3
Spearman Rank Intercorrelations Among Measures of
Field Dependence-Field Independence for 5-Year-Old
Chicano Boys and Girls

Measure	CEFT	BD	HFD
CEFT	—	.21	.19
BD	.12	—	.06
HFD	.34	.23	—

CEFT = Children's Embedded Figures Test; BD = Block Design; HFD = human figure drawing test. Coefficients above the main diagonal are for boys (n = 20), and those below it are for girls (n = 23).

DISCUSSION

Maternal Teaching Strategies and Maternal Cognitive Styles

The present data indicate that relatively field-dependent and field-independent mothers differed in the strategies that they used to teach their own children. The results provide support for the view that maternal teaching strategies are selected, organized, and controlled by mothers' own cognitive styles.[4] Relatively field-independent mothers were observed to use inquiry and praise as teaching strategies more frequently than did relatively field-dependent mothers. On the other hand, relatively field-dependent mothers more frequently taught through modeling.

The use of modeling, a relatively concrete, enactive mode of instruction, is likely to reflect a tendency toward field dependence. On the other hand, the choice of inquiry and praise, a self-discovery approach to instruction, is likely to reflect a tendency toward field independence. The present results thus provide support for the hypothesis that the contrasting tendencies toward greater or lesser self-nonself segregation and their cognitive and personality sequelae enter into the mothers' choices of teaching strategies. These findings are harmonious with Moore's (cited in Witkin, Moore et al., 1977), who found that field-independent classroom teachers used a self-discovery instructional approach more frequently than did those who were field-dependent.

The present results further indicate that field-independent mothers use teaching strategies that are likely to stimulate in their children the development of a field-independent cognitive style, and field-dependent

---

[4]I do not mean to imply that such choices are under the conscious control of the individual or that the individual is consciously aware of the psychological processes underlying her behavior.

mothers approach teaching in a manner that is likely to foster in their children a field-dependent cognitive style. Inquiry as a teaching strategy is likely to place a "demand" on the learner to engage in cognitive restructuring and to "place distance" between self and nonself. Similarly, the use of praise, in the context of the tasks used here, is likely to encourage the child to approach problem solving by "acting on the field." In contrast, teaching through modeling requires that the learner adhere to the field as given and rely on others as sources of information. Hence, the results support the hypothesis that each mother teaches her young child by using the type of strategy that is likely to stimulate in the child the development of a cognitive style similar to her own. Whether the child indeed develops a cognitive style similar to the mother's style probably depends on a variety of other environmental as well as biological factors (see Goodenough & Witkin, Note 1).

It is useful to place the latter finding against the backdrop of previous results that have indicated a tendency for people of similar cognitive style to feel greater attraction toward each other and perhaps to achieve greater progress in the goals of their interactions than do persons mismatched on cognitive style (Witkin, 1976; Witkin et al., 1977). Bases for this tendency may lie in the shared personality characteristics and interests and in the similarity in modes of communication of persons matched on cognitive style (Witkin et al., 1977). By encouraging her child to develop a cognitive style similar to hers, the mother, through her manner of interaction, may be unwittingly laying the foundation for a mutually satisfying and productive relationship with her offspring.

The results failed to support the hypothesis that mothers, regardless of their cognitive styles, adopt teaching strategies that are likely to encourage sex typing in their children's development of cognitive style. Recent findings indicating that traditional sex role stereotypes are more evident in the behavior of field-dependent than of field-independent people (Lockheed, 1977) suggest that field-dependent mothers, but not field-independent mothers, may encourage sex typing in their children's development of cognitive style. This notion, which requires a research design different from the one used in this study, warrants further investigation.

There was only modest support for the hypothesis that mothers adopt the teaching strategies that better meet the learning needs that emanate from each child's cognitive style. Trends indicate that mothers used visual cue, modeling, and negative physical control more frequently with field-dependent than with field-independent children. Because field-dependent people are particularly responsive to the dominant properties of the field and have difficulty separating the stimulus into its component parts and restructuring it, such teaching strategies as visual cue and modeling constitute stimulus aids concordant with their learning characteristics (Koran, Snow, & McDonald, 1971; Shapson, 1977). It also appears that field-dependent children learn faster than do field-independent children under conditions of social punishment but not under conditions of social reward (Goodenough, 1976). The lack of stronger evidence in support of this hypothesis may be related to the additional finding that field dependence–field independence was only just beginning to emerge as a coherent cluster in these 5-year-old children. Future research should test the hypothesis for older children with firmly established cognitive styles.

Maternal Teaching Strategies As Mediators of Children's Development of Cognitive Styles

The correlations between maternal teaching strategy variables and measures of children's field dependence–field independence were generally low and not highly consistent across the three measures of children's field dependence–field independence. This finding contrasts sharply with that involving *maternal* cognitive styles, in which the significant correlations between maternal teaching behavior and maternal field dependence–field independence were higher and more consistent across different measures of the cognitive style dimension. This is exactly what one would expect, based on the additional findings that the intercorrelations among the three maternal measures of field dependence–field independence were all significant and moderately high and that the intercorrelations among the three measures of children's field dependence–field independence were low and nonsignificant.

The present data nevertheless reveal trends that conform to the hypothesis that socialization practices that encourage strict parental dominance, coercive control, and harsh punishment are likely to encourage greater field dependence. Mothers who exercised negative physical control in teaching their children were more likely than mothers who did not use such control to have children who scored in a relatively field-dependent direction. In contrast, mothers who used positive physical control had children who scored in a relatively field-independent direction. The other trends obtained were also in line with field-dependence theory. Mothers who taught through modeling and visual cue were more likely than mothers who did not use such strategies to have field-dependent children. In contrast, mothers who used inquiry and praise were more likely to have daughters who scored in a relatively field-independent direction. Inquiry and praise as maternal teaching strategies make the types of cognitive demands on the child that are likely to stimulate the development of cognitive restructuring skills and autonomous functioning—or a field-independent cognitive style. On the other hand, as maternal teaching strategies, modeling and visual cues, as well as negative physical control, make the types of cognitive demands on the child that are likely to stimulate reliance on external referents—or to stimulate development of a field-dependent cognitive style. Together, the trends suggest that the teaching strategies to which the child is exposed may influence which cognitive style the child develops.

The findings discussed thus far in this article must be considered in light of the fact that it is difficult to ascribe directionality with correlational data. Indeed, one cannot entirely discard the possibility that the mother's behavior is an adaptation to characteristics of the child or that the process is one of mutual adaptation (Laosa, 1979). Nevertheless, together, the data do fall in line with stated hypotheses. Additional research is required to illuminate reciprocal effects in development. Of particular value would be longitudinal studies from the prenatal period through an age at which children have already firmly established cognitive styles.

Emergence of Cognitive Styles

A significant developmental question is at what point in ontogeny do the field-dependent and field-independent cognitive styles firmly emerge as a coherent construct? The present findings indicate that for adult Chicano females, the field dependence–field independence measures used represent a coherent cluster of measures. The data thus provide evidence of construct validity for field dependence–field independence in adult Chicano women. For the children, the intercorrelations among the measures were low, although positive, indicating that at 5 years of age field dependence–field independence is only just beginning to emerge as a coherent construct in Chicano children.

The intercorrelations among the various field dependence–field independence measures were slightly higher for girls than for boys, suggesting that a coherent construct of field dependence–field independence might emerge slightly earlier in female than in male Chicanos. A sex difference such as this has been found in samples of other cultural populations (Kogan, 1976). The present results thus suggest that one may extend to Chicanos the general finding that a coherent construct of field dependence–field independence emerges earlier in females than in males.

For a deeper understanding of the emergence of cognitive styles in children, additional studies are needed. Short-term longitudinal studies covering early and middle childhood would be of particular value.

REFERENCE NOTES

1. Goodenough, D. R., & Witkin, H. A. *Origins of the field-dependent and field-independent cognitive styles* (ETS RB 77-9). Princeton, N.J.: Educational Testing Service, 1977
2. Witkin, H. A., & Goodenough, D. R. *Field dependence revisited* (ETS RB 77-16). Princeton, N.J.: Educational Testing Service, 1977.
3. Witkin, H. A., Goodenough, D. R., & Oltman, P. K. *Psychological differentiation: Current status* (ETS RB 77-17). Princeton, N.J.: Educational Testing Service, 1977.
4. Laosa, L. M. *Measures for the study of maternal teaching strategies.* Princeton, N.J.: Educational Testing Service, 1979.

REFERENCES

Dyk, R. B., & Witkin, H. A. Family experiences related to the development of differentiation in children. *Child Development*, 1965, *30*, 21–55.

Goodenough, D. R. The role of individual differences in field dependence as a factor in learning and memory. *Psychological Bulletin*, 1976, *83*, 675–694.

Harris, D. B. *Children's drawings as measures of intellectual maturity*. New York: Harcourt, Brace & World, 1963.

Holtzman, W. H., et al. *Personality development in two cultures: A cross-cultural longitudinal study of school children in Mexico and the United States*. Austin: University of Texas Press, 1975.

Hoppe, C. M., Kagan, S. M., & Zahn, G. L. Conflict resolution among field-independent and field-dependent Anglo-American and Mexican-American children and their mothers. *Developmental Psychology*, 1977, *13*, 591–598.

Kogan, N. *Cognitive styles in infancy and early childhood*. Hillsdale, N.J.: Erlbaum, 1976.

Koran, M. L., Snow, R. E., & McDonald, F. J. Teacher aptitude and observational learning of a teaching skill. *Journal of Educational Psychology*, 1971, *62*, 219–228.

Laosa, L. M. Cognitive styles and learning strategies research: Some of the areas in which psychology can contribute to personalized instruction in multicultural education. *Journal of Teacher Education*, 1977, *18*, 26–30.

Laosa, L. M. Maternal teaching strategies in Chicano families of varied educational and socioeconomic levels. *Child Development*, 1978, *49*, 1129–1135.

Laosa, L. M. Social competence in childhood: Toward a developmental, socioculturally relativistic paradigm. In M. W. Kent & J. E. Rolf (Eds.), *Primary prevention of psychopathology:* Vol. 3. *Social competence in children*. Hanover, N.H.: University Press of New England, 1979.

Laosa, L. M., Swartz, J. D., & Diaz-Guerrero, R. Perceptual-cognitive and personality development of Mexican and Anglo-American children as measured by human figure drawings. *Developmental Psychology*, 1974, *10*, 131–139.

Lockheed, M. E. Cognitive style effects on sex status in student work groups. *Journal of Educational Psychology*, 1977, *69*, 158–165.

Questor Education Products. *Tinkertoy instruction and idea book*. Bronx, N.Y.: Author, 1972.

Ramírez III, M., & Castañeda, A. *Cultural democracy, bicognitive development, and education*. New York: Academic Press, 1974.

Shapson, S. M. Hypothesis testing and cognitive style in children. *Journal of Educational Psychology*, 1977, *69*, 452–463.

Wechsler, D. *Wechsler Intelligence Scale for Children manual*. New York: Psychological Corporation, 1949.

Wechsler, D. *Manual for the Wechsler Adult Intelligence Scale*. New York: Psychological Corporation, 1955.

Witkin, H. A. Cognitive style in academic performance and in teacher-student relations. In S. Messick (Ed.), *Individuality in learning*. San Francisco: Jossey-Bass, 1976.

Witkin, H. A., & Berry, J. W. Psychological differentiation in cross-cultural perspective. *Journal of Cross-Cultural Psychology*, 1975, *6*, 4–87.

Witkin, H. A., Dyk, R. B., Faterson, H. F., Goodenough, D. R., & Karp, S. A. *Psychological differentiation*. Potomac, Md.: Erlbaum, 1974. (Originally published by Wiley, 1962.)

Witkin, H. A., & Goodenough, D. R. Field dependence and interpersonal behavior. *Psychological Bulletin*, 1977, *84*, 661–689.

Witkin, H. A., Moore, C. A., Goodenough, D. R., & Cox, P. W. Field-dependent and field-independent cognitive styles and their educational implications. *Review of Educational Research*, 1977, *47*, 1–64.

Witkin, H. A., Oltman, P. K., Raskin, E., & Karp, S. A. *A manual for the Embedded Figures Test*. Palo Alto, Calif.: Consulting Psychologists Press, 1971.

18

Reading Comprehension and the Verbal Deductive Reasoning of Bilinguals

Richard P. Durán
Educational Testing Service

Although psychological research on the cognitive functioning of bilinguals is not new, few researchers have investigated how well bilinguals solve simliar problem solving tasks in each of their two languages, when due consideration is given to level of proficiency in each language.[1] Research of the sort described would appear compelling, because of educators' practical need to improve their understanding of the problem-solving capability of bilingual students. This chapter describes the outcome of a study which investigated 209 adult Puerto Rican college students' ability to solve comparable deductive reasoning problems occurring on four matched pencil-and-paper tests administered in Spanish and English. The objective of the work was to learn how assessed reading proficiency in each language predicted overall test performance in the same language and to compare the obtained pattern of prediction for both Spanish and English.

ISSUES AND PREVIOUS RESEARCH

Previous investigation of bilinguals' skill in solving problems in two languages stem from two sources: (a) psychometric studies of mental abilities; (b) experimental studies of problem solving. Major reviews of previous research on the mental abilities and achievement test performance of United States Latinos were given by Padilla (1979) and Zirkel (1975); a great many of

---

[1]The term *bilingual* in the present paper refers to persons who possess at least a minimal degree of functional or social competence in each of two languages. Throughout this paper, the term *Latino* is used to refer to persons of Latin-American or Spanish heritage.

the papers cited by these authors have been reprinted recently (Cordasco, 1978). Other recent papers summarizing testing issues pertaining to United States Latinos are by Garcia (1977); Olmedo (1977); and Laosa (1977). Only rarely have researchers investigated how Latinos' test performance in two languages is related to their bilingualism or proficiency in two languages. In addition, an overwhelming amount of testing research has tended to be concerned with assessing general intelligence rather than with more precisely defined, particular mental abilities—though there have been important exceptions.

Research on Latinos' test performance generally led to findings demonstrating that their success on performance (i.e., nonverbal) tests of general intelligence is superior to that on verbal general intelligence tests (see, for example, Garth, Elson, & Morton, 1936; Shotwell, 1945; Cook & Arthur, 1951; Darcy, 1952). Research investigating whether United States Latinos perform better on Spanish-version intelligence and achievement tests than on English-version counterparts has produced mixed findings. Some early studies (e.g., Mitchell, 1937; Mahakian, 1939) have shown that Latinos perform better on Spanish-version than on English-version tests. Other studies, however, have shown no difference (e.g., Palmer & Gaffney, 1972) or have shown that Latinos perform better on English-version than on Spanish-version tests (e.g., Keston & Jimenez, 1954). Each of these three patterns of findings is no doubt thoroughly confounded by the investigators' failure initially to establish the proficiency level of examinees in the vernacular or variety of Spanish and English used on tests. For example, in the Keston and Jimenez (1954) study, the Spanish version of Form L of the 1937 Stanford-Binet Intelligence test administered to the children in the study was translated from English into Spanish by a professor at the National Institute of Psychotechniques, in Madrid. It seems highly unlikely that the vernacular of Spanish used on the translated tests corresponded very well to the norms for Spanish usage most familiar to the New Mexico children studied; hence, without previous assessment of children's proficiency in each of the languages of testing there could be no way of averting the plausible conclusion that children's deficit performance in Spanish as compared to English reflected their relative unfamiliarity with the Spanish vernacular used in one test version and their familiarity with the English used in the other intelligence test version.

The role language ability plays in Latinos' mental test performance in Spanish and English has on occasion been more explicitly analyzed. For example, in two early papers (Sánchez, 1932, 1934) argued that some vocabulary items in (Spanish or English) intelligence tests often do not at all reflect the normative language experiences of Latino children. He argued, too, that simple, direct translation of English-version tests into Spanish is not necessarily an acceptable solution to the problem of improving control over the effects of vocabulary familiarity in testing. Development of translated forms of mental abilities tests mandates study of the difficulty of translated items for a population of examinees as well as investigation, in general, of the reliability and validity of the newly translated test forms. In closing his 1934 paper, Sánchez pointed out the critical importance of assessing reading comprehension ability of Latinos if one wishes to evaluate sensitively the level of cognitive test performance and its dependence on language factors.

Empirical research that specifically addressed how Latinos' cognitive test performance is allied with language factors has shown that some young Latino children almost exclusively prefer the use of Spanish rather than English during administration of a performance test of general intelligence (Anastasi & de Jesús, 1953). Other researchers have found that some Latino children's performance on general intelligence tests in English is constrained by English verbal comprehension skills and by ability to transfer English verbal skills to new situations (Christiansen & Livermore, 1970). Padilla (1979), discussing a study by Killian (1971), cites it as showing that bilingualism in a group of Spanish-American children is allied with low WISC intelligence test scores relative to the higher WISC scores manifested by a group of monolingual English Latino children and the still higher WISC scores of a group of non-Latino monolingual English children. Padilla (1979) in his summary, states that the Killian (1971) data showed Latino bilingual children to be deficient in comprehending sentences and related picture materials and quoted Killiam as stating that this deficiency might have arisen from the economic impoverishment of bilingual background children and the differences between their and other children's sociocultural experiences. These critical variables may have influenced the relatively lower WISC scores of the bilingual children.

In weighing the validity of results of studies such as those just mentioned one must consider that they have not systematically sampled among different Latino subgroups, nor has the proficiency level of subjects in the studies in two languages been controlled or accounted for with precision within studies. For example, it could be expected that Chicano third-generation bilingual-background persons, dominant in English rather than Spanish, would be most likely to perform better on cognitive tests in English.

A recent psychometric study of bilinguals' cognitive abilities by Duncan and De Avila (1979) included investigation of Spanish-English bilingual children. The results of this study revealed that first-grade and third-grade children who were simultaneously high in both Spanish and English proficiency also manifested a high ability perceptually to disembed parts of geometrical figures and to articulate different features in their drawings of human figures. Monolingual children from comparable backgrounds and grade levels who were of the same proficiency in their single language did not manifest similar high levels of cognitive ability on the tasks described. The Duncan and De Avila results are consistent with findings of other recent international studies surveyed by Cummins (1978) that have found positive enhancement of some cognitive skills among bilinguals possessing high levels of proficiency in two languages.

Although there has been very little detailed psychometric research on proficiency issues underlying mental test performance by bilinguals in two languages, there has, in contrast, been some interesting experimental research by cognitive psychologists of relevance to the present study. In this regard, Dornic (1977) has assembled a most comprehensive review of bilinguals' information-processing abilities in performing simple perceptual, memory encoding and retrieval, and linguistic tasks. Over the historical course of research in this area researchers have consistently found that bilinguals perform problem-solving tasks more slowly in a second language than in a first. This finding applies, regardless of the complexity of tasks. For very simple tasks, for example, Gutierrez-Marsh and Hipple Maki (1976) found that bilingual-background subjects performed a digit-naming task more slowly in their nondominant language. Other studies—e.g., by Lambert, Havelka, & Gardner (1959) and Kolers (1966)—have found that bilinguals' oral reading is characteristically slower in a nondominant second language than in a first language. A study by Lambert (1955), measuring simple response times to instructions delivered in two languages, showed that bilinguals were slower to respond to instructions in a weaker second language than in a first language, thus supporting the hypothesis that comprehension as well as production is slower in a nondominant language.

Research on memory information-processing skills of bilinguals has often centered on the issue of whether the semantic memory—i.e., memory for meanings of words and concepts—in bilinguals is divided into two separate storage systems, depending on language. According to Dornic (1977), the predominant evidence emerging from research on this issue suggests that bilinguals possess a single semantic memory system, words in one language or another often proving to be simply tags for underlying meanings retained in a single memory store. Kolers (1966), for example, found that facility in retaining words in short-term memory in one language also appeared to extend to their translated equivalents in another language. Research, by Young and Navar (1968),has shown that forgetting of paired-associate words in one language can be induced through the process of retroactive inhibition involving learning of new paired-associate words in the other languages. In other research, López and Young (1974) found that subject's reading of a list of words in either Spanish or English, before being asked to memorize a target list, facilitated memorization if the list consisted of the same words originally read or the translated equivalents of the original words.

Studies of bilingual information processing and solution of nontrivial problems mostly directly related to the kinds of problem solving investigated in the present study are rare. MacNamara (1967) and MacNamara and Kellaghan (1968) reported an extensive series of investigations of bilingual Irish children's ability to solve verbal arithmetic problems in Gaelic and

English. Their findings suggested that bilinguals were more likely to solve verbal arithmetic problems incorrectly in their weaker second language than were monolinguals in their single language, though bilinguals and monolinguals were found to be equally good at solving mechanical arithmetic problems. As part of their research program, MacNamara and Kellaghan (1968) reported another study, investigating problem-solving ability in two languages, that on this occasion focused on whether understanding the subparts of a verbal problem equally well in two languages would be allied with equal success in solving the same problem in the different languages. The findings showed that subjects solved fewer problems correctly in their second language despite their having evidenced an equal understanding of individual sentences making up problems in both languages. A much earlier study by the International Institute of Teachers College, Columbia University (1926), on the verbal arithmetic problem-solving ability of Puerto Rican bilinguals educated in Puerto Rico, found that twelfth-grade Puerto Ricans performed more poorly than monolingual United States mainland twelfth graders did, even though the Puerto Rican students had received their arithmetic lessons in English since the fifth grade. According to MacNamara, these results were evidence that problem-solving skill is constrained by linguistic proficiency difficulties that extend beyond the initial stages of learning a new subject matter in a weaker (second) language.

Research on deductive reasoning skills of bilinguals relevant to the present study was conducted by d'Anglejan and Tucker (1975). In this investigation, an analysis was made of occurrence of errors in solving three-term syllogism problems by two groups of bilingual French-English Canadians, whose first language was French and second language was English. Subjects were classified as either high or low in English proficiency according to results on an elaborate battery of diagnostic tests of reading, writing, aural comprehension, and oral production of English. The results showed that both high-proficiency and low-proficiency English-speaking subjects made more errors in solving three-term syllogism problems in their second language, English, than in their first language, French. An analysis of latency of problem solution showed that subjects, regardless of proficiency level in their second language, generally took longer to solve problems in that language than in their first language, though no test of statistical significance was reported for this difference.

The work that has been reviewed suggests verbal problem-solving by bilinguals might be profitably investigated in terms of several proficiency issues that influence problem-solving success in two languages. In the present study, four different tests of deductive reasoning skill in Spanish and English were used to measure problem-solving skill in order to explore whether language proficiency skills bore similar relationships to problem-solving performance, within as well as across languages. The four reasoning tests had been found, in previous psychometric studies, to identify one single cognitive reasoning factor. Each of the selected reasoning tests varied in its gross linguistic processing requirements—e.g., vocabulary recognition only, vs. comprehension of simple sentences, vs. comprehension of brief tracts of natural text.

Previous research cited suggested that an estimate of reading comprehension skills constraining bilinguals' deductive verbal problem-solving might be obtained by measures reflecting how well criterion problems were understood, and as well by other measures obtained on independent tests of reading comprehension in the language of reasoning problems. Reflection upon previous research, however, yields the conclusion that never have both types of measures been included in the same study for the purpose of learning whether measures of reading comprehension of criterion problems themselves were adequate to account for the total extent to which language proficiency skills usefully predict general problem-solving success in two languages. Thus, in the present work, both types of reading comprehension measures were included as predictors of overall performance on verbal reasoning tests. Measures of facility in comprehending reasoning problems on tests in a given language included (a) average reading time for problem items on a test; (b) number of times on a test when mental translation to the other language was necessary; (c) total number of words not understood on test problems; (d) total number of sentences not understood on tests whose problem items involved meaningful sentence material. Measures of generalized reading comprehension skills in a language were assessed by scores on matched Spanish and English advanced reading comprehension tests administered separate from reasoning tests. These latter tests yielded subscores pertaining to (a) vocabulary; (b) reading speed; (c) *level,* defined as ability to recognize paraphrase in a language.

METHOD

Subjects

Two hundred and nine Puerto Rican students (99 males and 120 females) enrolled in approximately 21 East Coast colleges and universities served as subjects, paid at the rate of $20.00 for a single 4½ hour testing session. A large majority of students, 175 out of 209 (83.7 percent), were enrolled in four-year institutions; 25 students (12) were enrolled in two-year institutions. Nine subjects (4.3 percent) did not specify whether their current or entering college was a two-year or four-year institution.

Before college, the subjects had averaged 4.3 years of schooling in Puerto Rico and 7.7 years of schooling in the United States mainland. Seventy-four of the 209 subjects (35.4 percent) had attended primary school in Puerto Rico; 109 subjects (52.2 percent) had attended primary school on the mainland.

Twenty-five subjects (12 percent) had attended primary school in both Puerto Rico and on the mainland.

Sixty-eight of 209 subjects (32.5 percent) had attended intermediate school (junior high school or grades 7 through 9) solely in Puerto Rico. Only 7 of the 209 subjects (3.4 percent) had attended intermediate school on both the island and the mainland.

The number of subjects who had attended high school only in Puerto Rico was 54 (25. 8 percent); 146 subjects (69.9 percent) reported having attended high school exclusively on the United States mainland. Only 3.8 percent of all subjects reported having attended high school in both Puerto Rico and the continental United States.

Subjects were asked to sign a standard consent and receipt-of-payment form that also explained the nature of the study, the rate of pay, provided a guarantee of anonymity and notification of the right to withdraw from testing without notice, should discomfort arise.

Deductive Reasoning Instruments and Assessment of Reading Comprehension on Reasoning Instruments

The four deductive reasoning tests used in the present study were based on the four reasoning tests, *Diagramming Relationships, Nonsense Syllogisms, Inference Test,* and *Logical Reasoning,* drawn from French, Ekstrom, and Price (1963) and Ekstrom, French, and Harman (1976). In the procedure followed, Spanish translations of parts 1 and 2 of the original English-version tests were developed. Subsequently subjects were administered part 1 of a test in one language and part 2 in the other language. Thus, all told, the study involved use of two alternative forms of a test in a single language based on whether items were drawn from part 1 or part 2 of the original full length English-version test. Counterbalancing procedures were followed to ensure that approximately equal numbers of subjects were exposed to the two forms of each test and to alternative orders of administering of test forms in each language.

In addition to the shortened length and possible occurrence in Spanish rather than English, the instruments in the current study also differed from the original instruments by the inclusion of three or four tasks not found on the originals. The tasks included:

1. Recording the time in hours, minutes, and seconds from a Heathkit model GC-1092D digital clock at the start and conclusion of the first reading of each test item.
2. After completing an item, checking "Yes" or "No" to a question inquiring whether a subject was aware (a) of thinking in a language

different from the one in which the item was stated; (b) of deliberate mental translating of an item from one language to another.

3. After working an item, underlining words in the item not understood in context or not understood clearly.

4. After working an item consisting of complete, meaningful sentences, placing a question mark after each sentence not understood fully in context.

The object of these tasks was to gain evidence on reading comprehension facility in Spanish or English at the moment that reasoning problems were being worked. In accordance with these task demands, total time allotted for completion of items on a test was increased by 1.5 to 2 times the total period allotted to work items on the original test versions.

Translation of English-language items into Spanish for all instruments was accomplished in four stages. In the first stage, a Mexican graduate student in psychology, experienced in professional translation, translated English items into Spanish. The instructions given the translator were to avoid literal translations that were awkward or changed meaning; attention was given also to noting vocabulary on the tests that was rare in Spanish or had a noticeably different meaning in Spanish than in English. In the second stage of translation, the principal investigator, a bilingual Chicano, English-dominant, checked the first translation and suggested minor changes in wording to reflect more common usage of terms in United States spoken Spanish than in Standard international Spanish. Subsequent stages of translation and revisions of translations involved bilingual Puerto Ricans exclusively. In the third stage of translation, a Puerto Rican graduate student of sociolinguistics, who was judged equivalently proficient in both Standard Spanish and English, modified the then-existing Spanish translations of items to reflect Spanish familiar to most Puerto Rican college students. In the fourth and final stage of translation, a graduate student research assistant, born and raised in Puerto Rico and dominant in Spanish, reviewed the Spanish translations for intelligibility and suggested revisions, which were then implemented. The consensus of the research team, following this procedure for translation and pilot testing, was that the Spanish-version items, although not always conforming to the highest standards of idiomatic usage in Standard international Spanish, were intelligible to Puerto Ricans identified as proficient in varieties of Spanish spoken in the United States by Puerto Ricans.

Description of Logical Reasoning Tests

The following is a description of the reasoning instruments administered in the present study in their English version. Each of the four tests requires subjects to reason from premises to a conclusion or to evaluate the correctness of a conclusion. The logical reasoning test with minimal linguistic processing requirements is the *Diagramming Relationships* test, which presents subjects with sets of three nouns such as:

dogs, mice, animals,

which then must be matched against one of the five diagrams of the form:

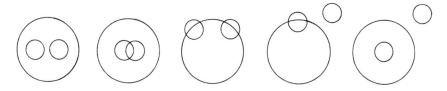

(answer)

that captures the category relationships among the classes of concrete objects referred to by nouns. In the case of the problem given, the first diagram is the correct solution since dogs and mice are both animals but are distinct from each other. In terms of linguistic processing, this test thus requires only recognition of isolated words.

In the *Nonsense Syllogisms* test, subjects are presented with a hypothetical three-term syllogism such as:

All trees are fish. All fishes are horses.
Therefore all trees are horses.

Subjects are requested to respond G (good) or P (poor) in a multiple-choice format and to base their decision on whether the argument is valid or not if the first two terms are assumed true, regardless of their pragmatic deficiencies. Linguistically, this test requires subjects to understand the syntactic form of a sentence and the meaning of terms of quantification, logical entailment, and predication of properties of objects.

The *Logical Reasoning* test is essentially identical to the *Nonsense Syllogisms* test in format, reasoning, and linguistic processing requirements, except that three-term syllogisms have valid pragmatic references to the properties of object; i.e., the syllogism terms are not nonsensical.

The fourth logical reasoning instrument, known as the *Inference Test,* presents subjects statements like the following:

All human beings fall into four main groups according to the composition of their blood: O, A, B, and AB. Knowledge of these blood types is important for tranfusions.

On the basis of these statements, subjects are required to select the unique correct conclusion that logically follows from a set of alternatives, such as:

1. The blood type is determined by genes.
2. Persons of group AB can receive blood from any other type.
3. Blood transfusions between members of the same group are always safe.
4. Certain percentages of all people belong to each type. (Correct answer)
5. Blood from persons of group O can safely be given to persons of any group.

Subjects are instructed to choose only that conclusion which follows from the original information given without bringing in other knowledge or beliefs not made explicit originally. Linguistically, this class of logical reasoning problems requires more extensive discourse comprehension and manipulation of syntactic and semantic information than the three previous tests mentioned.

Reading Comprehension Instruments

Generalized reading comprehension ability in Spanish and English was assessed by administration of the *Prueba de Lectura, Nivel 5—Advanzado— Forma DEs* and by the *Test of Reading Level 5—Advanced Form CE* (Guidance Testing Associates, 1962). Both these tests had been originally developed as reasonably approximate instruments of advanced reading comprehension proficiency for use with Puerto Ricans (Manuel, 1963). Although these instruments no doubt need renorming, given the date of their development, they are currently the best available advanced-level reading comprehension instruments in Spanish and English in parallel forms. Each generalized comprehension test in a language yields three subscores, assessing vocabulary, speed of comprehension, and paraphrase comprehension— termed *level*—and a separate composite total performance score.

The purpose of measuring generalized reading comprehension in each language was to evaluate how performance on logical reasoning tests in each language depends on reading comprehension ability in the same language.

RESULTS

Psychometric Characteristics of Test Data

Tables 1 and 2 display the mean score, standard deviation of scores and coefficient α reliability estimates of scores on forms 1 and 2 of each of the four pairs of deductive reasoning tests in Spanish and English. The means and

TABLE 1
Means, Standard Deviations, and Estimated Reliability Coefficients of Scores on Deductive
Reasoning Tests in Spanish*

Test	Form	Number of Items	Mean Score	Standard Deviation	Coefficient α Reliability Estimate
Spanish	1	15	6.67	2.44	.49
Nonsense	2	15	7.09	2.46	.43
Syllogisms	1 & 2 pooled	15	6.92	2.42	————
Spanish	1	15	5.14	2.80	.63
Diagramming	2	15	5.77	2.77	.45
Relationships	1 & 2 pooled	15	5.45	2.54	————
Spanish	1	10	3.26	2.01	.51
Inference	2	10	4.28	2.14	.58
Test	1 & 2 pooled	10	3.80	2.18	————
Spanish	1	20	7.49	3.69	.70
Logical	2	20	7.59	4.40	.77
Reasoning	1 & 2 pooled	20	7.48	3.89	————

*N = 98 subjects for Form 1 tests; N = 111 for Form 2 tests.

standard deviations and estimated reliabilities reported are reasonably homogeneous. Coefficient α reliability estimates for the various test measures ranged from the low forties to high seventies and low eighties. Although these reliability estimates are low for applied psychometric purposes, they are considered acceptable evidence that the reasoning instruments in the current

TABLE 2
Means, Standard Deviations, and Estimated Reliability Coefficients of Scores on Deductive
Reasoning Tests in English*

Test	Form	Number of Items	Mean Score	Standard Deviation	Coefficient α Reliability Estimate
English	1	15	7.07	2.31	.40
Nonsense	2	15	7.72	2.54	.50
Syllogisms	1 & 2 pooled	15	7.33	2.44	————
English	1	15	5.36	2.72	.61
Diagramming	2	15	6.32	3.51	.79
Relationships	1 & 2 pooled	15	5.80	3.22	————
Enlgish	1	10	3.74	2.08	.53
Inference	2	10	4.70	2.47	.70
Test	1 & 2 pooled	10	4.21	2.33	————
English	1	20	8.80	4.10	.75
Logical	2	20	8.72	4.81	.83
Reasoning	1 & 2 pooled	20	8.73	2.92	————

*N = 111 subjects for Form 1 tests; N = 98 for Form 2 tests.

study do possess adequate internal coherence for interpretation as hypothesized. In all subsequent discussions of the results, reference to deductive reasoning test scores in a given language will focus on pooled scores across the two forms in a language for each test.

Tables 3 and 4 display means and standard deviations for measures of reading comprehension obtained during administration of each deductive reasoning test in Spanish and English. The measures in question indicate information about how well subjects understood the linguistic statement of reasoning problems on each test as they worked problems.

Table 5 contains mean score, standard deviation of scores, and coefficient α reliability estimates for subscores and total score obtained on the *Prueba de Lectura* and *Test of Reading* instruments. The measures in question reflect subjects' generalized reading comprehension ability in Spanish and English— the term *generalized* referring to an assessment of reading skill not linked to a specific reading content or reading task domain. The coefficient α reliability estimates for Spanish and English generalized reading comprehension test subscores were quite good, ranging from a low of .88 to a high of .94.

Predicting Reasoning Test Performance From Reading Comprehension Skill

Table 6 presents the results of regression analyses indicating how well subjects' total score on each of the four Spanish-version deductive reasoning tests could be predicted from measures of reading comprehension ability in Spanish. The first four independent variables listed in Table 6 correspond to measures of reading comprehension ability in Spanish obtained during the administration of each reasoning test. The remaining three independent variables in each analysis correspond to subjects' generalized reading comprehension ability in Spanish assessed by subscores on the *Prueba de Lectura*. The results of the regression analyses showed that total score on three deductive reasoning tests—*Spanish Diagramming Relationships, Spanish Inference Test,* and *Spanish Logical Reasoning*— were significantly predictable ($p < .001$) from combined information about subjects' Spanish reading comprehension during reasoning test administration and from their generalized Spanish reading comprehension ability. As shown by the R^2 entries in Table 6, reading comprehension measures accounted for 30 percent to 38 percent of the variance on the three reasoning tests in question. The corresponding multiple correlation coefficient entries, R, ranged from .55 to .62—indicating, as expected, a substantial relationship between deductive reasoning performance in Spanish and reading comprehension ability in Spanish.

Performance on the *Spanish Nonsense Syllogisms* test was not significantly predictable from reading comprehension measures in Spanish, contrary to hypothesis.

TABLE 3

Means and Standard Deviations of Measures of Reading Performance on Deductive Reasoning Tests in Spanish

Measure of Reading Performance on a Test	Test Score									
	Spanish Nonsense Syllogisms		Spanish Diagramming Relationships		Spanish Inference Test		Spanish Logical Reasoning		
	Mean	S.D.	Mean	S.D.	Mean	S.D.	Mean	S.D.		
Average Reading Time per Item	13.87	4.96	9.47	4.38	15.87	7.10	10.36	5.05		
Number of Times Used English	1.75	3.50	2.02	4.33	1.28	2.82	2.46	5.38		
Number of Words Not Understood	.77	2.16	.71	1.97	.79	2.50	.85	2.31		
Number of Sentences Not Understood	——	——	——	——	.22	.91	.22	1.20		

323

TABLE 4

Means and Standard Deviations of Measures of Reading Performance on Deductive Reasoning Tests in English

Measure of Reading Performance on a Test	Test Score							
	English Nonsense Syllogisms		English Diagramming Relationships		English Inference Test		English Logical Reasoning	
	Mean	S.D.	Mean	S.D.	Mean	S.D.	Mean	S.D.
Average Reading Time per Item	11.80	4.77	8.77	4.89	12.84	5.82	9.21	5.27
Number of Times Used English	1.22	3.18	1.27	3.25	.96	2.40	2.17	5.16
Number of Words Not Understood	.08	.52	.11	.70	.28	1.45	.47	3.54
Number of Sentences Not Understood	——	——	——	——	.11	1.13	.22	2.27

TABLE 5

Means, Standard Deviations, and Estimated Reliability Coefficients of Subscores and Total
Scores on Spanish and English Reading Comprehension Tests*

Test	Subscore or Total Score	Number of Items	Mean Score	Standard Deviation	Subscore Coefficient α Reliability Estimate
Prueba de Lectura, Nivel 5-Advanzado	Spanish Vocabulary	45	22.74	9.55	.93
	Spanish Speed	30	8.23	5.55	.88
	Spanish Level	50	17.46	7.56	.88
	Spanish Total	125	48.47	20.72	—
Test of Reading, Level 5- Advanced Form	English Vocabulary	45	25.58	10.81	.94
	English Speed	30	11.95	5.64	.88
	English Level	50	21.78	9.12	.91
	English Total	125	59.45	23.61	—

*N = 209 subjects

Table 6 also includes estimates of the standardized regression weights (*Beta*) computed for each reading comprehension measure in predicting given criterion Spanish deductive reasoning scores, along with a significance test statistic F and a corresponding significance probability (P) for weights—the latter probability indicating the chance that each weight might actually be zero, given its computed estimate. Among reading measures, Average Reading Time per Item and Spanish Vocabulary would appear to be of most value in predicting scores on all three Spanish-version deductive reasoning tests that were found to be significantly related to all combined reading measures. Care, however, should be taken to avoid any claim that Average Reading Time per Item and Spanish Vocabulary are as important reading skills as they appear to be on the basis of the analyses described. The problem is that estimates of individual weights for independent variables in multiple regression analyses are known to be unstable when independent variables are highly intercorrelated—though the overall results of analyses, in terms of total variance predicted for in criterion measures, may be relatively stable, given sufficient numbers of subjects.

Table 7 displays results of regression analyses that indicate how well subjects' total score on each of the four English-version deductive reasoning

TABLE 6

Multiple Regression Analyses: Scores on Deductive Reasoning Tests in Spanish in Relation to Reading Comprehension Performance During Testing and Generalized Reading Comprehension Scores in Spanish

	Dependent Variable											
	Spanish Nonsense Syllogisms			Spanish Diagramming Relationships			Spanish Inference Test			Spanish Logical Reasoning		
Independent Variables	*Beta*	$F_{(1,101)}$	*P*	*Beta*	$F_{(1,101)}$	*P*	*Beta*	$F_{(1,100)}$	*P*	*Beta*	$F_{(1,100)}$	*P*
Average Reading Time per Item	-.03	.12	n.s.	-.18	4.55	$<.05$	-.16	3.43	$<.10$	-.19	4.82	$<.05$
Number of Times Used English	-.03	.09	n.s.	-.08	.75	n.s.	.07	.69	n.s.	.14	2.34	n.s.
Number of Words Not Understood	-.18	3.25	$<.10$	-.01	.00	n.s.	.06	.36	n.s.	.05	.20	n.s.
Number of Sentences Not Understood	-.31	3.44	$<.10$	-.26	3.82	$<.10$	.02	.06	n.s.	.01	.00	n.s.
Spanish Vocabulary	.34	4.60	$<.05$	.09	.42	n.s.	.34	6.67	$<.025$	.28	3.93	$<.05$
Spanish Speed	.02	.01	n.s.	.24	3.34	$<.10$	.16	1.41	n.s.	.19	1.83	n.s.
Spanish Level							.13	.99	n.s.	.07	.27	n.s.
Regression Statistics												
R	.30			.62			.62			.55		
R^2	.09			.38			.38			.30		
F	2.76			10.38			8.86			6.20		
df	6,101			6,101			7,100			7,100		
P	n.s.			$<.001$			$<.001$			$<.001$		

TABLE 7

Multiple Regression Analyses: Scores on Deductive Reasoning Tests in English in Relation to Reading Comprehension Performance During Testing and Reading Comprehension Scores in English

	Dependent Variable											
Independent Variables	English Nonsense Syllogisms			English Diagramming Relationships			English Inference Test			English Logical Reasoning		
	Beta	$F_{(1,101)}$	P	Beta	$F_{(1,101)}$	P	Beta	$F_{(1,100)}$	P	Beta	$F_{(1,100)}$	P
Average Reading Time per Item	-.32	11.33	<.005	-.32	17.46	<.001	-.14	3.46	<.10	-.23	8.51	<.01
Number of Times Used Spanish	-.03	.12	n.s.	-.07	.70	n.s.	.03	.25	n.s.	-.09	1.20	n.s.
Number of Words Not Understood	-.04	.15	n.s.	.04	.25	n.s.	.13	4.10	<.05	.09	1.23	n.s.
Number of Sentences Not Understood	—	—	—	—	—	—	.13	3.50	<.10	-.04	.23	n.s.
English Vocabulary	-.01	.00	n.s.	.15	1.54	n.s.	.46	17.83	<.001	.13	1.06	n.s.
English Speed	.04	.07	n.s.	.15	1.61	n.s.	.15	1.73	n.s.	.07	.26	n.s.
English Level	.16	.92	n.s.	.29	4.47	<.001	.15	1.59	n.s.	.39	8.59	<.01
Regression Statistics												
R	.39			.70			.76			.66		
R^2	.15			.48			.58			.44		
F	3.03			15.75			19.50			11.06		
df	6,101			6,101			7,100			7,100		
P	<.01			<.001			<.001			<.001		

tests could be predicted from measures of reading comprehension ability in English. Total score on three reasoning tests—*English Diagramming Relationships, English Inference Test,* and *English Logical Reasoning*—were significantly predictable ($p < .001$) from combined information about subjects' English reading comprehension during reasoning test administration and generalized English reading comprehension ability. These results strongly parallel a similar finding for the same Spanish-version reasoning tests and their relation to Spanish reading comprehension skills.

The proportion of variance accounted for by combined English reading measures on the three English-version reasoning tests in question, ranged from 44 percent to 58 percent—as shown by the R^2 entries; corresponding R statistics ranged from .66 to .76. The R^2 statistics for predicting scores on these three English-version reasoning tests were about one and one-half times higher than those obtained for predicting scores on the Spanish-version of the same reasoning tests.

Unlike the results of regression analyses for *Spanish Nonsense Syllogisms* test scores, results of the regression for *English Nonsense Syllogisms* test scores showed that scores on this test bore a statistically significant relation ($p < .01$) to combined reading comprehension ability measures in the same language. Combined reading measures in English accounted for 39 percent of the total variation among *English Nonsense Syllogisms* scores, this figure representing more than four times the proportion of variance accounted for in the parallel Spanish-version analysis.

Table 7 also includes estimates of the standardized regression weights (*Beta*) computed for each English reading comprehension measure in predicting performance on each English-version reasoning test. As with the results reported for predicting Spanish-version reasoning test performance, there is no sensible way of definitively concluding which reading measures are truly the most important determinants of reasoning test performance due to intercorrelation among reading measures. There is a lingering suspicion, however, based on the results for prediction of reasoning test performance in Spanish and English, that Average Reading Time per Item is an important determinant of reasoning performance. Although this latter conclusion may remain a hypothesis, there is no question, however, that taken in combination, all reading comprehension scores in English are excellent predictors of performance on all four English deductive reasoning tests.

Table 8 presents the results of stepwise multiple regression analyses intended to ascertain the relative importance of two classes of reading comprehension measures in predicting total scores on each of the four Spanish-version deductive reasoning tests. In these analyses, the first regression step involved computing how much variance in each Spanish-version deductive reasoning test was accounted for strictly by combined measures of reading comprehension proficiency obtained during administration of deductive reasoning tests. Recall that these measures

TABLE 8

Multiple Regression Analyses: Improvement in R^2 in Predicting Scores on Deductive Reasoning Tests in Spanish by Adding Independent Variables

	Dependent Variable										
	Spanish Nonsense Syllogisms			Spanish Diagramming Relationships			Spanish Inference Test			Spanish Logical Reasoning		
Classes of Independent Variables in a Regression	R^2	Increm.	Sig. of Increm.	R^2	Increm.	Sig. of Increm.	R^2	Increm.	Sig. of Increm.	R^2	Increm.	Sig. of Increm.
Reading Performance on Reasoning Tests	.04	—	—	.15‡	—	—	.13†	—	—	.10*	—	—
Reading Performance on Reasoning Tests + Generalized Spanish Reading Comprehension	.09	.05	n.s.	.38§	.28	.0005	.38§	.25	.0005	.30§	.20	.0005

Note
*$p < .05$
†$p < .01$
‡$p < .005$
§$p < .001$

included Average Reading Time per Item, Number of Times Used English, Number of Words Not Understood, and Number of Sentences Not Understood. The results showed that reading comprehension performance on reasoning tests accounted for a significant proportion of variance—10 percent to 15 percent on the *Spanish Diagramming Relationships, Spanish Inference Test,* and *Spanish Logical Reasoning* tests. The results for the *Spanish Nonsense Syllogisms* test showed that reading comprehension performance on this test accounted for only 4 percent of the variation in total scores on the test.

Step two of the stepwise multiple regression analysis was intended to assess how much additional variance in each Spanish-version deductive reasoning test was accounted for by including in the analyses generalized Spanish reading comprehension measures and also reading comprehension measures already considered in step one of the analyses. The regression analysis solutions obtained in this second phase correspond exactly to the results reported in Table 6—where all combined reading comprehension measures were used to predict Spanish reasoning test scores.[2] The focus of the new stepwise analyses, however, was on evaluating the increment in explained Spanish deductive reasoning test score variance between step one and step two. The results of this incremental analysis show that inclusion of generalized Spanish reading comprehension measures, in addition to measures of comprehension considered in step one, improved prediction of variance on the *Spanish Diagramming Relationships, Spanish Inference Test,* and *Spanish Logical Reasoning* tests by 20 percent to 30 percent; these increments in improvement were, of course, all of high statistical significance, as shown in Table 8. The simple conclusion to be drawn from these stepwise regression analyses for the three Spanish-version reasoning tests in question is that generalized reading comprehension skills in Spanish are important to consider in addition to the reading performance measures considered when predicting performance on reasoning tests.

Results of the stepwise regression analysis for predicting *Spanish Nonsense Syllogisms* test scores from reading measures did not lead to any statistically significant increment in reasoning test variance accounted for across steps one and two.

Table 9 displays the results of stepwise regression analyses for predicting English-version deductive reasoning test scores from reading comprehension measures. The design of these analyses was the same as for the Spanish-version reasoning tests, except for the use of corresponding measures of English rather than Spanish reading comprehension. The results of the first regression step showed that reading comprehension performance on all four English-version deductive reasoning tests predicted a statistically significant

---

[2]In the second phase of the stepwise regression analysis, all regression weights for independent variables in the analysis were estimated simultaneously.

TABLE 9

Multiple Regression Analyses: Improvement in R^2 in Predicting Scores on Deductive Reasoning Tests in English by Adding Independent Variables

	Dependent Variable										
	English Nonsense Syllogisms			English Diagramming Relationships			English Inference Test			English Logical Reasoning		
Classes of Independent Variables in a Regression	R^2	Increm.	Sig. of Increm.	R^2	Increm.	Sig. of Increm.	R^2	Increm.	Sig. of Increm.	R^2	Increm.	Sig. of Increm.
Reading Performance on Reasoning Tests	.12†	—	—	.22‡	—	—	.14*	—	—	.16†	—	—
Reading Performance on Reasoning Tests + English Reading Comprehension	.15*	.03	n.s.	.48‡	.26	.0005	.58‡	.44	.0005	.44‡	.28	.0005

Note
*p < .025
†p < .005
‡p < .001

proportion of variance on all tests; the accounted for variance on reasoning tests ranged from 12 percent to 22 percent. Interpretation of the increment in deductive reasoning test score variance, accounted for by additionally including generalized English reading comprehension measures in step two of the analyses, showed a highly significant statistical improvement in prediction of scores on the *English Diagramming Relationships, English Inference Test,* and *English Logical Reasoning* test. The magnitude of improved prediction ranged from 26 percent to 44 percent of the total variance in reasoning test scores.

Results of the stepwise regression analysis for predicting *English Nonsense Syllogisms* test scores from English reading comprehension measures revealed no significant increase in acounted-for variance in going from step one to step two of the analysis.

One final aspect of data analysis results deserves mention; namely, that the degree to which reading measures predicted reasoning test performance seemed not to be systematically interpretable according to the gross linguistic processing demands of different deductive reasoning tests—apart from the finding that scores on the Spanish and English versions of the *Nonsense Syllogism* test were not significantly predictable from comprehension measures. Overall, scores on three reasoning tests which could be predicted from reading measures showed no systematic differentiation in prediction attributable to the gross linguistic processing demands of tests.

SUMMARY AND DISCUSSION

The results of the present study indicate that performance on four verbal deductive reasoning tests in either Spanish or English can be significantly predicted by measures of reading comprehension in the language of tests, where reading measures represent facility in comprehension of deductive reasoning problems or else generalized comprehension skills in the language of problems. Interpretation of the importance of particular reading comprehension measures in predicting reasoning test performance is not unequivocal since the reading comprehension measures considered in the present work are moderately to highly intercorrelated. Thus, they do not permit us to make a simple interpretation of how important a measure is by evaluating the statistical significance of the corresponding standardized regression weight estimate computed in a regression analysis. The obtained results do, however, suggest that, quite possibly, the speed with which subjects read deductive reasoning problems in either language is a critical determinant of overall level of success in solving those problems. Recently, Durán (in preparation) investigated this effect more closely and found that average reading speed for deductive reasoning problems remained a highly significant predictor of overall success in solving problems, even when regression analyses included an additional independent variable representing number of deductive reasoning problems attempted on a reasoning test.

The hypothesis that reading speed is possibly an important contributor to success in verbal deductive reasoning problem-solving in either of two languages is somewhat consistent with findings of previous research on bilingual cognition (e.g., MacNamara, 1967; Kolers, 1966; Lambert et al., 1959; d'Anglejan & Tucker, 1975). Care should be taken, however, to note that relevant previous bilingual studies have focused on a different issue, stressing that slower reading speed of verbal problems in a weaker or second language leds to a detriment in performance of problem-solving tasks in the second language over the first. In contrast, the present work has found that speed in reading verbal problems is associated with a detriment in problem-solving success in either of two languages without consideration of which language is more dominant.

A second major finding of the present investigation was that prediction of performance on deductive reasoning tests in both Spanish and English is aided significantly by using information about generalized reading comprehension skills in a language, in addition to information about how well subjects understood problems on deductive reasoning tests. This finding applied to the *Diagramming Relationships, Inference Test* and *Logical Reasoning* tests and was slightly more prominent in predicting English-version reasoning test scores than in predicting Spanish-version reasoning test scores.

The improvement in prediction of reasoning test scores just cited may have arisen for two different reasons that are not mutually exclusive. First, the self-report methodology used to collect information about how well subjects understood reasoning problems on tests may have been statistically unreliable, although not totally useless in predicting reasoning test performance. Subsequent introduction of highly reliable generalized reading comprehension measures could thus have better tapped the very same kinds of reading skills addressed by measures of reasoning problem comprehension, but with more statistical reliability, thus leading to improved prediction of reasoning test performance.

A second possible reason for the improved prediction may have been that generalized reading measures are somehow drawing on language skills very much more related to solution of deductive reasoing problems than are simple measures of how well reasoning problems are understood. Bilingual cognitive research cited earlier (e.g., MacNamara, 1967; MacNamara & Kellaghan, 1968) suggested that success in solving verbal problems in a weaker language may not bear a trivial, direct relationship to whether individual statements of problem parts are completely understood. It does not seem unreasonable to suppose that proper comprehension of verbal problems requires facility in combining semantic information across sentences or statements in a problem in building a working representation of a problem in short-term memory. The requisite language facility involving ability to build representation of meaning across sentences may well have been better assessed by the measures of generalized reading comprehension (such as ability to recognize paraphrase) used in the present study, than by measures of skill and speed in comprehending reasoning problem statements alone.

In the final analysis, it may well be that deductive reasoning ability itself represents a very broad class of mental skills which might be involved not only in solving problems like those examined in the present study; it may also represent skills connected very closely to many forms of everyday language comprehension. Such a view of language comprehension has recently been presented by Hildyard and Olson (1978), who suggest a broader taxonomy of inference types implicated in everyday discourse comprehension Other views connecting comprehension of meaning in language directly to inference processes have been put forth by a number of researchers in cognitive psychology (see Bransford, 1979; Frederiksen, 1977; and Lachman et al., 1979, for recent surveys of relevant work).

These new views of language processing in relation to inference mechanisms represent unexplored issues in the study of bilinguals' cognition.

REFERENCES

Anastasi, A., & de Jesús, C. Language development and nonverbal IQ of Puerto Rican preschool children in New York City. *Journal of Abnormal Psychology,* 1953, *48*(3), 357–366.

Bransford, J. D. *Human cognition: Learning, understanding and remembering.* Belmont, Calif.: Wadsworth, 1979.

Christiansen, T., & Livermore, G. A. A comparison of Anglo American and Spanish American children on the WISC. *Journal of Social Psychology,* 1970, *81*(1), 9–14.

Cook, J. M., & Arthur, G. Intelligence rating of 97 Mexican-American children in St. Paul, Minn. *Journal of Exceptional Children,*1951, *18*(1), 14–15.

Cordasco, F. (Ed.). *The bilingual-bicultural child and the question of intelligence.* New York: Arno, 1978.

Cummins, J. Bilingualism and the devleopment of metalinguistic awareness. *Journal of Cross-Cultural Psychology,* 1978, *9,* 131–149.

d'Anglejan, A., & Tucker, G. R. *Solving problems in deductive reasoning: A study of the performance of adult second language learners.* Unpublished manuscript Toronto: Ontario Institute for Studies in Education, 1975.

Darcy, N. T. The performance of bilingual Puerto Rican children on verbal and nonverbal language tests of intelligence. *Journal of Educational Research,* 1952, *45*(7), 499–506.

Dornic, S. *Information processing and bilingualism.* Reports from the Department of Psychology, The University of Stockholm, November 1977.

Duncan, S. E., & De Avila E. A. Bilingualism and cognition: Some recent findings. *NABE Journal,* 1979, *4,* 15–50.

Durán, R. P. *Bilingual reading speed and success in solving verbal reasoning problems in two languages.* Princeton, N.J.: Educational Testing Service, in preparation, 1980.

Ekstrom, R. B., French, J. W., & Harman, H. H. *Manual for kit of factor-referenced cognitive tests.* Princeton, N.J.: Educational Testing Service, 1976.

Frederiksen, C. H. Semantic processing units in understanding text. In R. O. Freedle (Ed.), *Discourse production and comprehension.* Norwood, N.J.: Ablex, 1977.

French, J. W., Ekstrom, R. B., & Price, L. A. *Manual for kit of reference tests for cognitive factors.* Princeton, N.J.: Educational Testing Service, 1963.

Garcia, J. Intelligence testing: Quotients, quotas and quackery. In J. L. Martinez, Jr. (Ed.), *Chicano psychology.* New York: Academic Press, 1977.

Garth, T. R., Elson, T. H., & Morton, M. M. The administration of non-language intelligence tests to Mexicans. *Journal of Abnormal and Social Psychology,* 1936, *31*(1), 53–58.

Guidance Testing Associates. *Prueba de lectura,* Nivel 5-Advanzado-Forma DEs. San Antonio, Texas: Author, 1962.

Guidance Testing Associates. *Test of reading,* Level 5-Advanced, Form CE. San Antonio, Texas: Author, 1962.

Gutiérrez-Marsh, L., & Hipple-Maki, R. Efficiency of arithmetic operations in bilinguals as a function of language. *Memory and Cognition,* 1976, *4,* 459–464.

Hildyard, A., & Olson, D. R. Memory and inference in the comprehension of oral and written discourse. *Discourse Processes,* 1978, *1,* 91–117.

International Institute of Teachers College, Columbia University. *A survey of the public educational system of Puerto Rico.* New York: Bureau of Publications, Teachers College, 1926.

Keston, M. J., & Jimenez, C. A study of the performance on English and Spanish editions of the Stanford-Binet intelligence test by Spanish-American children. *Journal of Genetic Psychology,* 1954, *85*(2), 263–269.

Killian, L. R. WISC Illinois Test of Psycholinguistic Abilities, and Bender Visual-motor Gestalt Test performance of Spanish-American kindergarten and first-grade children. *Journal of Consulting and Clinical Psychology,* 1971, *37*(1), 38–43.

Kolers, P. A. Reading and talking bilingually. *American Journal of Psychology,* 1966, *79,* 357–376.

Lachman, R., Lachman, J., & Butterfield, E. C. *Cognititve psychology and information processing: An introduction.* Hillsdale, N.J.: Erlbaum, 1979.

Lambert, W. E. Measurement of the linguistic dominance of bilinguals. *Journal of Abnormal and Social Psychology,* 1955, *50,* 197–200.

Lambert, W. E., Havelka, J., & Gardner, R. C. Linguistic manifestations of bilingualism. *American Journal of Psychology,* 1959, *72,* 77–82.

Laosa, L. Nonbiased assessment of children's abilities: Historical antecedents and current issues. In T. Oakland (Ed.), *Psychological and educational assessment of minority children.* New York: Brunner/Mazel, 1977.

López, M., & Young, R. K. The linguistic interdependence of bilinguals. *Journal of Experimental Psychology,* 1974, *102,* 981–983.

Mahakian, C. Measuring intelligence and reading capacity of Spanish-speaking children. *Elementary School Journal,* 1939, *39*(10), 760–768.

MacNamara, J. The effects of instruction in a weaker language. *Journal of Social Issues,* 1967, *23*(2), 121–135.

MacNamara, J., & Kellaghan, T. P. Reading in a second language. In M. Jenkinson (Ed.), *Improving reading throughout the world.* Newark, Del.: International Reading Association, 1968.

Manuel, H. T. *The preparation and evaluation of inter-language testing materials.* Austin, Texas: University of Texas at Austin, 1963.

Mitchell, A. J. The effect of bilingualism in the measurement of intelligence. *Elementary School Journal,* 1937, *38*(1), 297.

Olmedo, E. L. Psychological testing and the Chicano. In J. L. Martinez (Ed.), *Chicano psychology.* New York: Academic Press, 1977.

19 Bilingualism and the Metaset

Edward A. De Avila and Sharon E. Duncan
De Avila, Duncan and Associates, Inc., Larkspur, CA.

INTRODUCTION

Bilingualism is a worldwide phenomenon, yet the implications for the individual or group which is able to communicate in more than one language vary greatly, from country to country, from one geographical area to another, even from one situation to another. Whether bilingualism is considered an asset or a liability, a necessity or an accepted way of life is also a factor of changing political and economical conditions.

Moreover, there seems to be such divergence of opinion as to what actually constitutes bilingualism,[1] that descriptions may range from "native-like control of two languages" (Bloomfield, 1946:56) to "... alternately using two languages" (Weinrich, 1953:1), to producing "... complete and meaningful utterances in the other languages..." (Haugen, 1953:6).[2]

Finally, as noted by a number of writers (Schumann, 1975, 1976; Gardner & Lambert, 1972; Gardner, 1973) being bilingual in certain languages and in certain places is a mark of education and cultural advantage; bilingualism in other languages in other places may be synonymous with poverty and supposed cultural deprivation.

Although the question of bilingualism has been seriously studied for over four decades in Western Europe—primarily in the tradition of historical

---

[1]Okaar (1972) notes "... vagueness of definition often correlates positively with the modernity of the linguistic publication."

[2]Given such diversity of definitions, one would expect equal difference of opinion as to what constitutes an adequate measure of bilingualism. This is, in fact, true. A discussion of this issue may be found in De Avila and Duncan (1978).

linguistics—the greatest impetus to modern research on bilingualism came from the United States and Canada in the 1960s. Currently, bilingualism as a topic for research is interdisciplinary, including, but not limited to, linguistics, psycholinguistics, psychology, sociology, and education. There continues to be an abundance of studies focusing on such issues as phonology, lexicology, contrastive analysis, "interference," and codeswitching, but far fewer studies have been aimed at investigating the effects of bilingualism on the intellectual development and skills of the individual.

Yet it is precisely these effects—seen by some as injuries, by others as advantages—which carry the heaviest linguistic and psychological impact. In the United States the most immediate of these implications fall within the realm of bilingual education.

The purpose of this chapter is threefold. First, we shall examine the issue of bilingualism as it relates to the educational treatment of language minority children living in the United States. Second, by integrating the findings of a number of studies in bilingualism with theories of cognitive development and learning, we shall propose a new approach to the issue of bilingualism and make some predictions with respect to the relationship between bilingualism and intellectual/cognitive functioning. Third, we shall summarize the findings of a recent study of bilingualism designed to test the general hypothesis drawn from the review.

Education of linguistic minorities in the United States is still in its infancy, although federal and state-supported bilingual programs have proliferated over the past two decades. This proliferation has been motivated primarily by the enforced recognition of the right to an education irrespective of language background—a right supported by Title VI guidelines[3] and mandated by numerous court decisions.[4] These decisions have concerned placement, traditional testing procedures and classroom methodology with linguistic minority children and have begun to stimulate a wide variety of research on related issues, ranging from studies which examine the relationship between self-concept and school achievement among Spanish-speaking children (Cervantes & Bernal, 1976), to the study of parent-child interaction patterns (Laosa, 1975).

Beginning with the massive Civil Rights Commission survey (1974) of the educational status of the Mexican-American, a common theme running through most of the research on Spanish-speaking minorities—as well as studies of Native Americans, Filipinos, Puerto Ricans, etc.—has been an

---

[3]"No person in the United States shall, on the ground of race, color or national origin, be excluded from participation in, be denied the benefits of, or be subjected to discrimination under any program or activity receiving federal financial assisatance" 42 U.S.C. 2000d (1970).

[4]See Teitlebaum and Hiller (1977) on the implications of *Lau* v. *Nichols* and subsequent cases for equitable education.

emphasis on studies directed toward describing the poor academic showing of children from various non-English speaking backgrounds. Thus, most of the research on language minority students has focused on the examination of ethnolinguistic differences believed to account for the poor academic performance of children from backgrounds where little or no English is spoken. One line of investigation has focused on the negative effects of bilingualism on academic performance (Darcy, 1946) and has shown that children from bilingual environments tend to perform substantially below the level of their monolingual English-speaking peers, particularly on tests requiring verbal skills. In contrast, other investigators have focused on the use of individual/difference variables to explain differences in academic performance which are attributed to cultural and personality incompatibilities between language minority students and the mainstream (Castañeda et al., 1974; De Avila et al., 1978).

A cursory review of the research, however, suggests certain limitations to both approaches, which follow from both methodological and theoretical confusion.

With respect to studies which have claimed to demonstrate the negative effects of bilingualism, most seem to suffer from a failure to control for language proficiency as well as from a lack of definition for bilingualism in either theoretical or operational terms. Yela (1975) concludes that bilingualism (described as characterized by "... el uso de la lengua primera en el hogar y en muchas situaciones de la vida cotidiana y el empleo de la segunda lengua en las tareas escolares y oficiales...) reduced subjects' performance on semantic tasks. Brown, Fournier, and Moyer (1977), in a study focusing on science concepts and Piagetian concrete reasoning, find that:

> ...the Mexican American children in this study scored significantly lower on both tests than the Anglo American children...The lag in development between the two groups...appears to be about 2 + years (Brown, Fournier, & Moyer, 1977; 332–332).

A review of these and other studies seems to suggest that the failure to operationalize and control for linguistic proficiency has resulted in the widespread belief that bilingual children must inevitably face a linguistic handicap with the ultimate effect of lowering both intellectual and academic performance (see De Avila & Duncan, 1979a).

In contrast to these approaches, recent work drawn from a variety of other fields, including linguistics and psycholinguistics, learning, developmental psychology, and organizational sociology suggest: that rather than causing intellectual deprivation, early bilingualism may offer benefits that far exceed any short-term educational deficits. In fact, as will be seen, studies in the areas of metacognition[5] and metalinguistics (Flavell et al., 1968; Cazden, 1972; Markham, 1973) seem to suggest that bilingual children may be potentially advanced with respect to concept formation and general mental flexibility. Therefore, a careful review of research on cognitive development, learning sets, and metacognition might serve to facilitate the development of successful educational models applicable to children who do not speak English as a first language, and perhaps, to provide a new theoretical direction in United States bilingual education as a whole.

COGNITION AND BILINGUALISM

Learning sets were first studied by Harlow (1949) who hypothesized that concepts such as triangularity, middle-sizedness, redness, number, smoothness, etc., evolve from learning set formation. Thus, a learning set may be experimentally formed as in the "oddity problem." In this paradigmatic task, the child (or subject, since learning set methodology has been used with a wide variety of species) is presented with a set of stimulus objects, one of which differs in some specifiable way (i.e., three red wooden shapes, two of which are rectangular, one of which is triangular). The child is then asked to say which object is different from the other two and is rewarded if a correct identification is made. If a correct response is not made, the stimulus objects are removed and presented again in a second trial in a different arrangement. The child then chooses and is rewarded for the correct choice. This procedure is repeated until the child reaches a criterion; then a second problem is introduced that differs from the first only in that a different set of stimulus objects is used (i.e., two blocks are round, and one is square). The "principle of solution" remains invariant across all trials. Hence, changes occur only on the irrelevant dimensions.

The concept of the learning set, as opposed to its methodology, bears great similarity to the notion of the "scheme" as used by Jean Piaget (1960). Furth (1969) following Piaget, has defined the *scheme* as "the structure common to all those acts which, from the subject's point of view, are equivalent." In a sense, the scheme bears great similarity to Tolman's (1959) *cognitive map,* and Miller, Galanter and Pribram's (1960) *plan of action.* Pascual-Leone (1970), however, points out that the scheme is a more general concept because it applies to *any* pattern of recurring behavior which is modifiable through experience. Hence, the scheme cuts across any number of affective, cognitive, or perceptual domains.

---

[5]*Meta:* a Greek-derived prefix denoting "after," "along with," "beyond," "among," "behind," used in the formation of compound words, such as metaphysics, metalinguistics, metacognition, etc.

Regarding perceptual, cognitive, and by simple extension, linguistic schemes, Pascual-Leone (1970) states "...a scheme corresponds to a predicate function (i.e., a property or a relation) which the child has stored in his repertory and which is used by him for assimilating (i.e., interpreting or categorizing semantically or pragmatically) the input." Within a Piagetian framework, a novel psychological act, such as one represented by a correct response to an oddity problem, takes place through the simultaneous integration of schemes within the child's repertory. Moreover, *it is this capacity to integrate schemes to produce novel acts that defines intelligence or capacity.*[6] Further discussion of this relation will be included below.

Blank and Solomon (1968) assert that poorly functioning preschoolers have failed to develop an "abstract attitude...[and that]...the mental attitude or set that impels well-functioning young children to think is an abstract attitude." They argue that the principal goal of teaching poorly functioning children should be developing in them the precursors of abstract thinking so that they will have an internalized readily available symbolic system. They conjecture that to be useful in preschool education, learning sets would almost always have to constitute a metaset—the learning set of all sets. The metaset, then, involves a metacognitive process which includes a general predisposition to use all learning sets and to shift flexibly among these as the situation demands. Confronted with a new problem, the child's metaset provides assurance that information is available to solve this problem or to meet this new situation. The child must then determine which of the available schemes, sets, or plans of action is applicable.

With respect to language acquisition, Hunt (1961) uses the concept of the learning set to explain Helen Keller's generalization of the notion that "things have names." The process of learning set formation, according to Hunt (1961), follows from direct experience and is

> ...attested to by the fact that Helen Keller (1903), who had been both blind and deaf following an illness in her first year of life, did not hit upon this generalization until the critical water-pump incident that came in her eighth year after a tedious period during which Teacher (Anne Sullivan) had repeatedly associated the various forms of the touch alphabet with objects. At the pump, however, Helen suddenly discriminated, with teacher's help, the signs for the water that overflowed onto her hand from the cup that she held in her hand, and to discriminate the signs of both of these from the sign for the act of drinking...The acquisition of this "learning set" in the development of language puts the child into the dual system of relationships: (1) that which he sustains in his interaction with concrete objects and events, and (2) that concerned in his communication with other people (Hunt, 1961:187–188).

---

[6] This is also what distinguishes a Piagetian theory from an S-R theory. Namely, in Piagetian theory, learning is based on the productions of a novel act. Under S-R theory, there is no explanation for novel acts since the S-R contingencies have never existed. Thus, S-R theory cannot account for inference.

Moreover, we might add that insofar as the object-referent bond is understood or broken through the formation of the learning set, then the formation of these learning sets may well lie (as suggested by Harlow) at the very basis of cognition itself. And this would apply across any series of comparisons the researcher might care to make.

Metacognition

Nowhere can the relationship between learning set formation and higher-order mental operations be more readily seen than in the recent interest in metacognition (Cazden, 1972; Markham, 1974).

Metacognition refers to an individual's awareness of his or her own cognitive processes. To that extent it represents one of the highest orders of thought; thinking about thinking, which has historically been the exclusive province of the philosopher.

Metacognition can be manifested in a variety of ways. The ability to make judgments of grammaticality (Gleitman, Gleitman, Shipley, 1972) serves as an example of metacognition in the domain of language whereas the ability to speak does not. Awareness of general properties of language would also be considered a metacognitive, or more specifically, a metalinguistic ability. For instance, recognizing the arbitrariness of words (e.g., that one could just as well have called the moon *boodle*) requires thinking about language (Osherson & Markham, 1973; Piaget, 1926).

Examples of metacognition concerning perception include an individual's realization that perspectives other than one's own exist (Flavell, et al., 1968) and knowledge of what other perspectives of a three-dimensional display actually are (Inhelder & Piaget, 1956). Notice that rather than thinking about or perceiving the *display* the individual is thinking about *perceptions* of the display. Or, one might contrast the ability to *predict* that one's memory span for a set of items is eight with the ability to remember eight times. The former is a *metacognitive* or *metamemorial* ability; the latter, is a cognitive or memorial ability. Other examples of metamemorial skills include knowledge of factors affecting recall and the realization that one has stored in memory some information which at the moment is inaccessible (Brown, 1965; McNeill, 1970).

The distinctive feature of these examples is that they involve knowledge about cognitive processes. Phenomena as diverse as predicting one's memory span and knowing grammatical rules have thus been subsumed under the concept of "metacognition."

An even more important feature of the present context is that the level of abstraction here is content-free. That is, metalinguistic awareness or, more generally, metacognition, is not tied to any particular language or set of sociocultural circumstances and is applicable to any situation or experience, whether it be Mexican-American, Anglo, or Serbo-Croatian. By the same token, one might argue that the formation of learning sets cuts across any number of content areas whether "affective" or "cognitive." In this way, one would expect to find effects attributable to the formation of learning sets to be general across cognitive and personality dimensions.

As just noted, one of the primary features defining metalinguistic awareness is an understanding of the arbitrary use of language. In fact, Miller (1965) admonishes us all when he warns:

> The meaning of an utterance should not be confused with its referent. I take this to imply that the acquisition of meaning cannot be identified with the simple acquisition of a conditioned vocalization in the presence of a particular environmental stimulus. It may be possible to talk about reference in terms of conditioning, but meaning is a much more complicated phenomenon that depends on the relations of a symbol to other symbols in the language (Miller, 1965:18).

In this very key feature one might expect bilinguals to have a headstart. The linguistic experience of the child growing up with more than one language should increase metalinguistic awareness. In fact, after extensive observations of his own child's linguistic development, Leopold (1949) concluded:

> ...I attribute this attitude to detachment from words confidently to the bilingualism. Constantly hearing the same things referred to by different words from two languages, she had her attention drawn to essentials, to content instead of form (Leopold, 1949).

This fact also seems to be indicated by the results of the longitudinal studies done by Lambert and Tucker (1972) and Edwards and Casserly (1973, cited in Tremaine, 1975) with French-English bilingual children in Canada, where it was found that French immersion not only facilitated certain mathematical skills, but also that "... increased exposure by basically Anglophone children to a second language benefits not only the acquisition of the second language, but also the development of the mother tongue" (Edwards & Casserly, cited in Tremaine, 1975:2).

Bilingual children are exposed to two different languages with different grammatical rules and different phonological patterns and so learn many different ways of saying the same things. Hence their knowledge is based, like Harlow's learning sets, on the "principle of solution" and is therefore transferable to any number of novel situations.

It would seem to follow that if bilingual children are potentially advanced with respect to metalinguistic awareness, then this headstart would manifest itself in superior performance on other tasks of general ability, such as tests of intelligence. Several relevant variables, however, may tend to obscure or even "wash away" this potential headstart. These have to do with cultural biases and variations in relative language proficiency of bilingual children. The cultural biases in currently available tests with respect to children from Spanish-speaking backgrounds have been well documented (see De Avila & Havassy, 1974). The issue of language proficiency has been somewhat less discussed. In fact, much previous research on bilingualism has tended to focus on establishing IQ differences between monolingual and bilingual populations; it has often found most of the differences to be with respect to verbal tests, suggesting the bilingual group to be less than proficient in the language of the monoglinguals, and therefore, the differences. Hence it would seem meaningless to compare monolingual and bilingual populations on verbal IQ when the two populations are equivalent with respect to linguistic proficiency. It would also seem equally meaningless to compare groups on verbal measures when the groups have not been equated. To do either would seem to focus the research on the subject sample population difference rather than on the effects of the linguistic characteristics upon the cognitive performance of two groups. On the other hand, when language is treated as an independent variable, cognitive advantages of bilingual children have been reported on measures of cognitive flexibility, creativity, and diversity.

In a rigorously controlled series of experiments on the relationship between language, intellectual development, and school-related achievement, Peal and Lambert (1962) matched monolingual and bilingual groups and reported superior performance for the bilinguals:

> The picture that emerges of the French/English bilingual in Montreal is that of a youngster whose wider experiences in two cultures have given him advantages which a monolingual does not enjoy. Intellectually, his experience with two language systems seems to have left him with a mental flexibility, a superiority in concept formation, and a more diversified set of mental abilities, in the sense that the patterns of abilities developed by bilinguals were more heterogeneous... In contrast, the monolingual appears to have a more unitary structure of intelligence which he must use for all types of intellectual tasks (Peal & Lambert, 1962:6).

Further review of the literature on bilingualism would tend to support the foregoing conclusions in research conducted throughout the world from Singapore (Torrance et al., 1970), Switzerland (Balkan, 1971), South Africa (Ianco-Worrall, 1972), Israel and New York (Ben-Zeev, 1972), Western Canada (Cummins & Gulutsan, 1974), and Montreal (Scott, 1973).

Bilingualism and Piagetian Development

The biases, instability, and general shortcomings of traditional testing approaches to assessment of bilingual children are well known. Therefore, there is little need to retrace the issues. One alternative has been suggested by the work of De Avila (1976) and De Avila and Havassy (1975) using a

Piagetian-based approach which controls for many of the biasing elements in IQ methodology through pretraining. This approach has been found to be useful in a variety of different educational-assessment contexts. The assessment of developmental stage is also consistent with Sigel and Coop's (1963) admonition that failure to consider developmental differences may produce spurious results, indicating cognitive style differences between groups which simply develop at different rates.

The application of Piagetian constructs to the study of bilingualism can be found in almost any review of the literature. Unfortunately, however, the results of these studies are equivocal for a variety of reasons. The primary flaw in previous studies, as suggested earlier, has been in the failure to control for the relative linguistic proficiency of the comparison groups.

In one of the earlist studies, Price-Williams (1969) studied illiterate West African children. He used conservation of quantities and concluded:

> There seems to be little doubt from the results that the progression of comprehension concerning conservation postulated by Piaget is evident in these African children (p. 207).

Most of the conservation studies have focused on cross-cultural comparisons which have examined the effects of schooling (see Gordon, 1923, cited in Al-Issa & Dennis, 1970; Husen, 1951; Heber et al., 1972), but more recent studies have been directly applied to the study of bilingualism within the United States.

In an often cited study on the effects of early childhood bilingualism, Feldman and Shen (1971) compared bilingual and monolingual subjects on Piagetian "object constancy" tasks in which various transformations were made on different objects, such as a cup, a paper plate, and a sponge. Two other types of tasks were used in which children were asked to recognize the arbitrary use of object names and to apply these names in simple sentences. Their results showed the bilingual group to be superior in performing all three tasks. Feldman and Shen argue that ability to use arbitrary names in statments involves the ability to see language as an instrument or set of strategies which varies with linguistic and social context. In the sense that there is a differentiation or distinction between object and referent, we are reminded of Helen Keller's insight which satisfied the conditions for metalinguistic awareness. By implication, we are arguing that the concepts underlying and defining metalinguistic awareness of this type are acquired through the formation of learning sets in the same way as one acquires the concept "triangularity," "middle-sizedness," and so on. Unfortunately, the results of Feldman and Shen's study are flawed because the criteria for the assignment to subject groups were somewhat questionable. For example, assignment to the bilingual group was made on the basis of the children's "understanding of several simple Spanish questions and ability to speak

Spanish at home." No information is provided as to the nature of these questions or how the ability "to speak Spanish at home" was defined or discovered. Moreover, the comparison monolingual group was confounded by both linguistic and ethnic variables since the group consisted of Mexican-American and Black children residing in the same neighborhood. Thus, although the results of this study are generally supportive of the notion of cognitive advantage for the bilingual groups, those results are weakened by poor control over relevant variables.

The problem evidenced in the Feldman and Shen study is similarly evidenced in a study by Liedtke and Nelson (1968). In this study, where bilingual and monolingual subjects were compared on a number of Piagetian tasks, the criterion for assignment to the bilingual group was based on teacher observation. The group was defined as "children who had used two languages before entering school and who were exposed to both languages at home." Unfortunately, no data are provided as to the actual level of proficiency for either the bilingual or monolingual groups. Similarly, the authors provide no information as to the comparability of the two groups across socioeconomic dimensions. As with the Feldman and Shen study, it appears that the results of this study, although generally supporting the hypothesis of a cognitive advantage for bilinguals, is weakened by the lack of appropriate linguistic controls.

Finally, similar criticism may be leveled against a more recent study (Dahl, 1976) which claimed to illustrate a superior performance for bilinguals on Piagetian tasks. In this study "children identified as speakers of Spanish upon entry [to a bilingual preschool program in southern California] were assumed to acquire English because this was the language modeled" (Dahl, 1976:59). Unfortunately, no other data are provided as to the actual linguistic comparability of the two groups (bilingual and monolingual) studied.

The danger in a failure to control for linguistic variables is particularly evident in a number of other studies which have chosen to use Piagetian constructs or tasks to support a negative view of bilingualism. As such, the failure to control for level of linguistic proficiency can even result in opposite results when Piagetian tasks are given. For example, in the recent study by Brown, Fournier, and Moyer (1977), Mexican-American children were found to perform significantly lower than Anglo-American children across a battery of 10 Piagetian concepts including various conservation tasks. The authors conclude from their study that the acquisition of a second language and, hence, bingualism, leads to a "developmental lag." This study, like those which have found positive results, employed no measure or control for language proficiency. In fact, not only was there no assessment of the linguistic proficiency of the two groups, but the tests were presented in written and oral form, thus making them more difficult for those with either poor reading skills (as is typical of language minority children) or linguistic deficiencies in English. The inherent bias in this approach has been extensively discussed by De Avila and Havassy (1974). Similar studies which have "shown" opposite results can be cited (for example, see Ramirez and Price-Williams, 1974).

It seems sufficient to say that the need for tighter linguistic control over the definition of bilingual and monolingual groups is readily apparent in the studies just cited. This need becomes even more important in light of both the notions of the metaset theory described earlier, and of other recent theoretical considerations or approaches, such as that of Cummins (1978). Cummins has offered a threshold hypothesis which "proposes that there may be threshold levels of linguistic competency which a bilingual child must attain, both in order to avoid cognitive disadvantages and to allow the potentially beneficial aspects of bilingualism to influence his cognitive and academic functioning" (Cummins, 1978:p.1).

If the Cummins proposal is correct and if, as suggested by the metaset theory and a number of the studies reviewed here, bilingualism "accelerates" cognitive functioning, then this cognitive advantage or acceleration should be apparent in studies which carefully control for relevant variables, such as culture bias and language proficiency. Further, this advantage should be apparent across any measure involving cognitive processing.

Bilingualism and Cognitive Functioning: Some Recent Findings

Several studies—recently reported (De Avila & Duncan, 1979b; Duncan & De Avila, 1979) and in progress (Duncan, 1979; Duncan & Fleming, 1979)— involving bilingualism and cognitive functioning to varying degrees, support the previously hypothesized cognitive advantages of bilingualism. The study to be summarized (De Avila & Duncan, 1979b) employed a measure of Piagetian intellectual development as well as tests of cognitive/perceptual processing (also referred to as *psychological differentiation* or *field dependence–independence*) and cognitive tempo (*impulsivity-reflectivity*).

De Avila and Duncan (1979b) assessed the relation between bilingualism and neo-Piagetian intellectual development, field dependence/independence, and cognitive tempo (impulsitivity-reflectivity). The subjects were 278 public school children in grades one and three in the United States and Mexico.* Based on oral language proficiency in English and/or Spanish, three comparison groups were selected as follows:

---

*The data used in this study were collected as part of a larger, three-year cross-cultural investigation of eight ethnolinguistic groups, supported by the National Institute of Education, Contract #400-65-0051, and the Southwest Educational Development Laboratory, Austin, Texas.

1. 130 lower-middle–middle-class Anglo-American monolingual English speakers from an urban community in the San Francisco Bay area, California
2. 105 lower-middle-class Mexican monolingual Spanish speakers from an urban area in the State of Chihuahua, Mexico
3. 43 lower-middle–middle-class Spanish/English bilinguals consisting of subjects pooled from four Hispanic background sites in Texas, California, New York, and Florida.

The dependent measures consisted of the Cartoon Conservation Scales (CCS), Level I, the Children's Embedded Figures Test (CEFT), the Draw-a-Person (DAP) Test, and the Matching Familiar Figures (MFF) Test. Highly significant differences at the .001 level are reported for both the CEFT and the DAP. In both cases, the bilingual group outperformed the other two groups.

No significant differences were reported between groups on the MFF. On the CCS a significant F at the .01 level was reported for total score. Between-group differences on the CCS "Distance" and "Egocentricity" subscales were also significant at the .01 level. (On Distance, the Bilingual and Monolingual Spanish groups performed similarly; on the Egocentricity subscale, the Bilingual group clearly outperformed the two Monolingual groups.)

Since this study controlled for relative linguistic proficiency and, to a degree, for SES, it would seem to support our predictions of cognitive advantages for bilinguals.

SUMMARY AND CONCLUSIONS

In the preceding material, we have discussed a number of research approaches to the problem of accounting for the low academic performance of language minority children. In an attempt to reverse the deficit-based and culturally deprived image of these children, we have discussed the concepts of metacognition and metalinguistic awareness as they relate to treatment of bilingual children. We then cited various studies—still too few—focusing on the positive effects of bilingualism which have shown that bilinguals may actually have a headstart through their formation of an operational metaset.

It was argued that much of the previous research on the effects of bilingualism was subject to both criticism and alternative interpretation. With respect to the former, it was argued that, to a large extent, studies trying to explain the low overall school achievement of language minority children had focused on linguistic differences without controlling for the relative linguistic proficiency of the comparison group. With respect to the latter, we have presented an argument or theoretical framework in which it would appear that children growing up in a bilingual setting are forced to acquire multiple referents for similar objects or concepts. This situation seems to mirror the learning set paradigm in which trials are repeated and varied according to social and linguistic variations (primarily referential) while deeper semantic meaning remains invariant. Moreover, the extraction or "abstraction" of semantic meaning would seem to require an adaptive flexibility on the part of the child. This flexibility would have direct stylistic implications which are contrary to previously reported personality characteristics of language minority children, particularly Chicanos.

Accordingly, it would seem to follow that bilingualism would require a mental flexibility which, rather than predicting lower social and intellectual development, should predict an enhanced set of social and intellectual strategies.

Thus, when two groups of monolingual speakers whose level of linguistic proficiency was equivalent were compared to a group of bilingual children whose relative proficiency in two languages was equal to the monolingual proficiency of two other groups (De Avila & Duncan, 1979b), it was found that the bilingual group produced significantly higher scores on two measures of psychological differentiation or field dependence/independence.

No significant differences were reported (De Avila & Duncan, 1979b) with respect to impulsivity/reflectivity, but it is, perhaps, important to note that the bilingual group tended to score at intermediate levels of latency on the MFF, suggesting that the group could (on the basis of these data) be characterized as neither impulsive nor reflective. In this sense, one might expect a situational variability or flexibility on the part of the bilingual group which would enable them to "switch hit," depending on task demands.

When De Avila and Duncan (1979b) made a comparison on the intellectual development measures, the bilingual group tended to outperform both of the monolingual groups on five of the six CCS subscales as well as on the total score.

These findings might be taken to suggest that the bilingual group was primarily made up of "high processors" in that their scores seem to suggest a consistently high level of performance across most of the measures employed. One might speculate that this tendency is reflective of simple differences in intelligence. This interpretation is not positively convincing, for, in the past, even though the bilingual groups scored higher on the CCS than the two monolingual groups, the scores of all three groups were within the normal range as indicated by published test norms (see De Avila & Pulos, 1979).

In general terms, the findings of this most recent work seem to support earlier, less well-controlled studies and the hypothesis of a cognitive advantage for the bilingual child. Moreover, as hypothesized from a consideration of metacognitive implications, De Avila and Duncan (1979b) found this advantage to cut across both the Piaget and Witkin tests, suggesting that the advantage may be general across a number of dimensions. This speculation is supported by the particularly striking difference between the three groups on the Egocentricity scale which has been shown to have wide social application. A number of researchers have demonstrated high correlations between performance on Piaget's basically perceptual task and performance in the role-playing situation (see Flavell et al., 1968). Similarly, other investigators have found performance on egocentrism tasks to be a significant predictor of various aspects of socioemotional maturity (Neale, 1966; Feffer & Gourevich, 1960).

Finally, it seems appropriate to speculate on the importance of the metaset notion for those children identified as "bilingual" who are experiencing difficulty in the schools and who, according to many, do not seem to be functioning as high processors in the same way as the "bilingual" groups discussed by Peal and Lambert (1962), Liedtke (1968), and De Avila and Duncan (1979b).

Cummins (1978) has suggested that a child's level of competence in the two languages which make up his or her bilingualism can be viewed as an intervening variable which mediates performance across cognitive and academic tasks. In the De Avila and Duncan (1979 study, there was an attempt to test the metaset hypothesis by comparing only "children who were fully competent in both languages with those fully competent in only one language." The threshold hypothesis proposed by Cummins would suggest that if children with limited bilingual competency (relative linguistic proficiency) were compared with fully competent monolinguals or bilinguals, the less-competent bilinguals would perform less well than the other groups.

According to Cummins, the lower overall performance of many language minority children is attributable to "low levels of competence in both languages," or "semilingualism," or "double semilingualism." The presumption that lower linguistic skills lead to lower overall cognitive functioning carries with it an implicit assumption regarding an interaction between language and thought similar to the concept of linguistic interdependence. This would suggest that, so far as the two languages are "interdependent," as evidenced in *codeswitching* (the alternate use of two languages within a single utterance or sentence), lower overall cognitive functioning will be evidenced. Unfortunately, Cummins offers not data to support this contention.

The position presented within the metaset approach would make no such prediction. In fact, it would suggest that the schemes carried by the "semilingual" are different from those of the competent monolingual, perhaps even academically deficient, but in no way indicative of a lower level of cognitive functions. The prediction drawn from the present theory would be that differences between double semilingual children and competent monolinguals would occur only on tasks requiring linguistic manipulations within the language of the monolingual (as in the case of verbal IQ), but would not hold for tasks more directly indicative of cognitive functioning, such as Piagetian tasks where in task elements are equally familiar to both. Moreover, we might speculate that in those cases where differences have been found, the lower performance of the "bilingual group" could be attributable to the failure of researchers to take into account possible linguistic idiosyncracies of the group.

In an attempt to test the scheme interpretation, Duncan (1979) is comparing different types of bilinguals (proficient bilinguals, partial bilinguals, etc.) with monolinguals across a wide variety of intellectual development, cognitive style, and demographic dimensions. In an early report of these data (Duncan & De Avila, 1979), confirmatory evidence was found for the cognitive advantages of the proficient bilingual. The final results of this study should provide additional information as to the nature of linguistic, intellectual, and stylistic development among language minority children and help to show how appropriate educational programs might be offered which would facilitate the gift of bilingualism.

In conclusion, we urge that the need for further research aimed at investigating the psychological and educational effects of bilingualism—where language proficiency and SES are controlled—is of utmost importance in the context of bilingual educational models, and perhaps for mainstream education as well. In 1928, Meillet (Oksaar, 1972) stated "...the linguistic state has often depended on the social state...," today, given the current needs of bilingual education, we suggest that the educational state might well depend on the linguistic state.

REFERENCES

Al-Issa, I., & Dennis, W. *Cross-cultural studies of beavior.* New York: Holt, Rinehart & Winston, 1970.

Balkan, L. *Les effets du bilinguisme Francais-Anglais sur les aptitudes intellectuelles.* Bruxelles: Aimav, 1971.

Ben-Zeev, S. *The influence of bilingualism on cognitive development and cognitive strategy.* Unpublished doctoral dissertation, University of Chicago, 1972.

Blank, M., & Solomon, F. A tutorial language program to develop abstract thinking in socially disadvantaged preschool children. *Child Development,* 1968, *39,* 379–389.

Bloomfield, L. *Language.* New York: Holt, 1946.

Brown, R. L., Fournier, J. F., & Moyer, R. H. A cross-cultural study of Piagetian concrete reasoning and science concepts among rural 5th grade Mexican- and Anglo-American students. *Journal of Research in Science Teaching,* 1977, *14,* 329–334.

Brown, R. B. *Social psychology.* New York: Free press, 1965.

Castañeda, A., Harold, P. L., & Ramirez, M. *New approaches to bilingual education.* Austin, Texas: Dissemination and Assessment Center, 1974.

Cazden, C. B. *Child language and education.* New York: Holt, Rinehart & Winston, 1972.

Cervantes, R. A., & Bernal, H. H. *Psychosocial growth and academic achievement in Mexican American pupils.* San Antonio, Texas: D.C. Development Associates, 1976.

Cummins, J. Bilingualism and the development of metalinguistic awareness. *Journal of Cross-Cultural Psychology,* 1978, *9*(2), 131–149.

Cummins, J., & Gulutsan, M. Some effects of bilingualism on cognitive functioning. In S. Carey (Ed.), *Bilingualism, biculturalism and education. Proceedings from the Conference Universitaire Saint-Jean, The University of Alberta,* 1974.

Dahl, R. J. *The attainment of conservation of mass and verbal synthesis between Latin-American children who speak one or two languages.* Unpublished doctoral dissertation, University of Southern California, June 1976.

Darcy, N. T. The effects of bilingualism upon the measurement of the intelligence of children of preschool age. *The Journal of Education Psychology,* 1946, *37*(1), 21–43.

De Avila, E. A. Mainstreaming ethnically and linguistically different children: An exercise in paradox or a new approach? In R. L. Jones (Ed.), *Mainstreaming and the minority child.* Minneapolis, Minn.: Leadership Training Institute/Special Education, 1976.

De Avila, E. A., & Duncan, S. E. *Definition and measurement: The East and West of bilingualism.* Paper prepared for the California State Department of Education, August 14, 1978.

De Avila, E. A., & Duncan, S. E. The developmental assessment model. In H. T. Trueba (Ed.), *Futures of bilingual education: Interdisciplinary perspectives.* Rawley, Mass.: Newberry House, 1979a.

De Avila, E. A., & Duncan, S. E. Findings on the intellectual/developmental effects of bilingualism: A cross-cultural study. (In preparation, 1979b).

De Avila, E. A., Duncan, S. E., Fleming, J., Cervantes, A., & Laosa, L. *Research on cognitive styles with language minority children.* Report presented at National Association for Bilingual Education, Seventh Annual International Bilingual Bicultural Education Conference, San Juan, Puerto Rico, April 26, 1978.

De Avila, E. A., & Havassy, B. E. The testing of minority children: A neo-Piagetian alternative. *Today's Education, Journal of the National Education Association,* November/December, 1974, pp. 72–75.

De Avila, E. A., & Havassy, B. E. Piagetian alternative to IQ: Mexican-American study. In N. Hobbs (Ed.), *Issues in the classification of exceptional children.* San Francisco: Jossey Bass, 1975.

De Avila, E. A., & Pulos, S. The group assessment of cognitive level by pictorial Piagetian tasks. 1979. (Send requests for reprints to Steve Pulos, Lawrence Hall of Science, University of California, Berkeley, Calif. 94720).

Duncan, S. E. *Child bilingualism and cognitive functioning: A study of four hispanic groups.* Unpublished doctoral dissertation, Union Graduate School—West, 1979.

Duncan, S. E., & De Avila, E. A. *Relative linguistic proficiency and field dependence/independence: Some findings on the linguistic heterogeneity and cognitive style of bilingual children.* Paper presented at the 13th Annual Convention of TESOL. Colloquium on ESL in Bilingual Education: Implementation and Other Practical Considerations, Boston, February 27–28, 1979.

Duncan, S. E., & Fleming, J. *Metacognition and categorical style.* (In preparation, 1979).

Feffer, M., & Gourevitch, V. Cognitive aspects of role-taking in children. *Journal of Personality.* 1960, *28,* 383–396.

Feldman, C., & Frank, E. *An exploratory study for possible effects of bilingualism on the language-related cognitive abilities of 4- to 6-year olds.* Unpublished paper, University of Chicago, n.d.

Feldman, C., & Shen, M. Some language-related cognitive advantages of bilingual 5-year-olds. *The Journal of Genetic Psychology,* 1971, *118,* 235–244.

Flavell, J. H., Botkin, P. T., Fry, C. L., Wright, J. J., & Jarvis, P. *The development of role taking and communication skills in children.* New York: Wiley, 1968.

Furth, H. G. *Piaget and knowledge: theoretical foundations.* Englewood Cliffs, N.J.: Prentice-Hall, 1969.

Gardner, R. C. Attitudes and motivation: their role in second language acquisition. In J. Oller & J. Richards (Eds.), *Focus on the learner: pragmatic perspectives for the language teacher.* Rawley, Mass.: Newbury House, 1973.

Gardner, R. C., & Lambert, W. *Attitudes and motivation in second language learning.* Rawley, Mass.: Newbury House, 1972.

Gordon, H. The intelligence of English canal children. In I. Al-Issa & W. Dennis (Eds.), *Cross-cultural studies of behavior*. New York: Holt, Rinehart & Winston, 1970.

Gleitman, L. R., Gleitman, H., & Shipley, E. F. The emergence of the child as grammarian. *Cognition*, 1972, *1*, 137–164.

Harlow, H. F. The formation of learning sets. *Psychological Review*, 1949, *56*, 51–56.

Haugen, E. *The Norwegian language in America: A study in bilingual behavior* (2 vols.). Philadelphia: University of Pennsylvania Press, 1953.

Heber, R., Garber, H., Harrington, S., Hoffman, C., & Falendar, C. *Rehabilitation of families at risk for mental retardation. Progress report*. Madison, Wisc.: University of Wisconsin, Waisman Center, 1972.

Hunt, J. McV. *Intelligence and experience*. New York: Ronald, 1961.

Husén, T. *Begåvning och miljö*. [Talent and environment.] Stockholm: Almqvist & Wiksell, 1951.

Ianco-Worrall, A. D. Bilingualism and cognitive development. *Child Development*, 1972, *43*, 1390–1400.

Inhelder, B., & Piaget, J. *The child's conception of space*. London: Routledge & Kegan Paul, 1956.

Lambert, W. E., & Tucker, G. R. *Bilingual education of children*. Rawley, Mass.: Newbury House, 1972.

Laosa, L. M. Bilingualism in three U.S. Hispanic groups. *Journal of Educational Psychology*, 1975, *5*, 617.

Leopold, W. F. *Speech development of a bilingual child* (Vols. I–IV). Evanston, Ill.: Northwestern University Press, 1937–1949.

Liedtke, W. W. *Linear measurement concepts of bilingual and monolingual children*. Unpublished master's thesis, The University of Alberta, Edmonton, 1968.

Liedtke, W. W., & Nelson, L. D. Concept formation and bilingualism. *Alberta Journal of Education Research*, 1968, *14*(4) 225–232.

Markham, E. *Factors affecting the young child's ability to monitor his memory*. Unpublished doctoral dissertation, University of Pennsylvania 1973.

Markham, E. *The development of metalinguistic abilities and their relationship to reading and logical thinking*. University of Illinois, 1974. (Invited proposal submitted to NIE.)

McNeill, D. The development of language. In P. H. Mussen (Ed.), *Carmichael's manual of child psychology* (3d Ed.; Vol. 1). New York: Wiley, 1970.

Miller, G. A. *Some preliminaries to psycholinguistics. American Psychologist*, 1965, *20*(1), 15–21.

Miller, G. A., Galanter, E. H., & Pribram, K. H. *Plans and the structure of behavior*. New York: Holt, Rinehart & Winston, 1960.

Miller, G. A., Galanter, E. H., & Pribram, K. H. *Plans and the structure of behavior*. New York: Holt, Rinehart & Winston, 1960.

Neale, J. M. Egocentrism in institutionalized and noninstitutionalized children. *Child Development*, 1966, *37*, 97–101.

Oksaar, E. Bilingualism. In T. Sebeok (Ed.), *Current trends in linguistics* (Vol. 9). Elmsford, N.Y.: Mouton, 1972.

Osherson, D., & Markham, E. *Language and the ability to evaluate contradictions and tautologies*. Unpublished paper, University of Pennsylvania, 1973.

Pascual-Leone, J. A mathematical model for the transition rule in Piaget's developmental stages. *Acta Psychologia*, 1970, *32*, 301–345.

Peal, E., & Lambert, W. E. The relation of bilingualism to intelligence. *Psychological Monographs*, 1962, *76*.

Piaget, J. *The language and thought of the child*. New York: Harcourt-Brace Jovanovitch, 1926.

Piaget, J. *Psychology of intelligence*. Paterson, N.J.: Littlefield, Adams, 1960.

Price-Williams, D. R. (Ed.), *Cross-cultural studies*. Harmondsworth: Penguin Books, 1969. (Reprinted from *Acta Psychologica*, 1961, *18*, 297–305.)

Ramírez M., III, & Price-Williams, D. R. Cognitive styles of children of three ethnic groups in the United States. *Journal of Cross-Cultural Psychology,* 1974, *5,* 212–219.

Schumann, J. Affective factors and the problem of age in second language acquisition. *Language Learning,* 1975, *25,* 209–235.

Scott, S. *The relation of divergent thinking to bilingualism: cause or effect.* Unpublished research report, Toronto: McGill University, 1973.

Sigel, I. E., & Coop, R. H. Cognitive style and classroom practice. In R. H. Coop & K. White (Eds.), *Psychological concepts in the classroom.* New York: Harper, 1974.

Teitelbaum, H., & Hiller, R. J. Bilingual education: the legal mandate. *Harvard Educational Review,* 1977, *47,* 138–170.

Tolman, E. C. Cognitive maps in rats and men. *Psychological Review,* 1959, *56,* 144–155.

Torrance, E. P., Gowan, J. C., Wu, J. J., & Aliotti, N. C. Creative functioning of monolingual and bilingual children in Singapore. *Journal of Educational Psychology,* 1970, *61,* 72–75.

Tremaine, R. V. *Syntax and Piagetian operational thought.* Washington, D. C.: Georgetown University Press, 1975.

U.S. Commission on Civil Rights. *Toward quality education for Mexican-Americans.* Report VI: Mexican-American Education Study, February 1974.

Weinrich, U. *Languages in contact.* New York: Mouton, 1953.

Yela, M. Comprehension verbal y bilinguismo. *Revista de Psicologia General y Aplicado,* 1975, *30,*1045.

Author Index

Subject Index